AI-Driven Policing and Urban Security in Smart Cities

Mamdooh Abdelhameed Abdelmottlep
University of St. Thomas, USA

IGI Global
Scientific Publishing
Publishing Tomorrow's Research Today

Published in the United States of America by
IGI Global Scientific Publishing
701 East Chocolate Avenue
Hershey, PA, 17033, USA
Tel: 717-533-8845
Fax: 717-533-7115
Website: https://www.igi-global.com E-mail: cust@igi-global.com

Library of Congress Cataloging-in-Publication Data

Names: Abdelmottlep, Mamooh, 1955- editor
Title: AI-driven policing and urban security in smart cities / [edited by] Mamooh Abdelmottlep.
Description: Hershey, PA : IGI Global Scientific Publishing, [2026] | Includes bibliographical references and index. | Summary: "This book explores the emerging nexus between AI-driven policing and urban security, offering a comprehensive perspective on how innovative technologies are reshaping the role of policing in the context of modern smart cities. The discussion spans a variety of critical themes, from predictive policing to ethical challenges, thereby offering a holistic view of how AI can transform public safety and the urban experience"-- Provided by publisher.
Identifiers: LCCN 2025004051 (print) | LCCN 2025004052 (ebook) | ISBN 9798337302454 hardcover | ISBN 9798337302461 paperback | ISBN 9798337302478 ebook
Subjects: LCSH: Police--Technological innovations | Smart cities | Artificial intelligence | Public safety
Classification: LCC HV7921 .A43 2026 (print) | LCC HV7921 (ebook) | DDC 363.20285--dc23/eng/20250425
LC record available at https://lccn.loc.gov/2025004051
LC ebook record available at https://lccn.loc.gov/2025004052
British Cataloguing in Publication Data
A Cataloguing in Publication record for this book is available from the British Library.

Table of Contents

Detailed Table of Contents

to examine the intersection of AIP, ethical governance, and data-driven city management, addressing a critical gap in understanding how advanced AI solutions can revolutionize public safety and strategic foresight in smart city environments.

Technology is evolving rapidly, leading to increasingly sophisticated terrorist threats that challenge global security. Efforts by states to mitigate these risks often fall short, as terrorists adapt their techniques, especially through new technologies like artificial intelligence (AI). Research in cybersecurity is essential for awareness and protection. Counterterrorism strategies must evolve to address advancements in technology and the complexities of the dark web, where terrorist activities proliferate. Effective monitoring and legislative measures are crucial for enhancing security and combating these emerging threats.

Digital forensics has evolved significantly with advancements in artificial intelligence (AI) to enable faster, more accurate, and more scalable criminal investigation evidence collection. Traditional forensic procedures are overwhelmed by the volume, complexity, and fragility of digital evidence. AI-based forensics merges machine learning, predictive analytics, and automation in order to make digital artifact identification, preservation, and analysis better. This essay describes cutting-edge AI-based methods of forensic investigation, including deep learning-based anomaly detection, decision trees-based forensic classification, and ensemble methods to variance reduction in forensic predictions. Using AI, forensic analysts can spot patterns, follow cybercrime patterns, and relate digital evidence with greater precision. AI-based applications also assist in automating routine forensic work, reducing human errors, and improving legal investigations.

Intelligent Transportation Systems (ITS) employ cutting-edge technologies like the Internet of Things (IoT), Artificial Intelligence (AI), and cryptographic security to improve mobility and public safety. ITS combines intelligent toll collection, real-time traffic monitoring, and automated payment mechanisms to make transportation efficiency smoother and secure financial transactions. The use of cryptographic protocols, e.g., the Enhanced Ecliptic Curve Algorithm (IECA) to secure key exchange and the Enhanced Hash Function (EHF) for data integrity, enhances security within ITS networks. Such innovations avert cyber attacks, i.e., data tampering, replay attacks, and unauthorized intrusion. Additionally, blockchain technology improves transaction immutability, providing toll payment transparency. By marrying effective encryption techniques with real-time observation, ITS reduces congestion, improves toll management, and also increases commuter safety.

Rescue Team Scheduling Mode is an essential part of disaster management that facilitates timely deployment of emergency response teams with optimal utilization of resources. Conventional scheduling models are likely to fail in accommodating dynamic environments, uncertain disaster scenarios, and real-time decision-making. To address these challenges, a robust scheduling algorithm is presented, which combines machine learning, reinforcement learning, and optimization techniques. The algorithm takes into account factors like the severity of emergencies, availability of teams, current traffic conditions, and environmental limitations to distribute resources optimally. Using algorithms such as Multi-Objective Genetic Algorithm (MOGA), Ant Colony Optimization (ACO), and Reinforcement Learning (RL), the model redistributes teams adaptively and optimizes routes. The suggested mode of scheduling also provides equitable load distribution, reduces response time, and improves coordination among different agencies.

Preface

INTRODUCTION

The rapid development of smart cities has brought forth a paradigm shift in how urban spaces are managed, experienced, and secured. At the heart of this transformation lies artificial intelligence (AI), whose increasing integration into law enforcement is redefining the scope and nature of public safety. With this edited volume, *AI-Driven Policing and Urban Security in Smart Cities*, we aim to illuminate the dynamic relationship between emerging AI technologies and the evolving landscape of urban security.

As urban populations continue to grow and cities become more interconnected and complex, traditional policing methods often fall short in addressing modern security challenges. AI offers a powerful set of tools—ranging from predictive analytics to real-time surveillance and automated forensic analysis—that promise to enhance the efficiency and responsiveness of law enforcement. However, alongside these technological advancements come significant ethical, legal, and societal considerations. This book was born out of the urgent need to critically examine these multifaceted developments and their implications for policing in smart urban environments.

This volume presents a curated collection of interdisciplinary perspectives that span key themes such as predictive policing, deep learning for digital forensics, anomaly detection, ethical governance, and the role of AI in counterterrorism. By incorporating global case studies and diverse viewpoints from scholars, practitioners, and policymakers, we seek to offer both breadth and depth in our analysis. The contributions in this book not only document innovative applications of AI in law enforcement but also interrogate their consequences for human rights, accountability, and public trust.

Our goal is to bridge the often siloed domains of technology, policy, and social science. We envision this book as a critical resource for academics, graduate students, law enforcement professionals, technologists, and urban planners—anyone who is invested in shaping the future of smart, secure, and ethical urban environments. Moreover, we hope this work catalyzes interdisciplinary dialogue and inspires actionable strategies for deploying AI in ways that uphold democratic values and social equity.

We extend our deepest gratitude to the contributing authors whose expertise and insights form the backbone of this collection. Their collective efforts offer a timely and necessary contribution to the ongoing discourse on the role of artificial intelligence in urban policing. As editors, we are honored to present this volume and contribute to the evolving conversation about how technology can—and should—shape the future of public safety in our cities.

ORGANIZATION OF THE BOOK

This volume opens with **Chapter 1**, *A Cyber-Physical Systems and the Smart City Vision: A Comprehensive Guide*, which lays a conceptual foundation for understanding how Smart Cyber-Physical Systems (SCPS) underpin the architecture of smart cities. The chapter articulates the interrelation between digital infrastructure and physical urban environments, highlighting how SCPS leverage the Internet of Things (IoT), artificial intelligence (AI), and big data analytics to drive real-time urban management and service optimization. It presents smart cities as integrated ecosystems where technology and governance coalesce to improve public service delivery and the quality of life.

Building on this foundation, **Chapter 2,***Role of Artificial Intelligence in Smart Cities*, explores the broader application of AI across urban domains. It focuses on the role of city planners in deploying AI technologies to meet the growing demands of urbanization, such as housing, transportation, ICT, and utilities. This chapter showcases various technology solutions—ranging from cloud computing to machine learning—that enable efficient city management and support economic development. The discussion underscores the critical role of AI in transforming smart cities into responsive, resilient, and resident-centric environments.

Chapter 3, *AI and the Rule of Law in Urban Security: Upholding Police Accountability in Smart Cities*, shifts the focus to the regulatory and ethical landscape of AI use in law enforcement. It raises urgent questions about the governance of AI and its alignment with human rights, ethical norms, and international legal frameworks. The chapter emphasizes the importance of balancing innovation with accountability, discussing topics such as open justice, privacy, and operational fairness. This chapter serves as a vital guide for understanding how AI can be harnessed to strengthen—not circumvent—the rule of law.

In **Chapter 4**, *Challenging the Boundaries of Urban Security: AIP, Ethical Governance, and the Future of Smart Cities*, the discussion advances toward the complex terrain of AI-driven policing (AIP) and municipal governance. The chapter introduces a comprehensive theoretical framework that links AI-enabled situational awareness with strategic foresight, ethical governance, and adaptive policy-making. It calls for a reimagining of urban security paradigms in light of advanced analytics and data-driven governance, offering insight into how smart cities can anticipate and respond to evolving security demands.

Chapter 5, *The Role of Artificial Intelligence in Combating Terrorism: Exploring Capabilities and Challenges in the Dark and Deep Web*, addresses the increasingly sophisticated security threats emerging in hidden corners of the internet. As terrorist networks exploit the dark and deep web, the authors examine the capabilities and limitations of AI in tracking and neutralizing these threats. The chapter underscores the necessity for evolving counterterrorism strategies, highlighting the role of legislative measures and proactive monitoring in safeguarding public spaces from digital extremism.

Turning to investigative practices, **Chapter 6**, *Deep Learning for Digital Forensics: Advancing Criminal Investigations*, delves into the intersection of forensic science and AI. This chapter demonstrates how deep learning, predictive analytics, and automation are transforming digital evidence processing—making it more precise, scalable, and responsive to the demands of modern investigations. With methods such as anomaly detection and decision-tree classification, AI-enhanced forensics is positioned as a cornerstone of future-ready criminal justice systems, empowering investigators to uncover patterns and link evidence in increasingly complex digital landscapes.

Chapter 7, *Forensic Linguistics and DBN: Automating the Analysis of Witness Statements and Testimonies in AI-Driven Policing*, presents an innovative convergence of forensic linguistics and Deep Belief Networks (DBNs) to enhance the credibility assessment of witness statements. This chapter explores how AI models can detect deception, identify inconsistencies, and streamline testimony analysis, thereby expediting investigations and reducing human bias. It also tackles the ethical imperatives surrounding algorithmic fairness, data privacy, and the importance of inclusive training datasets. The work reflects a growing movement toward multidisciplinary approaches that embed ethical safeguards within intelligent policing tools.

In **Chapter 8**, *Developing a Deep Learning-Based Framework for Real-Time Anomaly Detection and Alerting Mechanism using Embedded Systems*, the authors propose a real-time surveillance solution using embedded deep learning systems. Designed for smart city applications such as crowd monitoring, traffic analysis, and home security, the framework leverages video surveillance and machine learning to detect anomalies efficiently and alert authorities immediately. The chapter underscores the potential of intelligent surveillance to enhance public safety and disaster preparedness while also drawing attention to the need for responsible deployment and oversight.

Chapter 9, *Enhancing Smart Toll Security: Improved Ecliptic Curve Algorithm in Intelligent Transportation Networks*, addresses the role of AI and encryption in strengthening transportation infrastructure. Through the use of the Improved Ecliptic Curve Algorithm (IECA) and Enhanced Hash Function (EHF), this chapter highlights how intelligent transportation systems can resist cyberattacks while streamlining toll payments and reducing congestion. It offers insights into how blockchain and cryptographic techniques not only enhance security but also increase transparency and commuter trust in automated mobility networks.

Chapter 10, *Smart Disaster Management: Minimizing Response Time in Disaster Situations Using AI*, takes a systems-based approach to crisis response by presenting a hybrid AI model for emergency team deployment. Integrating reinforcement learning, ant colony optimization, and multi-objective genetic algorithms, the model intelligently allocates resources based on severity, traffic conditions, and team availability. The chapter demonstrates how AI can improve interagency coordination, equitable resource distribution, and response efficiency, particularly in unpredictable, high-stakes urban disaster scenarios.

Concluding the volume, **Chapter 11**, *AI for Urban Innovation in Developing Cities*, shifts the lens to the Global South, examining how cities in regions such as West Africa, South Asia, and Latin America are leveraging AI to overcome infrastructural and social challenges. Through case studies from Accra, Bangalore, Lagos, and Medellín, the chapter reveals how AI enhances waste management, water systems, urban planning, and traffic control. It stresses the importance of community engagement, ethical design, and inclusive governance in developing AI solutions tailored to the needs of diverse urban populations. This final chapter calls for bridging the digital divide and ensuring equitable AI deployment across all cityscapes.

CONCLUSION

As this volume illustrates, the integration of artificial intelligence into urban policing and public security is not merely a technological shift—it is a transformative development that touches the very foundations of governance, civil liberties, and urban life. Each chapter in this book contributes a unique perspective to the evolving landscape of AI-driven policing, from cutting-edge forensic tools and cybersecurity frameworks to ethical governance and human rights concerns. By weaving together theoretical insights, empirical research, and practical frameworks, this collection provides a comprehensive and multidisciplinary exploration of the promises and perils that AI presents in the context of smart cities.

Our goal as editors has been to present a balanced and nuanced account—one that neither blindly celebrates innovation nor succumbs to dystopian anxieties. Instead, we aim to stimulate critical inquiry, informed dialogue, and responsible action. The chapters reflect the urgent need for ethical foresight, regulatory clarity, and inclusive design as cities worldwide adopt intelligent technologies in the name of safety and efficiency.

We hope that this book will serve as both a reference and a catalyst—for researchers seeking to deepen academic discourse, for practitioners striving to improve public service delivery, and for policymakers tasked with navigating the ethical and legal frontiers of emerging technologies. Ultimately, securing the future of AI-driven urban security requires collaboration across disciplines, sectors, and societies. It is our hope that the contributions in this volume spark those essential conversations and inspire the thoughtful, equitable deployment of AI in building safer, smarter cities.

Chapter 1
A Cyber-Physical Systems and the Smart City Vision: A Comprehensive Guide

Khushboo Malik
https://orcid.org/0009-0005-3911-4122
Christ University, India

Kamal Upreti
https://orcid.org/0000-0003-0665-530X
Christ University, India

Onam Singh
https://orcid.org/0009-0008-7070-2944
Dr. B.R. Ambedkar University, India

Pratham Tiwari
Christ University, India

Shreya Rathi
HSBC, India

Malika Ara
Saint Louis University, USA

ABSTRACT

The process of urban areas' transformation into smart cities with the help of Smart Cyber-Physical Systems (SCPS) is one of the most defining trends of modern urbanism. It requires a multifaceted perspective of smart cities, thereby evaluating the facets of SCPS intently concerning the complexities of their integration in urban structures while exploring their influence that transcends the domains of social sciences and economics, which has become crucial. In this context, smart cities are constructed as integrated systems at the crossroads of the digital and the physical: they sustain, facilitate, and improve the performance of the city's functions and living environment. The importance of technological environments in orientation and close consideration of SCPS reveals the functions in gathering data, immediate analysis, and decision-making processes of urban management. The interconnection

DOI: 10.4018/979-8-3373-0245-4.ch001

of the Internet of Things (IoT), artificial intelligence (AI), and big data analytics considering their impact and the creation of sustainable enhancing the quality of public services.

INTRODUCTION

In the rapidly urbanizing world, the smart city is a new important strategy to meet the complex challenges of urbanization. Smart cities make use of cutting-edge technologies in enhancing the quality of life of citizens, achieving sustainability, and bringing about operational efficiency in urban services. At the very epicentre of this transformative vision lies Smart Cyber-Physical Systems, which embeds computation and communication capabilities in physical processes in a bid to render environments smart and responsive. SCPS is at the heart of the paradigm of the smart city, facilitating real-time monitoring, data collection, and analysis that inform decision-making and efficient resource management. These are followed by the IoT, AI, big data analytics—of which these three, when combined, form the backbone for smart city infrastructure. SCPSs empower cities with seamless integration of technologies in order to optimize operations and reduce costs while enhancing the overall urban experience.

The relevance of smart cities and SCPS in contemporary urban planning is very high. In the process, as the population of the urban areas continues to surge, conventional methods of city management are proving inadequate to address issues such as traffic, pollution, energy supply, and resource supply. Smart cities present a proactive way of handling these emerging challenges by infusing technology into making urban spaces more livable, efficient, and sustainable. SCPS also falls within the trends of global digitization and sustainability of urban planning. The contribution to the broader goals—that is, mitigation of climate change, resilient economy, and social equity—is what these systems can do to support smart infrastructure development. SCPS can be used to bring greater adaptability to cities while ensuring a better quality of life for their residents.

This chapter is an all-in-one tutorial about the overlap between cyber-physical systems and smart city vision. It covers aspects related to foundational concepts, technological frameworks, social implications, economic dimensions, and environmental sustainability of SCPS within smart cities. The chapter thus tries to analyze through these different facets how SCPS can be harnessed toward making urban environments smarter, more efficient, and definitely more sustainable.

CONCEPTUAL FOUNDATIONS

Core Technologies in SCPS

Smart Cyber-Physical Systems will undergird the ambitions of smart cities. They will enable physical and computational processes to be intertwined in a synergistic fashion. The technologies driving SCPS are the Internet of Things, Artificial Intelligence, and Big Data Analytics.

IoT (Internet of Things): This is the network of physical devices basically embedded with sensors, software, and other associated technologies in connecting and exchanging data with other devices and systems via the internet. It facilitates real-time data collection, monitoring, and management. In this regard, it is critical to various smart city applications related to smart grids, intelligent transport systems, and environmental monitoring. For example, the smart grids collect consumption data through smart meters to rationalize energy distribution and reduce a whole range of wastages (Gubbi et al., 2013).

AI (Artificial Intelligence): It would improve SCPS's data input processing capability and ability to make decisions based on the same. It would automatically predict traffic patterns, work out public services, and augment security systems. For example, AI-based traffic management systems, with the integration of changing signal timings based on real-time traffic conditions, have reduced congestion and improved flow, according to (Kommineni et al., 2024).

Big Data Analytics: Big Data Analytics is a process to extract and analyze large data for the discovery of patterns and trends, which is used to gain meaningful insights. Smart city technologies are applied to improve urban services and operations. An array of datasets is harnessed from different sources, such as social media, sensors, and public records, for more efficient city planning and resource usage to predict future needs. Big Data Analytics helps officials to be more efficient and effective in cities, hence promoting data-driven decision-making (Manyika et al., 2011).

Integration of SCPS in Urban Infrastructure

SCPS forms the base for developing smart cities as far as integration into urban infrastructures is concerned. There are two major areas in which SCPSs are making their impacts: smart grids and intelligent transportation systems.

Smart Grids: SCPS makes it possible for smart grids to improve efficiency, reliability, and sustainability in electricity distribution networks. Such grids are enabled by IoT devices and artificial intelligence that monitor energy use in real time, detect outages, and predict maintenance needs. This facilitates the integration of renewable sources of energy into the grid, hence assisting a city in meeting its goals of sustainability. Dynamic balancing of supply and demand contributes to preventing the wastage of energy while at the same time offering stable power supply (Gungor et al., 2011).

Intelligent Transportation Systems: ITS implements SCPS to enhance safety and efficiency across transportation networks. IoT sensors gather information about vehicle movements, traffic flows, and road conditions. AI algorithms analyze this data to manage the traffic signals, provide real-time traffic updates, and optimize routes of public transport. As reported by Bifulco et al. in 2014, ITS can dramatically reduce times of travel, lower emissions, and generally improve the commuter experience and quality.

Data Management and Real-Time Analysis

Data management is an intrinsic part of SCPS, aside from real-time data analytics, which ensures that vast amounts of data are harnessed efficiently and securely.

Sensors and Data Collection: Smart cities have their data collected through a complex system of sensors embedded in many urban elements. According to the measurement, the information data the sensors collect refers to environmental conditions, health infrastructures, human activities, and many other parameters. Here, therefore, options have to be taken into consideration for ensuring the accuracy and reliability of the data given by sensors, so that SCPS work properly (Sundmaeker et al., 2010).

Data Privacy and Security: With the proliferation of data in smart cities, there is a high requirement for data privacy and security assurance. In this respect, robust encryption methods, secure solutions to store data, and stringent control on access are some of the aspects that can help protect sensitive information. On the other hand, some of the steps towards ensuring that the people's right to privacy is assured and goes a long way in enhancing public trust include adherence to protecting data regulations, such as GDPR (Zhang et al., 2018).

Autonomous Decision-Making: Such data insights could be autonomous in SCPS decision-making—no human intervention is required. This feature enables SCPS in response time, including critical situations like emergency management or even traffic control. Much support in making accurate and timely decisions by these systems is brought by AI and machine learning algorithms, further enhancing resilience and responsiveness of smart city infrastructure (Sarker et al., 2018).

SOCIETAL IMPACT AND IMPLICATIONS

Social Equity and Inclusion

Bridging the Digital Divide

The smart city vision unfortunately remains one of the utopian ideals of technological improvement for a better life quality for all citizens. This ideal is tempered with the realities of the so-called digital divide, or the gap between those who have access to modern information and communication technology and those who do not. That is to say, inadequate consideration of it might entrench already existing social inequities (Foth, 2017). Digital divide mitigation in smart cities is making sure that all citizens are on an even playing field by providing them with the basic requisite infrastructure: effective access to high-speed internet and developing digital literacy. Therefore, it should have in place digital literacy programs, cheap Internet packages, and universal device distribution. Besides, policies have to be directed toward the unserved population to avoid increasing digital divide (Van Dijk, 2020).

Accessibility and Affordability

Two of the most primal features that make inclusivity a taken characteristic within smart cities are accessibility and affordability. Ideally, 'accessibility' means more than just physical access to the digital infrastructure of a city; it further underscores the use of its digital services by persons with disabilities. Universal design principles will need to be embedded in smart cities so that technology remains usable by all, irrespective of their diverse abilities. Another critical point here is that of affordability, as the technology cost may prove prohibitive for the underprivileged. Subsidized internet services or public access in community centers and libraries are other ways of stemming such challenges. Additionally, policy frameworks need to have provisions for dealing with the result of smart city development that sees vulnerable populations being forced out because of the high cost of living (Gurstein, 2003).

Governance and Citizen Engagement

Participatory Governance Models

On the other hand, smart cities provide active citizen participation in effective governance. Nam and Pardo argue that participatory models of governance, whereby citizens take a more central role in decision-making, will improve transparency, accountability, and trust in public institutions. Typically, such models are technology-enabled and offer an opportunity for citizens to raise their concerns, contribute towards policy making, and engage in neighborhood projects collaboratively. These can be, among others, discussion forums created online, mobile applications through which people can file complaints, or digital platforms in terms of civic engagement. Models such as these make sure that benefits resulting from smart city initiatives are distributed equitably and policies address various needs of the population.

Public-Private Partnerships

PPPs are an integral part in developing and implementing smart city projects. This kind of partnership brings together two large players with their individual strengths—public sector oversight and private sector innovation and efficiency. This can provide the necessary funds, technical expertise, and innovative solution that may be beyond the single capacity of a public entity (Siemiatycki, 2013). However, equally significant is how such types of partnerships help secure transparency and accountability for clear role and responsibility definitions. Besides, the interests of partners in the private sector must serve the public for good, and it must ensure that profit intends do not undermine social equity and inclusion (Mazzucato, 2013).

Ethical Considerations

Surveillance and Privacy

Large-scale data collection is often part and parcel of the integration of advanced technologies into smart cities, and it gives rise to important surveillance and privacy concerns. According to Lyon, such technologies of surveillance like CCTV cameras, sensors, and data analytics might, while improving security and efficiency, turn out as the pervasive control of citizens' activities. These technologies could be expected to serve ethical purposes with strong regulation in the sphere of data protection, transparency of data practices, and mechanisms of citizen oversight. People should be in control of their data, with insight into the way it is collected and stored, and for what purposes it is used.

Ethical Use of Data

Beyond privacy, the use of ethics in data encompasses consent, bias, and general miss-use of information. Algorithms and AI systems used in smart cities should be designed in a manner that avoids biases which have the potential to yield a host of disparate impacts, argues O'Neil in 2016. Transparent algorithms and accountability frameworks, with regular audits, are required with respect to fairness and justice in decisions arrived at through the use of big data. Moreover, informed consent should be at the forefront of data practices, thus in full realization of the role of the uses and purposes that citizens' data is serving (Floridi & Taddeo, 2016).

Digital Rights and Responsibilities

Smart cities also raise issues relating to articulating and protecting digital rights and responsibilities. Digital rights are those that guard the privacy, freedom of expression, and access to information for all citizens within the online space, (Hintz et al., 2018). On the other hand, digital responsibilities relate to the ethical use of digital tools and conformance to the rule of law and social norms in online behaviors. Digital literacy, rights, and responsibility education is key to having active and responsible participation in smart city ecosystems (Mossberger, Tolbert, & McNeal, 2007).

ECONOMIC PERSPECTIVES AND CONSIDERATION

Economic Impact of Smart Cities

It has enormous economic impacts and is being driven by what have become developed to be "cutting-edge" technologies-such as IoT, AI, and big data analytics. All these change the urban economy, offer new jobs, and develop markets in cities. Smart cities directly influence or, rather, drive urban growth and competitiveness by their appeal to talent, businesses, and investments.

Job Creation and New Markets

It provides enormous employment opportunities in almost all domains as the smart city projects develop. IoT, AI, and data-driven services integration demand a competent workforce that encompasses knowledge in technology, data analysis, planning, and management of projects. For example, AI and machine learning knowledge holders of the algorithm play significant parts in large dimensions; those who develop systems that predict traffic flow or optimize energy consumption; data analysts decoding high volumes of city data for improved service delivery (Batty, 2018).

This necessitates new jobs in tech and support positions for IoT installation, maintenance, and big data analysis. In addition, start-ups and established firms continue to innovate solutions answering the needs unique to smart cities. New ventures cut across the sectors of transportation, healthcare, public safety, and energy, diversifying and enhancing the resilience of the urban economy (Caragliu et al., 2011). The results stimulate entrepreneurship, innovation of the economy, and an active urban career structure with a wider spectrum of employment opportunities.

Enhancing Urban Competitiveness

The city's competitiveness increases because smart city technologies enhance the urban region's operational efficiency, and the quality of life enjoyed and its reputation as well. For example, traffic congestion decreases, commute becomes shorter, and consequently cuts pollution, making the cities livable and investable for residents and businesses as well. Smart city systems do contribute to improving the level of mobility that results in worker productivity and, of course, makes the attractiveness to talent in retaining as well as attracting a good employee even more relevant than access to business itself.

The effective energy management systems, typical of which are driven by artificial intelligence, reduce the costs of the public and private sectors undertaking the operations in the city. Through data-driven resource management, a better allocation of resources can be made to areas with high demand. Such benefits position a city on a higher level of performance, putting it on a competitive destination for tourism, investment, and human capital and thus allows sustainable economic development.

Investment and Financial Models

The large-scale amount of capital needed for such smart city projects makes it highly necessary to finance it innovatively with funding strategies and models for achieving economic sustainability.

Funding Strategies for Smart City Projects

There is mostly public and private funding put in the smart city projects, with PPPs usually at the helm. In such models, it will be mostly the private sector partners that will invest in technology and infrastructure, while it becomes the responsibility of governmental bodies to provide regulatory support and align the projects towards the benefits and interests of the public. The partnerships bring their expertise, share the risk profile, and leverage the resources on hand, meaning cities do not overleverage their public budgets.

International financial institutions and development agencies provide grants and loans to especially brilliant city projects in developing countries, which the international community recognizes the value that cities add to global issues through resilience and sustainability. Cities take this further by finding creative ways of funding, such as local bonds or crowdsourcing from citizens, to sponsor particular projects (Anthopoulos et al., 2016). All this eases financial constraints and widens the pool of assets needed for the metamorphosis of cities into technologically advanced urban centers.

Cost-Benefit Analysis

Research work by Cavada et al. (2016) has pointed out that the high initial investments in technologies and infrastructural systems should be weighed against long-term benefits such as reduced running costs, greater efficiency, and a better life. Undoubtedly, such investments are justified by saving costs, especially those related to consumption and maintenance of energy. For instance, a smart grid can save energy by leaps and bounds, reducing actual consumption, thereby generating massive savings in the long run, making smart cities all the more economically attractive.

Economic Sustainability

Smart cities ought to be financially sustainable to avoid becoming liabilities on public budgets or increasing economic inequality. Smart cities need proper financial models for self-reliance and viability in the long term. For example, value capture financing bases the source of revenue on increased values for property that will be an effect of investments in smart cities to finance future developments-consequently, maintaining a stream of revenue needed to sustain improvements. This approach will make smart city benefits available to a large number of people, thereby supporting the economic inclusiveness and stability for all its urban residents.

Interdependencies with Broader Economic Systems

Smart cities form part of a broader economic landscape, and they thrive on resilience and agility in the face of global challenges. As innovation centers, smart cities influence and are influenced by regional and international economies.

Economic Resilience

Economic resilience in smart cities can be defined as the capability of opposing or recovering from economic shock, such as a recession or natural disaster, or even something like a pandemic. The diversifying of economic activities and the integration of leading-edge technologies enable smart cities to react to an economic disturbance at a faster rate than any other city. For example, monitoring systems with real-time data can decisively respond to crisis situations with minimal financial loss and rapid recovery (Hollands, 2008). This agility helps keep smart cities stable and find investors even during volatile economic times.

Adaptability to Global Challenges

The ability of smart cities to adapt to global issues such as climate change and rapid technological shift is a prerequisite for their economic sustainability. Smart cities have, as a priority, sustainable urban planning and integration of green technology, making them leaders in solving the environmental woes of the world. Daptive strategies of change enhance the economic sustainability of cities. For instance, adaptive infrastructure that responds to climate risk is a form of protection for investments and attracts businesses that have a commitment to sustainability (Albino et al., 2015).

Impact on Local and Global Economies

This not only affects the local economy but also has regional and international influences on economies. Suitable smart city policies have catalytic models for regional development, promoting cooperation between cities and countries. As a central location for investments, talents, and innovations, smart cities add to the global economy, promoting economic integration and best practice sharing globally (Angelidou, 2014). The emergence of smart cities may provide an opportunity to develop a more connected and resilient global economy, since urban centers worldwide align their growth strategies with the principles of smart sustainable development.

Smart cities contribute to the transformation of local economies and shine as beacons of sustainable practices, hence supporting a global urban network that can stand together against economic and environmental challenges. Continuing growth and evolution, smart cities create a future-oriented global economic structure espousing resilience, sustainability, and inclusivity.

CHALLENGES AND PATHWAYS TO ENVIRONMENTAL SUSTAINABILITY.

Role of SCPS in Promoting Sustainability

Energy Efficiency

Smart Cyber-Physical Systems ensure much higher energy efficiency in cities by smart integration of such innovative technologies as IoT, AI, and big data analytics. IoT sensors and smart grids are able to detect and manage energy consumption in real-time so as to optimize its distribution and not lose any extra energy. As an example, smart grids can keep a tab on the balance of energy loads and integrate renewable sources of energy properly with the goal of reduction in GHG emissions. The AI algorithms predict the pattern of energy demand and modulate its distribution to minimize loss of energy and increase efficiency of the overall system (Khaleel et al., 2024).

Waste Management

SCPSs enable intelligent waste management systems in route optimization of waste collection, thereby reducing operational costs and the environmental impact. The IoT sensors in waste bins monitor fill levels and send signals to the services involved in waste collection to ensure timely and efficient collection. This minimizes extra journeys, saves fuel, and reduces CO2 production in the collection process (Goutam et al., 2021). Besides this, the data analytics module by itself may predict trends of waste generation to ensure better planning and resource allocation.

Water Conservation

Smart meters and sensors, leak detection, and consumption data for real-time monitoring have already been integrated into SPSC systems for better management of water. AI and analytics predict demand and optimize the supply distribution to avert wastages. These technologies also integrate sustainable sources such as rainwater harvesting into the urban networks promoting efficient use of resources (Mukhopadhyay, 2014).

Climate Change Mitigation and Adaptation

Smart City Solutions for Climate Resilience

SCPS is applied in smart cities to gain improved resilience in respect of climate change by adopting a few innovative solutions. Anticipating the events of natural disasters using real-time environmental conditions monitored from IoT sensors and using satellite imagery, through the adoption of appropriate response strategies, is carried out. For instance, a smart flood management system with the help of predictive analytics is capable of switching on the preventive procedures such as regulating the water level in the reservoir in order to mitigate the situation and even warn the residents about the risks of the flood phenomena (Anbarasan et al., 2019).

Green Technologies and Practices

Green technologies and sustainable practices have defined smart cities. Solar panels, besides efficient buildings, are integral constituents of the infrastructures in smart cities. Such elements help diminish the use of fossil fuels, thereby reducing carbon footprint. SCPS make smooth and effective integration of such technologies into urban infrastructures with respect both to their performance and environmental implications (Casini, 2017). The intelligent transport system also promotes using electric vehicles and public transport, therefore further reducing emissions.

Case Studies of Environmentally Sustainable Smart Cities

Other cities across the world have also adopted SCPS to ensure a greener environment. For instance, Copenhagen smart city strategies are geared at ensuring that the city is carbon neutral by 2025. This entails massive investments in smart grids, green building standards, and intelligent transportation systems (Krähmer et al., 2020). An example of one such innovation in Copenhagen is the smart lighting project, whereby adaptive street lighting is applied to make consumption of energy minimal; this is exemplary to other cities, according to Tunku et al. (2021).

The Copenhagen experience, among others, underlines the need for stakeholder collaboration in robust data management and innovation processes toward sustainability. Public-private partnerships and active citizen participation are considered essential ingredients in the successful implementation of SCPS. Moreover, all technologies need to be integrated seamlessly to avoid operational inefficiencies and maximize environmental gains (Cugurullo, 2018).

NAVIGATING OBSTACLES AND MITIGATING RISKS

Introduction of Smart City Platform Systems within smart cities implies a number of significant challenges and risks that need to be very well managed in order for the sustainability, security, and inclusiveness of urban environments are warranted. Strong SCPSs are essential to the speedy digitization of urban spaces but these systems bring in complexities of cybersecurity vulnerabilities; digital divides will continue. This section discusses three key challenges: cybersecurity threats, data privacy concerns, and the digital divide.

Cybersecurity Threats

Connectedness in the context of smart cities can be viewed as dependent; this can be seen from the deployment of sensor networks and IoT devices that collect, process, and then disseminate real-time data. Such dependence makes them vulnerable to cyber-attacks in which a breach in one component can cascade through an entire network with possibly severe disruptions. There are various entry points in SCPS technologies for cybercriminals. Alcaraz and Zeadally in (2015) suggest the SCPS infrastructure diverseness - as related to traffic management or power grids-is what increases the "attack surface" of their infrastructure, making cybersecurity that much tougher. As simple as data breaches, cyber-attacks can get quite complex by disrupting a whole city-endangering residents' safety.

Robust mitigation measures such as the use of encryption protocols, rigorous and regular security audits, and real-time threat monitoring are to be done to prevent breach events in real-time. Stakeholders would need awareness and regular training on cybersecurity in order to increase defence mechanisms against evolving threats. Adaptive or multi-layered frameworks need to be built says Roman et al. (2018) and it shall adapt itself according to new and emerging threats for continuous protection. To avoid cyber-attacks on such vital urban systems, governments and municipal authorities have a role to play in somehow collaboratively agreeing on national and international standards for the cybersecurity of infrastructures in smart cities.

Data Privacy Concerns

With the tremendous data processing involved in smart cities, there are severe privacy implications, as SCPS process a huge amount of personal and sensitive information. Citizens' data is being collected infinitely with various devices, sensors, and applications through which smart cities are exposed to misuse and breaches. Public trust relies on visible data management and the observance of privacy laws like GDPR with the high requirement of full protection of personal data. Binns (2018) posits that the SCPS should be designed with "privacy by design": that is, privacy protections are part of the core and should be well integrated from the beginning. This may prevent abuses in the exercise of power and ensure that privacy is treated as a critical feature of the smart city infrastructure.

Importantly, citizen identities can be anonymized through data methods such as the Gaussian method. Also, city officials should clearly point out well-informed citizen consent; citizens should be informed on how the data is being used, stored, and shared. The privacy policy shall be dynamic to change with time for novel technological advancement and threats. Strict compliance and development of public oversight can help create confidence in the hands of citizens; otherwise, they will resist the data collection, which is integral to SCPS.

Digital Divide

The digital divide is a core problem in smart cities. It creates obstacles for equal access and causes social differences. This is happening as the technology of smart city becomes the standard feature of urban life, thus separating people by income, education, and geographical location about their chances to participate and become effective users of these innovations. According to Van Deursen and van Dijk (2019), socio-economic inequalities restrict the access to digital services and may potentially exclude marginalized populations from the benefits of SCPS. For example, there is a low possibility that the respective poor neighborhoods will be introduced to cheaper, suitable, and abundant internet services. While this informs that such families will be limited in availing the necessary smart city services.

To this end, governments must prioritize enabling affordable internet access, digital device distribution, and digital skills training. As Norris (2001) cautions, unless such policy focus is available, smart cities will only serve to deepen social inequalities by favoring affluent and well-connected communities. Inclusiveness commitment obliges local governments to design policies to bridge gaps in access to digital and open the ways for all citizens to share in the benefits from digital transformation.

POLICY AND REGULATORY FRAMEWORKS

National and International Policies

National and international policies are very strong driving forces in the development process of smart cities and Smart Cyber-Physical Systems. Governments all around the world are exploiting the power of smart cities in mitigating urban challenges, improving quality life, and promoting sustainable development. Most of the countries have incorporated smart city strategies into their national agendas. For example, the Indian Smart Cities Mission has targeted the development of 100 smart cities by exploiting digital technology and infrastructural developments, as explained by Sharma in 2017.

At the international level, the United Nations' Sustainable Development Goals set a framework for the development of inclusive, safe, resilient, and sustainable cities in 2015. The European Union also supports smart city projects, through Horizon 2020, by funding innovation, energy efficiency, and sustainable mobility.

Yet, all the same, regulatory challenges are still a thorn in the way. Interoperability and standardization of technologies developed across different regions are very important. It requires quite stringent regulations for the balancing act between innovation, on the one hand, and privacy and security on the other. Indeed, efficient regulatory frameworks will not only protect citizens' rights but also stimulate innovation with ethical use of data.

Standardization and Interoperability

Standardization and interoperability of SCPS are fundamental in realizing smart cities, where diverse systems can be integrated for perfect functioning. If there are no uniform protocols developed in smart city solutions, fragmentation will cut down on their effectiveness. Global organizations, such as the International Organization of Standards and the Institute of Electrical and Electronics Engineers, comprise bodies that develop vital standards. ISO 37120 provides indicators for city services and quality of life, allowing cities to benchmark against global standards. On the other hand, interoperability amongst IoT devices and systems is encouraged by IEEE's P2413 standard.

Further, collaborative exercises like GSC3 directly support knowledge sharing for the creation of best practices that help in the creation of models for smart cities that are scalable and adaptable.

Future Directions for Policy Development

As smart cities and SCPS continue to evolve, the development of policies should be done simultaneously with technological developments. Some form of policies in the future must be able to address the complicated nature of smart city ecosystems and the dynamic configuration of urban set ups. With increasing use of AI in urban management, development is needed to be done in the area of ethical guidelines to avoid such problems as algorithmic bias (Smuha, 2021). In addition, appropriate and comprehensive cybersecurity policy is needed to be applied to protect critical infrastructure against potential cyberattacks (Clim et al, 2022).

Other policy recommendations are public-private partnerships, citizen engagement, and international collaboration with a view to addressing global urban challenges in action. Aligning policy frameworks toward goals of sustainability, inclusiveness, and resilience will ensure cities leverage SCPS potential optimally in creating smart and sustainable urban precincts.

CASE STUDIES PERSPECTIVE AND APPLICATIONS

Successful Smart City Implementations

Case Studies from Different Regions

Barcelona, Spain. Barcelona is one of the excellent examples in Europe that presents a Smart City Solution, making urban life more accessible and sustainable, aiming to achieve higher levels of energy efficiency by using smart lighting whose brightness automatically changes when it is noticed by the system because it does not notice movement. It makes use of the latest sensors on the flow of pedestrians or cars and therefore dim the lights on areas with less traffic, which has reduced the amount of energy consumption as well as their respective costs. As such, in the opinion of Navarro and Bousquet, 2015, the project not only reduced energy usage by over 30% but also costs relating to maintenance.One of the other important success factors in Barcelona is its intelligent parking system. There, the parking space floors are covered by sensors with real-time information being sent to a mobile application that can notify the driver of availability of vacant space nearby. This has eased traffic congestion and reduced the emission of pollutants that have further meant easier driving conditions, according to research done by Hernández-Muñoz et al. (2011).

Singapore Smart Nation Initiative. In Asia, Singapore emerged as the leader of innovation for the smart city through the ambitious Smart Nation initiative; a well-integrated program aimed at creating an urban environment advanced in technology, enhancing quality of life for citizens. Singapore has developed an extensive network of sensors and cameras to monitor almost every aspect of the urban environment, from traffic flow to levels of air quality. With such an infrastructure, real-time data will be available so that public authorities can take quick decisions on matters in public transport, hazards to the environment, and even urban planning. According to Chourabi et al. (2012), because it uses the data-centric approach, Singapore was able to optimize its services and improve resources for its citizens, thus making greater resilience in its urban areas. This move has also included a smart transportation system that has reduced the time needed in commuting and unclogged roads, significantly improving the Singaporean's everyday life (Phang, 2013).

New York City, USA. New York City in North America is one of the examples doing fantastic work towards public safety through its smart city plan. The city says DAS consolidates data across multiple sources, including CCTV cameras, public safety sensors, and environmental monitors, in order to make it easier to prevent crime and respond quickly in case of emergencies. It aggregates data, using a series of machine learning algorithms to identify crime patterns, potential hazards, and enforce law enforcement in the right places. In this context, the sort of technology has led to a drastic decline in crime rates and ensured effective law enforcement. So, Saheb (2023) believes that effectiveness of the project would depend on the collaboration between the city governments and private tech firms with public safety agencies.

Critical Success Factors

Other critical factors that can influence the sustainability of such a smart city project across different regions are governmental support, technological infrastructure, and public-private partnerships. It is through the launch of these factors that the smart city initiatives in Barcelona, Singapore, and New York City went perfectly well.

1. **Governmental Support and Policy Framework:** An effective policy framework together with pro-government involvement is one of the key factors. In the case of Barcelona, strong support by the city council spurred financing and regulatory support to move smart city projects forward (Navarro & Bousquet, 2015). Likewise, in Singapore, the government rendered substantial support and regulation in pushing for the Smart Nation initiative to ensure a well-coordinated plan in the investment areas towards infrastructure, IoT, and big data applications (Chourabi et al., 2012).
2. **Integration of Advanced Technologies:** The government has the ability to make real-time decisions on data-driven parameters through access to IoT, big data, and AI technologies. For example, in Barcelona's smart lighting and parking systems, IoT sensors will enable the city to decrease its cost of operations while improving efficiency, hence achieving greater resilience and sustainability (Hernández-Muñoz et al., 2011).
3. **PPPs:** Public-private collaboration is the only way to guarantee the efficient deliverability and upscaling of smart city projects. An example would be the relationship between New York City and private corporations, who involved the companies in developing novel solutions in public safety as well as sustainabil-

ity. Instead of just access to leading-edge technology, partnerships also helped relief of financial burden to carry out these large smart city initiatives.

In a nutshell, findings through case studies have led to lessons that capture how customized approaches with specific technologies and robust collaborative frameworks can make smart city initiatives successful and sustainable across different contexts.

Comparative Analysis

Differing Approaches and Outcomes

Although common to all successful smart city implementations are success factors, the approaches and outcomes sometimes differ significantly from one region to another. For instance, European cities, like Barcelona, place considerable emphasis on sustainability and social equity. Having a primary orientation toward reducing energy consumption and enhancing public services—hence improving the quality of life for all citizens—the smart city projects of Barcelona set a very good example.

On the other hand, the Asian cities like Singapore focus on economic growth and technological innovation. According to Phang, 2013, Smart Nation is a program aiming to make Singapore one of the leading technology and innovation hubs in the world so that to ensure economic competitiveness and woo investments. The move has overseen quite a massive infrastructural development of the urban infrastructure and public services but has also opened a can of worms regarding personal data privacy and surveillance.

City governments in North America, such as New York City, are more concerned with the issue of public safety and security. Although DAS implemented in New York has greatly enhanced counter crime and emergency prevention and response capabilities of the city, it also tends to raise surveillance issues and individual rights to privacy as stated by Saheb, 2023.

Recommendations for Policymakers and Planners

Case studies based on these kinds of aspects can be learned and utilized by policymakers and urban planners. First, securing public trust and safeguarding individual rights are considered highly essential, which would be captured through investment in good structure for data privacy and security. Second, finding public-private partnerships may bring onboard the necessary resources and expertise to ensure the delivery of successful smart city projects. The third is inclusiveness and equity in bridging the digital divide and promoting social equity (Chourabi et al., 2012).

Finally, smart city projects must be monitored and evaluated if errors are to be detected and long-term success is to be secured. Learning from experiences, especially in cities like Barcelona, Singapore, and New York, future smart city projects will be able to create much more sustainable, efficient, and inclusive urban environments by drawing on tested strategies and avoiding common mistakes.

CONCLUSION AND FINAL REFLECTION

In a nutshell, Smart City is one of the most extreme changes introduced by urban development. Here, technology and data meet to bestow more efficient, livable, and sustainable urban space. To that end, the present chapter has comprehensively discussed integrating SCPS in dimensions of urban planning as technological, social, economic, and environmental. At the core of these SCPS are technologies such as IoT, AI, and Big Data Analytics that actually give impetus to the building of smart city processes through real-time capture, processing, and decision-making. They help make concrete certain smart urban infrastructures like smart grids and intelligent transportation systems that optimize resource usage and the quality of life in urban settlements.

The chapter has also brought to the fore how SCPS is useful in enhancing social equity, inclusion, and participatory governance. In like manner, the book has raised ethical and public concerns around data privacy, surveillance, and digital rights that challenge one for a balanced approach, so it respects individual liberty while fostering innovation. Smart cities contribute to job creation, urban competitiveness, and economic sustainability; at the same time, they are closely related with broader global economic systems. The dimension of environmental sustainability in smart cities, which is being driven by SCPS, looks at sustainability from the angle of energy efficiency, waste management, and climate change mitigation. Case studies and empirical data in the chapter strongly illustrate smart cities' potential for responding to contemporary urban challenges but also bring out their complexities and risks for implementation.

Such insights that one derives while going through this chapter impose huge importance on future urban planning because SCPS can be incorporated in the framework of a city only by adhering to an interdisciplinary dimension that involves not only technological development but also looks into the social, economic, and environmental contexts. Urban planners need to collaborate with technologists, policymakers, and indeed the citizen body in the design of smart cities that are not only efficient and sustainable but also equitable and inclusive.

REFERENCES

Albino, V., Berardi, U., & Dangelico, R. M. (2015). Smart cities: Definitions, dimensions, performance, and initiatives. *Journal of Urban Technology*, *22*(1), 3–21. DOI: 10.1080/10630732.2014.942092

Anbarasan, M., Muthu, B. A., Sivaparthipan, C. B., Sundarasekar, R., Kadry, S., Krishnamoorthy, S., Samuel R, D. J., & Dasel, A. A. (2019). Detection of flood disaster system based on IoT, big data and convolutional deep neural network. *Computer Communications*, *150*, 150–157. Advance online publication. DOI: 10.1016/j.comcom.2019.11.022

Angelidou, M. (2014). Smart city policies: A spatial approach. *Cities (London, England)*, *41*, S3–S11. DOI: 10.1016/j.cities.2014.06.007

Anthopoulos, L., Janssen, M., & Weerakkody, V. (2016). A unified smart city model (USCM) for smart city conceptualization and benchmarking. [IJEGR]. *International Journal of Electronic Government Research*, *12*(2), 77–93. DOI: 10.4018/IJEGR.2016040105

Anttiroiko, A.-V. (2016). City-as-a-Platform: The rise of participatory innovation platforms in Finnish cities. *Sustainability (Basel)*, *8*(9), 922. DOI: 10.3390/su8090922

Caragliu, A., Del Bo, C., & Nijkamp, P. (2011). Smart Cities in Europe. *Journal of Urban Technology*, *18*(2), 65–82. DOI: 10.1080/10630732.2011.601117

Casini, M. (2017). Green Technology for Smart Cities. *IOP Conference Series. Earth and Environmental Science*, *83*, 012014. DOI: 10.1088/1755-1315/83/1/012014

Chourabi, H., ... (2012) "Understanding Smart Cities: An Integrative Framework," 2012 45th Hawaii International Conference on System Sciences, Maui, HI, USA. pp. 2289-2297, DOI: 10.1109/HICSS.2012.615

Clim, A., Toma, A., Zota, R. D., & Constantinescu, R. (2022). The Need for Cybersecurity in Industrial Revolution and Smart Cities. *Sensors (Basel)*, *23*(1), 120. DOI: 10.3390/s23010120 PMID: 36616718

Cugurullo, F. (2018). The origin of the Smart City imaginary: from the dawn of modernity to the eclipse of reason.

Floridi, L., & Taddeo, M. (2016). What is data ethics? *Philosophical Transactions. Series A, Mathematical, Physical, and Engineering Sciences*, *374*(2083), 20160360. DOI: 10.1098/rsta.2016.0360 PMID: 28336805

Goutam Mukherjee, A., Ramesh Wanjari, U., Chakraborty, R., Renu, K., Vellingiri, B., & George, A., C R, S. R., & Valsala Gopalakrishnan, A. (. (2021). A review on modern and smart technologies for efficient waste disposal and management. *Journal of Environmental Management*, *297*, 113347. DOI: 10.1016/j.jenvman.2021.113347 PMID: 34314963

Gurstein, M. (2003). Effective use: A community informatics strategy beyond the Digital Divide. *First Monday*, *8*(12). Advance online publication. DOI: 10.5210/fm.v8i12.1107

Hernández-Muñoz, J. M.. (2011). Smart Cities at the Forefront of the Future Internet. In Domingue, J. (Eds.), Lecture Notes in Computer Science: Vol. 6656. *The Future Internet. FIA 2011*. Springer., DOI: 10.1007/978-3-642-20898-0_32

Jaeger, P. T. (2012). *Disability and the Internet: Confronting a digital divide*. Lynne Rienner Publishers.

Khaleel, M., Yusupov, Z., Alfalh, B., Guneser, M. T., Nassar, Y., & El-Khozondar, H. (2024). Impact of smart grid technologies on sustainable urban development. Int. J. Electr. Eng. and Sustain., 62-82.

Kommineni, M., & Baseer, K. K. (2024). An Architecture and Review of Intelligence Based Traffic Control System for Smart Cities. *EAI Endorsed Transactions on Energy Web*, *11*. Advance online publication. DOI: 10.4108/ew.4964

Krähmer, K. (2020). Are green cities sustainable? A degrowth critique of sustainable urban development in Copenhagen. *European Planning Studies*, *29*(7), 1272–1289. DOI: 10.1080/09654313.2020.1841119

Lyon, D. (2014). Surveillance, Snowden, and Big Data: Capacities, consequences, critique. *Big Data & Society*, *1*(2), 2053951714541861. Advance online publication. DOI: 10.1177/2053951714541861

Mansur, T., Nizar, T. M., Ali, R., Baharudin, N., & Ananda-Rao, K. (2021). Performance analysis of smart lighting control system for sustainable campus operation. *International Journal of Advanced Technology and Engineering Exploration.*, *8*(74), 54–63. DOI: 10.19101/IJATEE.2020.S2762179

Mazzucato, M. (2013). *The Entrepreneurial State: Debunking Public vs. Private Sector Myths*. Penguin Books.

Mossberger, K., Tolbert, C. J., & McNeal, R. S. (2007). *Digital Citizenship: The Internet, Society, and Participation*. MIT Press. DOI: 10.7551/mitpress/7428.001.0001

Norris, P. (2001). *Digital divide: Civic engagement, information poverty, and the Internet worldwide*. Cambridge University Press. DOI: 10.1017/CBO9781139164887

O'Neil, C. (2016). *Weapons of Math Destruction: How Big Data Increases Inequality and Threatens Democracy*. Crown Publishing Group.

Saheb, T. (2023). Ethically contentious aspects of artificial intelligence surveillance: A social science perspective. *AI and Ethics*, *3*(2), 369–379. DOI: 10.1007/s43681-022-00196-y PMID: 35874304

Sharma, A. (2017). India's Smart Cities Mission: Smart for Whom? *Cities (London, England)*, *91*, 70–78.

Smuha, N. A. (2021). From a 'race to AI' to a 'race to AI regulation': Regulatory competition for artificial intelligence. *Law, Innovation and Technology*, *13*(1), 57–84. DOI: 10.1080/17579961.2021.1898300

Sundmaeker, H., Guillemin, P., Friess, P., & Woelfflé, S. (2010). Vision and challenges for realising the Internet of Things. European Commission, 3(3), 34-36. https://data.europa.eu/doi/10.2759/26127

Van Dijk, J. (2020). *The Digital Divide*. Polity Press.

Yigitcanlar, T. (2014). Smart cities: An effective urban development and management model? *Australian Plants*, *52*(1), 27–34. DOI: 10.1080/07293682.2015.1019752

Chapter 2
Role of Artificial Intelligence in Smart Cities

Lalit Kumar
https://orcid.org/0009-0005-0456-7930
MMEC, Maharishi Markandeshwar University, India

Ritu Gupta
https://orcid.org/0000-0002-2435-8440
Chandigarh University, India

Komal Bhardwaj
https://orcid.org/0000-0002-9378-5542
Maharishi Markandeshwar Institute of Management, Maharishi Markandeshwar University, India

ABSTRACT

City planners are starting to have serious concerns about urbanization. Rapid, efficient, and affordable services are among the many needs of the world's residents as the urban population grows and puts more strain on available resources. To manage their city efficiently, city planners must crucially offer the necessary infrastructure support. These comprise, among other things, clean drinking water, power, infrastructure such as roads. bridges etc., housing, transit, and Information and Communications Technology (ICT). In response to growing demand in their cities, planners have turned to technology to improve service delivery, enhance residents' lives, and stimulate local and national economic growth. An overview of the many technology options accessible to planners to help them facilitate the efficient and quick delivery of services to their inhabitants is given in this chapter. Few examples of these technical solutions include big data, cloud computing, the

DOI: 10.4018/979-8-3373-0245-4.ch002

Internet of Things (IoT), artificial intelligence (AI), and machine learning (ML), among others.

INTRODUCTION

The 'obvious' starting point for discussion around smart cities and big data The first and the primary most thing which can comes to our mind is that: What actually is a smart city? The idea of the "smart city" is in fact an elusive one and varies greatly from one city and country to another.

What Are Smart Cities?

A "Smart City" as an urban area uses information and communications technology (ICT) and other technology to help manage resource and city in a more efficient, sustainable and environmentally friendly way.

Artificial intelligence is making it possible for cities to continually reinvent themselves. AI technology and smart cities The Cities can predict energy usage, pollution levels and environmental impact as well as control traffic, garbage and maintenance by using AI technology. Here are seven ways computers could help make smart cities a reality, from reduced climate change effects to better quality of life, and better decision-making, (Ward, Kim, & Dey, 2015) (Kumar & Ailawalia, 2024) (Saini, Dutta, & Marques, 2020).

AI applications such as UAVs, EVs, and AVs have led to substantial developments in urban mobility. Yet, security issues persist, and more work is needed to investigate this area.

Smart Cities: How Does AI Make Cities Smarter?

This chapter investigates the disruptive potential of Artificial Intelligence (AI) in the planning and governance of smart cities. Urban systems can be more efficient, responsive, and sustainable when AI technologies take advantage of real time data, advanced analytics, and machine learning algorithms. AI is pervasive in smart cities across domains from traffic, energy, waste, security, and healthcare.

For instance, an AI-based traffic system can foresee traffic jams and control traffic flow with the help of real-time data available from sensors and cameras. In energy distribution grids, AI can appreciate demand and support balancing the load, which increases energy efficiency and reduces waste. AI-driven systems monitor our movements and activities in the smart cities, helping to identify, for example, criminal behaviour with facial recognition algorithms and activity patterns; and large-scale AI-driven, churned models that are based on locals' behaviour through chatbots and digital platforms that improve citizen engagement and serve.

Moreover, AI also encourages the environmental supervision, by monitoring the level of pollution and the possibility of forward activeness. AI simulations looking at growth possibilities or infrastructure requirement are also profitable for urban planning. Overall, the chapter underlines that AI is the brain of smart cities, as smart cities are enhanced and made possible through automation, intelligent prediction decisions, and personalised services. Yet it also shows that when it comes to smart cities, we must also focus on addressing ethical considerations, data privacy and the digital divide in order to keep smart cities inclusive and human-centred. Rapid urbanization of the world is underway. It also showed growth in the number of people moving to cities in search of a good life. This inflow has increased the need for smart city services to contribute to elaborating favourable, efficient, and sustainable conditions which can improve urban residents' quality of life. Planners have long worked to make these metrics as favourable as possible. But many of the existing urban systems are either obsolete or incapable of sustaining a population that is ever-increasing. It is high time the government should begin using modern means of technology to moderate and make endurable the life and existence of its citizens.

Inspired by this, the idea of "smart cities" that utilise cutting-edge smart city technology has been born. Figure 1: Some the most important components of the smart city.

Figure 1. Leading components of smart cities

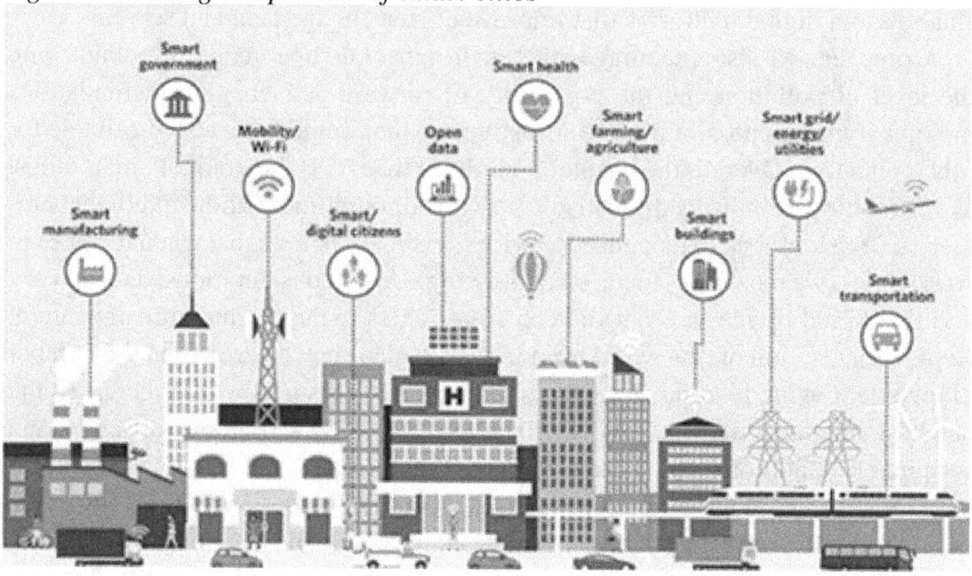

(Gupta & Kumar, 2025)

Digital technology by IoT and AI are reshaping the future cities. In cities, for example, these advanced capabilities help to reduce pollution and disaster risks, enhance public safety, better manage waste, improve traffic flow, and much more Scale cities' digital infrastructure with technology, smart, connected networks that can easily process data. An "intelligent" solution which facilitates such a technological improvement is the Internet of Things (IoT), (Gupta & Kumar, 2025). The rise of IoT development and use has exploded in recent years and there are projected to be over 27 billion connected IoT devices in use by 2025 as per a report by IoT Analytics.

Cities can also find new value in their existing infrastructure and generate value through their existing infrastructure through smart city applications. Governments and citizens save money as a result of the upgrades, and the upgrades open new revenue streams and operational savings. Smart cities also utilize other technologies other than their mesh of IoT devises in order to enhance people's QoL and promote economic activities, (Albino, Berardi, & Dangelico, 2015) (Heratha & Mittal, 2022) (Appleton, 2021).

Smart cities that are successful, go through the following four major steps:

a) Collection: Live information is collected by smart sensors located all over the city.
b) Analysis: The intelligent sensors do not extract any significant knowledge that the smart sensor data must be analysed.

c) Communication: Powerful communication mechanisms are employed to communicate the knowledge gained through the analysis to decision makers.
d) Action: Cities use data-driven insights to generate solutions, improve asset management and operations, and increase the quality of life for their residents.

ROLE OF AI IN SMART CITIES

Due to its ability to analyze big data rapidly and accurately, Artificial Intelligence can be leveraged to support city officials to help them to easily recognize patterns and trends which will lead to more informed decision making on how to manage their resources. AI has the potential to be applied in many of the smart city issues, for example, traffic management, security, garbage management, parking problem solving, etc., (Albino, Berardi, & Dangelico, 2015).

So, building smart cities depends so much on artificial intelligence and machine learning algorithms, which increasingly become so fundamental in a range of sectors. The space of cyber-physical is generated through the use of Intelligent equipment AI-driven based on machine learning. Some examples of the above devices are, meter reading devices, traffic sensors, industrial control devices, video cameras and environment sensors. When analyzed, all that information collected by these ingenious gadgets contribute to predictive analysis and decision-making in crafting smart cities.

Figure 2 represents the increases in the keywords "Smart City" and "Artificial Intelligence" during 2014. The figure shows the increase level of interest on smart cities and artificial intelligence.

Figure 2. The popularity of the keywords "Smart City" and "Artificial Intelligence" since 2014

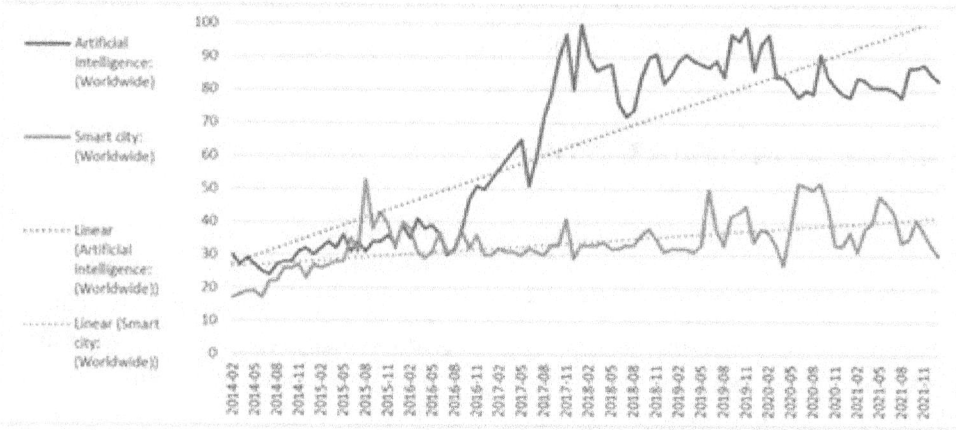

(Albino, Berardi, & Dangelico, 2015)

With an emphasis on rational decision-making, tackling climate change, and improving the lives of the populace, some of the AI applications that can be enormously beneficial in a Smart City are discussed in this chapter, (Butler & Lachow, 2016a) (Appleton, 2021) (Butler & Lachow, 2016b).

Predicting Future Needs

Artificial intelligence powered smart cities can predict what citizens will need in the future. Energy tracking devices can help cities to see how close they are to adopting greener options, when to switch to a new fuel, or when more energy is needed. Some AI may even predict and help in city planning and real estate development, putting up houses for sale when they are actually needed.

The ability to forecast what you might need down the line is an important feature of any contemporary planning, from government to business to health care, education, or environmental stewardship. In this ever changing world of rapid technological development, globalization and demographic shifts, the ability to foresee future becomes essential in staying competitive and ensuring sustainable development. Proper detection and prediction of future needs allows organizations and policymakers to plan resources, shape adaptive systems, and ultimately avoid disasters. For all of these subject areas, whether it be predicting job markets, healthcare needs, urban infrastructure, or technological trends- predicting the future need is one of the first steps in creating flexible systems that can survive and flourish despite uncertain futures.

One of the primary purposes of forecasting is to plan for the future. In today's rapidly moving world, businesses and countries can't afford to "wait and react." Instead, they are required to create long-term visions from credible projections. For example, planning for an increase in electric vehicles enables cities to adequately plan charging infrastructure ahead of time, without creating traffic hot spots. On the same note, schools who are forward thinking and see the shift in importance of AI and data science can start building out their curriculums to make sure students are ready to enter the job market when they graduate. Strategic foresight enables decision makers to design policies, investments and operations that are attuned not to yesterday's paradigm but to tomorrow's reality.

There are many tools and approaches to help forecasting the future. More conventional methodologies, like trend analysis and forecasting, are still prevalent as well. Trend analysis is using past data to predict future results. For instance, stable urban population growth would give a way to compute future housing or transport needs. More advanced approaches are, for example, scenario planning in which various possible futures are created based on ongoing trends and newly appearing uncertainties. This is especially beneficial in high return industry sectors like energy and defence where making decisions in uncertainty is common place. The Delphi process is another useful methodology to apply in tactical planning and policy formulation, as it pools expert's opinion across rounds until consensus is reached.

The deployment of artificial intelligence (AI) and big data analytics has transformed the latest prediction space over the past few years. Certainly, although not with the eyes of a human, AI can process databases of structured and unstructured data to discover patterns, correlations and anomalies. For instance, you'll find machine learning algorithms being employed in retail to estimate consumer demand, in healthcare to predict the outbreak of diseases, and in finance to predict shifts in the markets. Such tools provide insight as data streams in, correct inaccuracy in any forecasts and learn with each piece of new data, ensuring that forecasting remains a dynamic and reliable game. Now, with more access to data and more mature AI applications, predicting future trends is not only more accurate, but also more actionable.

One area in which it is especially important to anticipate what will be needed in the future is with healthcare. Given aging, prevalence of chronic conditions, and health care cost trends, anticipation of future needs can be used for two reasons: to make an effective policy and/or to plan for infrastructure. Predictive models can also predict the future needs of the population with regard to diseases such as diabetes, or cancer which can help healthcare systems to prepare for the future, in terms of staff, resources, and budgeting. Prior predictions during the SARS-CoV-2 pandemic included projections of infection rates, need for hospital beds and allocation of vaccine. That was because of advanced planning. It demonstrates the value of predictive capabilities in public health.

Another domain in which future focussed planning is encroaching is in education. As professions change, so do the skills needed to get jobs. Foreseeing which skills will be valuable to employers is valuable not just for academic institutions designing practical programmes but also for governments formulating policies to fill skills gaps. For example, with the advent of automation and AI, we are seeing a growing emphasis on STEM (Science, Technology, Engineering, and Mathematics), critical thinking, digital literacy. Future-ready education systems teach for jobs that have not yet been invented, in addition to jobs that exist today.

Urban planning and development of infrastructure also depend on accurately predicting future needs. As more than half the world's population now live in cities, a trend that's expected to continue, planners need to think ahead about what housing, transportation, energy and sanitation will look like in the future. Smart city efforts combine information from sensors, traffic cameras and public feedback to determine immediate conditions as well as long-range predictions. For example, predictive analytics can be used to identify which regions will experience a population boom — and thus require more schools, roads, or hospitals. Furthermore, for sustainable cities, cities can plan ahead for environmental impacts and deploy green infrastructure accordingly.

The business world has long relied on forecasting to make investments, plan product launches and manage supply chains. Yet, with companies making their way into the Digital World, markets are fanning out on the use of real-time data, predictive algorithms to get on the end trending side. Amazon, for example, applies predictive analytics to control inventory, suggest products to customers and help with logistics. By predicting consumer needs, companies can minimize waste, increase customer satisfaction and improve their bottom line. In finance, predictive models are used to evaluate credit risk, detect fraud, and inform investment strategies. Competitive advantage Becoming more competitive - This has therefore led to accurate 'forecasting' becoming a competitive advantage in the global economy.

Environmental sustainability is also a field where anticipating the requirements in the future is critical. These are complex problems related in an intricate fashion to climate change, resource depletion and loss of biodiversity which need long term vision and strategy. Prediction (for example, charactering of the impact of the outfield management at the present on the future climates, which enable adaptation and mitigation measures). For instance, they can demonstrate how continued deforestation might alter these patterns, or how rising sea levels might affect coastal cities. They are used by governments, NGOs and institutions to create policy, prepare for disaster response and inform the public. Anticipating ecological trends allows us to reconcile development and preservation for the sake of the future of humankind.

But job forecasting has never been easy. One of the biggest problems is data quality. If the information is incorrect, adverse, or biased, such predictions would be misleading. There is also the issue rapid changing of conditions what is true today may not be true tomorrow. Furthermore, human behavior is inherently unpredictable and shaped by many vagaries such as culture, emotion and the chance occurrences of international events. There is also the issue of ethics, especially when relying on AI predictions. For one, predictive policing has been accused of entrenching systemic biases. Hence ethical practises should be integrated in all predictive systems, such that transparency, accountability, and fairness should be encouraged in all models in order to prevent unintended impacts.

Nonetheless, the forecasting of needs is promising for the future. With the coming of superior computational technology like quantum computing, speed and precision of predictions will be greatly enhanced. When you combine IoT devices, 5G networks and edge computing, you give rise to real-time forecasting across important industries such as healthcare, manufacturing and disaster management. Moreover, the integration of predictive models between data scientists, sociologists, economists, or environmentalists will boost the capacity and competition of the predictive models.

The bottom line is that we can no longer afford the luxury of failing to anticipate our future requirements in a highly networked world that is becoming increasingly complex and changeable. Whether it's anticipating the next technological wave, addressing healthcare challenges, designing cities, or adapting to climate change, foresight is the basis of resilience as well as innovation. Through adopting data-driven tools and fostering an anticipation culture while also adopting responsibilities for ethical forecasting practices, we can do better by responding aggressively to the perils and potential promise of tomorrow.

AI can contribute fundamentally to the prediction of future needs of individuals in different fields by making use of data analysis and processing of intelligent systems, machine learning and predictive modeling, (Albino, Berardi, & Dangelico, 2015) (Pratama & Suswanta, 2021) (Angelidou *et al.,* 2017) (Caragliu & Del Bo, 2018) (Yigitcanlar, Lee, & Kamruzzaman, 2019). Here are some of the ways in which AI can be used:

1. **Tailor-made Suggestions:** E-commerce/retailing AI algorithms have the capability to automatically process buying history, browsing pattern, demographics to forecast future buying behavior and recommend the appropriate products to the customers.
2. **Content Streaming:** Using AI to know what kind of content (movie, music, article, etc.) a user may be interested in, even before the user searches for it based on past interactions and likes.

3. **Healthcare:** Predictive Diagnostics: AI could potentially predict future health problems for patients, which in turn allows preventive care early in the process. Resource prediction AI can predict what resources (e.g. medical supplies, hospital beds, staffing) are going to be required in the future for a better preparedness.
4. **City Planning and Urban Design:** Traffic Control: AI can forecast and make recommendations on traffic, for example infrastructure changes or decisions related to control of traffic.
5. **Public Services**: Plan the demand for services, e.g., waste, and public transportation, power etc.
6. **Finance Market Trends:** AI can assess the macroeconomic conditions and market trends for upcoming trajectories in stock markets which again can be beneficial for investors to take more rational decisions.
7. **Consumer Financial Planning:** AI can assist individuals in estimating their financial requirements and handle their personal budget planning in a better way by forecasting the future expenses and changes in income.
8. **Supply Chain and Logistics:** Demand Forecasting: AI can forecast upcoming demand for items, enabling companies to optimize inventory levels and avoid waste. Route Optimization – Predictive analytics can optimize delivery routes, thereby decreasing the time taken for shipping, and increasing the satisfaction level of the customers.
9. **Education:** Personalized Learning: AI can analyze how is student learning and where does the student need to go, so that more customized education plans and resources can be made available. Planning the Curriculum for Future Workforce: Forecasting future job market trends to help schools plan current curricula that will provide students with the skills needed for their careers in the future.
10. **Environmental Management:** Climate prediction: AI can forecast the climate and natural disaster in the future to help develop action plans for mitigation and adaption.
11. **Resources:** Looking into the future availability of gifts and planning for sustainable use.
12. **Customer Service:** Chatbots and Virtual Assistants: AI based tools can anticipate frequent consumer queries and anticipate best-fit solutions, resulting in enhanced consumer satisfaction.
13. **Customer Sentiment Analysis:** Forecasting the customer sentiment and feedback pattern to improve product and service i.e. offerings.
14. **Talent Management:** Identify strength of current talent and predict future hiring needs based on growth patterns in the company and industry as a whole.
15. **Staff Retention:** Examining the staff behavior and engagement to forecast the turnover and take actions to retain the precious staff. Connecting AI in these realms means that gathering and analyzing of data is ongoing, thus keeping

predictive models valid and current. By doing this, AI can empower companies and people to make better decisions, forecasting and filling our needs before we even realize we have them. If local government can ensure that the private investments meet public needs, then private-sector investment can be a useful source of capital. The establishment of impactful locally originated mild-circular carbon economy initiatives and the maximization profits can be encouraged by the government offering monetary reward to the developers and stakeholders to motivate them in the construction of urban culture and a sense of belonging, (Zanella *et al.,* 2014) (Al-Garadi, Mohamed, & Du, 2017).

Security

Modern data technologies make it possible to collect vast amounts of data from a variety of sources in real time. There's smart technology that pools data from different sources, such as from sensors, cameras, and citizens' feedback, stationed across cities that are growing in both people and physical size.

The smart city concept is a disrupt & transformative paradigm that uses the latest technologies, such as IoT, AI, big data and cloud computing, to provide better public services, improve the quality of life and to ensure the sustainable ecosystems. But as cities become more connected, and wired, the need to secure more control systems, and more data, become ever more important. Security in smart cities goes beyond physical protection and covers the concerns of cybersecurity, data privacy, ethical surveillance, protection of infrastructure, and emergency response system. Standalone, smart city advancement may expose its mediatory successes to side effects of having millions of local citizens grow with a habitat ripe to exploit.

Cybersecurity is one of the basic prerequisites of security in the smart city. With tens of thousands of sensors, cameras, and IoT devices collecting and communicating data, the attack surface is exploding for cybercriminals. A vulnerability in any part of the city's digital foundations — traffic lights or power grids or public Wi-Fi — can disrupt services, result in stolen data or, worse, a citywide meltdown. For example, a ransomware assault on a smart city's transportation network may freeze even the latter, in turn breeding chaos. So, cyber strategies like encryption, secure authentication systems, intrusion detection tools and deploy regular search for vulnerabilities are necessary for the protection of citywide digital networks.

Data protection is also a serious threat in the security aspect of smart cities. These cities generate enormous volumes of data regarding residents' location, facial recognition, biometric status, behavior, and the like. Although this information can be crucial for improved services and policy-making, it gives rise to ethical and legal concerns regarding consent, surveillance, and misuse. Keeping citizens' personal data transparently collected, safely stored and ethically used is a must.

Compliance with data protection laws and regulations, e.g. GDPR and privacy-by-design approaches are some of the important steps towards gaining public trust in smart city projects.

Physical security in smart cities is also going through a transition by digital technology's involvement. AI-enabled facial recognition on security cameras can assist the police on recognising any suspects, monitoring the crowd during public gatherings and reacting promptly to evens. Intelligent lighting systems can also illuminate dark alleys once movement is detected, discouraging potential criminal activity. Yet, these surveillance powers must be weighed against civil liberties. Too much surveillance can result in an invasion of privacy and loss of individual freedom. Consequently, there need to be boundaries in place as to the scope of surveillance, how long the data is to be kept on file, and citizen oversight.

Security of critical infrastructure is another important aspect of smart city security. In a digitally controlled city, the energy grid, water treatment, the flow of traffic and emergency services are all interconnected and dependent on real-time data and automation. When bugged or broken, these systems can cripple governments. For instance, by commandeering the water treatment system, an attacker could poison the water supply, resulting in a public health emergency. Cities must, therefore, deploy multiple layers of defence, with redundant systems, physical security at data centres, regular security audits, and cybersecurity risk analysis, to mitigate such risks.

Smart cities have enhanced emergency response and disaster management and rely heavily on dependable networks. The ICCC gather all forms of data from the departments to manage any trouble that may occur due to natural calamities, mishap or a terrorist strike. Immediate communication among medical teams, hospitals, and utility companies optimizes a more coordinated response. But in times of crisis, communication infrastructure is frequently a target, and one that aims to destroy civil society. These systems will need careful protection and therefore it is necessary for smart cities to invest in the redundancy/reliability of their communications infrastructure as well as backup systems with integrated power solutions to ensure continued operation.

Additionally, IoT security is becoming another big issue. The rise of internet-connected devices, whether in the form of smart meters and traffic lights, or public kiosks, and even garbage bins, has created additional points of vulnerability for cyber hacks. Most IoT devices are resource-constrained, so it is challenging to enforce heavyweight security mechanisms. Furthermore, they may be at risk due to the use of default passwords, lack of frequent updates to their firmware, and inadequately secured APIs. Manufacturers and city authorities must ensure that security guidelines stipulate advanced security features, like secure boot processes, end-point encryption, and over-the-air (OTA) update capabilities to help ensure vulnerabilities can be patched as they are disclosed.

In addition, the public transportation in the smart cities is also being automated and more digital communication dependent. … Smart ticketing, GPS tracking, automated traffic signals and AI-enabled traffic flow systems all increase efficiency – but they all require robust cybersecurity to maintain integrity, and prevent tampering or abuse. Hackers would, for example, be able to tamper with traffic lights and disrupt traffic, or cause accidents. As a result, transportation organizations will need to regularly assess their risks and will use AI-based threat detection systems all along the supply chain to detect any strange patterns or unauthorized access attempts.

For successful smart city, citizen should be aware and participate in the city. No city, however technologically sophisticated, can be secure if its citizens don't know the ABCs of digital hygiene. City safety City safety: Cybersecurity education programmes, Community policing projects, Citizen feedback mechanisms empowering citizens to play an active part in maintaining city safety Cities can also tap the crowd for intelligence via mobile apps that enable citizens to report suspicious activities or infrastructure problems on the fly.

Inter-agency cooperation is a key factor to any success in the security of our smart city environment. Departments from police, to fire, to health, to utilities must function on integrated platforms, so they can share information, detect threats, and respond together. Consolidated dashboards and AI-driven analytics support the authorities to identify any anomalies and to anticipate the potential risks and to act proactively. Specifically, AI can process things like data derived from social media trends, weather and traffic to predict where incidents may take place and deploy resources in advance. This kind of intelligence-based policing and crisis response demands interoperability and data standards between departments.

But the push towards smart cities can grow only when policy and governance issues are solved too. Clearing defining who owns the data, the roles/responsibilities of private tech partners, audit mechanisms and paths for redressal in case of breach, will have to be there in the regulatory frameworks. Smart cities require public-private partnerships (PPP), however they do bring locks of concerns (control fittedness, accountability, financial benefit). The latter practice also needs monitoring (with transparent contracts, regular public consultations and independent oversight bodies).

Finally, safety, resilience and future preparardness are important characteristics of a safe smart city. The city — and others are surely watching — must be prepared to stay ahead of continually evolving types of threats. This entails implementing AI-based threat intelligence, quantum resistant encryption methods, token based blockchain authentication and zero trust security frameworks. By envisioning future threats and cultivating resilience, cities can protect themselves and foster public confidence for the long term.

Conclusion The security of smart cities is a many-layered problem that cannot be solved by simply adding firewalls or cameras. It needs an integrated strategy of technological robustness, ethical supervision, citizen engagement, and antifragility. With cities becoming increasingly digitalized and interconnected, security needs to be integral to any smart scheme. Then, and only then, will smart cities deliver on their promise of safe, efficient and inclusive cities for all.

Huge amounts of data about ordinary crimes are now generated. A surveillance system that utilizes artificial intelligence (AI), can partner the threat, trends of crimes and can contribute in application of security measures. Yes, almost everywhere in the world has mass CCTV that read facial features, and this has helped with public safety especially in major cities. AI security camera technology is game changing when it comes to the ability to respond rapidly to threats. But local entities have to be able to harness this new cascade of data to gain real insights, creating an authentically intelligent system.

A recommendation engine is employed to assign patrolling cars to high criminal activity regions based on resource and expertise utilizing. Issues such as mislocating events or crime incidents, not preserving personal information as name, gender, age, etc., so as not to bias the model. One other benefit is that companies will be able to monitor, and largely reduce, traffic accidents by using their AI-enabled cameras, sensors, and traffic infraction detection systems.

Maintenance

A company called RoadBotics, an artificial intelligence startup, has built a system that assesses road snapshots and pinpoints them, then recommends cheap solutions. By knowing when and where repairs are called for, cities can manage fixes more affordably. This sort of technology also makes cities safer because problems can't go unattended. Digital transformation is driving the manufacturing industry to change their ways as efficiency and quality in production and manufacturing processes are on increased demand across sectors. The advent of digital technology has made it possible for maintainers to gather a vast amount of data, but now they need ways of addressing it that will help them to sift through it and uncover useful information and insights.

The machine-of-choice for all of this data is artificial intelligence — it's the only thing powerful enough to parse through complex machine data on a large scale and, most importantly, spit out the key insights that can drive better maintenance. Using techniques of Machine Learning, this software processes different types of machine data which in turn, provides current information about the health of the machines. When applied correctly, it is capable of detecting the slightest deviation in machine performance and conduct root-cause analysis to prevent equipment failures and downtime.

Due to the fact that industrial equipment works repetitively, it is prone to failure and downtimes worldwide. But as production and manufacturing are optimized to be just-in-time or just-in-sequence, your maintenance operation is put under increasing pressure to keep the equipment working, ensuring that unscheduled downtime does not occur and cause delays – and the loss of customers – and in a worst-case scenario loss of revenue and profits for the organization. So, the unscheduled shutdown has to be as little as possible. Predictive maintenance solution can help in achieving this.

Predictive maintenance is a data-driven approach using the condition of the equipment to predict when it will fail. Although, when the manufacturing entities make use of proper predictive maintenance methods, they could significantly extend the life and improve the performance of the equipment.

The objective of predictive maintenance is to predict when maintenance should be performed on industrial assets as to minimise the inconvenient of an unexpected failure and optimize the maintenance cost.

Controlling Pollution

Scientists have developed hardware that analyzes the types of pollutants in the air and can predict their levels over the next two hours using a machine learning technique called artificial intelligence. With such a technology police could reduce their environmental footprint by coming to conclusions prematurely. Air pollution and CO2 emissions are rapidly increasing due to this rapid urbanization.

It does this by analyzing data from many sensors, satellites and meteorological stations to track waste management, water quality, noise levels and air quality and waste disposal. AI machine learning systems can identify patterns, predict environmental risks, and trigger actions for pollution and resource management prevention. For public health, urban air pollution exposure provided adverse public health associations (Kumar & Ailawalia, 2024), apart from those of the climate, atmospheric, and disruptive changes to the ecosystem, (Angelidou *et al.,* 2017). Air pollution is a major cause of premature death of 5.5 million people annually across the world (GBD 2013 Risk Factors Collaborators, 2015). The researchers concluded that the air quality where we live also affects this phenomenon, so it's important to have clean air to extend life. Bad air quality has been associated with a range of health problems, such as respiratory disease and cardiovascular disease, from infections to chronic illnesses and cardiovascular problems, cancer and pregnancy and delivery issues.

It is of urgent need to establish an AI-based predictive system to conduct intelligent air quality monitoring. Predicting air pollution, or air quality management, and the impact of such on the creation of low-carbon cities can be significantly advantageous for the government or authorities through the AI-based prediction system. The analysis of pollution interactive patterns was a direct demand to reach this goal. At present, pollutant levels are monitored in the stations, which maintain the quality of air through existing sensor networks. Thereafter, the pollutants are checked at their levels remotely to ensure that the levels are not beyond the prescribed limits as per the U.S Environmental Protection Agency (USEPA) guidelines and mandate passed by World Health Organisation (WHO). AI can thus help in extending the air control monitoring network for example by processing measurement signals from sensor devices

Parking Systems

Parking lots could potentially spot cars that have overstayed their allotted hours and levy fines and tickets via licence plate recognition technology. Users waiting can be alerted about available spots in parking lots where AI systems have been implemented. Advanced technologies can even recommend based on the type of car. This aspect facilitates an easier understanding of demand patterns for different time of the year—both festival and non-festival time.

AI can maximise parking revenue for in-city parking spots "On-the-fly pricing" allows AI to also optimise parking income for parking spots inside a city. AI can also help city officials set the right price for parking spots that would allow them to generate maximum income yet still leave enough demand for the spaces.

The congestion has made it increasingly more difficult to find parking, thanks to the regrowth of street traffic from folks gathering in cities. Some commercially saturated areas take active use of their parking zones to new levels. The city hall cannot tweak the price dynamically to generate a better revenue for the parking infrastructure depending on the demand.

In commercially dense areas, parking zone occupancy and parking cost increase during peak hours, while in these denser locations, cheaper parking spots in nearby zones are not fully utilized to equalize occupancy. In that there, artificial intelligence (AI) is the answer allowing predicting the demand for parking zones in different areas or corners of the city and adjusting the parking slots supply on a need basis.

Applications with out-of-the box AI model pipelines for parking demand and fare recommendation Once a user gets access to the ridership insights and patterns, he or she can use the data science model pipeline in applications for forecasting, prediction, and recommendation. Maximized parking could help to make sure that parking remains reasonable for both locals and tourists, while also helping the city to generate the revenue needed to maintain and improve the parking stock.

Public Transportation

AI has been deployed to revolutionize mass transit for smart cities. This application increases consumers' satisfaction and punctuality by providing public transit users with the opportunity to have real time information and position updates. The application of self-driving buses to urban areas, which can reduce emissions, improve routes, and frequency of service, is also considered.

Even if we had the most advanced AI tools and technology, managing public transit is one of the most interesting urban challenges. City traffic is a highly time variant complex systems where thousands of people use different means of transport, leading to very complex interactions. Other such decisions must be taken on the spot in order to ensure the safety and well-being of all traffic participants.

AI-based public transport can be created that enables to work within the smart city. This system enables public transport users to gain live up dates and tracking to increase timing and customer satisfaction. There are also future plans to operate these city services using automated buses, these can help reduce emissions, improve the route as well as run more frequently.

Smart city public transportation systems What AI can do to smart city public transportation Don't just imagine it—you can use our tech for it! And here are three ways AI can help public transportation:

a) Predictive Maintenance:

Monitoring Sensors: AI can use data from sensors attached to vehicles and infrastructure to predict when maintenance will be required, preventing breakdowns and minimizing downtime.

Cost effectiveness: Supported by condition prediction, cities can manage their budgets and avoid costly emergency repairs.

b) Optimal Routing and Scheduling:

Dynamic scheduling: AI can dynamically modify bus and train schedules on the fly in response to demand, traffic or other data, helping optimize the system and minimize time in between rides.

Route optimization. By analyzing traffic patterns and passenger preferences, AI can suggest optimal routes for vehicles to minimize travel time and avoid congested areas. Smart traffic lights that drivers can control dynamically to prioritize buses and penalize private vehicle use are another example of how it may be done through AI.

c) Integrations with Other Smart City Platforms:

Multi-Modal Transportation: AI can help to connect various transportation forms (e.g., buses, trains, bike-sharing) to achieve a seamless travel experience. Smart Ticket: By optimizing ticketing system through AI-enabled dynamic pricing, automatic payment and seamless connection to other city services.

Minimization of Environmental Impact: Emission monitoring: AI can monitor and analyse the emission of public transportation vehicles supporting the cities to plan actions to reduce the green cover.

Sustainable Planning: AI could help to plan more sustainable public transportation networks, by analyzing data on environmental impact and proposing sustainable alternative routes.

With the use of AI, smart cities can build better public transportation systems, which are more efficient, reliable and user-friendly, thus enhancing the quality of life of their residents and ensuring sustainability in urban development.

Traffic Management

To reduce the level of accidents and traffic, AI is being integrated into transportation. A traffic-management system, known as CIRCLES, uses deep learning algorithms to predict and alleviate traffic — and hence reduce the pollution associated with transportation. To make traffic cameras more umbrage, easier to manage, and artificial intelligence (AI) may also be integrated into traffic camera systems to recognize the objects in real-time.

With increasing urbanization globally, cities find it increasingly difficult to manage transportation networks efficiently. One of the problems is road congestion which not only results in more time spent on the road and more fuel being consumed, but it is also responsible for environmental pollution and poor quality of life. Smart cities are expected to solve these problems with the help of advanced technology and data analytics. It is not about regulating traffic but about taking advantage of intelligent systems, real-time data and automation to build an efficient, safe, and sustainable urban transportation ecosystem.

The Smart City and Traffic Management Concept

A smart city relies on information and communication technologies (ICT), the Internet of Things (IoT), artificial intelligence (AI), and big data to increase the efficiency and quality of infrastructure and services, including transportation. The traffic control and management in smart cities is focused on the blending of these technologies for monitoring, analyzing, and control of traffic flow to improve road safety and to maintain a sustainable environment.

Existing legacy traffic control systems are predominantly reactive systems. Smart city traffic control systems however are more proactive and predictive, and help the authorities to prevent traffic jams and make routes faster and assist police response to the events as early as possible. These changes are enabled by integrated systems, real-time monitoring, and sophisticated analysis.

Smart Traffic Management, Key Technologies

Smart traffic systems are built on the infrastructure of IoT devices and sensors. These data can originate in various equipment implanted within the road, for example, road sensors, GPS devices, radio frequency identification (RFID) tags, and cameras that are wired and capable of monitoring speed and volume of vehicle, condition of the road, and the environment. This immediate and current data makes it possible to act in real time on data.

Artificial Intelligence Artificial Intelligence (AI) algorithms process a large volume of traffic data, in order to identify trends and foresee future traffic. AI can be used to optimize traffic signals, predict congestion and identify accident hotspots. Machine learning models become more accurate over time as they analyse historical data and results.

Big Data and Cloud Computing

While there are tens of thousands of cars in the city and hundreds of surveillance points – the mass of data is huge. These data are stored, processed, and analyzed with big data tools. Data can be accessed and shared in the cloud across departments and parties in real time.

Intelligent Traffic Signals

Smart traffic lights react to real-time traffic flow the team's traffic lights can respond to real-time traffic flow. For instance, if there is more congestion along one of the roads the time of the green light will be automatically adjusted according to that number. This minimizes idle, cuts down on fuel consumption and reduces emissions.

GPS and Navigation Systems

The use of GPS along with information in real-time guides drivers to less congested roads. Airlines share real-time airliner locations with air traffic controllers to ensure there are no collisions, and navigation apps such as Google Maps and Waze rely on users' reports to alert drivers about traffic jams, accidents and road closures.

Command, Communication, and Control Centres

These serve as centers where a mass of data from different sources is processed, and strategic decisions are taken. Operators can look at the traffic flow, respond to emergencies, manage traffic lights, and communicate with public safety agencies.

Public Implementations of Smart Traffic Management in Cities

Among its other most important uses is congestion control. Predictive analytics and adaptive signal control will allow smart systems to predict traffic congestion and act to prevent it. For example, drivers can be re-routed, or signal timings changed using a computer system.

Smart cameras and sensors can sense crashes or stalled autos. Alerts are automatically transmitted to the emergency services, providing faster response times. Moreover, derailment diverted traffic to avoid other collisions and gridlock.

Public Transport Management

Smart traffic systems are connected to public transport networks to offer live information to travelers. Buses and trains can be prioritized to keep to their schedules, and passengers can be informed of arrival times or delays or alternative routes.

Pollution Measurement and Abatement

Ferry vehicle emissions can be monitored, and air quality data can aid in reducing pollution through the employment of smart traffic systems. But in extremely polluted places, authorities can enact odd-even car days, congestion charges, and low-emission zones.

Smart Parking Systems

One of them is parking that is a significant cause of traffic congestion in the city. Sensors identify open parking spaces in smart parking systems and direct drivers through mobile applications. This eliminates the search for parking time and reduces unnecessary traffic movement.

Integration to the Vehicle as an Autonomous Vehicle

Smart traffic systems supporting vehicle-to-infrastructure (V2I) communication as autonomous vehicles are introduced take on great importance for the safe and efficient operation of these communication systems in the cities of the future.

Smart Traffic Management in Practice

Singapore is a world leader in ITS. The city-state regulates congestion through its use of Intelligent Transport Systems (ITS) such as the Electronic Road Pricing (ERP) system. The ERP system levies vehicles according to the level of congestion and the location, incentivising off-peak travel and easing jams in congested areas.

Barcelona collects real-time traffic data through a network of sensors and cameras. The Urban mobility plan of the city covers the measures such as a dynamic traffic light system, a public bicycle sharing system, and an optimal facilities of the public transportation system. These actions have resulted in reduced traffic emissions and low carbon mobility.

AI-driven adaptive traffic control systems are now being introduced by Delhi at select locations. Cameras, vehicle sensors and traffic signals all are tied together to monitor traffic flow and signal timing. There are pilot projects with a significant saving as regards waiting times and emissions.

In Amsterdam: Prioritizing traffic signals for bicycles, and public buses, to promote clean transport — part of the city's smart mobility approach. The real-time data is also employed by the city to help direct traffic for special events and emergencies.

Advantages of Smart Traffic Control

Less time on the road: Dynamic PWS and real-time path guidance reduces travel time and shorten commute.

Fuel Saving: Save fuel by minimizing stagnant condition of vehicles & easy traffic movement.

Environmental Protection: Enhanced traffic efficiency associated with decreased vehicle emissions and improved air quality.

Improved Safety: Automated incident detection and quicker emergency response prevents accidents and fatalities.
Better Use of Public Transport -Easier interconnectivity and information leads to higher confidence in public transportation and usage.
Growth: Productive transport systems enable trade and minimize the economic burden of congestion.

Smart traffic management is a key part of the smart urban planning process. AI systems for traffic management are a huge help for metropolitan transport. Some of the real-time traffic data analysis methods based on machine learning: These machine learning (ML) techniques are utilized in the field of AI accelerate to know the traffic condition and interchange the signaling times, thereby enhancing the traffic flow and minimizing congestion.

Traffic management has undergone a rapid evolution with the emergence of intelligent technology, such as artificial intelligence (AI)-based video analytic, which has led to active traffic management (ATM). Traffic can be dynamically controlled, as based on actual or expected traffic condition, by ATMs.

By using AI, models can process past and present traffic data. This way we converge the data and look for patterns and trends in the traffic. Traffic managers use predictive analysis to predict future situations better so that employees can more effectively plan the allocation of resources, the optimum route to avoid traffic congestion, or the timing of traffic signals. AI-based systems can help identify traffic incidents like crashes, speeding, wrong way driving and objects on the road etc.

Waste Management

Artificial intelligence is starting to be used by smart cities for trash management. With the help of this technology, communities can track recycling and determine what may be recycled locally. Some Sydney communities go one step further and employ robots with artificial intelligence (AI) to sift trash and clean up places like rivers and lakes.

AI can revolutionize waste management in smart cities by enhancing efficiency, reducing costs, and promoting sustainability. Here are several ways AI can contribute to waste management:

1. Smart Waste Collection:
    - Optimized Collection Routes: AI can analyze data from waste bins equipped with sensors to determine the optimal collection routes, reducing fuel consumption and operational costs.

- Dynamic Scheduling: Based on the fill levels of waste bins, AI can dynamically schedule collection times, ensuring timely collection and avoiding overflow.

2. Waste Sorting and Recycling:
    - Automated Sorting: AI-powered robots and machines can sort waste more accurately and quickly than humans, improving recycling rates and reducing contamination.
    - Material Identification: AI systems can use computer vision to identify and sort different types of materials (e.g., plastics, metals, paper), enhancing the efficiency of recycling processes.
3. Predictive Maintenance:
    - Equipment Monitoring: AI can monitor waste management equipment (e.g., trucks, compactors) in real-time to predict maintenance needs and prevent breakdowns, ensuring continuous operation.
    - Cost Efficiency: Predictive maintenance can reduce unexpected repair costs and extend the lifespan of equipment.
4. Waste Generation Forecasting:
    - Demand Prediction: AI can analyze historical data and trends to predict future waste generation, helping cities plan for adequate waste management resources and infrastructure.
    - Event Planning: For special events or peak times, AI can forecast increased waste generation and suggest additional resources or services.
5. Route and Fleet Optimization:
    - Fleet Management: AI can optimize the use of waste collection vehicles, ensuring they operate at maximum efficiency and reducing idle times.
    - Traffic Integration: By integrating real-time traffic data, AI can suggest alternative routes to avoid congestion, improving the speed and efficiency of waste collection.
6. Public Engagement and Education:
    - Awareness Campaigns: AI can tailor public awareness campaigns to specific demographics, promoting recycling and waste reduction practices effectively.
    - Feedback Systems: AI can analyze feedback from residents to identify issues in waste management services and suggest improvements.
7. Smart Waste Bins:
    - Sensor Integration: Waste bins equipped with sensors can monitor fill levels, temperature, and waste composition, providing valuable data for AI analysis.

    - Alert Systems: AI can trigger alerts for collection services when bins are full or if there are any anomalies (e.g., fire risk), ensuring prompt action.
8. Illegal Dumping Detection:
    - Surveillance and Monitoring: AI can analyze footage from cameras to detect and report illegal dumping activities, helping authorities take swift action.
    - Pattern Recognition: AI can identify patterns in illegal dumping, allowing for targeted enforcement and prevention measures.
9. Resource Recovery:
    - Energy from Waste: AI can optimize processes that convert waste to energy, improving efficiency and maximizing energy recovery from waste materials.
    - Composting and Biogas Production: AI can enhance organic waste processing by optimizing composting conditions and biogas production.
10. Environmental Impact Analysis:
    - Emissions Tracking: AI can monitor and analyze emissions from waste management activities, helping cities implement strategies to reduce their carbon footprint.
    - Sustainability Metrics: AI can provide insights into the environmental impact of waste management practices, guiding policy decisions and sustainability initiatives.
11. Data-Driven Decision Making:
    - Performance Analytic: AI can analyze the performance of waste management systems, identifying areas for improvement and optimizing resource allocation.
    - Policy Development: Insights from AI can inform policy development, helping cities create effective waste management regulations and incentives.

By leveraging AI, smart cities can create more efficient, sustainable, and responsive waste management systems, ultimately improving urban living conditions and environmental health.

Energy Tracking

Artificial intelligence may be used in smart cities to monitor and analyze consumer and commercial energy consumption. Based on this information, decisions can be made on where to integrate renewable energy sources. This may also demonstrate to cities where energy is squandered and how to prevent it.

One goal of sustainable development, especially in cities, is to slow down the car system to allow for more environmentally friendly transportation that aligns with the goals of the energy and ecological transition. These days, announcements of such a policy are made at all tiers: regional, national, and worldwide. Reducing the harmful influence of automobiles seems to be a fundamental principle in all programs.

AI can play a crucial role in tracking and managing energy usage in smart cities by providing detailed insights, optimizing energy consumption, and promoting sustainability. Here are several ways AI can contribute to tracking energy usage:

1. Smart Meters: AI can analyze data from smart meters to provide real-time monitoring of energy consumption at the household, building, and city levels.
    - Energy Usage Patterns: AI can identify and analyze patterns in energy usage, helping to pinpoint inefficiencies and areas where energy savings can be achieved.
2. Predictive Maintenance:
    - Equipment Monitoring: AI can monitor the performance of energy-consuming equipment and predict when maintenance is needed to prevent energy wastage due to malfunctioning equipment.
    - Preventive Actions: By anticipating equipment failures, AI can suggest preventive actions to ensure optimal performance and energy efficiency.
3. Demand Forecasting:
    - Load Prediction: AI can predict future energy demand based on historical data, weather conditions, and other relevant factors, allowing for better planning and management of energy resources.
    - Peak Demand Management: AI can help manage peak demand periods by predicting when they will occur and suggesting measures to reduce load during these times.
4. Energy Optimization:
    - Dynamic Pricing: AI can facilitate dynamic pricing models that encourage consumers to use energy during off-peak times, reducing strain on the grid and lowering energy costs.
    - Smart Grid Management: AI can optimize the distribution of energy across the grid, ensuring efficient use of resources and minimizing losses.

5. Renewable Energy Integration:
   - Resource Forecasting: AI can predict the availability of renewable energy sources such as solar and wind, helping to balance supply and demand.
   - Storage Management: AI can optimize the use of energy storage systems, ensuring that excess renewable energy is stored and used when needed.
6. Building Energy Management:
   - Smart HVAC Systems: AI can control heating, ventilation, and air conditioning (HVAC) systems to optimize energy use based on occupancy and weather conditions.
   - Lighting Control: AI can adjust lighting based on occupancy, time of day, and natural light availability, reducing energy consumption.
7. Energy Consumption Feedback:
   - User Insights: AI can provide consumers with detailed insights into their energy usage, highlighting areas where they can reduce consumption and save money.
   - Behavioral Nudges: AI can use behavioral insights to encourage energy-saving practices among consumers through personalized recommendations and incentives.
8. Infrastructure Management:
   - Street Lighting: AI can manage street lighting systems to ensure they operate efficiently, adjusting lighting levels based on time of day, traffic conditions, and weather.
   - Public Buildings: AI can monitor and manage the energy usage of public buildings, identifying opportunities for energy savings and optimizing operations.
9. Policy and Planning:
   - Data-Driven Decision Making: AI can provide city planners and policymakers with detailed analyses of energy consumption patterns, helping to inform energy policies and sustainability initiatives.
   - Scenario Analysis: AI can simulate different scenarios to assess the impact of various energy policies and interventions, aiding in the development of effective energy strategies.
10. Grid Stability and Security:
   - Anomaly Detection: AI can detect anomalies in energy consumption patterns that might indicate issues such as energy theft, grid instability, or cuber-attacks.
   - Response Management: AI can help manage responses to detected issues, ensuring quick and effective mitigation to maintain grid stability.

By leveraging AI, smart cities can achieve more efficient, reliable, and sustainable energy management, leading to reduced costs, lower environmental impact, and improved quality of life for residents.

ROLE OF AI IN CONTROLLING THE ENVIRONMENT

AI can be utilised by digital cities to track their contribution towards pollution, global warming and local ecology. To minimize pollution and lower energy use, governments and cities can use AI and machine learning to make smart decisions that not only impact the environment positively. CO2 is also detected by AI in smart cities, for instance, which could assist transportation choices.

Smart infrastructure and smart services held promise, but various barriers, including lack of know-how, stalled deployment. and lack of institutionalisation, poor legislation, not being in line with silo management approach, financial constraints and very limited risk of the private sector. The aspiration to smartly change city services and infrastructure appeared highly challenging to achieve without extensive national and regional interventions. There have been two events recently that have made the cry for smart city change grow louder Notes [a href="#back"]a[/a]. The first of them relates to ecological and digital transformations of government and services that are anticipated by the public, (Al-Garadi, Mohamed, & Du, 2017) (Cellary, 2013) (Lee & Ji-In, 2019).

Taking into consideration the environmental concerns, Solar Bike Highway in Hyderabad was developed under the leadership of Kalvakuntla Taraka Rama Rao (KTR) an Indian politician serving as the Minister for Municipal Administration and Urban Development; Industries and Commerce; and Information Technology, Electronics and Communications of Telangana. The state-of-the-art solar cycle track launched in Hyderabad is pioneering endeavour to promote non-motorised transport, and sets a benchmark for other cities in India and the rest of the world to follow in developing world class cycling infrastructure conducive to their local conditions. This road has comfort services such as drinking water, restrooms, baby rooms, a food truck, bicycle parking, service station. And it was the second such highway after South Kora. And frankmingly such type of steps has to be taken in order to solve environment problem.

Micro-Climate Analysis

Landscapes have different roles with respect to the environment, human welfare and ecological sustainability and are partly the cause of their intricacy. Landscapes provide green recreational areas and have a cultural and historical value, provide spaces to grow food and agriculture, support habitats for biodiversity, regulate temperature and microclimate, manage water resources through absorption and filtering and also have a social and psychological impact on humans. In essence, landscapes have many different ecological, social, and economic functions that contribute to life in general and sustainable life in particular. In areas of hot and humid climate such as the Gulf countries (UAE, Qatar, Saudi Arabia, Kuwait, etc.) the landscape is expected to have a large influence on the microclimate.

Also, and this is important, the species are planted that can endure the hot summers those nations typically have. Conserve was invited to study the microclimate for a prestigious project. In this case study, we will show you how to simulate a microclimate in a landscape with CFD.

1. To comprehend the variations in temperature that are seen in and around the Garden in the most extreme weather (summer and winter).
2. To comprehend the temperatures of the leaves and how they survive and flourish in the local microclimate.
3. To comprehend the impact of the microclimate on softscape elements like grass, lower shrubs, and pavers—their survival and growth in the surrounding microclimate—it is important to understand the surface temperatures at lower heights (<0.5m).
4. Specialists will be better able to make decisions and comprehend the growth of both native and non-native species and their healthy growth if they have a foundational grasp of local conditions.

A primary obstacle in creating the digital twin of the microclimate is obtaining real-time meteorological data for predicting in the short term. In order to achieve this, a Grasshopper model is created with the goal of regenerating the epw fle using forecasting data. The JSON-formatted forecast weather data are obtained from the Open Weather Map API, which offers short-term weather forecasts. For the epw fle to regenerate, the API fle must provide the following four parameters: wind speed, sky cover, relative humidity, and dry bulb temperature. These components produced the global solar radiation, hourly dew point temperature, and as well as models of diffuse and direct breakdown. Because Grasshopper cannot communicate directly with EnergyPlus, an automated procedure to rewrite an epw fle depending on the current epw fle was created by connecting Open Studio, Energy Plus, Radiance, and Daysim using the Honeybee tool. The hourly format of the automated procedure was used to replace the weather elements. These weather data will be used in the upcoming simulation steps.

CONCLUSION

To conclude, the inclusion of AI to the smart city can bring more smart, efficient, and sustainable to the cities. Through the application of AI in areas such as energy management, transportation, waste management, public safety, healthcare, environmental monitoring, infrastructure management, citizen engagement, and data-driven decision-making, cities can realize a number of advantages.

With the help of AI, they can monitor in real time, predict through analytics, optimise resources, automate and make AI–based decisions that lead to increased efficiency, a capital efficient savings, a clean environment and deliver better living experiences to the citizens. AI allows cities to tackle complex issues and adapt to evolving urban environments – from optimising energy use and easing traffic congestion to improving waste management and boosting public safety.

In addition, AI promotes innovation and encourages the creation of smart technologies to make cities more resilient, responsive, and equitable. Using the power AI, Smart cities would be able to build future urban spaces which are sustainable-environmentally and economically - and equitable.

Essentially, AI is the fuel accelerating the development of smart cities and the progress to a future where our cities will be not only more technologically advanced, but also more livable, resilient and economically viable for all dwellers. By making strategic investments in AI-powered projects and leveraging the data AI requires, cities can make mobilizing AI work to their advantage and create a smarter, more sustainable tomorrow for generations to come.

REFERENCES

Al-Garadi, M. A., Mohamed, A., & Du, X. (2017). Exploring the impact of artificial intelligence on smart city research: A bibliometric analysis. *Sustainability*, *9*(5), 681.

Albino, V., Berardi, U., & Dangelico, R. M. (2015). Smart cities: Definitions, dimensions, performance, and initiatives. *Journal of Urban Technology*, *22*(1), 3–21. DOI: 10.1080/10630732.2014.942092

Angelidou, M., Psaltoglou, A., Komninos, N., Kakderi, C., Tsarchopoulos, P., & Panori, A. (2017). Enhancing sustainable urban development through smart city applications. Journal of Science and Technology Policy Management.

Anthopoulos, L. G. (2017). *Understanding Smart Cities: A Tool for Smart Government or an Industrial Trick?* Springer International. [REMOVED HYPERLINK FIELD], DOI: 10.1007/978-3-319-57015-0

Appleton, J. (2021). *What is IoT and why is it important for smart cities*. Emerald Publishing Limited.

Appleton, J. (2021, May 11). What is IoT and why is it important for smart cities. Emerald Publishing Limited. Butler, R. J., & Lachow, I. (2016). Smart cities and the internet of things: Benefts, risks, and options. New America. http://www.jstor .com/stable/resrep10510.5

Butler, R. J., & Lachow, I. (2016). Smart cities and the internet of things: Benefts, risks, and options. New America. http://www.jstor.com/stable/resrep10510.5

Caragliu, A., & Del Bo, C. (2018). Smart cities: A review of definitions, metrics, and initiatives. *International Journal of Urban Sciences*, *22*(2), 168–186.

Cellary, W. (2013). Smart governance for smart industries. In *Proceedings of the 7th International Conference on Theory and Practice of Electronic Governance*. 91-93.

Cugurullo, F. (2020). Urban Artificial Intelligence: From Automation to Autonomy in the Smart City. In Frontiers in Sustainable Cities 2. 38.

Gupta, R., & Kumar, L. (2025). Analysis of Bit Rate vs SNR in Coded FSO Communication Systems. 2025 3rd IEEE International Conference on Industrial Electronics: Developments & Applications (ICIDeA), Bhubaneswar, India, pp. 1-5, DOI: 10.1109/ICIDeA64800.2025.10963345

Heratha, H. M. K. K. M. B., & Mittal, M. (2022). Adoption of artificial intelligence in smart cities: A comprehensive review. *International Journal of Information Management Data Insights*, *2*(1), 2. DOI: 10.1016/j.jjimei.2022.100076

Komninos, N. (2013). *Intelligent cities: Innovation, knowledge systems and digital spaces*. Routledge. DOI: 10.4324/9780203857748

Kumar, A., & Navdeep, M. (2021). An approach-driven: Use of artificial intelligence and its applications in civil engineering. In Manoharan, K. G., Nehru, J. A., & Balasubramanian, S. (Eds.), *Artificial Intelligence and IoT: Smart Convergence for Ecofriendly Topography* (pp. 201–221). Springer Singapore., DOI: 10.1007/978-981-33-6400-4_10

Kumar, L., & Ailawalia, P. (2024). Advances in Answer Set Planning: A Comprehensive Survey and Integration with Mixed Integer Programming. *15th International Conference on Advances in Computing, Control, and Telecommunication Technologies (ACT 2024)*, vol. 2, pp. 4210-4214.

Kumar, L., & Ailawalia, P. (2024). Knowledge Extraction from Answer Set Programming based Encoding Selection. *15th International Conference on Advances in Computing, Control, and Telecommunication Technologies (ACT 2024)*, vol. 1, pp. 1494-1499, 2024.

Kummitha, R. K. R., & Nathalie, C. (2017). How do we understand smart cities? An evolutionary perspective. *Cities (London, England)*, *67*, 43–52. DOI: 10.1016/j.cities.2017.04.010

Lee, J. Y., & Ji-In, C. (2019). The evolution of smart city policy of Korea. In Emergence, S. C. (Ed.), *Leonidas Anthopoulos* (pp. 173–193). Elsevier., DOI: 10.1016/B978-0-12-816169-2.00008-0

Navarathna, P. J., MalagiInternational, V. P.,(2018). Artificial Intelligence in Smart City Analysis. In Conference on Smart Systems and Inventive Technology (ICSSIT). DOI: 10.1109/ICSSIT.2018.8748476

Pratama1, I., Suswanta, S., (2021). Artificial Intelligence in Realizing Smart City through City Operation Center, In Proceedings of the International Conference on Public Organization. 209.

Saini, J., Dutta, M., & Marques, G. (2020). Indoor Air Quality Monitoring Systems Based on Internet of Things: A Systematic Review. *International Journal of Environmental Research and Public Health*, *17*(14), 4942. DOI: 10.3390/ijerph17144942 PMID: 32659931

Tan Yigitcanlar, T., & Cugurullo, F. (2020). The Sustainability of Artificial Intelligence: An Urbanistic Viewpoint from the Lens of Smart and Sustainable Cities. In State of the Art and Future Perspectives in Smart and Sustainable Urban Development. 12(20), 8548; DOI: 10.3390/su12208548

Ward, J., Kim, J., & Dey, A. K. (2015). Smart city sensors: A survey. *ACM Computing Surveys*, *48*(1), 1–34.

Yigitcanlar, T., Lee, S. H., & Kamruzzaman, M. (2019). Artificial intelligence and machine learning for smart cities: A bibliometric and systematic literature review. *Cities (London, England)*, *89*, 186–201.

Zanella, A., Bui, N., Castellani, A., Vangelista, L., & Zorzi, M. (2014). Internet of things for smart cities. *IEEE Internet of Things Journal*, *1*(1), 22–32. DOI: 10.1109/JIOT.2014.2306328

Chapter 3
AI and the Rule of Law in Urban Security: Upholding Police Accountability in Smart Cities

Sheikh Inam Ul Mansoor
https://orcid.org/0000-0001-8636-4769
Dayananda Sagar University, India

ABSTRACT

The global governance of AI is an essential theme for scientific research and reflection since AI technologies actively or passively influence various sectors worldwide. The subject of this chapter is the necessity of an adequate framework that can support innovation processes and consider ethical factors at the same time. It provides the current status of regulation of AI and the problem of how to guide technological progress towards respecting fundamental human values and rights and international cooperation. The authors explore and re-affirm the effects of AI at the societal level before outlining the possible research directions on the regulatory frameworks for AI, ethics, and cooperation internationally. This chapter is devoted primarily to AI in security and policing in smart cities and its further application to law, regulation, and governance. Non-technical considerations like open justice, privacy, and operational justice as applied to AI in law enforcement are discussed under the auspices of properly utilizing AI to execute the rule of law.

DOI: 10.4018/979-8-3373-0245-4.ch003

INTRODUCTION

The application of AI in management of cities particularly under smart city frameworks represents a revolution in police and public security. Fast developing cities with a focus on technological advancement, connectivity, and the use of data in managing services create an appropriate environment for implementation of AI systems for management and maintenance of order (Ullah et al., 2024). These cities use technologies to control resources and infrastructure, supervise and solve societal necessities where AI is essential to improve the capability of urban systems (Wolniak & Stecuła, 2024). Against this background, the convergence between AI and policing has brought in complex legal and ethical concerns, giving rise to rather questions concerning ordering and regulation, responsibility, as well embracing of rights and freedoms (Sachoulidou, 2024). This chapter looks at how AI technologies for smart cities can enhance or threaten urban security and assures the use of principles of the rule of law in the application of these technologies and technologies.

The main concept behind smart cities is the utilisation of data as a means to improve living in urban environment. AI technologies are at the core of this eco-system, since they support predictive analytics, automation and real-time decision-making (Kandt & Batty, 2021). Stable urban management in today's society requires efficient policing mechanisms through which crime has been mechanized, public safety, and proper enforcement of the law the application of AI has been embraced widely (Manning & Agnew, 2020). Examples of such applications include; predictive policing algorithms in crime analysis, facial recognition systems in surveillance, and automated surveillance mechanisms in policing work. These innovations being heralded for their accuracy and efficiency hold the potential to completely transform policing through efficient response, effective resource management and the use of analytical tools to inform crime-fighting strategies (Jenga et al., 2023). However, integration of such tools into policing requires analysis of their compliance with legal standards especially on the cardinal values of openness, responsiveness, and equal treatment. The use of AI in policing presents questions of concern that complicate the polity's constitutional and human rights. The country's principle that informs the governance of societies that are democratic requires that any actions, including those of law enforcement agencies, must be legal. This principle make it possible for power to be exercised under law, afford parity and put into check the exercise of power (Završnik, 2020). Further, in the case of AI-supported police work, the rule of law presupposes that tools should be chosen both effective and legal and meet the standards of legal permissibility. We are also seeing rampant AI misapplication leading to sabotage of due process, loss of public confidence, and perpetuation of bias in the society (Blount, 2024). Consequently, this chapter argues that there is need to enhance accountability mechanisms, follow procedural fairness, and respect to the fundamental rights in the usage of AI in the practice of law enforcement (Wani & Mansoor, 2025). Furthermore, the role that is played by AI in contributing to police creates nexus with democracy by dealing with the relationship between human rights and state authority. Democracies prescribe freedom of civil liberties and fairness of justice. It is the essence of policing, and any adoption of AI technologies in policing should not stray away from these objectives but should build upon it (Jungherr, 2023). For example, facial recognition systems aimed at improving security have been criticized for invasion of personal privacy and therefore violation of the right on privacy. Accordingly, an application of historical data to predict future activities, as in case with the so-called predictive policing, may lead to the reproduction of bias and discrimination if the corresponding measures are not taken (Sarabdeen, 2022). These problematics exemplify the need to engraft democratic principles in AI decision making to encourage its applicability to the cause of justice and fairness.

This chapter examines the relationship between the rule of law and policing exercised in the context of legitimizing the action of the state, especially in the modern age, where algorithms and machine learning are becoming the norm for decision-making models. There are problems of executive control associated with "black boxes" of opaque AI systems. These points raise questions about how exactly these systems work given the vagueness of their operation creates doubt and impedes the way that regulatory bodies can efficiently monitor them for efficiency and fairness (Hassija, Chamola, Mahapatra, et al., 2024). Concerning this, it is possible to familiarize with the European Union's General Data Protection Regulation (GDPR) as the significant legal tool whose objective is to improve the transparency of the automated decision-making process (Hoofnagle et al., 2019). Such examples should remain in the backdrop that both policymakers and policing agencies have to build strong frameworks adhering to non-arbitrary usage of AI in the policing function. Also on the procedural fairness front, AI is clearly connected to the rule of law. Procedural justice that is the other principle of justice deals with justice in decision-making procedures and hence refers to fair and impartial decisions made appropriately (Decker et al., 2025). With regards to AI policing this means that individuals who are affected by policing decisions made by AI should have a chance to correct these decisions or sue for them. Lack of such mechanisms erode the authority of AI tools besides being a violation of due process law as provided in the constitution and international law (Sachoulidou, 2024). Therefore, the cases supporting programming AI systems with the principles of justice and fairness regulations require a foundation for procedural safeguard integration.

Urban policing is not an area that can be immune to transformative AI potentiality. Employing big data and analytics solutions, the functioning of law enforcement agencies can dramatically improve its outcomes and optimize work to fight crime. However, at the same time, this potential has to be approached with a very proper compliance with the legal and ethical requirements (Kandt & Batty, 2021). When it comes to adopting AI for SMAC, attention must be given to its understanding of the driver of governance, rights, as well as democracy. As scholars and technologists, such an approach allows AI technologies to be the tools of justice and equity, and not as the maintainers of the array of existing inequities and challenges to the rule of law.

LEGAL AND ETHICAL CHALLENGES IN AI POLICING

Implementation of AI technology in the policing approach especially within the smart city concept has raised significant discussion on the legal and Ethics implications (Davies & Krame, 2023). Although the use of AI in public safety and crime prevention has great potential to create a significant change than starting a revolution in law enforcement, the decision has raised multiple controversies in disenchantment transparency and accountability, bias and discrimination, privacies, and data protection (Fontes et al., 2022). These issues, based in the technology aspects of some human rights, require adequate legal regulation of AI-based policing so that the latter would not deviate from the principles of the rule of law and justice. The first of the major complications in the use of AI in police work concerns the account of decision-making within algorithmic systems (Rodrigues, 2020). Dubbed 'black-box models' such algorithms tend to provide no explanation of how the ultimate decisions are arrived at, thus often, it becomes challenging to determine why a particular decision was made. This opaqueness is a straight up affront to the principles of accountability and due process since anyone affected by decisions made by an AI algorithm may never understand or have the ability to challenge such a decision (Hassija et al., 2024). Not only do machine-learning models that had learned and acted with no possibility of explainability erode citizens' trust, but also they may continue and reinforce unfair practices. Transparency is thus a legal necessity – the use of AI has to be explained and made accessible to those outside the scope of the algorithm, to the oversight bodies and courts (Mansoor & Wani, 2025). To facilitate independent audits current legislation needs to require that organisations reveal the algorithm that underlies the functioning of their AI systems and that they function in a manner that is constitutional and compliant with international human rights laws (Balasubramaniam et al., 2023).

Another major issue to do with AI policing relates to accountability, which, as we know, is pinioned strongly to the issue of transparency. The conventional models of police are managed by sound system of responsibility, according to which police departments and specific officers hold responsibility for their behaviours (Hung & Yen, 2021). However, delegation of decision-making power to the AI systems make this relation challenging. Real doubts emerge as to who is held legally accountable for the mistakes, prejudice, or detriment AI systems deliver—developers, vendors, or the law enforcement organizations using such systems. This diffusion of responsibility means there is legal void that has to be filled with concrete accountability mechanisms (Novelli et al., 2024). These frameworks must distinguish the roles of multiple actors and include some pathways for compensation in case of damage. Moreover, the principle of accountability requires scrap and bonafide proactive assessment to check violations of the AI legal and ethical guidelines. Another controversy in AI policing is biased and discriminative results from algorithm base systems that are used are now in operation. In AI systems, the algorithms are built and trained on past information that contains known unfair social patterns and discrimination. This is because when such data is used to develop predictive policing models it ends up fortifying such plenary discriminations (Joseph, 2024). For instance, algorithms may over police the black community because the police have always policed it in a disproportionate manner. This concern is especially real in territories whose police forces have been reliably implicated in racially or socio-economically discriminatory policing (DaViera et al., 2024). This principle, legally protected in recent constitutional and international legal documents, requires creating and implementing AI systems that cannot give discriminative results. It means that legal protections must also encompass algorithmic review to determine bias and require direct effects use in terms of testing the possible effects of AI instruments on certain population categories (Zuiderveen Borgesius, 2020).

This issue of bias does not start and end in feeding AI models with certain training data but encompasses the housing, implementation and widespread of the AI. Implementers of AI systems may incline towards developing the tools with certain biased ideas to predispose their decision-making systems. This highlight the need for multi-disciplinary team where lawyer, ethicist and technologist come together in order to analyze problem areas that relate to bias (Ortega-Bolaños et al., 2024). In addition, the use of such systems should be preceded by specific rules so that the law enforcement agencies met the constitutional standards and norms of human rights while applying artificial intelligence systems (Venkatesh, 2022). Privacy and data protection is still another very significant area and feature of the legal and ethical aspects of using AI policing. AI applications including facial recognition systems and predictive reports require large databases with personal information. While these systems can improve the security of individuals in the public, these systems remain dangerous concerning the right to privacy as enshrined in the constitution bill of rights and other international human rights conventions (Smith & Miller, 2022). AI Systems that assist mass surveillance are considered as being violative of the principle of proportionality, and their deployment has been questioned repeatedly for their efficacy in the absence of sufficient precaution or judicial review (Karliuk, 2023). The principle of proportionality, familiar to every constitutional lawyer, is designed as a possible restriction of a fundamental right in relation to the aim pursued by limitation and the extent to which such limitation is justified (Sikri, 2021). In the concept of AI policing, this principle requires that surveillance technology should only be utilized where it is in the public interest, moreover, the implementation of the technology should be heavily protected from misuse (Fontes et al., 2022).

Privacy can be considered as a subset of data protection especially in those jurisdictions where there is no sufficient legislation governing the subject. The collection, storage, and processing of personal data by the AI systems are the issues that increase questions about the legal sufficiency of the established instruments. Of those aspects, data protection, especially consent and the right to erasure are especially important in this context (Sun et al., 2021). For example, the bad intention of people or hackers gaining access to data such as personal information, health records or financial information that have been gathered through the AI systems may cause the individuals serious and unnecessary loss their identities, or reputations (Hammouchi et al., 2019). Legal enables governing instruments should define concrete rules for data protection with reference to the principles of minimization, purposes limitation and storage security. In addition, the subjects should have the rights to access, erasure and rectification of their personal data and can exercise free control over their data (Lynskey, 2023). Specifically, the innovation process, including AI policing as one of the application fields of AI technology, should address privacy and data protection concerns that are well regulated by European Union's General Data Protection Regulation (GDPR) (Meszaros & Ho, 2021). Originally enacted to regulate the EU's data protection law, the GDPR is comprised of general provisions that provide insight into how, in theory, law can govern AI technologies in law enforcement such as automated decision-making and profiling provisions, coupled with the obligation of transparency and accountability (Ishii, 2019). Nevertheless, due to the global application of AI, there is required the collaboration of countries for the development of standardized regulation of personal data processing and protection (Zaidan & Ibrahim, 2024). Domestically, it is important to use codes of conduct and protect human rights, while multilateral agreements and other international legal instruments can supplement the Trans-national application of artificial intelligence in policing.

Explicating privacy concern and public safety adds another strimmer to ethical and legal debate about the use of AI in policing. As the information's privacy is viewed as a constitutional right, the right has to be safeguarded in balance with state responsibilities within preservation of public order and crime prevention. This raises the problem/solution dilemma, where on the one hand, the quality and efficiency offered by these technologies are considered, while on the other hand potential threat to human rights are assessed (Friedewald & Pohoryles, 2013). The efficiency of the use of artificial intelligence in policing is required to be assessed taking in to account the legal landmarks of necessity, proportionality and non-discrimination so that incorporation cannot breaches the core value of justice and equity (Blount, 2024).

IMPACT OF AI POLICING ON PUBLIC TRUST AND LEGITIMACY

The incorporation of AI for policing, as innovative as it is, affects one of the most sensitive variables familiar to society: the police's and the police force institutions' credibility (Bowers & Johnson, 2024). Policing as a function of the state is essentially warrantied by the willingness of the governed, as well as the rule of law and its equitable justice. However, the use of the AI system in law enforcement activities highlights the relationship between efficiency and the technological aspect of AI, perception of the public and their rights. Therefore, as the use of various AI based analytical tools in law enforcement becomes widespread it is of great importance to grasp the social effects coupled with the development of the technique that will guide the method of constructing and enhancing community trust (Gans-Combe, 2022). In addition, it is crucial to promote technological developments and human rights together with the equal safeguarding of the legal bases for these rights so that democratisation can continue. AI in law enforcement has positive impacted in the organisational effectiveness of policing organisations. New technologies such as, predictive analytics, technologies for facial recognition and automated police surveillance systems are expected to improve crime prevention and crime investigation (Fontes et al., 2022). However, an analysis of these advancements in giving solutions cannot exclude their impact on the society. Use of such technologies largely results to a notion of over policing especially among specific groups in the society or region or those most likely to encounter the police. This is because mutual trust between people and the police breaches the social covenant thus leading to creation of a prejudicial climate (Mukto et al., 2024). It can be seen that trust in policing institutions and its organisations is not solely born out of its efficacy but its fairness and abilities to include all in its daily practise. The tremendous transparency-related deficit raiser is the kind of artificial intelligence where their methods are difficult to comprehend, combined with cases of biased or wrong decisions (Zuiderwijk et al., 2021).

AI technologies implementation in policing also has implications to emergent shifts of power relations within the state and between the state and an individual. The state utilizes AI for intelligence and surveillance in analysis of individuals' behaviours that poses a test on the proper use of power in the state Ohio (Davies & Krame, 2023). That change is detrimental to the doctrine of proportionality that calls on states to intervene in individual rights where it is necessary and where the interference would be least invasive. If efficient legal protection is not provided, the use of AI tools concerns the creation of an atmosphere of an unobserved society in which people are monitored as if they are criminals or terrorists (Karliuk, 2023). The mentioned perceptions erode public confidence and call into question law enforcement agencies that are expected to be guardian rather than violator of civil liberties. In order to overcome these challenges and earn the confidence of the public, police all around the world have to employ strategies that involve openness, responsibility and representation. Everything related to the application, functionality and area of implementation of AI should be clearly communicated (Balasubramaniam, et al., 2023). Fundamental misinformation of and misconception about AI technologies adapts easily to advocacy outreach strategies, specifically public awareness campaigns coupled with community engagement programs. Furthermore, the police need to guarantee that the AI systems are approved by some other governing agency and audited periodically. They increase confidence of the public because it shows that the government is competent in its legal conducts (Bewersdorff et al., 2023). Other structures which are of equal importance include accountability mechanisms, which contribute to development of trust as well. To this end, the integration of AI in the policing process can only be achieved when the necessary measures that set out the critical roles and sanative measures in case of complaint for unfair recourse to the technology are put in place (Novelli, et al., 2024). Creation of outside boards and committees for overseeing of the deployment and use of AI technologies guarantees that all such technologies will be employed absolutely appropriately in relation to legal and moral frameworks. In addition, the use of design and deployment of machine learning, big data and other forms of artificial intelligence should include legal voices and ethicists as well as other citizens' representatives to check for bias and match with community values (Lavin et al., 2022).

Procedural justice which asserts ideals of fairness, impartiality and respect regarding the measure adopted by the police is equally important in relation to policing facilitated by AI. The implications of ensuring that the general use of integrated AI systems in various domains corresponds with these principles are that public acceptability of AI systems can be significantly boosted (de Oliveira et al., 2022). For instance, allowing people to challenge the decision made by the AI system, or request any decision made by such, increases the notion of being fair to individual's rights. Despite some distortions made within the framework of procedural safeguards mentioned above, these measures both strengthen the authority of law enforcement and restore the focus on justice as one of the key values of the pursuit of public safety (Taylor, 2023). Citizen rights against the advancement of information technology is may be the most sensitive issues to do with use of AI in policing. Introduction of the AI technologies should not be without preserving and protecting some of the key rights freedom of expression, privacy and public presumption of innocence

(Rodrigues, 2020). The legal frameworks for AI policing should, therefore, have measures that would ensure the impact of the rights herein is accomplished while reinforcement of the use of such technology. As in most human rights balancing tests, proportionality is used to check that benefits derived out of such tools are not inordinately infringing on freedoms of individuals (Castets-Renard, 2021). This idea is probably best served by the concept of consent in this context. This is to mean that the outcome of AI policing will depend on the social acceptance of the technologies involved will in turn depend on the views of the community on the usage of the technologies for the common good of society and democracy (Manning & Agnew, 2020). AI's implementation can gain from public consultations and participatory decision-making processes for it will increase its legitimacy. Besides, these approaches do not raise the unfair concern with overreach and misuse, and encourage ownership of responsibilities among the police organizations and the communities they work with (Zuiderwijk et al., 2021).

Another aspect civil liberties relate to is issue of data protection since machine learning mostly relies on big data to feed the AI systems, the users' data is collected and processed. The right to privacy of one's information is a crucial element in the fight and safeguarding of Personal data is a crucial factor in promoting the fundamental rights of personal freedom (Becker, 2019). Legal frameworks liberal for data protection as presented in the EU GDPR proscribe guidelines that govern the lawful, fair and transparent collection and processing of data. It means that similar standards have to be incorporated into the national regulation of AI policing; the usage of data has to be compliant with the principle of purpose limitation, data minimization, the right to informed consent (de Carvalho et al., 2020).

A new way of offering response to the clients' concern with legitimacy and trust of AI policing is through espousing integration of ethical considerations to AI policing. The usage rationality for Ethical AI should be described as actually pushing for fairness, quality, and humane interfacings with the applications (Laufs & Borrion, 2022). The use of ethical standard entails that procured, developed and deployed AI systems are in within the social expectations and provisions of the laws. Furthermore, the idea of teams consisting of technologists and legal and social scientists in order to come up with proper solutions supported by AI systems is rather encouraging (Hickok, 2024). This chapter argues that judicial supervision has a critical function in preserving the balance between the use of technology and people's rights. Courts use their judicial discretion in relation to implementation and determination of legal norms on AI policing. Through analysing the regulation of AI technologies and preventing rights' infringement, rescuing interventions shed light on how constitutional maxims are prioritized in public safety' administration (Gorlamudiveti & Sethu, 2023). Besides, the case laws offer helpful guidance for law enforcement authorities in equal to mean that the use of AI tools is legal.

GLOBAL PERSPECTIVES ON AI IN POLICING

Engagement of Artificial Intelligence (AI) in policing across the globe presents a broad continuum of uses and results that can be attributed to differences in legal systems, culture and organizational objectives (Sarzaeim et al., 2023). Some case studies originating from different parts of the world will shed light on the potential and risks that exist in Smart Policing. The United States, Europe as well as Asia have one way or the other succeeded or failed in the efficacies of their procedures and they are all controversies that call for stringent regulatory controls although with legal and societal considerations different from one another (Feldstein, 2023). These examples indicate that liberals should pay justice, accountability and civil liberties while assimilating new technologies.

In the US, the category of prescriptive analytics has garnered a lot of attention when deployed in the police force. Counting on crime statistics, AI algorithm define areas or people potentially involved in criminal dealings and thereby, help the police to distribute security more efficiently. Software like PredPol (Predictive Policing) is used across the country's cities to predict crimes including burglary, theft, and assault (Feldstein, 2023). As these systems purport to offer increased efficiency and crime deterrence, they have elicited a lot of concern about their reliability and impartiality, let alone the possibilities of forging artificial biases. However, relying on past data in an attempt to prevent future crimes is highly likely to reproduce old discrimination patterns (Benbouzid, 2019). For example, if one or several groups of people were targeted by police work in the past, the same can be applied to the predictive models, meaning that some groups will be targeted more than others will, so the circle of over-policing is created. This only opens the floodgates to targeting the subgroups causing again violation of the Fourteenth Amendment provision that guarantees the rights to equal protection from the law. Critics have claimed that prejudicial analysis in prediction policing leads to discrimination based on colour, race, or class legal and ethical concerns. AI Transparency and accountability are also the major issues in the U.S. Most predictive policing software's exist as closed source algorithms that are also not amenable to public scrutiny due to issues to do with copyright (Memarian & Doleck, 2023). This leads to a lack of clear accountability and understanding making AI-predictions as biased and inaccurate as the data they are based on, which drastically reduces citizen's confidence in law enforcement institutions. Lack of well-defined best practices for deploying and overseeing predictive policing tools increases these problems, strengthening the need for corrective legal and juridical frameworks (Jobin, Ienca, & Vayena, 2019).

The mainstream deployment of facial recognition technology in policing in the Europe region has caused a lot of controversy indicating the region's strict focus on data protection and privacy laws (Hill, O'Connor, & Slane, 2022). Facial recognition is used with various degrees of success in such countries as the United Kingdom and France for crowd control and suspects identification in criminal cases. These deployments are evidence of the technology's ability to improve societal safety; however they have also given rise to pressing question concerning the technology's operation as per the principles of proportionality, necessity, and potential misuse (Taskiran et al., 2020). Data protection laws in Europe where in particular the GDPR has very high standards before personal data that includes biometric data can be processed. Facial recognition applications and systems have to follow certain key principles such as data protection by design and by default and data minimization (Hoofnagle et al., 2019). They complained that in some cases there has been non-compliance and inadequate monitoring and supervisory mechanisms by legal scholars and human rights organizations. For instance, the use of real time facial identification technology is used by the police in the public, courts have considered it a violation of the right to privacy under Article 8 of the ECHR (Blind et al., 2023).

The case of the South Wales Police in the United Kingdom best captures the above-discussed tensions. Facial recognition technology used by the force was banned in the Bridges v. South Wales Police the very force where the Court of Appeal affirmed that the use of the technology in police work was unlawful due to violation of privacy and data protection legislation (Gordon, 2021). The court also noted that there is the need to protect citizens' rights by putting measures that prevent the implementation of such technologies In addition; there should be legal certainty on how such technology may be used, as well as applied, with the concept of proportionality being a critical benchmark. This decision identifies the role of the judiciary requiring that; technological growth does not exceed human rights standards (Urquhart & Miranda, 2021). Privacy loss is another issue that European society associates with the use of facial recognition technology and Deepuyu The technology is also accused of increasing biases and discriminations. Many academic analyses have demonstrated that facial recognition technologies have low accuracy when used for persons of color, thus there are concerns about prejudiced identification and practice (Barnard-Wills, 2013). These are recent problem areas within the EU that the European Commission has acknowledged and advanced regulatory strategies to counter the moral and legal dilemmas of Artificial intelligence. For instance, the current draft of the AI Act aims at creating a unified legal base for high-risk AI uses, such as facial recognition assessing compliance with the EU Charter of Fundamental Rights and key ethical principles (Palmiotto et al., 2023).

In Asia, the use of AI surveillance technologies has attracted quite a bit of attention, especially in China and India. These systems have multi-uses that include security and police work, social control and even regulation depending on the political and legal traditions of this region (Roberts et al., 2021). Most prominently, China is in the forefront of using AI in political policing using facial recognition, video analysis and social credit scores to track the citizenship (Sarker et al., 2021). AI surveillance in China therefore poses legal and ethical issues mainly based on issues to do with security and privacy. While Chinese officials speak of reliance on artificial intelligence as a tool to fight crime and maintain social order, observers consider that the analysed technologies facilitate mass surveillance and violate privacy and free speech rights (Roberts et al., 2021). It remains worrying though that there are no ideal privacy laws and a lack of judicial control within these states, which means that they can turn into an authoritarian regime when using AI technologies. Mainly, the case of Xinjiang will show what the use of AI surveillance may entail in a situation where human rights violations are already suspected (Coffey, 2021). The surveys have shown that technology-assisted Face Recognition among others has been employed to supervise and manage the mobility of ethnic groups, especially the Uighur people (United Nations OHCHR, 2022). These practices have been deplored globally and legal scholars have been arguing that they amount to the violations of international human rights especially the rights to non- discrimination and freedom of movement as spelt by the International Covenant on Civil and Political Rights (ICCPR).

India has a similar but equally as complicated a story to tell when it comes to AI surveillance. Its attempts at deploying the use of Artificial Intelligent in crime fighting and management of societies demonstrate the country's desire for technology led development and order (Marda, 2018). However, several issues affect the realization of data protection such as; inadequate legal framework for data protection in the region. Those agencies of Indian law enforcement agencies, applying facial recognition systems, have been cited for their lack of transparency, low legal standards of application, non-respect for privacy rights (Sayyed, 2024).

While the DPDP Act is now in place, several months had passed before its enactment, leaving Indian citizens exposed to the potential dangers of public and government surveillance using AI without adequate protection and safeguards. Nevertheless, the enactment of the Act is incomplete without proper rules and raises uncertainty over its full functionality (Malhotra & Malhotra, 2024). On the other hand, mass surveillance and application of Artificial Intelligence in political settings have been established to compromise people's freedom as well as democracy. There is a need to recommend protection including an independent oversight committee and judicial safeguards to ensure that AI surveillance fits within the constitution; especially the right to privacy as dictated in *Justice K.S. Puttaswamy v. Union of India, 2019 (1) SCC 1* (Kumar, 2019).

POLICY RECOMMENDATIONS AND LEGAL FRAMEWORKS

The independence and use of artificial intelligence (AI) in the police require that there be proper laws and policies to govern its use in order to be effective, fair and committee-free. To that end, policymakers have to find ways to counteract all the multiple problems arising from the use of AI technologies through a series of measures that would consolidate a renewed system of checks, erase biased elements, protect individuals' data, and engage the public in the decision process (Zuiderwijk et al., 2021). All these actions have to be built based on justice, openness and conformity with the law, so that technical progress leads only to positive changes of the existing situation, to strengthen and protect civil liberties. One of the indispensable components of the AI regulation to address the use of the technology in policing is providing ways for algorithmic responsibility. Since many AI systems are complex and described as 'black boxes,' there is a need to focus on common guidelines that will allow the scrutiny of decision-making (Erdélyi & Goldsmith, 2022). This can be done by making it compulsory for developers of AI models to document their reasons for arriving at its decisions and the data used, so that outside auditors and government regulators could check the inputs used in the model. Since police forces, use AI technologies to exercise police powers public and private entities creating and implementing the technologies should meet legal disclosure duties. Such steps help in making sure that the AI system work in the approved and ethical legally defined parameters.

Finally, liability to explain which principal shares accountability for harm done by AI systems is also a requirement of accountability. Currently, it is for policymakers to define who is responsible for the erroneous and biased AI outcomes in cases where such tools are used (Novelli et al., 2024). This may involve prescribing new remedies into the tort law systems or extending existent tort law doctrines or prescribing other legislative regimes. Moreover, independent watchdog agencies empowered to conduct probe and address complaints of wrongdoing by individuals or organizations on use of AI should be set. These bodies act as observers to the activities of stakeholders and observe whether they are within the legal precisions set down.

Reducing bias in AI is an important policy concern as algorithmic discrimination erodes the cannons of equality in the laws. One of the biggest challenges that come within the implementation of bias is brought about by the training data; this usually contains certain biases corresponding to past unfair treatment that has taken place (Alvarez et al., 2024). Regulations should require the policy models to be built from diverse data that adequately represents the population and this process should be followed by some testing to estimate and remove the biases. In the current state, developers should be mandated to carry out impact assessments that seek to determine likelihood of discrimination and the results should be disclosed to the public. There is also a need for regulatory to put in place standards on the ethical manner in which AI systems should be designed which include; who to harm no one & be fair on all (Mennella et al., 2024). Pre-deployment biases can be detected and prevented with further means that include algorithmic fairness metrics, adversarial testing. This tool may also be applicable in this rating to avoid the pre-deployment bias. In addition, the involvement of multidisciplinary supervision teams, that is, lawful advisers, ethicists, and societal members, can assist in offering a comprehensive vision of the entailing societal impact of AI policing devices. This makes sure that Artificial Intelligence working parity with the democratic values and standards of the human rights.

Another aspect that requires a legal enhancement to regulate representatives of artificial intelligence in law enforcement is improving privacy measures. Much of AI and predictive policing including facial recognition entails the processing of large quantities of people's data (Zaidan & Ibrahim, 2024). Due to the risk of abusing of the personal information gathered by the organizations, and to safeguard personal identity, there must be legal measures that set out the extent to which information may be gathered, stored and used. Most of these limitations should be subjected to principles like data minimisation, use limitation and consent so that the necessity and proportionality of the data processing practices are met. It should also be noted that any sufficiently developed legislation guaranteeing privacy must also regulate threats connected with the penetration and interception of information. In order to increase the safeguards for such information, the policy makers should enforce the execution of stringent security features like encryption and control of access (Erdélyi & Goldsmith, 2022). Further, people shall be given the freedom to have their data, correct them and even delete them which will allow people control over personal details. For these rights to be effectively upheld a number of countries have developed independent data protection authorities with the authority to compel compliance and which can impose sanctions for non-compliance.

The equity issues should also be incorporated into the policing of artificial intelligence As such and before describing how due process should be deployed in public policy, it is crucial to understand its general meaning (Decker et al., 2025). Risk assessments or sentencing recommendation made with the help of AI systems prompt questions pertaining to procedural justice and the right to appeal an adverse decision of an organ charged with administrative discretion. Some individuals can get AI decisions that affect them and they do not have any way of challenging these decisions and getting to know why certain decisions were made. For this there is a need to come up with explainability of AI, by which users are able to comprehend the outcome of the various algorithms. On this front, it is therefore important for the public to be involved in the policy-making processes to have the AI technologies that are adopted as a true reflection of the society's values and with an ability to tackle most of the issues within this society (Han et al., 2022). The dark and complex aspect of AI and big data instruments evaporates the public, policymakers, and technologists' accountability mechanism. To fill this gap, policymakers require policies that compel decision makers to engage a range of stakeholders including civil society organizations, advocacy groups and marginalized communities. These processes should afford the relevant form of participation and therefore allow stakeholders to shape some of the decisions concerning the design and (or) deployment of the AI systems as well as the kind of regulation that needs to be applied.

There is also an important aspect that can be supported through transparency is publishing impact assessments and policy reasons. Through disclosure of relevant information on the soul and potential advantages and dangers of AI innovations, administrations can promote society's trust in the approach they have made to manage such innovations (Ho, Hancock, & Miner, 2018). In addition, legal and public education and awareness can make the citizens gain necessary knowledge as to proactive and informed engagements against AI tended police work. Adding to the calls for coordination in dealing on AI, the cross-border nature of AI also add to the call for legal ad policy response. Since many Artificial Intelligence technologies are developed and implemented across borders, and since data exchange also occurs globally, certain standards would have to be brought into conformity (Tallberg et al., 2023). Governments must collaborate to establish good practices guiding organizations working in the international environment on issues regarding data exchange, algorithmic explanation, and accountability. International conventions and more particularly regional systems like the AI Act of the European Union may be emulated to harmonize domestic laws with those of the international standards.

Contrary to the principles of proportionality, necessity and legality, any other principles devised when it comes to the use of Artificial Intelligence in policing need to be banned. There is huge potential for growth in people and society's potentialities through technology, but there is also a great risk in providing unlimited freedom to some technological developments that may harm individual rights and/or general societal values. It must be emphasized that such utilization of the legal regulation of AI deployment entails thorough comprehension of the circumstances under which AI systems apply; legal frameworks should be sufficiently adaptable to address new challenges while being faithful to justice and equality.

CONCLUSION

The use of AI within policing brings a shift in the application of technology in government and polices as well as the law. AI and specifically, Machine Learning has evolved and brought awareness to both opportunity and risk that may exist within judicial system. Several generalizations and lessons can be derived from the analysed discourse about expanded uses of AI in law enforcement, for distilling the future course of missioned poly-legal transformation with provision for foundational principles of law and social acceptability. Perhaps the most obvious findings from the analysis of AI application in policing concerns the fact that it increases productivity whilst raising social justice issues. Governments around the world are embracing AI technologies like the predictive analytics and facial recognition, autonomous surveillance, since they open the door for better allocation of resources in policing, and crime detection and prevention, and safety of the society. Nevertheless, their use triggers important legal and ethical issues especially on the rights to privacy, equity and natural justice as well as accountability. This distinction must be acknowledged to capture AI in its potential to revolutionize the world by also underlining ways in which this technology has the ability to transgress human rights and further enshrine discrimination.

Holding the AI technology's developer responsible for the consequences of the AI technology becomes the main legal assertion to alleviate the risks of applying the AI technologies. The general idea of black box decision making a result of algorithms, and the fact that these are not easily understandable by the nonprofessional, raises issues regarding transparency of decision-making processes and related accountability. It is unreasonable to avoid presenting high requirements for legal responsibility regarding all the parties involved in the design and introduction of AI systems. This also encompasses requiring recording of processes common in algorithms, datasets and decisions in order to enhance audit and review processes. Furthermore, liability structures have to articulate who bears how much risk for AI-produced mistakes or discriminations and tie accountability for such to legal remedies. The final key lesson drawn is pertains to the role of bias in proper deployment of AI in police work. Socio-political bias: A given society has been designed in a certain unfair way and this is transferred into the data by gathering data in a systematic way, therefore whatever data that is fed to the AI system will be prejudiced. It highlights the necessity for inclusionary and responsible stock gathering sets that are valuable, reasonably various, and valid for fair testing and tuning before being released. Furthermore, the training of fairness metrics, adversarial evaluation and ethical review as integral parts of AI development and deployment in the justice system means that the risks of AI algorithmic bias are well managed and people place their confidence in the efficacy of using artificial intelligence in the justice delivery system.

This chapter has identified that the privacy protection is still one of the most significant issues when it comes to the use of artificial intelligence in law enforcement. Due to the wide area coverage made possible by the application of Artificial Intelligence to closely monitor the individuals, this area has major problems in the area of private privacy and data protection. Law and regulations should incorporate principles like data minimization, purpose limitation and collection, informing consent, guarantees that the collection and processing of individuals' data applied proportion and necessity principles. Stronger privacy is needed not only because of the rights to privacy of citizens but also on the grounds of avoiding using data in ways involving manipulative tools which undermine people's trust and democracy. Before we discuss the future of AI in policing, its future should focus on integrating the formally into the context of the rule of law. It is imperative that it be done with complete adherence in accordance with the best principles of AI, justice, equity and human dignity in the advancement of the objectives of the law enforcement departments. This matter requires a new thinking about legal regulation and its evolution parallel to developments in current technology for the safeguarding of human and civil rights.

It is beyond doubt that the use of artificial intelligence in policing will not only go on developing but will also change due to breakthroughs in many areas, including machine learning and data analysis, as well as the growing computational capabilities of contemporary computers. New and innovative uses will disrupt the current perception of security and public safety by offering capabilities that go beyond real-time threat identification, behaviour forecasting, and self-controlled response mechanisms. However, their application must be determined legally and ethically, to ensure that those innovations are used and applied in a correct manner that respects human rights on the society. The role of International partnership and standardization in police use of artificial intelligence will remain central to framing the future of this technology. The internationality of artificial intelligence technologies compels different countries and nations to apply the proper foundation to cope with worldwide issues like information exchange, international responsibility, and explaining algorithms. Efforts that have been made and are currently ongoing, such as the EU's proposed AI Act, present good examples of how to promote a coordinated approach. Through use of international treaties, dialogues to engage all nations, best practices are developed and used in policing involving AI technology. Words such as participation and engagement must not be removed from the discourse on AI policing. It is crucial for managers to invite other stakeholders into policymaking processes so that the use of AI technologies can be in congruence with the needs of the community. Sustaining clear and open consultation structures offers civil society organizations, campaigners for human rights, and other groups an opportunity to share their views and to demand for their rights. This kind of approach does not only increase the acceptability of the actionable principles for regulating Artificial Intelligence but also cultivates trust in the responsible use of technologies.

This means that using and implementing AI in justice requires a reinvention of approaches to teaching law and developing human resources. Police officers, solicitors, and legislators should be ready to deal with all the challenges of using AI systems. There is need for reinvention concerning AI and justice in training and developing the capacity of legal learners. Whatever is generated with the use of artificial intelligence should be made understandable to police officers, attorneys, and those who make the laws. This refers to the practical implementation of AI including technology specifications including the algorithms and data processing in addition to the legal considerations relating to implementation of the technology. Integrative practical courses with the focus on the connection between legal and technological aspects as well as ethical considerations will enable stakeholders to navigate the world of justice domain in the contemporary Information Age.

REFERENCES

Alvarez, J. M., Colmenarejo, A. B., Elobaid, A., Fabbrizzi, S., Fahimi, M., Ferrara, A., Ghodsi, S., Mougan, C., Papageorgiou, I., Reyero, P., Russo, M., Scott, K. M., State, L., Zhao, X., & Ruggieri, S. (2024). Policy advice and best practices on bias and fairness in AI. *Ethics and Information Technology*, *26*(2), 31. DOI: 10.1007/s10676-024-09746-w

Balasubramaniam, N., Kauppinen, M., Rannisto, A., Hiekkanen, K., & Kujala, S. (2023). Transparency and explainability of AI systems: From ethical guidelines to requirements. *Information and Software Technology*, *159*, 107197. DOI: 10.1016/j.infsof.2023.107197

Barnard-Wills, D. (2013). Security, privacy and surveillance in European policy documents. *International Data Privacy Law*, *3*(3), 170–180. DOI: 10.1093/idpl/ipt014

Becker, M. (2019). Privacy in the digital age: Comparing and contrasting individual versus social approaches towards privacy. *Ethics and Information Technology*, *21*(4), 307–317. DOI: 10.1007/s10676-019-09508-z

Benbouzid, B. (2019). To predict and to manage. Predictive policing in the United States. *Big Data & Society*, *6*(1), 2053951719861703. Advance online publication. DOI: 10.1177/2053951719861703

Bewersdorff, A., Zhai, X., Roberts, J., & Nerdel, C. (2023). Myths, mis- and preconceptions of artificial intelligence: A review of the literature. *Computers and Education: Artificial Intelligence*, *4*, 100143. DOI: 10.1016/j.caeai.2023.100143

Blind, K., Niebel, C., & Rammer, C. (2023). The impact of the EU General Data Protection Regulation on product innovation. *Industry and Innovation*, *31*(3), 311–351. DOI: 10.1080/13662716.2023.2271858

Blount, K. (2024). Using artificial intelligence to prevent crime: Implications for due process and criminal justice. *AI & Society*, *39*(1), 359–368. DOI: 10.1007/s00146-022-01513-z

Bowers, K., & Johnson, S. (2024). Facing the future of crime: A framework for police use of technology. *The Political Quarterly*, *95*(3), 480–488. DOI: 10.1111/1467-923X.13426

Castets-Renard, C. (2021). Human Rights and Algorithmic Impact Assessment for Predictive Policing. In Micklitz, H.-W., Pollicino, O., Reichman, A., Simoncini, A., Sartor, G., & De Gregorio, G. (Eds.), *Constitutional Challenges in the Algorithmic Society* (pp. 93–110). Cambridge University Press. DOI: 10.1017/9781108914857.007

Coffey, T. 2021. "Under the Watchful Eye of the CCP: Chinese Surveillance in Xinjiang." *Human Rights Pulse*. April 21, 2021. Accessed [date]. https://www.humanrightspulse.com/mastercontentblog/under-the-watchful-eye-of-the-ccp-chinese-surveillance-in-xinjiang

DaViera, A. L., Uriostegui, M., Gottlieb, A., & Onyeka, O. C. (2024). Risk, race, and predictive policing: A critical race theory analysis of the strategic subject list. *American Journal of Community Psychology, 73*(1-2), 91–103. DOI: 10.1002/ajcp.12671 PMID: 37067014

Davies, A., & Krame, G. (2023). Integrating body-worn cameras, drones, and AI: A framework for enhancing police readiness and response. *Policing. Policing (Oxford, England), 17*, paad083. Advance online publication. DOI: 10.1093/police/paad083

de Carvalho, R. M., Del Prete, C., Martin, Y. S., Araujo Rivero, R. M., Önen, M., Schiavo, F. P., Rumín, Á. C., Mouratidis, H., Yelmo, J. C., & Koukovini, M. N. (2020). Protecting citizens' personal data and privacy: Joint effort from GDPR EU cluster research projects. *SN Computer Science, 1*(4), 217. DOI: 10.1007/s42979-020-00218-8

de Oliveira, L. F., da Silva Gomes, A., Enes, Y., Castelo Branco, T. V., Pires, R. P., Bolzon, A., & Demo, G. (2022). Path and future of artificial intelligence in the field of justice: A systematic literature review and a research agenda. *SN Social Sciences, 2*(9), 180. DOI: 10.1007/s43545-022-00482-w

Decker, M., Wegner, L., & Leicht-Scholten, C. (2025). Procedural fairness in algorithmic decision-making: The role of public engagement. *Ethics and Information Technology, 27*(1), 1. DOI: 10.1007/s10676-024-09811-4

Erdélyi, O. J., & Goldsmith, J. (2022). Regulating artificial intelligence: Proposal for a global solution. *Government Information Quarterly, 39*(4), 101748. DOI: 10.1016/j.giq.2022.101748

Feldstein, S. (2023). Evaluating Europe's push to enact AI regulations: How will this influence global norms? *Democratization, 31*(5), 1049–1066. DOI: 10.1080/13510347.2023.2196068

Fontes, C., Hohma, E., Corrigan, C. C., & Lütge, C. (2022). AI-powered public surveillance systems: Why we (might) need them and how we want them. *Technology in Society, 71*, 102137. DOI: 10.1016/j.techsoc.2022.102137

Friedewald, M., & Pohoryles, R. J. (2013). Technology and privacy. *Innovation (Abingdon), 26*(1–2), 1–6. DOI: 10.1080/13511610.2013.768011

Gans-Combe, C. (2022). Automated justice: Issues, benefits and risks in the use of artificial intelligence and its algorithms in access to justice and law enforcement. In O'Mathúna, D., & Iphofen, R. (Eds.), *Ethics, integrity and policymaking* (Vol. 9, pp. 185–199). Springer., DOI: 10.1007/978-3-031-15746-2_14

Gordon, B. J. (2021). Automated Facial Recognition in Law Enforcement: The Queen (On Application of Edward Bridges) v The Chief Constable of South Wales Police. *Potchefstroom Electronic Law Journal (PER/PELJ)*, 24.. Available at *SSRN*: https://ssrn.com/abstract=3959617DOI: 10.17159/1727-3781/2021/v24i0a8923

Gorlamudiveti, L. P., & Sethu, S. G. (2023). Role of Artificial Intelligence in the Indian Judicial System. In *2023 International Conference on Computational Intelligence and Knowledge Economy (ICCIKE)* (pp. 305-310). Dubai, United Arab Emirates. DOI: 10.1109/ICCIKE58312.2023.10131795

Hammouchi, H., Cherqi, O., Mezzour, G., Ghogho, M., & El Koutbi, M. (2019). Digging deeper into data breaches: An exploratory data analysis of hacking breaches over time. *Procedia Computer Science*, *151*, 1004–1009. DOI: 10.1016/j.procs.2019.04.141

Han, S., Kelly, E., Nikou, S., & Svee, E.-O. (2022). Aligning artificial intelligence with human values: Reflections from a phenomenological perspective. *AI & Society*, *37*(4), 1383–1395. DOI: 10.1007/s00146-021-01247-4

Hassija, V., Chamola, V., Mahapatra, A., Singal, A., Goel, D., Huang, K., Scardapane, S., Spinelli, I., Mahmud, M., & Hussain, A. (2024). Interpreting black-box models: A review on explainable artificial intelligence. *Cognitive Computation*, *16*(1), 45–74. DOI: 10.1007/s12559-023-10179-8

Hickok, M. (2024). Public procurement of artificial intelligence systems: New risks and future proofing. *AI & Society*, *39*(3), 1213–1227. DOI: 10.1007/s00146-022-01572-2 PMID: 36212228

Hill, D., O'Connor, C. D., & Slane, A. (2022). Police use of facial recognition technology: The potential for engaging the public through co-constructed policy-making. *International Journal of Police Science & Management*, *24*(3), 325–335. DOI: 10.1177/14613557221089558

Ho, A., Hancock, J., & Miner, A. S. (2018). Psychological, relational, and emotional effects of self-disclosure after conversations with a chatbot. *Journal of Communication*, *68*(4), 712–733. DOI: 10.1093/joc/jqy026 PMID: 30100620

Hoofnagle, C. J., van der Sloot, B., & Borgesius, F. Z. (2019). The European Union General Data Protection Regulation: What it is and what it means. *Information & Communications Technology Law*, *28*(1), 65–98. DOI: 10.1080/13600834.2019.1573501

Hung, T. W., & Yen, C. P. (2021). On the person-based predictive policing of AI. *Ethics and Information Technology*, *23*(3), 165–176. DOI: 10.1007/s10676-020-09539-x

Ishii, K. (2019). Comparative legal study on privacy and personal data protection for robots equipped with artificial intelligence: Looking at functional and technological aspects. *AI & Society*, *34*(3), 509–533. DOI: 10.1007/s00146-017-0758-8

Jenga, K., Catal, C., & Kar, G. (2023). Machine learning in crime prediction. *Journal of Ambient Intelligence and Humanized Computing*, *14*(5), 2887–2913. DOI: 10.1007/s12652-023-04530-y

Jobin, A., Ienca, M., & Vayena, E. (2019). The global landscape of AI ethics guidelines. *Nature Machine Intelligence*, *1*(9), 389–399. DOI: 10.1038/s42256-019-0088-2

Joseph, J. (2024). Predicting crime or perpetuating bias? The AI dilemma. *AI & Society*. Advance online publication. DOI: 10.1007/s00146-024-02032-9

Jungherr, A. (2023). Artificial intelligence and democracy: A conceptual framework. *Social Media + Society*, *9*(3), 20563051231186353. Advance online publication. DOI: 10.1177/20563051231186353

Kandt, J., & Batty, M. (2021). Smart cities, big data, and urban policy: Towards urban analytics for the long run. *Cities (London, England)*, *109*, 102992. DOI: 10.1016/j.cities.2020.102992

Karliuk, M. (2023). Proportionality principle for the ethics of artificial intelligence. *AI and Ethics*, *3*(2), 985–990. DOI: 10.1007/s43681-022-00220-1

Kumar, V. (2019). Dynamics of the "right to privacy": Its characterization under the Indian Constitution. *Journal of the Indian Law Institute*, *61*(1), 68–96. https://www.jstor.org/stable/27097351

Laufs, J., & Borrion, H. (2022). Technological innovation in policing and crime prevention: Practitioner perspectives from London. *International Journal of Police Science & Management*, *24*(2), 190–209. DOI: 10.1177/14613557211064053

Lavin, A., Gilligan-Lee, C. M., Visnjic, A., Ganju, S., Newman, D., Ganguly, S., Lange, D., Baydin, A. G., Sharma, A., Gibson, A., Zheng, S., Xing, E. P., Mattmann, C., Parr, J., & Gal, Y. (2022). Technology readiness levels for machine learning systems. *Nature Communications, 13*(1), 6039. DOI: 10.1038/s41467-022-33128-9 PMID: 36266298

Lynskey, O. (2023). Complete and effective data protection. *Current Legal Problems, 76*(1), 297–344. DOI: 10.1093/clp/cuad009

Malhotra, C., & Malhotra, U. (2024). Putting interests of digital nagriks first: Digital Personal Data Protection (DPDP) Act 2023 of India. *The Indian Journal of Public Administration, 70*(3), 516–531. DOI: 10.1177/00195561241271575

Manning, M., & Agnew, S. (2020). Policing in the Era of AI and Smart Societies: Austerity, Legitimacy, and Blurring the Line of Consent. In H. Jahankhani, B. Akhgar, P. Cochrane, & M. Dastbaz (Eds.), *Policing in the Era of AI and Smart Societies* (pp. 17–34). Advanced Sciences and Technologies for Security Applications. Springer, Cham. DOI: 10.1007/978-3-030-50613-1_2

Mansoor, S. I., & Wani, S. A. (2025). Harnessing ethical AI: Measures of redressing hate speech in the social media context. In Chakraborty, S. (Ed.), *Ethical AI solutions for addressing social media influence and hate speech* (pp. 37–62). IGI Global Scientific Publishing., DOI: 10.4018/979-8-3693-9904-0.ch003

Marda, V. (2018). Artificial intelligence policy in India: A framework for engaging the limits of data-driven decision-making. *Philosophical Transactions. Series A, Mathematical, Physical, and Engineering Sciences, 376*(2133), 20180087. DOI: 10.1098/rsta.2018.0087 PMID: 30323001

Memarian, B., & Doleck, T. (2023). Fairness, Accountability, Transparency, and Ethics (FATE) in Artificial Intelligence (AI) and higher education: A systematic review. *Computers and Education: Artificial Intelligence, 5*, 100152. DOI: 10.1016/j.caeai.2023.100152

Mennella, C., Maniscalco, U., De Pietro, G., & Esposito, M. (2024). Ethical and regulatory challenges of AI technologies in healthcare: A narrative review. *Heliyon, 10*(4), e26297. DOI: 10.1016/j.heliyon.2024.e26297 PMID: 38384518

Meszaros, J., & Ho, C. (2021). AI research and data protection: Can the same rules apply for commercial and academic research under the GDPR? *Computer Law & Security Review, 41*, 105532. DOI: 10.1016/j.clsr.2021.105532

Mukto, M. M., Hasan, M., Al Mahmud, M. M., Haque, I., Ahmed, M. A., Jabid, T., Ali, M. S., Rashid, M. R. A., Islam, M. M., & Islam, M. (2024). Design of a real-time crime monitoring system using deep learning techniques. *Intelligent Systems with Applications*, *21*, 200311. DOI: 10.1016/j.iswa.2023.200311

Novelli, C., Taddeo, M., & Floridi, L. (2024). Accountability in artificial intelligence: What it is and how it works. *AI & Society*, *39*(4), 1871–1882. DOI: 10.1007/s00146-023-01635-y

Ortega-Bolaños, R., Bernal-Salcedo, J., Germán Ortiz, M., Galeano Sarmiento, J., Ruz, G. A., & Tabares-Soto, R. (2024). Applying the ethics of AI: A systematic review of tools for developing and assessing AI-based systems. *Artificial Intelligence Review*, *57*(5), 110. DOI: 10.1007/s10462-024-10740-3

Palmiotto, F., & Menéndez González, N. (2023). Facial recognition technology, democracy and human rights. *Computer Law & Security Review*, *50*, 105857. DOI: 10.1016/j.clsr.2023.105857

Roberts, H., Cowls, J., Morley, J., Taddeo, M., Wang, V., & Floridi, L. (2021). The Chinese approach to artificial intelligence: An analysis of policy, ethics, and regulation. *AI & Society*, *36*(1), 59–77. DOI: 10.1007/s00146-020-00992-2

Rodrigues, R. (2020). Legal and human rights issues of AI: Gaps, challenges and vulnerabilities. *Journal of Responsible Technology*, *4*, 100005. DOI: 10.1016/j.jrt.2020.100005

Sachoulidou, A. (2024). Harnessing AI for law enforcement: Solutions and boundaries from the forthcoming AI Act. *New Journal of European Criminal Law*, *15*(2), 117–125. DOI: 10.1177/20322844241260114

Sarabdeen, J. (2022). Protection of the rights of the individual when using facial recognition technology. *Heliyon*, *8*(3), e09086. DOI: 10.1016/j.heliyon.2022.e09086 PMID: 35309394

Sarker, I. H., Furhad, M. H., & Nowrozy, R. (2021). AI-driven cybersecurity: An overview, security intelligence modeling and research directions. *SN Computer Science*, *2*(1), 173. DOI: 10.1007/s42979-021-00557-0

Sarzaeim, P., Mahmoud, Q. H., Azim, A., Bauer, G., & Bowles, I. (2023). A Systematic Review of Using Machine Learning and Natural Language Processing in Smart Policing. *Computers*, *12*(12), 255. DOI: 10.3390/computers12120255

Sayyed, H. (2024). Artificial intelligence and criminal liability in India: Exploring legal implications and challenges. *Cogent Social Sciences*, *10*(1), 2343195. Advance online publication. DOI: 10.1080/23311886.2024.2343195

Sikri, A. K. (2021). Proportionality—A balancing act for achieving constitutional rights: A comparative study. In M. John, V. H. Devaiah, P. Baruah, M. Tundawala, & N. Kumar (Eds.), *The Indian Yearbook of Comparative Law 2019* (pp. [specific pages if known]). Springer, Singapore. DOI: 10.1007/978-981-16-2175-8_6

Smith, M., & Miller, S. (2022). The ethical application of biometric facial recognition technology. *AI & Society*, *37*(1), 167–175. DOI: 10.1007/s00146-021-01199-9 PMID: 33867693

Sun, L., Zhang, H., & Fang, C. (2021). Data security governance in the era of big data: Status, challenges, and prospects. *Data Science and Management*, *2*, 41–44. DOI: 10.1016/j.dsm.2021.06.001

Tallberg, J., Erman, E., Furendal, M., Geith, J., Klamberg, M., & Lundgren, M. (2023). The global governance of artificial intelligence: Next steps for empirical and normative research. *International Studies Review*, *25*(3), viad040. Advance online publication. DOI: 10.1093/isr/viad040

Taskiran, M., Kahraman, N., & Erdem, C. E. (2020). Face recognition: Past, present and future (a review). *Digital Signal Processing*, *106*, 102809. DOI: 10.1016/j.dsp.2020.102809

Taskiran, M., Kahraman, N., & Erdem, C. E. (2020). Face recognition: Past, present and future (a review). *Digital Signal Processing*, *106*, 102809. DOI: 10.1016/j.dsp.2020.102809

Taylor, I. (2023). Justice by Algorithm: The Limits of AI in Criminal Sentencing. *Criminal Justice Ethics*, *42*(3), 193–213. DOI: 10.1080/0731129X.2023.2275967

Ullah, A., Anwar, S. M., Li, J., Nadeem, L., Mahmood, T., Rehman, A., & Saba, T. (2024). Smart cities: The role of Internet of Things and machine learning in realizing a data-centric smart environment. *Complex & Intelligent Systems*, *10*(3), 1607–1637. DOI: 10.1007/s40747-023-01175-4

United Nations Office of the High Commissioner for Human Rights (OHCHR). (2022). *China's algorithms of repression: Reverse engineering a Xinjiang police mass surveillance app*. Retrieved from https://www.ohchr.org/en/press-releases/2022/08/un-human-rights-office-issues-assessment-human-rights-concerns-xinjiang

Urquhart, L., & Miranda, D. (2021). Policing faces: The present and future of intelligent facial surveillance. *Information & Communications Technology Law*, *31*(2), 194–219. DOI: 10.1080/13600834.2021.1994220

Venkatesh, V. (2022). Adoption and use of AI tools: A research agenda grounded in UTAUT. *Annals of Operations Research, 308*(1), 641–652. DOI: 10.1007/s10479-020-03918-9

Wani, S. A., & Mansoor, S. I. (2025). Criminal justice system in the age of artificial intelligence: Exploring rights, risks, and responsibilities in the digital era. In Kaunert, C., Raghav, A., Ravesangar, K., Singh, B., & Riswandi, B. (Eds.), *Artificial intelligence in peace, justice, and strong institutions* (pp. 67–92). IGI Global Scientific Publishing., DOI: 10.4018/979-8-3693-9395-6.ch004

Wolniak, R., & Stecuła, K. (2024). Artificial intelligence in smart cities—Applications, barriers, and future directions: A review. *Smart Cities, 7*(3), 1346–1389. DOI: 10.3390/smartcities7030057

Zaidan, E., & Ibrahim, I. A. (2024). AI governance in a complex and rapidly changing regulatory landscape: A global perspective. *Humanities & Social Sciences Communications, 11*(1), 1121. DOI: 10.1057/s41599-024-03560-x

Završnik, A. (2020). Criminal justice, artificial intelligence systems, and human rights. *ERA Forum, 20*(4), 567–583. DOI: 10.1007/s12027-020-00602-0

Zuiderveen Borgesius, F. J. (2020). Strengthening legal protection against discrimination by algorithms and artificial intelligence. *International Journal of Human Rights, 24*(10), 1572–1593. DOI: 10.1080/13642987.2020.1743976

Zuiderwijk, A., Chen, Y.-C., & Salem, F. (2021). Implications of the use of artificial intelligence in public governance: A systematic literature review and a research agenda. *Government Information Quarterly, 38*(3), 101577. DOI: 10.1016/j.giq.2021.101577

Chapter 4
Challenging the Boundaries of Urban Security:
AIP, Ethical Governance, and the Future of Smart Cities

Antonio Pesqueira
https://orcid.org/0000-0003-1530-6451
ISCTE, University Institute of Lisbon, Portugal

Andreia de bem Machado
https://orcid.org/0000-0002-4404-0341
Universidade Federal de Santa Catarina, Brazil

ABSTRACT

In an era marked by a heightened emphasis on proactive urban security, municipal governance faces escalating complexities and demands for adaptive interventions in response to dynamic demographic shifts, stringent regulatory frameworks, and unpredictable disruptions. The convergence of AI-driving Policing (AIP) solutions has emerged as a transformative force, enabling public officials and law enforcement agencies to enhance situational awareness through advanced analytics, targeted interventions, and synergy-driven governance orchestration within smart city infrastructure. This chapter develops a comprehensive theoretical framework to examine the intersection of AIP, ethical governance, and data-driven city management, addressing a critical gap in understanding how advanced AI solutions can revolutionize public safety and strategic foresight in smart city environments.

DOI: 10.4018/979-8-3373-0245-4.ch004

INTRODUCTION

The urban security sector, particularly within the realm of AI-driving Policing (AIP) and ethical governance, is encountering a surge in complexity regarding real-time situational oversight, propelled by escalating expectations for proactive interventions, civic resilience, and compliance with rigorous regulatory frameworks in the evolving landscape of integrated smart city solutions. Central to these challenges are persistent inefficiencies in coordinated security frameworks, such as conventional patrol strategies and fragmented surveillance infrastructures, which remain inadequately equipped to accommodate the evolving demands of modern urban ecosystems. These shortcomings manifest in disjointed data analytics, misaligned resource allocation, and insufficient responsiveness to security threat fluctuations, heightening risks to public safety and community trust (Ebrahimi & Bridgelall, 2021).

The urgency to resolve these issues transcends mere procedural refinement. Developing robust Artificial Intelligence (AI) enhanced security frameworks ensures adaptability, regulatory adherence, and sustained innovation in a domain where emergent threats can have immediate repercussions for public welfare and civic stability. Advanced AI technologies—encompassing predictive analytics, automated threat detection, and dynamic resource coordination—are poised to radically reformulate conventional policing strategies, bridging the gap between strategic security objectives and day-to-day governance. However, theoretical models that systematically integrate AI-driven insights into urban security management remain disparate, leaving gaps in understanding the interplay among technological adoption, administrative culture, and continuous capability development. Resolving these gaps is indispensable for refining conceptual foundations and shaping ethically grounded and technologically responsive governance pathways in smart city contexts (Gebhardt et al.,2022).

While extant literature underscores AI's capacity to deliver high-precision forecasting, operational efficiencies, and real-time visibility in various urban contexts, it often neglects AIP's role in bolstering ethically accountable governance for modern cities. Established models of municipal oversight—largely anchored in reactive and compartmentalized enforcement tactics—offer valuable insights into crime reduction and community relations but seldom incorporate the transformative influence of advanced AI-based paradigms. Although recent investigations have begun exploring digital transformation imperatives in urban security, the multidimensional convergence of AI, proactive governance strategies, and dynamic capability development remains insufficiently examined. Additionally, explorations of ethical considerations within technology-driven policing frequently treat these facets as peripheral, overlooking their interplay with AI-based personalization and data governance (Kant, Anjali, 2021; Dillard-Wright, Shields-Haas, 2021; Javaid, Haleem, Singh, 2023).

Against this backdrop, the present chapter introduces a unified theoretical framework synthesizing advanced AIP approaches, ethical governance principles, and dynamic capability enhancement to address the intricacies of urban security within smart cities. The principal objective is to deepen our understanding of how AI-facilitated oversight can bolster adaptability and strategic foresight in municipal governance networks. Complementary aims include tracing the evolution of these security frameworks and evaluating their alignment with ethical imperatives. By consolidating multidisciplinary insights, this chapter aspires to offer actionable guidelines for city officials, policymakers, and stakeholders intent on leveraging AI-enabled solutions for both effective urban security and principled accountability. The core research concern resides in the absence of a cohesive theoretical model that coherently merges AI-driven strategies with existing policing paradigms while adequately accommodating ethical and citizen-focused considerations. To fill this lacuna, the investigation centers on two pivotal queries: How do current conceptualizations of proactive interventions and dynamic capabilities (DC) account for the complexities of AI integration within urban security? Which critical components must a conceptual framework include to align AIP strategies with ethical mandates?

This chapter adopts a concept-centric theoretical research approach, prioritizing rigorous conceptual scrutiny and systematic literature synthesis to construct a holistic framework. The analysis leverages a comprehensive review of scholarly articles, policy briefs, and illustrative case studies, thereby capturing pivotal knowledge gaps and integrating insights from public administration, AI innovation, and governance ethics. This approach ensures alignment between the research objectives and theoretical contributions, while simultaneously laying the groundwork for future empirical inquiries. Findings from this chapter are anticipated to advance scholarly discourse by demonstrating how ethical imperatives and DC can be productively interwoven into emergent urban security strategies, particularly amid volatile conditions in global cityscapes. The proposed framework also generates pragmatic recommendations, including methods for synchronizing AIP with ethical guidelines and leveraging AI functionalities to strengthen municipal resilience and adaptive capacity. Ultimately, these insights aim to guide city leaders and organizations in navigating contemporary urban security's complexities, ensuring operational excellence and ethical responsibility.

LITERATURE SURVEY

Revolutionizing Urban Security and Policing with AI

The historical evolution of AIP offers critical insights into its current capabilities and applications within urban security frameworks. The initial adoption of AIP was predominantly exploratory, focusing on using video analytics to monitor suspicious activities and detect early signs of criminal behavior. Early applications were characterized by limitations in data accuracy and system interoperability, however, the subsequent convergence of machine learning (ML) and cloud computing enabled real-time data processing, laying the groundwork for its application in complex urban environments. These technological advancements have transformed traditional reactive policing into a more dynamic and proactive system, emphasizing predictive analytics and targeted interventions. Despite these strides, the evolution of AIP has been marked by uneven progress across regions and socioeconomic strata. High-income cities rapidly adopted these technologies, while resource-constrained municipalities struggled due to limited infrastructure, regulatory ambiguities, and cultural barriers. Understanding this trajectory underscores the need for equitable and inclusive strategies that align technological innovations with the diverse needs of global urban security systems (Ebrahimi, Bridgelall, 2021; Jacob, Bourke, Heuss, 2022; Dillard-Wright, Shields-Haas, 2021).

AIP constitutes a pivotal domain within contemporary urban security practice, functioning as the critical interface between real-time surveillance data and strategic law enforcement interventions. The theoretical foundations of such policing can be traced to early inquiries in criminology, predictive analytics, and public administration sciences. Foundational models, including data-driven crime prevention frameworks, underscore the seamless alignment of community-specific insights with policing protocols to achieve optimized crime management and public safety outcomes. In recent years, the field has undergone a decisive shift toward AI-centric methodologies that harness ML and predictive modeling. Scholars emphasize AI's transformative impact on enhancing threat anticipation, personalized policing strategies, and cross-functional coordination, particularly in high-stakes urban security contexts characterized by fluctuating crime patterns and stringent regulatory standards for public accountability. However, persistent constraints—such as data fragmentation, limited interoperability across security platforms, and insufficient integration among municipal service tiers—continue to impede the realization of truly agile AIP frameworks (Gebhardt et al.,2022; Breaux et al.,2023; ElBaih, 2023).

The discourse within the literature also highlights substantial debates about the extent and depth of technological integration in AIP initiatives. Proponents of AI-centric paradigms advocate for their capacity to uncover latent patterns in extensive crime datasets, thereby reducing human error and bias in law enforcement analytics. Critics, however, contend that in contexts marked by sparse or unreliable data, common in underserved or rapidly evolving urban areas, AI may falter without nuanced human oversight. A further unresolved challenge lies in the uneven incorporation of ethical frameworks into AIP protocols. This discrepancy underlines the urgent need to reconcile operational objectives with holistic security imperatives, ensuring that advanced data-driven insights align with broader responsibilities to citizen rights and community trust. In addition to these perspectives, contemporary scholarship increasingly scrutinizes the synergistic relationship between technological innovation and the essential human elements of urban policing in the AI-empowered era. Ethical concerns, public expectations, and cross-jurisdictional regulatory complexities introduce further intricacies, spurring calls for frameworks that extend beyond algorithmic sophistication to include socio-emotional welfare. This growing emphasis on holistic value generation accentuates the necessity of addressing both theoretical and pragmatic limitations that currently restrict the potential of AI-led personalized policing (Kant, Anjali, 2021; Dillard-Wright, Shields-Haas, 2021; Javaid, Haleem, Singh, 2023).

The theoretical foundations underlying AI-driven crime monitoring have evolved through iterative refinements, highlighting the interplay between quantitative analytics and law enforcement acumen. Traditional prognostic paradigms—ranging from evidence-based patrol strategies to linear crime progression models—have garnered widespread acceptance due to their interpretability and consistency. Their reliance on historical crime data, however, limits their utility in dynamic environments where emergent technologies and unpredictable crime patterns frequently arise. Consequently, the adoption of agile, AI-driven monitoring becomes indispensable in navigating unpredictable trajectories in urban security. Adaptive modeling strategies, such as Bayesian updating techniques, exemplify the progression of AIP by integrating real-time data streams (e.g., surveillance feeds and sensor inputs) and continuously recalibrating insights to reflect evolving crime trends. Additionally, hybrid approaches that synthesize ML algorithms with established policing frameworks have demonstrated notable efficacy in security settings grappling with rapid changes in criminal behavior or the sudden emergence of innovative threats. These adaptive strategies signify a key breakthrough, offering both predictive accuracy and operational agility in addressing the multifaceted demands of urban security management. Another methodological milestone is the emergence of comprehensive frameworks that unify AIP with system-wide processes, particularly integrated security pathways. While integrated security has gained considerable traction, its limitations in adapting to real-time fluctuations and incorporating ethically grounded metrics underscore the necessity for further methodological refinements (Jacob, Bourke, Heuss, 2022; ElBaih, 2023; Kasneci et al., 2023).

A key debate within the field centers on finding an equilibrium between algorithmic precision and human insight in AIP. Proponents of purely data-driven strategies maintain that ML systems can detect complex patterns and early indicators of criminal activity unattainable through conventional methods alone, thereby improving law enforcement reliability. Conversely, detractors emphasize that human discernment is essential in interpreting atypical trends or ethical dilemmas where rigid algorithms might overlook nuanced contextual or moral considerations. This tension reveals a critical research gap in envisioning frameworks that unite algorithmic rigor with expert oversight. Another salient shortfall pertains to embedding citizen-centered ethics within AIP protocols. Although value-based models are increasingly recognized, their direct application to AI-powered personalized policing remains inconsistent. Conventional approaches seldom address the broader sociocultural or civic implications of real-time data-driven interventions, such as potential privacy invasions or concerns regarding data security. The role of secure cloud-based solutions in augmenting AIP capabilities has also attracted growing scholarly interest. While proponents point to the potential for real-time data synchronization, streamlined predictive analytics, and on-demand computational resources, empirical validations in sensitive urban contexts remain limited. This gap is especially pertinent to AIP management, where confidentiality requirements, varied regulatory statutes, and complex community dynamics introduce unique challenges. Furthermore, ethical concerns relating to data governance, algorithmic fairness, and citizen consent underscore the necessity for personalized policing frameworks that balance technological efficacy with respect for individual rights and community trust (Breaux et al.,2023; Javaid, Haleem, Singh, 2023; Kwok & Treiblmaier, 2023).

Ethical Frameworks and Case-Based Analysis

The ethical implications of deploying AI in mental healthcare extend beyond standard concerns of data privacy and security. Ethical frameworks must address issues such as algorithmic bias, informed consent, and equitable access to ensure that AI and Internet of Medical Things (IoMT) applications uphold patient autonomy and social justice. For example, the General Data Protection Regulation (GDPR) in Europe emphasizes robust data governance but often clashes with the need for real-time data sharing in AI systems. In contrast, countries like the United States, guided by the Health Insurance Portability and Accountability Act (HIPAA), offer a more compliance-driven approach, which can limit cross-border interoperability. Case studies demonstrate how ethical principles are implemented—or sometimes compromised—in practice. Addressing these issues required community-driven solutions, including localized consent protocols and culturally adapted training materials. Such examples highlight the importance of embedding ethical frameworks within the lifecycle of AIoMT applications. Adaptive approaches that combine stakeholder engagement, regulatory compliance, and real-world validations can bridge gaps and create more accountable systems (Dillard-Wright & Shields-Haas, 2021; Kasneci et al., 2023).

The integration of theoretical frameworks with empirical evidence is critical for advancing the understanding of AIoMT in mental healthcare. Two key frameworks—DC and the Resource-Based View (RBV)—provide foundational insights into how organizations adapt to technological innovations and optimize resource utilization. The DC theory emphasizes the importance of sensing, seizing, and transforming capabilities in navigating rapidly evolving environments. In the context of AIoMT, these capabilities manifest as the ability of mental health providers to identify emerging technological opportunities (sensing), deploy AIoMT systems to meet patient needs (seizing), and restructure operational processes to enhance care delivery (transforming). For example, Scandinavian healthcare systems, known for their high levels of innovation, have successfully integrated AIoMT solutions into ADHD monitoring programs. These systems leverage predictive analytics to detect early relapse indicators, enabling swift intervention and reducing long-term treatment costs. The adaptability demonstrated in these cases highlights the practical application of DC in advancing patient outcomes through technology-driven care (ElBaih, 2023; Kwok, Treiblmaier, 2023; Secinaro et al.,2021).

Then the RBV complements DC by focusing on the strategic value of tangible and intangible resources, such as proprietary AI algorithms, secure data governance mechanisms, and skilled personnel. An empirical study conducted in the United States revealed how healthcare providers leveraged AIoMT tools like wearable sensors and ML algorithms to refine therapeutic pathways. The study highlighted the critical role of clinician expertise in interpreting AI-generated insights, ensuring that technology complements rather than replaces human judgment. By aligning organizational resources with patient-centric goals, healthcare providers not only improved outcomes but also achieved operational efficiencies. Empirical evidence supports the integration of these frameworks, particularly in addressing challenges unique to mental healthcare. Concurrently, the clinic utilized RBV by training its staff to optimize the use of these tools, ensuring seamless patient engagement despite external disruptions. Future research should explore longitudinal studies that assess how DC and RBV interact over time, especially in dynamic mental health contexts like ADHD and OCB. These insights can help refine theoretical constructs, fostering a more comprehensive understanding of how AIoMT drives sustainable innovation in mental healthcare (Javaid, Haleem, Singh, 2023; Pesqueira, Sousa, Pereira, 2023; Kotcher et al., 2021).

Adaptive Urban Resilience in AI-Driven Urban Security and Smart City Governance

Adaptive Urban Resilience (AUR) represents a fundamental theoretical construct for understanding how urban security systems adapt to evolving technological, sociopolitical, and regulatory conditions by identifying community-centric opportunities, optimizing resource allocation, and reshaping governance processes. This framework has been extensively examined in diverse contexts, highlighting the synergy between strategic responsiveness and resource orchestration. In urban security, particularly for challenges such as crime prevention and public safety, where citizen trust, service quality, and intricate compliance demands converge, AUR emerges as indispensable for enhancing municipal resilience and sustaining a competitive edge in a rapidly shifting environment. Advanced AIP has taken shape as a transformative enabler, poised to elevate AUR by offering sophisticated threat analytics, predictive modeling, and real-time decision support. Recent studies reveal how AIP sharpens the detection facet of AUR by uncovering emergent crime patterns, identifying security gaps, and enhancing operational efficiencies through ML and deep learning algorithms. Likewise, AI-driven tools streamline resource allocation, reinforcing the capacity to seize critical opportunities in integrated urban security pathways (Kasneci et al., 2023; Secinaro et al.,2021; Ullah et al., 2023). Furthermore, AIP's role in recalibrating administrative procedures has been linked to improved system agility, particularly when dealing with unpredictable fluctuations in crime rates or shifting regulatory mandates. However, despite these strides, the integration of AIP within the AUR framework in urban security contexts remains insufficiently explored, leaving open questions about how AI-driven capabilities truly foster organizational adaptability and transformative innovation. The foundational tenets of AUR are anchored in strategic and organizational management paradigms, wherein scholars emphasize the alignment of internal competencies with shifting community needs and policy expectations. Traditional inquiries often adopt qualitative case analyses or cross-sectional research designs to explore the evolution of these capabilities. Although these methods yield valuable insights, they do not always capture the granular influence of technology, specifically AIP, on AUR. Recent research initiatives have begun incorporating algorithmic and predictive methods to elucidate how AI-driven insights can bolster governance flexibility. Yet critics argue that prevailing models frequently fail to account for the distinctive constraints of urban security, where privacy concerns, collaborative protocols, and multi-stakeholder trust fundamentally shape technology adoption. Methodological shortcomings persist as well, with few longitudinal investigations tracing the progressive interplay between AI-driven solutions and AUR development. A notable gap in contemporary literature is the absence of integrative models that fuse AI-driven functionalities with AUR in personalized urban security governance. Though research underscores AIP's capacity to optimize strategic provision and administrative workflows, its impact on higher-level strategic agility, particularly in delivering sustained crime prevention and ensuring long-term community well-being, remains elusive (Kwok & Treiblmaier, 2023; Kotcher et al., 2021; Wani et al.,2022). This shortfall is especially relevant in areas such as hybrid security programs for smart cities, where disruptions in service delivery can severely compromise safety continuity and violate compliance standards. Another unsettled discussion concerns the equilibrium between AI-driven automation and managerial judgment in cultivating AUR. Advocates posit that algorithmic intelligence offers unmatched scalability and predictive precision, whereas skeptics caution that excessive reliance on automated systems may overlook the nuanced human judgment often essential in complex urban security scenarios. This dichotomy underscores the need for hybrid paradigms that unite machine-driven capabilities with expert oversight to optimize interventions under high-stakes conditions. Additionally, the literature scarcely addresses how ethical guidelines and strict regulatory measures interface with AI-driven AUR. Urban security enterprises operate under heightened scrutiny concerning data protection and governance accountability, yet few studies outline strategies for harmonizing AI innovations with these rigorous frameworks. Such considerations demand new models that blend AI-driven technical promise with the ethical and regulatory mandates characteristic of urban governance systems (Pesqueira, Sousa, Pereira, 2023; Ullah et al., 2023; Vlasta, 2023).

Table 1 provides an integrated perspective on each theme's theoretical lineage, current empirical focus, methodological orientations, knowledge gaps, and pragmatic applications in both operational and administrative settings. AIP, serving as a disruptive catalyst, is depicted as a game-changer capable of amplifying these competencies by supplying real-time analytics, automated decision support, and strategic resource optimization. Nevertheless, while AUR has been widely scrutinized in broader organizational contexts, its specific application within urban security, particularly when aligned with AI-driven monitoring and proactive policing, remains insufficiently characterized. The key contributions of the literature portion evaluate prevailing work on AUR and AIP, detailing each stream's achievements and constraints. AUR literature offers significant perspectives on fostering adaptive urban security services yet leaves questions unanswered regarding technology's role in restructuring governance pathways. AIP-focused investigations have demonstrated efficacy in enhancing predictive precision and strategy alignment but often neglect broader governance issues crucial to urban security, including holistic community welfare and multi-tiered regulatory compliance. Hybrid models that harness the precision of algorithmic tools while retaining space for expert discernment present a promising path forward, offering both optimized performance metrics and enhanced trustworthiness in community-facing contexts. These convergent perspectives aim to remedy conceptual and empirical limitations, ultimately strengthening the adaptability and sustainability of urban security operations. Collectively, the synthesis underscores the potential of AIP-augmented AUR to transform Personalized Urban Security Intelligence, urging interdisciplinary research and the development of integrative models that address the complexities of modern smart city service delivery (Secinaro et al.,2021; Wani et al.,2022; Kendzerska et al., 2021).

Table 1. Urban security, adaptive urban resilience in AI-driven urban security and smart city governance

Key Concepts	Dimensions	Theories
Adaptive Urban Resilience (AUR)	- Strategic responsiveness	- Strategic Management Theory
	- Resource optimization	- Organizational Resilience Theory
	- Governance process reshaping	
AIP	- Threat analytics	- Predictive Policing Theory
	- Predictive modeling	- Technology Adoption Models
	- Real-time decision support	
Smart City Infrastructure	- Integrated surveillance systems	- Smart City Frameworks
	- IoT sensor networks	- Systems Theory
	- Data interoperability	
Ethical Governance	- Data privacy	- Ethical Theory in Technology
	- Algorithmic fairness	- Governance Theory
	- Citizen rights	
Predictive Analytics	- Crime pattern detection	- Data-Driven Decision Making
	- Early threat identification	- Predictive Modeling Theory
	- Predictive accuracy	
Resource Allocation	- Strategic resource distribution	- Resource-Based View (RBV)
	- Operational efficiency	- Efficiency Theory
	- Scalability	
Community-Centric Opportunities	- Citizen engagement	- Community Engagement Theory
	- Trust-building	- Social Capital Theory
	- Socio-emotional welfare	
Real-Time Data Processing	- Immediate data analysis	- Real-Time Systems Theory
	- Dynamic response	- Information Processing Theory
	- Continuous monitoring	

continued on following page

Table 1. Continued

<table>
<tr><th>Key Concepts</th><th>Dimensions</th><th>Theories</th></tr>
<tr><td rowspan="3">Hybrid Policing Models</td><td>- Integration of AI and human judgment</td><td>- Hybrid Decision-Making Models</td></tr>
<tr><td>- Expert oversight</td><td>- Human-AI Collaboration Theory</td></tr>
<tr><td colspan="2">- Algorithmic and discretionary balance</td></tr>
<tr><td rowspan="3">Regulatory Compliance</td><td>- Adherence to laws and standards</td><td>- Regulatory Compliance Theory</td></tr>
<tr><td>- Policy alignment</td><td>- Public Administration Theory</td></tr>
<tr><td colspan="2">- Governance Accountability</td></tr>
<tr><td rowspan="3">Longitudinal Studies on AI Integration</td><td>- Progressive technology adoption</td><td>- Longitudinal Research Design</td></tr>
<tr><td>- Evolution of governance</td><td>- Evolutionary Theory</td></tr>
<tr><td colspan="2">- Impact assessment over time</td></tr>
</table>

Integration of Conceptual Frameworks with Empirical Evidence

Empirical evidence, such as the integration of AIP systems in large-scale urban security initiatives in metropolitan areas, demonstrates how these frameworks can guide implementation. The RBV complements AUR by highlighting the strategic importance of leveraging proprietary AI algorithms, robust data governance mechanisms, and law enforcement expertise. For instance, a longitudinal study in a major U.S. city revealed how law enforcement agencies optimized AIP pathways by aligning these resources with community-centric goals. The ethical implementation of AIP is essential to ensure that technological advancements uphold public trust, fairness, and accountability. This section explores the intersection of AIP with privacy, consent, and equity, highlighting case-based examples and best practices for embedding ethics into technology deployment (Kotcher et al., 2021; Vlasta, 2023; Junaid et al.,2023). Privacy concerns are paramount in urban security, where sensitive citizen data is frequently collected, transmitted, and analyzed. AIP systems must adhere to strict regulations such as the GDPR in Europe and the Privacy Act in various jurisdictions. For example, a smart city initiative in Germany utilized blockchain-based solutions to ensure secure data exchanges, offering citizens greater control over their information. By integrating encryption protocols and decentralized storage systems, the initiative mitigated risks associated with data breaches while fostering public trust in digital security interventions. Informed consent processes often face challenges in AIP applications, particularly in regions with low digital literacy. A case study from rural India highlighted these challenges, where community members struggled to understand the implications of continuous surveillance devices. To address this, the implementing organization developed visual aids and culturally adapted training sessions, ensuring that community members could make informed decisions. These practices underscore the need for context-sensitive consent mechanisms that respect local norms and values. Equitable access to AIP tools remains a critical concern, especially in underserved urban areas. While high-income cities have benefited from advanced AIP implementations, regions such as Sub-Saharan Africa and Southeast Asia face high costs and limited infrastructure barriers. An initiative in Nairobi demonstrated how low-cost surveillance devices, combined with community-driven data collection, enabled effective crime monitoring in underserved neighborhoods. This model not only improved accessibility but also empowered local law enforcement officers, fostering a sense of ownership and sustainability (Ullah et al., 2023; Kendzerska et al., 2021; Jalil et al., 2023).

Another ethical dimension involves maintaining a balance between algorithmic decision-making and human oversight. While AIP systems offer predictive accuracy, they can sometimes perpetuate biases or overlook nuanced community contexts. For example, an algorithm used in the United States to prioritize areas for increased patrols disproportionately favored urban neighborhoods with extensive data representation, neglecting rural areas with limited data. This finding prompted the organization to incorporate officer reviews alongside AI recommendations, ensuring a more equitable approach. To embed ethical considerations into AIP applications, organizations should adopt strategies that include conducting regular ethical audits to identify potential biases and risks, implementing transparency initiatives that provide clear explanations of how AI algorithms process and utilize citizen data, fostering community engagement by involving citizens, law enforcement officers, and local stakeholders in the design and deployment of AI-driven tools, and promoting global harmonization through international collaboration to establish consistent ethical standards across diverse urban security systems (Vlasta, 2023; Jalil et al., 2023; Alawida et al.,2023). By aligning technological advancements with robust ethical frameworks, urban security organizations can ensure that AIP serves as a force for equitable and accountable public safety. AIP applications extend far beyond traditional crime prevention, encompassing a diverse range of urban security functions. For instance, AI-driven systems have demonstrated significant potential in managing public safety by monitoring traffic patterns, predicting and preventing traffic accidents, and optimizing emergency response times. Similarly, AI-driven surveillance has been deployed to track and mitigate the spread of violent incidents through real-time data analysis and rapid intervention strategies. Expanding AIP's scope to include areas such as cybercrime, counter-terrorism, and community policing can further transform urban security management. For example, predictive analytics tools, coupled with AI-driven monitoring, are being used to detect and respond to cyber threats, providing law enforcement with the ability to anticipate and neutralize potential attacks. These examples highlight the untapped potential of AIP in broadening its impact on diverse urban security challenges (Wani et al.,2022; Junaid et al.,2023; Eager, Brunton, 2023).

The success of AIP hinges on its acceptance and usability by law enforcement officers and community members. Studies reveal that officers appreciate the real-time monitoring and predictive interventions AIP offers, but express concerns about data privacy, system reliability, and the potential for over-surveillance. Community members, on the other hand, value the enhanced safety these systems provide but often report a lack of transparency or clear guidelines on how AI-driven tools are used effectively and ethically. The ethical and legal dimensions of AIP are critical for ensuring public trust and compliance with global standards. Legal frameworks such as GDPR and the Privacy Act govern data privacy, but the rapid evolution of AIP technologies demands updated policies that address issues like algorithmic transparency, bias in predictive analytics, and liability in AI-driven decisions. Ethical concerns include the potential for over-reliance on algorithms, the commodification of sensitive civic data, and unequal access to AIP technologies. Organizations must adopt multi-stakeholder approaches that incorporate input from community members, law enforcement officers, ethicists, and regulators to design fair and transparent systems (Kendzerska et al., 2021; Eager & Brunton, 2023; Amini & Jahanbakhsh Javid, 2023).

The implementation of AIP in urban security is often hindered by high costs and limited accessibility, particularly in low- and middle-income cities. For instance, the upfront investment required for surveillance devices, infrastructure, and training can be prohibitive for smaller law enforcement agencies. A case study in Nairobi addressed this by using low-cost sensors and leveraging cloud-based analytics to monitor crime patterns in underserved areas. This model demonstrated that cost-effective AIP solutions can enhance accessibility without compromising quality. To address economic barriers, strategies such as public-private partnerships, subscription-based models, and philanthropic funding can support the adoption of AIP in underserved regions. Accessibility can also be improved by designing AIP systems that function with minimal connectivity requirements, ensuring their usability in remote or resource-constrained areas. The integration of AIP with existing urban security systems poses significant challenges. Many legacy systems lack the interoperability needed to exchange data seamlessly with AI-driven devices, leading to fragmented security efforts and inefficiencies. Standardization efforts, such as adopting open data protocols, can facilitate smoother integration across diverse platforms (Junaid et al.,2023; Alawida et al.,2023; de Bem Machado, Sousa, Pesqueira, Rocha, 2024).

AIP implementation necessitates significant organizational changes, from restructuring workflows to redefining roles and responsibilities. While these shifts can improve efficiency and outcomes, they also introduce challenges such as resistance to change, workforce realignment, and financial strain. A phased implementation strategy, supported by clear communication and change management processes, can mitigate these risks. Sustainability is another critical consideration. AIP systems must align with environmental, social, and governance (ESG) principles to ensure long-term viability. For instance, using energy-efficient devices, recycling electronic waste, and promoting equitable access are essential components of a sustainable AIP strategy. Incorporating sustainability metrics into organizational goals can drive both innovation and accountability (Eager, Brunton, 2023; de Bem Machado, Sousa, Pesqueira, Rocha, 2024; Masih, 2022). To enhance the global applicability of AIP solutions, the following strategies can be adopted: regional customization, international collaboration, scalable models, and equity-driven design. Regional customization involves adapting AIP systems to local cultural, regulatory, and infrastructural contexts, ensuring relevance and acceptance. International collaboration is critical to fostering partnerships between governments, non-governmental organizations, and technology providers to share resources and expertise. Additionally, developing modular AIP platforms that can be scaled up or down based on regional needs and resource availability is essential for widespread adoption. By aligning technological advancements with robust ethical frameworks and addressing economic and accessibility challenges, urban security organizations can ensure that AIP serves as a transformative force for equitable and accountable public safety. Expanding the scope of AIP to include diverse urban security challenges and fostering interdisciplinary research will further enhance the adaptability and sustainability of smart city governance systems (Jalil et al., 2023; Amini & Jahanbakhsh Javid, 2023; Haleem et al., 2022).

Personalized Policing in Urban Security and AI-Driven Smart Cities: Emphasis on Security Integrity

Advancements in AIP have ushered in a new era of personalized urban security for metropolitan areas. By integrating real-time surveillance data, predictive analytics, and secure data exchange protocols, AIP seeks to optimize public safety management while upholding stringent standards of security integrity. The following discussion provides a deeper exploration of the critical dimensions that shape this emerging paradigm. In the realm of adaptive monitoring and individualized response strategies, AI-driven surveillance systems and smart sensors facilitate continuous tracking of urban activities, environmental indicators such as traffic flow and crowd density, and behavioral triggers that may signify potential security threats. This highly detailed data allows law enforcement agencies to adjust interventions rapidly and personalize policing strategies in near real time. ML algorithms, which analyze city-specific patterns, enhance the precision of intervention scheduling by identifying optimal points for patrol deployment, resource allocation, or community outreach programs. These insights enable a feedback mechanism in which policing plans are iteratively refined based on actual situational responses, reducing the likelihood of both over-policing and under-policing (Alawida et al.,2023; Haleem et al., 2022; Pesqueira, Sousa, 2022).

AI-driven diagnostics and predictive analytics further empower law enforcement by generating early detections of potential security breaches or criminal activities. Subtle changes in behavioral or environmental metrics can be flagged automatically, offering timely alerts for potential escalations or recurrence of security incidents. This capability supports evidence-based decision-making, as real-time guidance can incorporate historical crime data, established policing protocols, and broader population insights. The integration of multi-layered data sources—ranging from biometric information to community feedback—allows for targeted risk stratification and a more nuanced understanding of emerging threats. By minimizing human error in strategic decision-making, these AI-driven systems contribute to more accurate threat assessments and improved public safety outcomes (Amini & Jahanbakhsh Javid, 2023; Masih, 2022; Tariq et al.,2022). Holistic security ecosystems and collaboration benefit from AIP platforms that unify diverse stakeholders—police officers, security personnel, urban planners, and community leaders—within a single interface. Centralizing security data fosters consistent communication regarding incident responses, resource adjustments, and scheduling follow-up protocols, thereby reducing fragmentation across different security teams. Citizens themselves gain immediate access to public safety insights, enhancing their autonomy and commitment to community well-being. Moreover, AI-driven telesecurity solutions enable remote monitoring and interventions, widening access to specialized security services for underserved neighborhoods and reducing logistical barriers such as response time and resource allocation (de Bem Machado, Sousa, Pesqueira, Rocha, 2024; Pesqueira, Sousa, 2022; Wada et al.,2022).

Security integrity serves as a critical pillar in this landscape, particularly given the sensitivity of urban surveillance data. End-to-end encryption, rigorous authentication protocols, and secure communication channels guard against unauthorized access or data breaches. Through proactive cybersecurity measures that include frequent risk assessments and penetration testing, urban security organizations can fortify their AI-driven infrastructures against evolving threats while maintaining public trust and confidence in digital interventions. Finally, the sustainability and outlook of AI-driven personalized policing hinge on the capacity to integrate responsible resource management and ethical data stewardship. Continuous monitoring and predictive analytics help optimize resource usage and interventions, thereby limiting operational waste and environmental impact. Ethically guided governance, which underscores citizen confidentiality and equitable access, ensures that technological innovation unfolds alongside social and environmental responsibility. As AIP platforms become more secure, interoperable, and user-friendly, they hold the potential to democratize urban security services for broader populations, including those with limited resources or residing in remote areas. In doing so, these platforms advance both strategic innovation and sustainable security practices, establishing a robust framework for the future of urban security management (Haleem et al., 2022; Tariq et al.,2022; Shiwlani et al., 2023).

FUTURE IMPERATIVES AND STRATEGIC ADVANCEMENTS

Charting the Future of AIP in Urban Security and Smart Cities

AIP in the evolving landscape of urban security operates under a complex web of ethical and operational imperatives, reflecting the dual need for comprehensive crime prevention strategies and robust public protection measures. Central to these imperatives are rigorous standards that harmonize advanced surveillance, adaptive response protocols, and global interoperability of connected security devices. In this setting, institutional guidelines such as the GDPR in the European Union and the Privacy Act in various jurisdictions exemplify the heightened emphasis on data confidentiality and compliance, serving as baseline requirements for integrated planning and real-time decision-making in urban security ecosystems. Harmonization efforts led by international organizations, including INTERPOL and the United Nations Office on Drugs and Crime (UNODC), mitigate discrepancies across jurisdictions, while ISO-based frameworks enhance consistency in operational quality. From an operational perspective, these standards feed into the broader aims of personalized policing by ensuring coherent data governance and strategic alignment across interdisciplinary units. As the complexity of managing urban security continues to grow, consistent operational quality systems help organizations not only fulfill ethical mandates but also unlock synergies for advanced AIP adoption, especially in high-stakes security contexts (Masih, 2022; Wada et al.,2022; Pesqueira, Sousa, 2022).

Overcoming logistical and ethical barriers remains a critical challenge for law enforcement agencies striving to adopt AIP at scale. Issues such as continuous surveillance for crime detection underscore the intricacies of collecting accurate behavioral and environmental data, necessitating precision devices and algorithms to maintain real-time public oversight. Extended timelines for regulatory approvals, driven by stringent data protection requirements, add further layers of complexity to integrative security pathways. Heterogeneous guidelines in emerging markets can exacerbate these hurdles, demanding heightened adaptability and robust analytics to ensure equitable access to advanced policing interventions. Coupled with the threat of data breaches, these factors elevate the importance of advanced encryption mechanisms and transparent audit trails, including distributed ledger technologies that can reinforce privacy and strengthen public trust. Technological evolution plays a decisive role in addressing both operational and governance demands. AI serves as a central pillar of this evolution, facilitating predictive assessments that deepen AUR in policing management. However, concerns regarding algorithmic bias, public consent, and institutional endorsement persist, particularly in domains where individual rights and community trust are paramount. Similarly, blockchain technologies offer transparent transaction histories that can bolster policing authenticity but must adhere to confidentiality regulations, mirroring the stipulations set forth by entities like GDPR. Digital twin systems provide another promising avenue, enabling scenario-based simulations to optimize policing flows while maintaining close alignment with stringent ethical requirements (Pesqueira, Sousa, 2022; Shiwlani et al., 2023; Patil et al.,2022). Beyond operational imperatives, the growing influence of socially responsible security goals is reshaping how organizations approach oversight and innovation in urban policing. The drive toward holistic community well-being has led agencies to explore eco-conscious surveillance platforms, equitable resource distribution, and reduced environmental footprints, aligning operational achievement with conscientious security practices. Governments and professional associations increasingly incorporate these dimensions into policing guidelines, reinforcing the notion that integrated security should encompass not only operational outcomes but also sustainability benchmarks and socially mindful standards. To develop a resilient AIP infrastructure, law enforcement institutions must integrate compliance procedures with dynamic capability models and advanced analytics. This integration involves building adaptive oversight systems that encapsulate citizen data protection, secure device connectivity, and real-time analytics, all while actively detecting ethical risks or inefficiencies. Integrating socially responsible principles into these processes ensures that strategic adaptability coexists with ethical considerations, creating a paradigm in which community-centric excellence, adherence to data privacy, and public accountability converge. Through the synergistic use of AIP, personalized intervention design, and dynamic organizational practices, urban security networks can achieve the resilience and adaptability vital for sustainable progress in public safety management (Tariq et al.,2022; Pesqueira & Sousa, 2022; Leffa et al.,2022).

The global implementation of AIP reveals stark disparities influenced by regional regulations, socioeconomic conditions, and cultural practices. In high-income countries, AIP adoption has benefited from robust infrastructure, enabling sophisticated applications like predictive modeling and personalized patrol strategies. For example, Japan's law enforcement system leverages advanced AI technologies to streamline security interventions, integrating predictive analytics with smart surveillance platforms for effective crime management. Conversely, in low- and middle-income countries (LMICs), challenges such as limited internet access, fragmented regulatory frameworks, and high costs of deployment hinder widespread adoption. However, innovative low-cost solutions have emerged in regions like Sub-Saharan Africa, where community policing units use AI-driven devices to monitor crime patterns and provide real-time feedback to officers. These interventions demonstrate the potential of localized strategies to mitigate disparities and improve access. A comparative analysis of these regional dynamics underscores the need for flexible implementation models that accommodate varying levels of technological readiness and regulatory maturity. By fostering international collaborations and knowledge exchange, stakeholders can address socioeconomic and cultural barriers, ensuring that AIP benefits extend across diverse security ecosystems. AI-driven urban security, particularly in crime prevention and public safety management, constitutes a dynamic and cross-cutting discipline shaped by a mosaic of strategic frameworks that reflect diverse economic, cultural, and regulatory conditions. While these frameworks are critical for ensuring real-time threat detection, resource optimization, and community-centric adherence, the disparity among regions presents both challenges and opportunities for stakeholders operating in an increasingly digital and interconnected world. Establishing a foundational grasp of these regional paradigms entails not only recognizing their conceptual distinctions but also examining their operational ramifications and how they influence the broader trajectory of personalized policing strategies in the digital era (Wada et al.,2022; Patil et al.,2022; Kaplan & Hays, 2022).

Standards for AIP adoption vary from meticulously codified mandates to adaptive, fragmented protocols, mirroring the uneven pace of technological uptake worldwide. In North America, for instance, the United States enforces a rigorous oversight environment through frameworks such as the Privacy Act, which mandates exacting data privacy and traceability requirements. Such regulations protect security data pipelines but demand substantial infrastructure and analytic capabilities. Canada likewise imposes consistent standards, focusing on the entire continuum of data collection and strategic decision-making. Europe adopts a harmonization-oriented model, coordinated by entities such as INTERPOL and further enhanced by GDPR, thus ensuring unified citizen protections while accounting for localized nuances among member states. In contrast, Asian security systems display significant heterogeneity. Japan features innovation-friendly approaches, whereas emerging regions in China or India may confront infrastructural gaps. Nonetheless, rising investments in AIP have begun to standardize crime monitoring practices, although robust consensus remains elusive in large, diverse populations. Regions like Africa and Latin America continue to refine coherent guidelines, often facing limited resources and fragmented policies. Initiatives such as pan-regional security alliances show a growing commitment to alignment, underscoring a collective emphasis on data-driven progress in urban security management (Shiwlani et al., 2023; Leffa et al.,2022; Cifuentes-Faura, 2022).

These regional intricacies shape how law enforcement organizations structure and manage their AIP models. In high-compliance areas like North America and Europe, the obligation to adhere to frameworks such as the Privacy Act and GDPR prompts extensive investments in secure analytics and real-time monitoring. The adoption of blockchain or other tamper-evident systems often emerges as a pragmatic way to track interventions and community engagement while meeting evolving standards for data protection. Beyond fulfilling regulatory guidelines, such infrastructures foster operational clarity, which is essential for isolating bottlenecks or predicting service disruptions. In regions with variable oversight, including parts of Asia, Africa, and Latin America, organizations frequently adopt a dual-layer strategy. They embed global best practices when catering to more strictly regulated markets while adopting flexible models in areas with constrained infrastructure or looser policy enforcement. This balance alleviates tensions between worldwide obligations and local realities, though the diversity of compliance requirements can introduce inefficiencies and necessitate platforms that endure across varied regulatory and technological environments (Pesqueira & Sousa, 2022; Kaplan & Hays, 2022; Kouba et al., 2023).

Despite these divergences, numerous regions embrace innovative policy directions aligned with their respective operational and societal priorities. The United States implements streamlined pathways to expedite AI solutions aimed at bridging gaps in public safety services, aligning cost-effectiveness with rigorous adherence to citizen data safeguards. Europe emphasizes collaborative frameworks that encourage sustainability in digital security, weaving social responsibility into the fabric of AIP governance. Numerous Asian nations demonstrate advances in employing big data for security policy enforcement, offering examples of how emergent technologies can enhance response times and ensure regulatory oversight in urban security management. In emerging areas such as Africa and Latin America, joint ventures with global research partners reinforce foundational guidelines and promote digitization. These cooperative efforts herald an inclusive model where local constraints intersect with aspirations for robust AIP care, fostering an environment where technology serves as a bridge between diverse operational needs and strategic security objectives (Patil et al.,2022; Cifuentes-Faura, 2022; Spiel et al.,2022).

Advanced technologies, including blockchain, AI, and secure cloud infrastructures, have surfaced as effective instruments for navigating operational complexities and promoting harmonization. Blockchain's decentralized configuration guarantees validated chains of secure data, aligning with regions that emphasize data authenticity and continuity of public safety efforts. In markets with less sophisticated oversight frameworks, blockchain can compensate for infrastructural deficiencies by establishing shared ledgers accessible to multiple authorized stakeholders. AI and ML refine these oversight models by automating threat screening, predictive analysis, and ethical evaluations, enabling agencies to pivot swiftly amid shifting regulatory landscapes. Secure cloud systems enhance cross-border cooperation through unified data repositories, ameliorating fragmentation in contexts where enforcement varies widely. The infusion of socially responsible directives contributes another layer of strategic complexity across global urban security ecosystems. Europe's leadership in integrating sustainability and digital innovation illustrates the feasibility of weaving ecological consciousness into advanced surveillance platforms, producing synergy between social welfare and data governance. In North America, stakeholder pressure and market incentives, more than direct mandates, drive the incorporation of sustainability and inclusivity into AIP solutions. Meanwhile, resource-limited regions often must reconcile pressing service demands with sustainability objectives, relying on partnerships and international frameworks, such as the United Nations Sustainable Development Goals (SDGs), to facilitate incremental but impactful progress (Leffa et al.,2022; Kouba et al., 2023; Vallentin, Thórisson, Latapie, 2023).

Establishing a common foundation for AIP in urban security requires aligning diverse regional regulations with universal aims of public safety, operational rigor, and adaptive continuity. Law enforcement organizations must cultivate robust frameworks that respect jurisdictional distinctions yet leverage advanced technologies to secure data protection, expedite interventions, and enable real-time security adjustments. Embedding socially conscious elements into policing strategies ensures that organizational aims remain attuned to both local community interests and larger global expectations. Through heightened awareness of regional nuances and the judicious use of innovative AI-driven tools, law enforcement institutions can navigate these intricacies while capitalizing on strategic opportunities. This multifaceted model not only addresses immediate operational and ethical challenges but also lays a foundation for the long-term resilience, public trust, and accountability demanded in an era characterized by rapid innovation and heightened societal scrutiny (Kaplan & Hays, 2022; Spiel et al.,2022; Wamba et al., 2023).

Charting the Future of AIP in Urban Security and Smart Cities

AIP in the evolving landscape of urban security operates under a complex web of ethical and operational imperatives, reflecting the dual need for comprehensive crime prevention strategies and robust public protection measures. Central to these imperatives are rigorous standards that harmonize advanced surveillance systems, adaptive response protocols, and global interoperability of connected security devices. In this setting, institutional guidelines such as the Privacy Act in the United States and the GDPR in the European Union exemplify the heightened emphasis on data confidentiality and compliance, serving as baseline requirements for integrated planning and real-time decision-making in urban security ecosystems. Harmonization efforts led by international organizations, including INTERPOL and the United Nations Office on Drugs and Crime (UNODC), mitigate discrepancies across jurisdictions, while ISO-based frameworks enhance consistency in operational quality. From an operational perspective, these standards feed into the broader aims of personalized policing by ensuring coherent data governance and strategic alignment across interdisciplinary units. As the complexity of managing urban security continues to grow, consistent operational quality systems help organizations not only fulfill ethical mandates but also unlock synergies for advanced AIP adoption, especially in high-stakes security contexts (Pesqueira, Sousa, 2022).

Overcoming logistical and ethical barriers remains a critical challenge for law enforcement agencies striving to adopt AIP at scale. Issues such as continuous surveillance for crime detection underscore the intricacies of collecting accurate behavioral and environmental data, necessitating precision devices and algorithms to maintain real-time public oversight. Extended timelines for regulatory approvals, driven by stringent data protection requirements, add further layers of complexity to integrative security pathways. Heterogeneous guidelines in emerging markets can exacerbate these hurdles, demanding heightened adaptability and robust analytics to ensure equitable access to advanced policing interventions. Coupled with the threat of data breaches, these factors elevate the importance of advanced encryption mechanisms and transparent audit trails, including distributed ledger technologies that can reinforce privacy and strengthen public trust. Technological evolution plays a decisive role in addressing both operational and governance demands. AI serves as a central pillar of this evolution, facilitating predictive assessments that deepen AUR in policing management. However, concerns regarding algorithmic bias, public consent, and institutional endorsement persist, particularly in domains where individual rights and community trust are paramount. Similarly, blockchain technologies offer transparent transaction histories that can bolster policing authenticity but must adhere to confidentiality regulations, mirroring the stipulations set forth by entities like GDPR. Digital twin systems provide another promising avenue, enabling scenario-based simulations to optimize policing flows while maintaining close alignment with stringent ethical requirements (Kaplan & Hays, 2022; Spiel et al.,2022; Wamba et al., 2023).

Beyond operational imperatives, the growing influence of socially responsible security goals is reshaping how organizations approach oversight and innovation in urban policing. The drive toward holistic community well-being has led agencies to explore eco-conscious surveillance platforms, equitable resource distribution, and reduced environmental footprints, aligning operational achievement with conscientious security practices. Governments and professional associations increasingly incorporate these dimensions into policing guidelines, reinforcing the notion that integrated security should encompass not only operational outcomes but also sustainability benchmarks and socially mindful standards. To develop a resilient AIP infrastructure, law enforcement institutions must integrate compliance procedures with dynamic capability models and advanced analytics. This integration involves building adaptive oversight systems that encapsulate citizen data protection, secure device connectivity, and real-time analytics, all while actively detecting ethical risks or inefficiencies. Integrating socially responsible principles into these processes ensures that strategic adaptability coexists with ethical considerations, creating a paradigm in which community-centric excellence, adherence to data privacy, and public accountability converge. Through the synergistic use of AIP, personalized intervention design, and dynamic organizational practices, urban security networks can achieve the resilience and adaptability vital for sustainable progress in public safety management (de Bem Machado, Sousa, Pesqueira, Rocha, 2024; Pesqueira, Sousa, 2022; Wada et al.,2022).

The global implementation of AIP reveals stark disparities influenced by regional regulations, socioeconomic conditions, and cultural practices. In high-income countries, AIP adoption has benefited from robust infrastructure, enabling sophisticated applications like predictive modeling and personalized patrol strategies. For example, Japan's law enforcement system leverages advanced AI technologies to streamline security interventions, integrating predictive analytics with smart surveillance platforms for effective crime management. Conversely, in LMICs, challenges such as limited internet access, fragmented regulatory frameworks, and high costs of deployment hinder widespread adoption. However, innovative low-cost solutions have emerged in regions like Sub-Saharan Africa, where community policing units use AI-driven devices to monitor crime patterns and provide real-time feedback to officers. These interventions demonstrate the potential of localized strategies to mitigate disparities and improve access. A comparative analysis of these regional dynamics underscores the need for flexible implementation models that accommodate varying levels of technological readiness and regulatory maturity. By fostering international collaborations and knowledge exchange, stakeholders can address socioeconomic and cultural barriers, ensuring that AIP benefits extend across diverse security ecosystems. AI-driven urban security, particularly in crime prevention and public safety management, constitutes a dynamic and cross-cutting discipline shaped by a mosaic of strategic frameworks that reflect diverse economic, cultural, and regulatory conditions. While these frameworks are critical for ensuring real-time threat detection, resource optimization, and community-centric adherence, the disparity among regions presents both challenges and opportunities for stakeholders operating in an increasingly digital and interconnected world. Establishing a foundational grasp of these regional paradigms entails not only recognizing their conceptual distinctions but also examining their operational ramifications and how they influence the broader trajectory of personalized policing strategies in the digital era (Amini & Jahanbakhsh Javid, 2023).

Standards for AIP adoption vary from meticulously codified mandates to adaptive, fragmented protocols, mirroring the uneven pace of technological uptake worldwide. In North America, for instance, the United States enforces a rigorous oversight environment through frameworks such as the Privacy Act, which mandates exacting data privacy and traceability requirements. Such regulations protect security data pipelines but demand substantial infrastructure and analytic capabilities. Canada likewise imposes consistent standards, focusing on the entire continuum of data collection and strategic decision-making. Europe adopts a harmonization-oriented model, coordinated by entities such as INTERPOL and further enhanced by GDPR, thus ensuring unified citizen protections while accounting for localized nuances among member states. In contrast, Asian security systems display significant heterogeneity. Japan features innovation-friendly approaches, whereas emerging regions in China or India may confront infrastructural gaps. Nonetheless, rising investments in AIP have begun to standardize crime monitoring practices, although robust consensus remains elusive in large, diverse populations. Regions like Africa and Latin America continue to refine coherent guidelines, often facing limited resources and fragmented policies. Initiatives such as pan-regional security alliances show a growing commitment to alignment, underscoring a collective emphasis on data-driven progress in urban security management (Wani et al.,2022).

These regional intricacies shape how law enforcement organizations structure and manage their AIP models. In high-compliance areas like North America and Europe, the obligation to adhere to frameworks such as the Privacy Act and GDPR prompts extensive investments in secure analytics and real-time monitoring. The adoption of blockchain or other tamper-evident systems often emerges as a pragmatic way to track interventions and community engagement while meeting evolving standards for data protection. Beyond fulfilling regulatory guidelines, such infrastructures foster operational clarity, which is essential for isolating bottlenecks or predicting service disruptions. In regions with variable oversight, including parts of Asia, Africa, and Latin America, organizations frequently adopt a dual-layer strategy. They embed global best practices when catering to more strictly regulated markets while adopting flexible models in areas with constrained infrastructure or looser policy enforcement. This balance alleviates tensions between worldwide obligations and local realities, though the diversity of compliance requirements can introduce inefficiencies and necessitate platforms that endure across varied regulatory and technological environments (Vlasta, 2023).

Despite these divergences, numerous regions embrace innovative policy directions aligned with their respective operational and societal priorities. The United States implements streamlined pathways to expedite AI solutions aimed at bridging gaps in public safety services, aligning cost-effectiveness with rigorous adherence to citizen data safeguards. Europe emphasizes collaborative frameworks that encourage sustainability in digital security, weaving social responsibility into the fabric of AIP governance. Numerous Asian nations demonstrate advances in employing big data for security policy enforcement, offering examples of how emergent technologies can enhance response times and ensure regulatory oversight in urban security management. In emerging areas such as Africa and Latin America, joint ventures with global research partners reinforce foundational guidelines and promote digitization. These cooperative efforts herald an inclusive model where local constraints intersect with aspirations for robust AIP care, fostering an environment where technology serves as a bridge between diverse operational needs and strategic security objectives.

Advanced technologies, including blockchain, AI, and secure cloud infrastructures, have surfaced as effective instruments for navigating operational complexities and promoting harmonization. Blockchain's decentralized configuration guarantees validated chains of secure data, aligning with regions that emphasize data authenticity and continuity of public safety efforts. In markets with less sophisticated oversight frameworks, blockchain can compensate for infrastructural deficiencies by establishing shared ledgers accessible to multiple authorized stakeholders. AI and ML refine these oversight models by automating threat screening, predictive analysis, and ethical evaluations, enabling agencies to pivot swiftly amid shifting regulatory landscapes. Secure cloud systems enhance cross-border cooperation through unified data repositories, ameliorating fragmentation in contexts where enforcement varies widely. The infusion of socially responsible directives contributes another layer of strategic complexity across global urban security ecosystems. Europe's leadership in integrating sustainability and digital innovation illustrates the feasibility of weaving ecological consciousness into advanced surveillance platforms, producing synergy between social welfare and data governance. In North America, stakeholder pressure and market incentives, more than direct mandates, drive the incorporation of sustainability and inclusivity into AIP solutions. Meanwhile, resource-limited regions often must reconcile pressing service demands with sustainability objectives, relying on partnerships and international frameworks, such as the United Nations Sustainable Development Goals (SDGs), to facilitate incremental but impactful progress (Jalil et al., 2023; Amini & Jahanbakhsh Javid, 2023; Haleem et al., 2022).

Establishing a common foundation for AIP in urban security requires aligning diverse regional regulations with universal aims of public safety, operational rigor, and adaptive continuity. Law enforcement organizations must cultivate robust frameworks that respect jurisdictional distinctions yet leverage advanced technologies to secure data protection, expedite interventions, and enable real-time security adjustments. Embedding socially conscious elements into policing strategies ensures that organizational aims remain attuned to both local community interests and larger global expectations. Through heightened awareness of regional nuances and the judicious use of innovative AI-driven tools, law enforcement institutions can navigate these intricacies while capitalizing on strategic opportunities. This multifaceted model not only addresses immediate operational and ethical challenges but also lays a foundation for the long-term resilience, public trust, and accountability demanded in an era characterized by rapid innovation and heightened societal scrutiny (Haleem et al., 2022; Tariq et al.,2022; Shiwlani et al., 2023).

Table 2 presents a comprehensive overview of the multifaceted landscape of AIP within Urban Security and Smart Cities, highlighting fifteen key themes that interconnect to form a robust security ecosystem. Central to this framework is AUR, which emphasizes strategic agility and resource reorganization, enabling law enforcement agencies to dynamically respond to evolving threats and changing urban environments. This resilience is underpinned by theories from Strategic Management and Organizational Resilience, ensuring that policing strategies remain flexible and effective. AIP emerges as a pivotal theme, leveraging predictive analytics and real-time monitoring to enhance crime prevention and operational efficiency. Supported by Predictive Policing Theory and Technology Adoption Models, AIP utilizes machine learning algorithms to identify crime patterns and optimize resource allocation, thereby increasing the precision and responsiveness of law enforcement efforts. Ethical Governance and Regulatory Compliance are critical themes that ensure AI-driven initiatives uphold public trust and accountability. By adhering to frameworks like GDPR and the Privacy Act, and guided by Ethical Theory in Technology, these themes address data privacy and algorithmic fairness, mitigating biases and safeguarding citizen information. The integration of Smart City Infrastructure through IoT sensors and data interoperability facilitates cohesive surveillance and data sharing across urban security systems. This integration is supported by Smart City Frameworks and Systems Theory, which enable seamless communication and operational consistency. Predictive Analytics and Machine Learning Algorithms further enhance AIP by providing sophisticated tools for early threat detection and accurate data analysis. These concepts are grounded in Data-Driven Decision Making and AI Theory, driving proactive policing measures (Kotcher et al., 2021; Vlasta, 2023; Junaid et al.,2023).

Table 2. AIP and urban security in smart cities: Concepts and key dimensions

Key Theme	Key Concepts	Key Points	Related Theories/ Frameworks
Ethical Governance	Data privacy, algorithmic fairness	Ensures AIP upholds public trust, accountability, and ethical standards	Ethical Theory in Technology, Governance Theory
Smart City Infrastructure	IoT sensors, data interoperability	Facilitates integrated surveillance and data sharing across urban security systems	Smart City Frameworks, Systems Theory
Predictive Analytics	Crime pattern detection, early threat ID	Utilizes ML algorithms to anticipate and prevent criminal activities	Data-Driven Decision Making, Predictive Modeling Theory
Resource Allocation	Efficient deployment, scalability	Optimizes the distribution of policing resources based on predictive insights	Resource-Based View, Efficiency Theory
Community-Centric Opportunities	Citizen engagement, trust-building	Enhances public cooperation and community trust through transparent and participatory policing	Community Engagement Theory, Social Capital Theory
Machine Learning Algorithms	Pattern recognition, data analysis	Improves the accuracy and efficiency of threat detection and response	Machine Learning Theory, Artificial Intelligence Theory
Real-Time Data Processing	Immediate analysis, dynamic response	Enables law enforcement to make swift decisions based on live data	Real-Time Systems Theory, Information Processing Theory
Hybrid Policing Models	AI and human oversight, collaborative decision-making	Balances technological capabilities with human judgment to ensure nuanced and ethical policing	Hybrid Decision-Making Models, Human-AI Collaboration Theory
Regulatory Compliance	GDPR, Privacy Act	Mandates adherence to data privacy laws to protect citizens' information	Regulatory Compliance Theory, Public Administration Theory
Longitudinal Studies on AI Integration	Progressive technology adoption, impact assessment	Tracks the long-term effects and effectiveness of AIP systems	Longitudinal Research Design, Evolutionary Theory
Blockchain Technologies	Data integrity, secure ledgers	Ensures secure and tamper-proof records of policing data	Blockchain Theory, Data Security Frameworks
Digital Twin Systems	Scenario simulations, strategic optimization	Simulates policing scenarios to refine strategies before real-world implementation	Digital Twin Theory, Scenario Planning Framework
Sustainable Security Practices	Eco-conscious surveillance, resource efficiency	Integrates sustainability into urban security through low-energy devices and eco-friendly practices	Sustainability Theory, Environmental Governance

Integrated Personalized Policing and Adaptive Frameworks

Personalized surveillance and integrated response strategies remain pivotal in contemporary AIP, providing a structural backbone for coordinating law enforcement, community engagement, and technological initiatives. Collectively, they offer a coherent method for synchronizing data collection, interpreting security signals, and aligning long-term objectives across various security teams. Their growing significance in an era of heightened emphasis on public safety arises from the escalating diversity of urban challenges, expansive digital possibilities, and evolving societal norms. In this high-impact environment, ensuring seamless coordination among police officers, community leaders, and security specialists carries added weight. Complementing these key frameworks is the concept of AUR, which underscores the processes of sensing, seizing, and reorganizing organizational assets to maintain strategic agility in the face of unpredictable circumstances. Examining personalized surveillance and integrated response in conjunction with AUR provides essential insights into how community-focused security services can remain innovative, resilient, and effective amid rapid societal and technological transformations.

Personalized surveillance can be viewed as a broader evolution of conventional monitoring, widening the scope from basic observational methods to advanced AI-driven approaches. While traditional processes often emphasize patrol logs and periodic check-ins, personalized surveillance incorporates smart sensors, real-time behavioral analytics, and cross-domain data integration. Within urban security, these strategies merge daily operations with strategic interventions and resource allocation schedules. A salient advantage of personalized surveillance is its capacity to unify tactical decisions, such as adjusting patrol routes or deploying resources, with the community's evolving safety profiles. For instance, when initiating a novel crime prevention program, personalized surveillance enables the consolidation of environmental data, threat impact assessments, and community feedback measures, thereby supporting both security outcomes and community-centered safety goals. Such end-to-end synchronization minimizes resource mismatches and heightens operational impact. Personalized surveillance's effectiveness depends on robust data sharing and close collaborative engagement. By aggregating inputs from law enforcement officers, community members, security analysts, and municipal administrators, personalized systems create a holistic snapshot of urban safety dynamics. This shared perspective equips decision-makers to identify threats, fine-tune security services, and address arising disruptions swiftly. The participatory ethos in personalized surveillance further guarantees that interventions do not operate in silos but adhere to a unified framework. Technologies like ML are increasingly integrated into these platforms, refining the reliability of early-warning indicators and scenario planning to respond more effectively to subtle security changes.

Integrated response strategies, though narrower in scope than comprehensive surveillance, remain the cornerstone for harmonizing tailored interventions and community-based initiatives in response to real-time insights. Their fundamental objective is to produce a concrete plan that aligns a community's safety needs with available law enforcement resources, ensuring that patrol schedules and community outreach programs coalesce optimally. In security networks focusing on urban crime and public safety, integrated response often dictates the sequencing and intensity of service delivery, guaranteeing that crucial interventions, such as emergency response, community policing initiatives, or resource reallocation, are coordinated and timely. Its iterative orientation enables a swift recalibration of security plans when real-world factors shift, whether due to changes in community dynamics, economic pressures, or sudden security threats. During social crises, for instance, law enforcement agencies utilize integrated response strategies to direct more resources toward particularly vulnerable neighborhoods, balancing patrol presence with community support initiatives. The success of these strategies depends on accurate threat projections and inclusive decision-making. By harnessing historical crime data, feedback from community members, and security metrics, response teams construct an informed overview of demand, aligning resources and scheduling interventions with situational factors. Equally pivotal is transparent dialogue among all stakeholders, spanning law enforcement administrators, community leaders, families, and the citizens themselves. Such cross-functional engagement reduces duplicative efforts and lowers the probability of missed security threats. Digital transformation has further invigorated integrated response, as cloud-based systems, predictive modeling, and automated notifications have become more widespread, enabling agile responses to community relocations or shifts in resource availability. Though personalized surveillance and integrated response are systematic approaches that structure the continuum of urban security management, their potential is significantly magnified when merged with AUR. AUR highlights an entity's aptitude for detecting novel challenges, harnessing resources effectively, and restructuring security pathways to seize emergent opportunities. Within community-focused policing, AUR's relevance is especially pronounced due to age-specific developmental windows, fluctuating policy landscapes, and the rapid scaling of digital technologies. For example, the ability to detect changing crime patterns or policy modifications early allows agencies to modify program configurations in time-sensitive ways. Acquiring updated tools or forging cross-sector partnerships further helps organizations optimize novel security delivery models. Redesigning legacy processes for advanced AIP integration can ensure communities receive the most timely and accurate interventions possible.

Incorporating AUR into personalized surveillance and integrated response provides a strategic advantage by driving proactive engagement rather than reactive adjustments to unforeseen challenges. During pandemic-related lockdowns, agencies adept in dynamic sensing quickly recognized heightened security needs in communities that lost the stability of regular patrol routines. By linking these insights to response programs, they introduced remote monitoring modules, deployed smart surveillance devices, and ensured continuity of security through mobile units. Similarly, organizations supported by robust monitoring systems swiftly adapted their protocols to maintain crime prevention efforts and community outreach programs. Nonetheless, blending AUR with these frameworks entails cultural and procedural adaptation. A high degree of teamwork, an open attitude toward novel data streams, and dedication to iterative learning are essential for embedding AUR in everyday policing. In particular, the sensing component thrives on regularly gathering and analyzing community feedback, external research trends, and public perspectives. Achieving this breadth of vision frequently involves retraining security staff and upgrading legacy infrastructures. Meanwhile, the seizing component relies on cross-functional alignment, ensuring that budgetary, technical, and operational resources are promptly deployed in ways that maximize benefit. Transformative steps may include discontinuing outdated policing models, onboarding AI-enabled analytics, or reorganizing patrol schedules based on dynamic real-world constraints. Overcoming these hurdles requires resolute leadership, candid communication, and a commitment to ongoing refinements.

AUR's salience grows further in an era typified by global unpredictability and convergent technological shifts. Security networks operating across multiple regions must remain nimble in the face of emerging public safety mandates, infrastructural challenges, and surging demand for personalized urban security. AUR ensures that personalized surveillance and integrated response remain relevant by continually updating analytical tools, forging collaborative alliances, and exploring innovative telesecurity options. For instance, an unexpected surge in cybercrime may demand immediate reshuffling of security assignments or accelerated training of community policing units. By embedding AUR into established frameworks, institutions can mitigate security disruptions and sustain the timely provision of indispensable support. Personalized surveillance and integrated response are complementary concepts that coordinate day-to-day interventions with overarching goals, allocate resources efficiently, and respond flexibly to the volatile realities of urban security. Their synergy with AUR enhances these structures further, furnishing the agility and insight required to manage the complexities of modern urban security. By integrating AI-driven data platforms, interdisciplinary cooperation, and forward-thinking capabilities into standard protocols, security providers can surmount resource constraints, accommodate shifting community circumstances, and promote innovation for the benefit of cities and their inhabitants. As the sector continues its swift evolution, the interplay among personalized surveillance, integrated response, and AUR will remain pivotal to maintaining robust, inclusive, and ethically grounded security networks.

Figure 1 delineates a comprehensive theoretical framework that encapsulates the multifaceted dynamics of AIP within Smart Cities. At its core, AIP integrates advanced technologies such as predictive analytics, real-time monitoring, and machine learning algorithms to enhance crime prevention, resource allocation, and operational efficiency. Surrounding this central hub are four primary themes—AUR, Ethical Governance, Smart City Infrastructure, and Community-Centric Opportunities—each representing critical dimensions that collectively shape the efficacy and sustainability of AI-driven security initiatives. AUR, positioned to the top-left, underscores the importance of strategic agility and resource reorganization in responding to dynamic urban challenges. Grounded in Strategic Management and Organizational Resilience theories, AUR facilitates law enforcement agencies in adapting to evolving threats and changing urban landscapes, ensuring continuous operational effectiveness. Ethical Governance, located at the top-right, emphasizes the necessity of maintaining data privacy, algorithmic fairness, and regulatory compliance. This theme is pivotal in building public trust and ensuring that AIP practices adhere to ethical standards. Supported by Ethical Theory in Technology and Governance Theory, Ethical Governance acts as a safeguard against potential biases and abuses of surveillance technologies.

Smart City Infrastructure, situated to the bottom left, highlights the role of IoT sensors, data interoperability, and integrated surveillance systems in creating a cohesive and efficient urban security network. Smart City Frameworks and Systems Theory provide the foundational principles that enable seamless data sharing and operational integration across diverse security platforms. Community-Centric Opportunities, located at the bottom-right, focuses on enhancing citizen engagement, trust-building, and participatory policing models. By fostering strong relationships between law enforcement and communities, this theme ensures that AIP is both effective and socially acceptable. Community Engagement Theory and Social Capital Theory underpin strategies that promote collaborative and transparent security practices. The secondary themes—Predictive Analytics and Machine Learning, Hybrid Policing Models, Blockchain Technologies, Digital Twin Systems, and Sustainable Security Practices—interlink these primary themes, illustrating the complex interdependencies and reinforcing the framework's robustness. For instance, Predictive Analytics and Machine Learning enhance AIP by providing sophisticated tools for early threat detection and efficient resource allocation. Hybrid Policing Models balance AI technologies with human oversight, ensuring ethical and nuanced policing practices. Blockchain Technologies and Digital Twin Systems introduce secure data management and scenario-based simulations, respectively, further strengthening the integrity and strategic planning capabilities of urban security systems. Sustainable Security Practices integrate eco-friendly measures and resource efficiency, aligning operational goals with environmental stewardship and societal expectations. The interactions and flow depicted by the arrows indicate a dynamic and iterative process where continuous feedback loops and mutual reinforcement between themes foster an adaptive and resilient policing ecosystem. This holistic approach ensures that AIP not only addresses immediate security concerns but also evolves in tandem with technological advancements and societal changes (Figure 1).

Figure 1. Theoretical framework for AIP in smart urban security systems

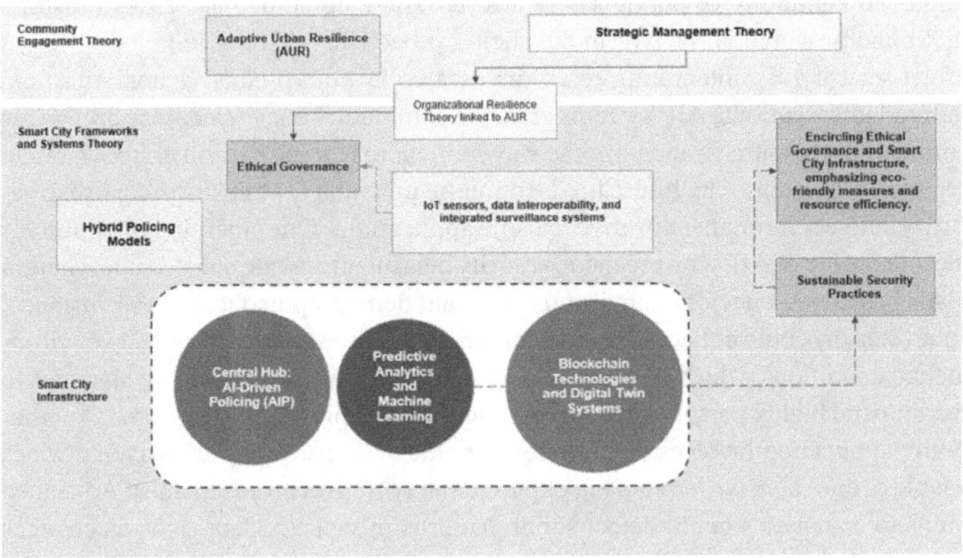

Opportunities and Current Real-Life Examples

AIP offers transformative opportunities across various aspects of urban security, particularly in enhancing crime prevention, real-time monitoring, and proactive interventions. For example, one law enforcement initiative combined smart sensors and AI algorithms to monitor traffic patterns and detect unusual activities. By analyzing data such as vehicle speeds and movement patterns, the system identified early warning signs of potential traffic accidents or suspicious behavior, allowing officers to intervene before incidents escalated. Another example involves a remote monitoring program for neighborhood safety, where AI-driven devices tracked real-time crime data and provided personalized recommendations for patrol adjustments. This approach not only improved public safety outcomes but also reduced the burden of frequent patrol deployments, demonstrating how AIP can empower communities in self-monitoring while maintaining close law enforcement oversight. In a separate application, AI-driven systems were used to support emergency response in urban areas. Smart devices monitored environmental indicators and alerted response teams to deviations from expected safety norms, ensuring timely adjustments to emergency protocols. This reduced response times and improved adherence to safety standards. Lastly, in public safety management, AI-driven surveillance systems have been employed to monitor and mitigate the spread of violent incidents through real-time data analysis and rapid intervention strategies. These systems facilitated the early detection of deteriorating security conditions, enabling timely intervention and improved continuity of public safety efforts. These combined use cases illustrate the immense potential of AIP in advancing proactive, personalized, and efficient urban security. By integrating real-time data collection, predictive analytics, and tailored interventions, AIP systems enhance community engagement, optimize law enforcement resources, and pave the way for a more responsive and effective urban security ecosystem. The future holds immense potential for transforming urban security delivery through innovative real-life applications. One emerging possibility is the integration of AIP with precision security measures to create tailored intervention plans based on behavioral, environmental, and demographic factors. For instance, smart sensors could collect data on community activities, traffic flows, and environmental conditions, which AI algorithms would analyze alongside crime statistics to recommend highly personalized patrol schedules and preventive measures. Another future application involves community-at-home systems, where AI-driven devices enable comprehensive monitoring of public safety from centralized hubs. Advanced predictive analytics could detect subtle patterns in security data, such as changes in crowd behavior or environmental anomalies, signaling early signs of potential security threats. This would allow law enforcement to intervene remotely, reducing the need for extensive patrols and enhancing public safety and quality of life.

AIP also offers opportunities in cybercrime and counter-terrorism, where smart diagnostic tools combined with AI-powered predictive models could monitor and respond to cyber threats in real-time. For example, AI systems could analyze data from various sources to predict and neutralize potential cyberattacks, providing law enforcement with the ability to anticipate and prevent security breaches. Additionally, the future may see AIP embedded into autonomous drones and robotic patrol units, where AI-guided devices provide real-time surveillance and threat detection during operations. These forward-looking applications highlight the transformative potential of AIP in creating more predictive, personalized, and equitable urban security systems. By bridging current technological capabilities with evolving security needs, AIP could redefine how public safety is managed, emphasizing prevention, precision, and community empowerment on a global scale.

FUTURE SCENARIOS AND FUTURE-BASED CONCEPTS

Future Perspectives: Anticipating Disruption and Strategic Opportunities

AIP in urban security is approaching a pivotal juncture, influenced by the intersection of rapidly advancing digital surveillance technologies, evolving ethical mandates, and a globally interconnected environment. Prospective directions, nascent conceptual frameworks, and forward-oriented principles offer vital insights into managing this fluid landscape. These perspectives function not only as a guide for preempting and addressing potential operational or technological hurdles but also as a platform for reconfiguring policing protocols to enhance public resilience, equitable access, and security responsiveness. Comprehending how these dimensions merge and co-evolve is paramount for constructing adaptive, future-ready urban security systems that thrive amid ongoing change.

Looking forward, emerging scenarios for AIP revolve around several interdependent themes, notably the proliferation of advanced threat-tracking algorithms, evolving data governance structures, and heightened concern for personalized and sustainable security interventions. These potential developments envision a more decentralized, interactive, and real-time urban security network, marked by enhanced transparency in policing outcomes and strengthened collaboration among law enforcement, community stakeholders, and technological innovators. A frequently cited scenario foresees the extensive deployment of "intelligent policing modules." Novel configurations—such as modular AI-driven threat assessments and localized analytics nodes—could facilitate on-demand adjustments to policing strategies, reducing response times and minimizing resource wastage. This model also aligns with community-specific security designs, enabling near-instant feedback to tailor interventions based on real-time situational data. However, actualizing such a system requires advanced interoperability standards, continuous data protection measures, and an overarching ethical framework to ensure responsible AI usage. Another future path underscores the amplified role of predictive analytics and AUR in structuring proactive security processes. By employing sophisticated forecasting models, agencies can swiftly detect potential threat triggers or predict fluctuations in crime patterns, recalibrating interventions or resource allocation as necessary. While this approach augments agility, it invites concerns about data bias, model interpretability, and the need for specialized competencies among professionals managing AI-centric applications. Regulatory clarity and transparent governance will serve as indispensable pillars of this envisioned transformation.

Emphasis on sustainable, community-centered security also undergirds possible trajectories, as urban security advocates intensify calls for socially accountable practices and citizen empowerment. This emphasis includes adopting outcome-driven strategies that streamline community engagement, reduce surveillance-related resource consumption, and incorporate ethical guidelines for AI-driven data collection. Multiple jurisdictions, including those shaping international security standards, are broadening directives around data stewardship and equitable resource distribution, prompting holistic integration of community-focused priorities within AI-augmented policing ecosystems. These scenarios collectively highlight the need for robust models that interlace operational efficiencies with broader social imperatives.

Conceptual Foundation: Linking Current Practices and Emerging Principles

The conceptual architecture for projecting future scenarios in AIP builds upon established theories, notably resource-based perspectives, systems thinking, and AUR. These theoretical angles illustrate how practitioners and organizations can optimize knowledge-sharing, remain attuned to evolving security landscapes, and innovate across intricate policing networks. AUR remains a cornerstone, highlighting how law enforcement and administrative bodies identify shifts in threat trajectories, leverage existing resources, and redesign policing pathways to maintain comprehensive, evidence-based security. Within urban policing, AUR assumes particular importance due to the confluence of stringent privacy norms, the complex interplay of societal factors, and rapidly emerging digital interventions. For example, recognizing changes in real-time regulatory guidelines or urban crime demographics enables policing teams to tailor new outreach programs or incorporate advanced AI-driven tools. The capacity for transformative adaptation proves vital, permitting the overhaul of outdated patrol protocols, seamless adoption of smart surveillance technology, and realignment of strategic objectives around community-centric safety and accountability. Resource-centric viewpoints complement AUR by spotlighting the ways distinctive assets, such as proprietary predictive algorithms, specialized sensor arrays, or integrated monitoring frameworks, can generate competitive or operational advantages. This lens is particularly salient for institutions that make substantial investments in next-generation platforms, be they advanced data analytics or blockchains, ensuring data integrity. However, a resource-based perspective equally stresses the value of human competency, driving the refinement of operational oversight, institutional culture, and training initiatives needed to maximize the benefits of AIP.

Systems thinking adds depth to this discussion, underscoring how seemingly independent components of threat monitoring, response coordination, and resource management interconnect in one unified continuum of urban security. Adopting a systemic stance allows organizations to project how new AI applications in early threat detection might influence community outreach or how emergent ethical standards may reverberate across global security networks. Systems-based approaches also emphasize the roles of cross-sectoral alliances—linking law enforcement agencies, community organizations, policymakers, and technology vendors—to foster synergy in delivering integrated and responsive urban security services. Forward-oriented paradigms in AIP are anchored in the goal of uniting advanced AI technologies with transformative security designs to enhance adaptability, efficiency, and ethical mindfulness. A key paradigm is the concept of an "intelligent security network," bringing together AI, secure data ledgers, and connected monitoring devices within a comprehensive, digitized infrastructure. Intelligent networks exhibit continuous data-sharing, strong predictive capacities, and automated updates to policing pathways, enabling law enforcement and communities to anticipate threats rather than merely react. For instance, smart sensors might capture fluctuations in crowd behavior or environmental anomalies, while a tamper-proof ledger ensures data authenticity and privacy.

Opportunities and Current Real-Life Examples

AIP offers transformative opportunities across various aspects of urban security, particularly in enhancing crime prevention, real-time monitoring, and proactive interventions. For example, one law enforcement initiative combined smart sensors and AI algorithms to monitor traffic patterns and detect unusual activities. By analyzing data such as vehicle speeds and movement patterns, the system identified early warning signs of potential traffic accidents or suspicious behavior, allowing officers to intervene before incidents escalated. Another example involves a remote monitoring program for neighborhood safety, where AI-driven devices tracked real-time crime data and provided personalized recommendations for patrol adjustments. This approach not only improved public safety outcomes but also reduced the burden of frequent patrol deployments, demonstrating how AIP can empower communities in self-monitoring while maintaining close law enforcement oversight.

In a separate application, AI-driven systems were used to support emergency response in urban areas. Smart devices monitored environmental indicators and alerted response teams to deviations from expected safety norms, ensuring timely adjustments to emergency protocols. This reduced response times and improved adherence to safety standards. Lastly, in public safety management, AI-driven surveillance systems have been employed to monitor and mitigate the spread of violent incidents through real-time data analysis and rapid intervention strategies. These systems facilitated the early detection of deteriorating security conditions, enabling timely intervention and improved continuity of public safety efforts. These combined use cases illustrate the immense potential of AIP in advancing proactive, personalized, and efficient urban security. By integrating real-time data collection, predictive analytics, and tailored interventions, AIP systems enhance community engagement, optimize law enforcement resources, and pave the way for a more responsive and effective urban security ecosystem.

The future holds immense potential for transforming urban security delivery through innovative real-life applications. One emerging possibility is the integration of AIP with precision security measures to create tailored intervention plans based on behavioral, environmental, and demographic factors. For instance, smart sensors could collect data on community activities, traffic flows, and environmental conditions, which AI algorithms would analyze alongside crime statistics to recommend highly personalized patrol schedules and preventive measures. Another future application involves community-at-home systems, where AI-driven devices enable comprehensive monitoring of public safety from centralized hubs. Advanced predictive analytics could detect subtle patterns in security data, such as changes in crowd behavior or environmental anomalies, signaling early signs of potential security threats. This would allow law enforcement to intervene remotely, reducing the need for extensive patrols and enhancing public safety and quality of life.

AIP also offers opportunities in cybercrime and counter-terrorism, where smart diagnostic tools combined with AI-powered predictive models could monitor and respond to cyber threats in real-time. For example, AI systems could analyze data from various sources to predict and neutralize potential cyberattacks, providing law enforcement with the ability to anticipate and prevent security breaches. Additionally, the future may see AIP embedded into autonomous drones and robotic patrol units, where AI-guided devices provide real-time surveillance and threat detection during operations. These forward-looking applications highlight the transformative potential of AIP in creating more predictive, personalized, and equitable urban security systems. By bridging current technological capabilities with evolving security needs, AIP could redefine how public safety is managed, emphasizing prevention, precision, and community empowerment on a global scale.

Integrated Personalized Policing and Adaptive Frameworks

Personalized surveillance and integrated response strategies remain pivotal in contemporary AIP, providing a structural backbone for coordinating law enforcement, community engagement, and technological initiatives. Collectively, they offer a coherent method for synchronizing data collection, interpreting security signals, and aligning long-term objectives across various security teams. Their growing significance in an era of heightened emphasis on public safety arises from the escalating diversity of urban challenges, expansive digital possibilities, and evolving societal norms. In this high-impact environment, ensuring seamless coordination among police officers, community leaders, and security specialists carries added weight. Complementing these key frameworks is the concept of AUR, which underscores the processes of sensing, seizing, and reorganizing organizational assets to maintain strategic agility in the face of unpredictable circumstances. Examining personalized surveillance and integrated response in conjunction with AUR provides essential insights into how community-focused security services can remain innovative, resilient, and effective amid rapid societal and technological transformations.

Personalized surveillance can be viewed as a broader evolution of conventional monitoring, widening the scope from basic observational methods to advanced AI-driven approaches. While traditional processes often emphasize patrol logs and periodic check-ins, personalized surveillance incorporates smart sensors, real-time behavioral analytics, and cross-domain data integration. Within urban security, these strategies merge daily operations with strategic interventions and resource allocation schedules. A salient advantage of personalized surveillance is its capacity to unify tactical decisions, such as adjusting patrol routes or deploying resources, with the community's evolving safety profiles. For instance, when initiating a novel crime prevention program, personalized surveillance enables the consolidation of environmental data, threat impact assessments, and community feedback measures, thereby supporting both security outcomes and community-centered safety goals. Such end-to-end synchronization minimizes resource mismatches and heightens operational impact. Personalized surveillance's effectiveness depends on robust data sharing and close collaborative engagement. By aggregating inputs from law enforcement officers, community members, security analysts, and municipal administrators, personalized systems create a holistic snapshot of urban safety dynamics. This shared perspective equips decision-makers to identify threats, fine-tune security services, and address arising disruptions swiftly. The participatory ethos in personalized surveillance further guarantees that interventions do not operate in silos but adhere to a unified framework. Technologies like ML are increasingly integrated into these platforms, refining the reliability of early-warning indicators and scenario planning to respond more effectively to subtle security changes.

Integrated response strategies, though narrower in scope than comprehensive surveillance, remain the cornerstone for harmonizing tailored interventions and community-based initiatives in response to real-time insights. Their fundamental objective is to produce a concrete plan that aligns a community's safety needs with available law enforcement resources, ensuring that patrol schedules and community outreach programs coalesce optimally. In security networks focusing on urban crime and public safety, integrated response often dictates the sequencing and intensity of service delivery, guaranteeing that crucial interventions, such as emergency response, community policing initiatives, or resource reallocation—are coordinated and timely. Its iterative orientation enables a swift recalibration of security plans when real-world factors shift, whether due to changes in community dynamics, economic pressures, or sudden security threats. During social crises, for instance, law enforcement agencies utilize integrated response strategies to direct more resources toward particularly vulnerable neighborhoods, balancing patrol presence with community support initiatives.

The success of these strategies depends on accurate threat projections and inclusive decision-making. By harnessing historical crime data, feedback from community members, and security metrics, response teams construct an informed overview of demand, aligning resources and scheduling interventions with situational factors. Equally pivotal is transparent dialogue among all stakeholders, spanning law enforcement administrators, community leaders, families, and the citizens themselves. Such cross-functional engagement reduces duplicative efforts and lowers the probability of missed security threats. Digital transformation has further invigorated integrated response, as cloud-based systems, predictive modeling, and automated notifications have become more widespread, enabling agile responses to community relocations or shifts in resource availability. Though personalized surveillance and integrated response are systematic approaches that structure the continuum of urban security management, their potential is significantly magnified when merged with AUR. AUR highlights an entity's aptitude for detecting novel challenges, harnessing resources effectively, and restructuring security pathways to seize emergent opportunities. Within community-focused policing, AUR's relevance is especially pronounced due to the confluence of stringent privacy norms, the complex interplay of societal factors, and rapidly emerging digital interventions. For example, recognizing changes in real-time regulatory guidelines or urban crime demographics enables policing teams to tailor new outreach programs or incorporate advanced AI-driven tools. The capacity for transformative adaptation proves vital, permitting the overhaul of outdated patrol protocols, seamless adoption of smart surveillance technology, and realignment of strategic objectives around community-centric safety and accountability.

Incorporating AUR into personalized surveillance and integrated response provides a strategic advantage by driving proactive engagement rather than reactive adjustments to unforeseen challenges. During pandemic-related lockdowns, agencies adept in dynamic sensing quickly recognized heightened security needs in communities that lost the stability of regular patrol routines. By linking these insights to response programs, they introduced remote monitoring modules, deployed smart surveillance devices, and ensured continuity of security through mobile units. Similarly, organizations supported by robust monitoring systems swiftly adapted their protocols to maintain crime prevention efforts and community outreach programs. Nonetheless, blending AUR with these frameworks entails cultural and procedural adaptation. A high degree of teamwork, an open attitude toward novel data streams, and dedication to iterative learning are essential for embedding AUR in everyday policing. In particular, the sensing component thrives on regularly gathering and analyzing community feedback, external research trends, and public perspectives. Achieving this breadth of vision frequently involves retraining security staff and upgrading legacy infrastructures. Meanwhile, the seizing component relies on cross-functional alignment, ensuring that budgetary, technical, and operational resources are promptly deployed in ways that maximize benefit. Transformative steps may include discontinuing outdated policing models, onboarding AI-enabled analytics, or reorganizing patrol schedules based on dynamic real-world constraints. Overcoming these hurdles requires resolute leadership, candid communication, and a commitment to ongoing refinements.

AUR's salience grows further in an era typified by global unpredictability and convergent technological shifts. Security networks operating across multiple regions must remain nimble in the face of emerging public safety mandates, infrastructural challenges, and surging demand for personalized urban security. AUR ensures that personalized surveillance and integrated response remain relevant by continually updating analytical tools, forging collaborative alliances, and exploring innovative telesecurity options. For instance, an unexpected surge in cybercrime may demand immediate reshuffling of security assignments or accelerated training of community policing units. By embedding AUR into established frameworks, institutions can mitigate security disruptions and sustain the timely provision of indispensable support. Personalized surveillance and integrated response are complementary concepts that coordinate day-to-day interventions with overarching goals, allocate resources efficiently, and respond flexibly to the volatile realities of urban security. Their synergy with AUR enhances these structures further, furnishing the agility and insight required to manage the complexities of modern urban security. By integrating AI-driven data platforms, interdisciplinary cooperation, and forward-thinking capabilities into standard protocols, security providers can surmount resource constraints, accommodate shifting community circumstances, and promote innovation for the benefit of cities and their inhabitants. As the sector continues its swift evolution, the synergy among personalized surveillance, integrated response, AUR, and forward-thinking constructs will be critical for addressing the nuanced demands of 21st-century urban security. Stakeholders that adopt these frameworks and invest in the requisite digital infrastructure, comprehensive analytics capabilities, and interdisciplinary collaborations will be best positioned to navigate disruptions, satisfy emerging regulatory expectations, and deliver meaningful benefits to communities and their inhabitants. Such a cohesive paradigm guarantees that AIP ecosystems remain not only efficient and innovative but also grounded in the fundamental goals of resilience, ethical guardianship, and equitable access for all.

Opportunities and Current Real-Life Examples

AIP offers transformative opportunities across various aspects of urban security, particularly in enhancing crime prevention, real-time monitoring, and proactive interventions. For example, one law enforcement initiative combined smart sensors and AI algorithms to monitor traffic patterns and detect unusual activities. By analyzing data such as vehicle speeds and movement patterns, the system identified early warning signs of potential traffic accidents or suspicious behavior, allowing officers to intervene before incidents escalated. Another example involves a remote monitoring program for neighborhood safety, where AI-driven devices tracked real-time crime data and provided personalized recommendations for patrol adjustments. This approach not only improved public safety outcomes but also reduced the burden of frequent patrol deployments, demonstrating how AIP can empower communities in self-monitoring while maintaining close law enforcement oversight.

In a separate application, AI-driven systems were used to support emergency response in urban areas. Smart devices monitored environmental indicators and alerted response teams to deviations from expected safety norms, ensuring timely adjustments to emergency protocols. This reduced response times and improved adherence to safety standards. Lastly, in public safety management, AI-driven surveillance systems have been employed to monitor and mitigate the spread of violent incidents through real-time data analysis and rapid intervention strategies. These systems facilitated the early detection of deteriorating security conditions, enabling timely intervention and improved continuity of public safety efforts. These combined use cases illustrate the immense potential of AIP in advancing proactive, personalized, and efficient urban security. By integrating real-time data collection, predictive analytics, and tailored interventions, AIP systems enhance community engagement, optimize law enforcement resources, and pave the way for a more responsive and effective urban security ecosystem.

The future holds immense potential for transforming urban security delivery through innovative real-life applications. One emerging possibility is the integration of AIP with precision security measures to create tailored intervention plans based on behavioral, environmental, and demographic factors. For instance, smart sensors could collect data on community activities, traffic flows, and environmental conditions, which AI algorithms would analyze alongside crime statistics to recommend highly personalized patrol schedules and preventive measures. Another future application involves community-at-home systems, where AI-driven devices enable comprehensive monitoring of public safety from centralized hubs. Advanced predictive analytics could detect subtle patterns in security data, such as changes in crowd behavior or environmental anomalies, signaling early signs of potential security threats. This would allow law enforcement to intervene remotely, reducing the need for extensive patrols and enhancing public safety and quality of life.

AIP also offers opportunities in cybercrime and counter-terrorism, where smart diagnostic tools combined with AI-powered predictive models could monitor and respond to cyber threats in real-time. For example, AI systems could analyze data from various sources to predict and neutralize potential cyber-attacks, providing law enforcement with the ability to anticipate and prevent security breaches. Additionally, the future may see AIP embedded into autonomous drones and robotic patrol units, where AI-guided devices provide real-time surveillance and threat detection during operations. These forward-looking applications highlight the transformative potential of AIP in creating more predictive, personalized, and equitable urban security systems. By bridging current technological capabilities with evolving security needs, AIP could redefine how public safety is managed, emphasizing prevention, precision, and community empowerment on a global scale.

CONCLUSION

AIP in urban security is undergoing a paradigmatic shift, propelled by breakthroughs in data-driven analytics, stricter community-protection frameworks, and intensified emphasis on holistic well-being. As law enforcement agencies endeavor to function within this increasingly multifaceted landscape, concepts such as personalized surveillance, integrated response, and AUR emerge as indispensable instruments for reinforcing adaptability, ethical rigor, and alignment with evolving security standards. When harmonized with progressive theoretical insights and the most recent digital innovations, these concepts form a robust platform for cultivating responsive, future-proof security ecosystems. The analysis underscores the strategic value of anticipating emergent scenarios. By actively recognizing challenges such as inconsistent data regulations, variable access to digital infrastructure, and escalating demand for community-centric interventions, security providers can shift course expeditiously and leverage opportunities. Foundational constructs, including AUR and systems thinking, bridge the gap between top-level security goals and day-to-day operational practices. They enable community-focused services to interpret external signals, secure pivotal resources, and overhaul core processes in reaction to unexpected disruptions—an imperative in a domain defined by continuous technological progress and intricate ethical mandates. Key forward-looking constructs, encompassing intelligent security networks, robust operational architectures, and socially conscientious frameworks, illustrate how organizations can merge operational efficiency with social accountability. Intelligent security systems unite AI-driven technologies, blockchain-based verification, and real-time analytics to foster data-driven decision-making. Resilient service models champion the diversification of security channels and fortified digital infrastructures, ensuring that organizations remain equipped to deliver ongoing support despite external challenges. In tandem, sustainable security initiatives integrate responsible device usage and fair resource allocation, aligning outcome-based security with broader public calls for conscientious, community-friendly practices.

This convergence of strategies marks a shift from reactive to anticipatory security governance, where organizations not only prepare for looming threats but also stand poised to pursue transformative endeavors and generate new pathways for growth. By refining operational models around both security priorities and ethical responsibilities, law enforcement agencies can secure a decisive edge in an environment characterized by ever-evolving community needs and persistent innovation. As the sector continues its swift evolution, the synergy among personalized surveillance, integrated response, AUR, and forward-thinking constructs will be critical for addressing the nuanced demands of 21st-century urban security. Stakeholders that adopt these frameworks and invest in the requisite digital infrastructure, comprehensive analytics capabilities, and interdisciplinary collaborations will be best positioned to navigate disruptions, satisfy emerging regulatory expectations, and deliver meaningful benefits to communities and their inhabitants. Such a cohesive paradigm guarantees that AIP ecosystems remain not only efficient and innovative but also grounded in the fundamental goals of resilience, ethical guardianship, and equitable access for all.

REFERENCES

Alawida, M., Mejri, S., Mehmood, A., Chikhaoui, B., & Isaac Abiodun, O. (2023). A Comprehensive Study of ChatGPT: Advancements, Limitations, and Ethical Considerations in Natural Language Processing and Cybersecurity. *Information (Basel), 14*(8), 462. DOI: 10.3390/info14080462

Amini, M., & Jahanbakhsh Javid, N. (2023). A multi-perspective framework established on diffusion of innovation (DOI) theory and technology, organization and environment (TOE) framework toward supply chain management system based on cloud computing technology for small and medium enterprises. Organization and Environment (TOE) Framework Toward Supply Chain Management System Based on Cloud Computing Technology for Small and Medium Enterprises (January 2023). *International Journal of Information Technology and Innovation Adoption, 11*, 1217–1234.

Breaux, R., Shroff, D. M., Cash, A. R., Swanson, C. S., Carlton, C., Bertollo, J. R., & Dahiya, A. V. (2023). Telehealth delivery of the RELAX intervention for families of adolescents diagnosed with ADHD: Preliminary treatment outcomes and evidence of acceptability and feasibility. *Evidence-Based Practice in Child and Adolescent Mental Health, 8*(1), 24–38. DOI: 10.1080/23794925.2021.1970053

Cifuentes-Faura, J. (2022). European Union policies and their role in combating climate change over the years. *Air Quality, Atmosphere & Health, 15*(8), 1–8. DOI: 10.1007/s11869-022-01156-5 PMID: 35035604

de Bem Machado, A., Sousa, M. J., Pesqueira, A., & Rocha, A. (2024). Metaverse for Education Information Systems: A Systematic Literature Review. Metaverse Driven Intelligent Information Systems: Emerging Trends and Future Directions, 29-47.

Dillard-Wright, J., & Shields-Haas, V. (2021). Nursing with the people: Reimagining futures for nursing. *Advances in Nursing Science, 44*(3), 195–209. DOI: 10.1097/ANS.0000000000000361 PMID: 33624989

Eager, B., & Brunton, R. (2023). Prompting higher education towards AI-augmented teaching and learning practice. Journal of University Teaching & Learning Practice, 20(5), 02.

Ebrahimi, S., & Bridgelall, R. (2021). A fuzzy Delphi analytic hierarchy model to rank factors influencing public transit mode choice: A case study. *Research in Transportation Business & Management, 39*, 100496. DOI: 10.1016/j.rtbm.2020.100496

ElBaih, M. (2023). The Role of Privacy Regulations in AI Development (A Discussion of the Ways in Which Privacy Regulations Can Shape the Development of AI). Available at *SSRN* 4589207. DOI: 10.2139/ssrn.4589207

Gebhardt, M., Kopyto, M., Birkel, H., & Hartmann, E. (2022). Industry 4.0 technologies as enablers of collaboration in circular supply chains: A systematic literature review. *International Journal of Production Research, 60*(23), 6967–6995. DOI: 10.1080/00207543.2021.1999521

Haleem, A., Javaid, M., Singh, R. P., & Suman, R. (2022). Medical 4.0 technologies for healthcare: Features, capabilities, and applications. *Internet of Things and Cyber-Physical Systems, 2*, 12–30. DOI: 10.1016/j.iotcps.2022.04.001

Jacob, C., Bourke, S., & Heuss, S. (2022). From Testers to Cocreators—the Value of and Approaches to Successful Patient Engagement in the Development of eHealth Solutions: Qualitative Expert Interview Study. *JMIR Human Factors, 9*(4), e41481. DOI: 10.2196/41481 PMID: 36102548

Jalil, S., Rafi, S., LaToza, T. D., Moran, K., & Lam, W. (2023). Chatgpt and software testing education: Promises & perils. In *2023 IEEE International Conference on Software Testing, Verification and Validation Workshops (ICSTW)* (pp. 4130-4137). IEEE. DOI: 10.1109/ICSTW58534.2023.00078

Javaid, M., Haleem, A., & Singh, R. P. (2023). ChatGPT for healthcare services: An emerging stage for an innovative perspective. BenchCouncil Transactions on Benchmarks. *Standards and Evaluations, 3*(1), 100105.

Junaid, M., Zhang, Q., Cao, M., & Luqman, A. (2023). Nexus between technology enabled supply chain dynamic capabilities, integration, resilience, and sustainable performance: An empirical examination of healthcare organizations. *Technological Forecasting and Social Change, 196*, 122828. DOI: 10.1016/j.techfore.2023.122828

Kant, N., & Anjali, K. (2021). Blockchain Technology: A Strategic Resource. In Blockchain for Healthcare Systems (pp. 1-15). CRC Press. 13

Kaplan, R. M., & Hays, R. D. (2022). Health-related quality of life measurement in public health. *Annual Review of Public Health, 43*(1), 355–373. DOI: 10.1146/annurev-publhealth-052120-012811 PMID: 34882431

Kasneci, E., Seßler, K., Küchemann, S., Bannert, M., Dementieva, D., Fischer, F., Gasser, U., Groh, G., Günnemann, S., Hüllermeier, E., Krusche, S., Kutyniok, G., Michaeli, T., Nerdel, C., Pfeffer, J., Poquet, O., Sailer, M., Schmidt, A., Seidel, T., & Kasneci, G. (2023). ChatGPT for good? On opportunities and challenges of large language models for education. *Learning and Individual Differences*, *103*, 102274. DOI: 10.1016/j.lindif.2023.102274

Kendzerska, T., Zhu, D. T., Gershon, A. S., Edwards, J. D., Peixoto, C., Robillard, R., & Kendall, C. E. (2021). The effects of the health system response to the COVID-19 pandemic on chronic disease management: A narrative review. *Risk Management and Healthcare Policy*, *14*, 575–584. DOI: 10.2147/RMHP.S293471 PMID: 33623448

Kotcher, J., Maibach, E., Miller, J., Campbell, E., Alqodmani, L., Maiero, M., & Wyns, A. (2021). Views of health professionals on climate change and health: A multinational survey study. *The Lancet. Planetary Health*, *5*(5), e316–e323. DOI: 10.1016/S2542-5196(21)00053-X PMID: 33838130

Kouba, P., Kohout, P., Haddadi, F., Bushuiev, A., Samusevich, R., Sedlar, J., Damborsky, J., Pluskal, T., Sivic, J., & Mazurenko, S. (2023). Machine Learning-Guided Protein Engineering. *ACS Catalysis*, *13*(21), 13863–13895. DOI: 10.1021/acscatal.3c02743 PMID: 37942269

Kwok, A. O., & Treiblmaier, H. (2023). Blockchain technology as a driver of economic development in small economies: A dynamic capabilities framework. *Journal of Decision Systems*, •••, 1–26.

Leffa, D. T., Grevet, E. H., Bau, C. H. D., Schneider, M., Ferrazza, C. P., da Silva, R. F., Miranda, M. S., Picon, F., Teche, S. P., Sanches, P., Pereira, D., Rubia, K., Brunoni, A. R., Camprodon, J. A., Caumo, W., & Rohde, L. A. (2022). Transcranial direct current stimulation vs sham for the treatment of inattention in adults with attention-deficit/hyperactivity disorder: The TUNED randomized clinical trial. *JAMA Psychiatry*, *79*(9), 847–856. DOI: 10.1001/jamapsychiatry.2022.2055 PMID: 35921102

Masih, E. A. (2022). Feasibility of using QR code for registration & evaluation of training and its ability to increase response rate–The learners' perception. *Nurse Education Today*, *111*, 105305. DOI: 10.1016/j.nedt.2022.105305 PMID: 35220149

Patil et al. (2022). "Utilization of Artificial Intelligence in Healthcare System, Pharmaceutical Industry & Education". International Journal of Advanced Research in Science, Communication and Technology.

Pesqueira, A., & Sousa, M. J. (2022). *12 Social Analytics Influencing KOLs Profiling in the Dissemination of Innovations and Scientific Knowledge in the Life Sciences Industry*. Innovations and Social Media Analytics in a Digital Society.

Pesqueira, A., & Sousa, M. J. (2022). Life Sciences Industry Blockchain Value Management, Investments, and Finance Impact Assessment: Global Questionnaire Survey of 1524 Industry Professionals and Executives. In Incorporating AI Technology in the Service Sector (pp. 67-107). Apple Academic Press.

Pesqueira, A. M., Sousa, M., & Pereira, R. (2023). Individual dynamic capabilities influential factors in blockchain technology innovation from hospital settings.

Secinaro, , Calandra, D., Secinaro, A., Muthurangu, V., & Biancone, P. (2021). The role of artificial intelligence in healthcare: A structured literature review. *BMC Medical Informatics and Decision Making*, *21*(1), 125. DOI: 10.1186/s12911-021-01488-9 PMID: 33836752

Shiwlani, A., Khan, M., Sherani, A. M. K., & Qayyum, M. U. (2023). Synergies of AI and Smart Technology: Revolutionizing Cancer Medicine, Vaccine Development, and Patient Care. International Journal of Social. *Humanities and Life Sciences*, *1*(1), 10–18.

Spiel, K., Hornecker, E., Williams, R. M., & Good, J. (2022). ADHD and technology research–investigated by neurodivergent readers. In *Proceedings of the 2022 CHI Conference on Human Factors in Computing Systems* (pp. 1-21). DOI: 10.1145/3491102.3517592

Tariq, , Awan, M. J., Alshudukhi, J., Alam, T. M., Alhamazani, K. T., & Meraf, Z. (2022). Software Measurement by Using Artificial Intelligence. *Journal of Nanomaterials*, *2022*(1), 7283171. DOI: 10.1155/2022/7283171

Ullah, H., Manickam, S., Obaidat, M., Laghari, S. U. A., & Uddin, M. (2023). Exploring the Potential of Metaverse Technology in Healthcare: Applications, Challenges, and Future Directions. *IEEE Access : Practical Innovations, Open Solutions*, *11*, 69686–69707. DOI: 10.1109/ACCESS.2023.3286696

Vallentin, A., Thórisson, K. R., & Latapie, H. (2023). Addressing the Unsustainability of Deep Neural Networks with Next-Gen AI. In International Conference on Artificial General Intelligence (pp. 296-306). Cham: Springer Nature Switzerland. DOI: 10.1007/978-3-031-33469-6_30

Vlasta, M. (2023). Methodological framework for European regulation of (artificial) intelligence and its limits.

Wada, M., Noda, Y., Iwata, Y., Tsugawa, S., Yoshida, K., Tani, H., Hirano, Y., Koike, S., Sasabayashi, D., Katayama, H., Plitman, E., Ohi, K., Ueno, F., Caravaggio, F., Koizumi, T., Gerretsen, P., Suzuki, T., Uchida, H., Müller, D. J., & Nakajima, S. (2022). Dopaminergic dysfunction and excitatory/inhibitory imbalance in treatment-resistant schizophrenia and novel neuromodulatory treatment. *Molecular Psychiatry*, *27*(7), 2950–2967. DOI: 10.1038/s41380-022-01572-0 PMID: 35444257

Wamba, S. F., Queiroz, M. M., Jabbour, C. J. C., & Shi, C. V. (2023). Are both generative AI and ChatGPT game changers for 21st-Century operations and supply chain excellence? *International Journal of Production Economics*, *265*, 109015. DOI: 10.1016/j.ijpe.2023.109015

Wani, . (2022). Utilization of Artificial Intelligence in Disease Prevention: Diagnosis, Treatment, and Implications for the Healthcare Workforce. *Health Care*. PMID: 35455786

Chapter 5
The Role of Artificial Intelligence in Combating Terrorism:
Exploring Capabilities and Challenges in the Dark and Deep Web

Abderrahim Khoumich
University Ibn Tofail, Morocco

Mohamed Mliless
https://orcid.org/0000-0003-4153-2524
School of Arts and Huminaities, University Moulay Ismail, Morocco

Mohamed Achamrah
University Sultan Moulay Sliman, Morocco

ABSTRACT

Technology is evolving rapidly, leading to increasingly sophisticated terrorist threats that challenge global security. Efforts by states to mitigate these risks often fall short, as terrorists adapt their techniques, especially through new technologies like artificial intelligence (AI). Research in cybersecurity is essential for awareness and protection. Counterterrorism strategies must evolve to address advancements in technology and the complexities of the dark web, where terrorist activities proliferate. Effective monitoring and legislative measures are crucial for enhancing security and combating these emerging threats.

DOI: 10.4018/979-8-3373-0245-4.ch005

INTRODUCTION

Artificial intelligence offers potential and difficulties in the fight against terrorism, especially when it comes to the deep and dark web. New threats from organised and self-organised individuals or groups are joining the classic risks as terrorism activities move more and more into the internet. Therefore, improving knowledge of the new ways terrorists communicate is essential to counterterrorism initiatives (Ebner et al., 2022). The possibility of terrorists abusing AI is threatening. The way that terrorists exploit the Internet and cutting-edge technologies has created a new dynamic environment that counterterrorism will need to adjust to in order to defeat their tactics. The encrypted nature of social network conversations, for instance, makes intelligence collection extremely difficult. There are possible advantages to integrating artificial intelligence with counterterrorism initiatives, though.

Some progress has been achieved by integrating behavioural cues and language processing (Thorley and Saltman, 2023). Although socio-semantic network analysis has shown promise in identifying individuals who inspire violence in radical networks (Bérubé et al., 2023), it is not always possible to derive a social network for study. As we will explore, evaluating anonymous and dispersed communications platforms requires linguistic research exclusively, as there are no social network structures to examine.

However, before pursuing any action, Leveraging AI's potential requires understanding both terrorism and AI's function. Understanding the roots of terrorism may orient Intelligence services to effectively use AI in surveillance and monitoring systems, predictive analytics and threat assessment, and data analysis and pattern recognition. Through social networks, forums, and markets on the dark web, these capabilities could prominently improve the battle against terrorism.

By analysing citizen big data, artificial intelligence techniques are essential for anticipating terrorist attacks (Kathleen, August 2019). However, they also present human rights issues and practical application challenges that raise concerns about the limitations of their predictive uses in counterterrorism and the implications of opportunities and risks (Kathleen, August 2019).

Notwithstanding its potential, applying AI to counterterrorism presents many difficulties. Significant challenges include privacy and security hazards, legal and ethical issues, adversarial attacks, and false information (McKendrick, 2019). To make matters even more complicated, terrorist operations find refuge on the deep and dark web. AI solutions for monitoring the dark and deep web include web scraping and crawling technologies, natural language processing for text analysis, as well as image and video recognition for content detection. However, challenges in monitoring the dark and deep web, such as anonymity and encryption technologies, volume and velocity of data, and deception and disinformation tactics, must be addressed.

In our case studies, investigators employed multiple techniques to follow criminals and terrorists, including network analysis, behavioural analysis, and real-time social media monitoring. This took them thousands of hours of human investigation, which could be minimised into seconds if they could use algorithms to detect potential criminal or terrorist entities, evaluate terrorist threats, and analyse the large quantity of data disseminated for criminal and terror purposes (UNICRI and UNCCT, 2021). AI could also retrieve relevant open-source data needed for a meticulous threat assessment of potential terrorism.

Indeed, integrating AI into counterterrorism efforts presents both opportunities and challenges. The effective utilisation of AI in monitoring and combatting terrorism on social networks, as well as the dark and deep web, has the potential to significantly predict and analyse terrorist behaviour and, improve security and safety measures.

BACKGROUND AND HISTORY

Since the beginning of time, there has been an ongoing conflict between right and wrong. The dictionary defines terrorism as "the unlawful use of violence and intimidation, especially against civilians, in the pursuit of political aims" (Oxford, 2024), characterising it as unlawful and, therefore, against accepted values. It is crucial to overview terrorism's history while discussing the subject briefly. As was already mentioned, there is disagreement on what constitutes terrorism. Terrorism, in my opinion, has existed for as long as history has been written. One hypothesis holds that terrorism originated in France during the Reign of Terror in the late 18th century when the government used terror as a tactic and intimidated citizens (Hoffman, 2017).

Terrorism has a lengthy history that dates back millennia; it is not a recent occurrence. Nonetheless, there has been a discernible increase in terrorist activities in recent decades. For Chaliand and Blin (2007), terrorism started with the Zealots and the Assassins, whose attempts are portrayed as essentially a religious and political conflict. Like the Zealots, the Assassins (also called in Arabic "Al Hashshashin) only used daggers to kill their targets and planned their murders in marketplaces or mosques while their victims were doing their prayers. As we dig deeper into the history of the Assassins, we conclude that there is a strong link "between it and the terrorist organisations of the modern world, including those that have emerged from and are ideologically modeled" (Chaliand and Blin, 2007, p. 60).

Just like in any other traditional organisation, Imams, warriors, diplomats, and teachers were all part of the Assassin organisation. The sect's careful division of labour and organisational structure, along with its fervent devotion to its leader

(Hassan Essabbah) and dynamic ideological activism, made it an actor that, despite its marginal status, had to be considered at all times.

The ideology upon which all radical Islamic movements based their Jihadi actions is the call (Da'wa) to the conversion into Islam (their proper understanding of Islam). In terms of intellectual and ideological motivations, the phenomenon of terrorism has increased due to many factors, including the misinterpretation of religious principles and provisions, the dependence of young people on one another without consulting scholars, the intellectual void and ignorance of the valid religious rules, the ignorance of Sharia's purposes, extremism, and radicalisation in thought.

However, since the dawn of Islam, da'wa has mainly been a nonviolent exhortation to non-Muslims to convert to Islam. Notable early outliers are the Ismailis (Daftary, 2011) and the Abbasids, who were in power during the Umayyad House and whose goal was to overthrow the current monarch (Lewis, 1970). Beginning with the Ismailis, who were the first to do so, Da'wa also addressed Muslims over the years, encouraging them to stay on the straight and encouraging them to follow the example of various Islamic organisations or movements. Then, there is a conflict about what constitutes faithful Islam. Now, the primary conflict of jihadism is with other Muslims. According to ideology, da'wa is meant to convert other Muslims. Its political goals are to establish Islamic law and establish a Caliphate. To do this, heretical regimes must be overthrown. It states militarily that Muslims who openly oppose jihadism or aid the unbelievers must be opposed by real believers. This entails disparaging Shi'a, Sufis, liberal, and secular Muslims, among others (Habeck, 2006).

This is not to say that terrorism's roots are only Islamic but also Jewish portrayed by Zionism, whose conviction of supremacy makes them exterminate other races and occupy their lands, and of European origins in the conceptual framework of contemporary political theories, such as anarchist, Marxism, nihilism, and fascism, which all led to wars that killed millions of people; Also, American manifested in the Ku Klux Klan (KKK) terrorist organisation whose hatred to other ethnicities (particularly Afro-Americans) urged them to assault and kill their leaders. The aforementioned terrorist groups are just a few of the ideologies and movements that have been linked to terrorism over the years. Terrorism "has been practiced by political organisations with both rightist and leftist objectives, by nationalistic and religious groups, by revolutionaries, and even by state institutions such as armies, intelligence services, and police" (Britannica, 2024)

Numerous unsettling incidents have occurred in the twenty-first century thus far, including the September 2001 terrorist attacks and the current coalitions of transnational terrorist groups. The goal of Al Qaeda's 9/11 attack on the Pentagon was to make the mujahideen aware of the American state's fragility. In August and September 2014, the Islamic State of Iraq and the Levant (ISIL) decapitated two American journalists, and their orange jumpsuits resembled the jumpsuits used by the Guantanamo Bay captives, giving the impression that the executions were a form of revenge for the way the United States treated Muslims (Klausen, 2014). The 9/11 attacks significantly impacted the sense of safety and security in the US. The last time the United States experienced domestic terrorism comparable to the events of 9/11 was in 1814, when the British set fire to the White House. Americans appear to have lived in a state of invulnerability to foreign threats ever since. The 9/11 events undoubtedly destroyed that illusion. Shughart (2006) stated in his paper "An Analytical History of Terrorism, 1945-2000" that "creating a climate of fear requires fostering the belief that everyone is a potential target.". Since at least 263 US government groups had been established or reorganised by 2014 in response to the security lapse following 9/11, it appears that Al-Qaeda was successful in this endeavour.

Fighting terrorism does not mean fighting al-Qaeda or other radical Islamist organisations. Academics or the law do not agree upon the definition of terrorism. Any act intended to incite fear is considered terrorism in its broadest definition, whereas terrorism in its narrowest sense can be viewed as a political objective. Typically, religious and nationalist organisations, revolutionaries, right- and left-wing political parties, and governing governments use terrorism as a tactic to achieve their goals. Notably, many of the most problematic concepts and terrorist activities are not exclusive to extreme organisations.

Terrorists began using digital platforms more frequently since the 2000s. Nowadays, terrorist organisations recruit terrorists and radicalise people using digital channels for propaganda, including cyberterrorism. According to reports, a considerable number of juveniles were recruited to carry out public beheadings and terrorist assaults in 2016 (United Nations, 2017). In the twenty-first century, terrorists use digital preaching on a variety of platforms in addition to traditional in-person preaching. Modern terrorist leaders like Ayman al-Zawahiri understood the importance of media in winning wars. He wrote to the now-deceased leader of Al Qaeda in Iraq, Abu Musab al-Zarqawi: "We are in a battle, and more than half of this battle is taking place in the battlefield of the media. And that we are in a media battle in a race for the hearts and minds of our Ummah." (in Klausen, 2014, p. 3).

Social media sites like Facebook, Twitter, YouTube, and other online mediums are among the most popular channels the new Islamic preachers use to spread Da'wa (Weismann, 2020). As a result of this effect, terrorists have utilised social media to plan and carry out attacks. Islamic State (ISIS) used social media to propagate its ideas and propaganda the most successfully of any terrorist organisation. They stood out for their capacity to spread information via social media and the caliber of the content they offered. ISIS also employed high-velocity content that was executed quite effectively.

The use of social media by terrorist organisations to recruit and spread information leaves them open to attack. Social media uses open, worldwide platforms that leave digital traces that law enforcement can use to find users. Open-source information has been used to stop malicious activity and identify the perpetrators. Localisation and terrorist elimination are made possible by the intelligent tools and techniques used to analyse the information now available. It is also feasible to prevent issues before they happen by responding quickly to the information that is currently accessible.

However, these routes are unsafe for them because many foreign authorities consider it unlawful for anonymous people to join Islamic movements or commit acts of terrorism. Also, algorithms have impacted terrorist groups' capabilities. Consequently, there is a need for an alternative platform that can conceal preachers from law enforcement or intelligence services. This leads to the use of the deep web and dark web (Weimann, 2019). According to research, terrorists and extremists established several safe havens where they developed schemes, obtained fresh funding, and attracted supporters (Malik, 2018).

In 2014, it was discovered that terrorist groups posted a significant number of tweets every day, and from September 2014 to September 2015, these groups posted a lot of tweets from a variety of accounts (Klausen, 2014). Because of the easiness of following posts and spotting their localisations in the surface net, terrorist groups now use the deep web and the dark web extensively for propaganda, recruitment, and purchases of weapons and explosive materials. Another biggest benefit they gain in this large dark swamp is finding money in the absence of formally constituted institutions. With an extraordinary rise in funding based on cryptocurrency, the digital age has also altered the goals of terror-relevant capitalisation. The proliferation of terrorist groups operating in the deep and dark webs, along with the flow of digital extremism, makes it imperative that we strengthen our security and stop the acts that occur in this area.

DEMOGRAPHICS OF TERRORISTS

It appears that there is no one profile of the modern terrorist, whether it be "an ideal personality pattern," "criminal profile," "terrorism genes," or "physical characteristics", just like there is no single profile of criminals. The vast majority of terrorists and fighters, however, are not of low socioeconomic status; rather, the middle class, if not the bourgeoisie, is the one that engages in armed political activities, according to one of the researchers who examined the socioeconomic and educational profiles (Borum, 2004). The same can be said for the leaders, such as Oussama Ben Laden, the historical leader of Al Qaeda who belonged to one of the wealthiest families in Saudi Arabia. In other words, the fact that the terrorists are impoverished people is absolutely not true according to research and "there is little to suggest that growing up in (relative) poverty is over-represented among individuals who will later radicalise to extremism" (Schuurman & Sarah, 2023, p. 959).

Current studies (Korotayev, et al., 2021; Sun, et al., 2022; Luo & Qi, 2021; Ajide & Alimi, 2021; Piazza, 2023) concentrate on investigating the educational and socio-economic backgrounds of recruits and operatives as well as the backgrounds of terrorist leaders. This sort of understanding would offer some insights into decision-making processes, which could help identify issues at intelligence agencies, assist them in improving and, ideally, rebuilding local communities, and mitigate concerns that have put them on a terrorist nation watch list. It could also help create more effective community-based counter-extremism programs locally, nationally, and internationally. Further understanding of terrorist demography has been found to be essential to combating and preventing terrorism (Danzell, et al., 2020).

Researchers have not given much thought to the sociology and socioeconomic profile of militant organisations and their leadership up to this point. The majority of empirical research has relied on assumptions about the rank-and-file militants' political and ethnic identities as the primary motivators for their involvement in militant activities, which has led to the stereotype that any Muslim with a beard is a terrorist.

Terrorist organisations recommend that for leaders to effectively lead the terror movement, they need to be knowledgeable about the following crucial subjects: the code of conduct, "jihadi" literature, recruiting tactics, public relations guidelines, and strategic planning (Doctor, et al., 2023). However, local leaders are required to carry out a variety of duties, such as collecting contributions and taxes (also called "Zakat" in Muslim jargon, whose first and most noble purpose is to help the poor and the vulnerable), organising meetings, visiting swamp regions, reciting holy texts, and giving advice on actions that are worthy of commendation.

Being aware of the magnificent importance of a leader, law enforcement agencies frequently target them in the hope that the terrorist group will disintegrate if the leader is killed or captured. However, there are equally as many instances of ineffectiveness as there are of effectiveness in the history of this "leadership targeting" tactic (Freeman, 2014). According to Michael Freeman, a leader's operational or inspirational role can impact the likelihood of success in pursuing them. Leadership targeting may, nevertheless, backfire, according to some research. The unintended outcomes include the development of a martyrdom effect, increasing recruitment, retaliatory attacks, a strengthening of group commitment and strength, and an increase in attack frequency and intensity (in Jordan, 2014).

DEEP AND DARK WEB

The US government first developed the technology that gave rise to the Dark Web in the middle of the 1990s so that intelligence services and spies could communicate anonymously. Because it is anonymous, it is easy to see that it is suitable for various activities that people would not dare undertake on the surface of the web.

Due to the anonymity and data encryption offered by programs like Tor, they are used by those who wish to sell illegal goods and services (such as hacking for hire, guns, drugs, explosive materials, etc.), as well as by terrorists and extremists who wish to spread their message and evangelise others. Therefore, comprehending this facet of cyberspace is crucial to investigating the precise ways in which artificial intelligence (AI) might be employed to prevent and track such terrorist and extremist activity in online spaces. It's important to realise that these are frequently just one facet of their criminal personalities; they are actors who can behave in both the actual and virtual worlds as needed to further their objectives.

Since Dark Web sites are growing at a rate far faster than Law Enforcement Agencies (LEAs) have been able to stop, the exponential growth of websites offering illegal goods and services, closed forums, and websites related to radicalisation, extremism, and terrorism, along with the anonymity they offer, present ongoing challenges to LEAs. Additionally, it appears that the tools available today are insufficient to stop activities occurring on the Dark Web altogether, and the cybercriminals' tools, strategies, and methodology are constantly changing.

Everybody has the right to anonymity, but the jurisdictional issues brought about by the Internet's nature make it even harder for those in charge of protecting society. Lastly, while LEAs must combat other types of cybercrime, it may be hard to justify the expense and person-months of operations required to monitor and regulate the Dark Web. As a result, LEAs are always searching for technological tools that will help them actively identify radicals, extremists, and terrorists, as well as identify and analyse illegal content on the Dark Web while protecting the privacy of legitimate users (Kavallieros et al., 2021).

Case Studies: Stories of AI Success and Failure in Counterterrorism and Cybercrimes

According to fundamental sociological principles, we must examine our underground and black markets in order to gain a deeper understanding of our changing human societies and the potentially unlawful actions of individuals inside them. The rules of what can be free to say, control, and do have been changed by technological advancements. The question of why a trader would operate online is a research issue posed by sociologists. The rise in digital anonymity, which is often frequently presented as a problem for law enforcement agencies, has been and continues to be the obvious answer.

According to Liggett et al., (2020), the advent of internet forums in the early 21st century allowed those interested in illegal goods or services to meet and trade in a more secure and private setting than they could on the street. Despite the extremely non-fungible nature of their service, which puts buyers and sellers at greater risk than markets for tangible items, these online marketplaces quickly gained popularity, particularly among Libertarians who believe that people have all the right to buy and sell anything they like. Terrorists who find themselves in these markets secure purchases of weapons and explosive materials to ensure their anonymous identities. They leave no transactional footprints using bitcoin and the blockchain to finish their deals.

All Dark Web markets are reported to be an operation of the original Silk Road from 2011, which is specifically defined as being English-speaking, based in Europe, North America, or the developing Asia-Pacific area, and requiring registration in order to purchase or sell within the market, along with verified seller accounts. This market was operated by Ross Ulbricht, a young university graduate, under the pseudonym "Dread Pirate Roberts", who was arrested and sentenced to life in federal prison in 2015.

Following over two and a half years of operation, the first large-scale Dark Web market was destroyed by a series of law enforcement investigations. To take concerted action to shut down some of the online markets, they first carefully examined them in order to determine their weaknesses. Authorities mostly focused on DPR's coding flaws and mistakes when utilising technology they believed was essential to the market's dependability. Dread Pirate Roberts was in danger because of how he employed the software and encryption principles, even if they were sound and well within the bounds of federal law. Consequently, the FBI gathered multiple pieces of evidence as soon as they found the server. In addition, the investigations questioned their ability to handle complicated embedded systems and exposed certain other technological flaws that were unknown to the public. This technological conversation demonstrates the tight ties between law enforcement as well as the growth of Dark Web marketplaces. Along with that, some criminal activities were aborted, and the culprits involved in the Munich gun murders were arrested.

On December 11th, 2017, a federal jury found Brooklyn, New York resident Akayed Ullah, 27, a permanent resident of Bangladesh, guilty of charges relating to the explosion and attempted detonation of a bomb in a subway station close to the New York Port Authority Bus Terminal in New York City. Prior to the explosion, Ullah was seen on surveillance tape strolling around the station before setting off the device. Ullah was arrested shortly after the explosion when the first responders found him lying on the ground in the station where he had set off the homemade explosive device (US.DOJ, 2021).

Court records and the evidence used during the trial indicate that Ullah started to become radicalised around 2014. Ullah started looking for online resources endorsing extreme Islamic terrorist ideology because he disapproved of American foreign policies in the Middle East. Ullah was particularly motivated by ISIS propaganda, such as a video in which the group told its fans that if they couldn't travel abroad to join, they should carry out attacks in their own countries. About a year before his attack, Ullah started studying how to make a bomb. In the weeks before the attack, he constructed his pipe bomb in his Brooklyn apartment (US. DOJ, 2021).

After digging into extensive data, Intelligence services found out that the bomber already contacted someone from Pakistan. Figuring out the operative's email address, the intelligence community discovered that other people were using it to send emails. AI algorithms designed to identify different indicators in the raw email data for those connections—such as elevated alert status, the activation of a sleeper cell, the construction of a bomb, and so on—were used to process the data (Freeman, 2021).

Nevertheless, it is unrealistic to anticipate that AI will instantly solve complex problems, particularly detecting potential terrorism with extremely high effectiveness. When US Immigration and Customs Enforcement tried to apply machine learning models in data mining across multiple online sources to help with the vetting of visa applicants, they figured out that this was a failure (Harwell & Miroff, 2018). It was determined that no such capability was available for immediate procurement. Hence, the search for a technical solution to this task was dropped. Moreover, 55 million Pakistani mobile phone users' metadata was examined by the US National Security Agency's SKYNET program in order to find possible terrorist couriers. About 15,000 people were mistakenly classified as suspects, even though the reported false positive rate was only 0.008% given the size and type of the data, which resulted in false accusations and demonstrated how even tiny mistake rates can cause serious harm when applied to huge populations in delicate situations like counterterrorism (Robbins, 2016). Indeed, The model was ineffective on its own.

Evolution and Application of AI in Counterterrorism

The use of AI in counterterrorism operations represents a significant shift from traditional surveillance methods. What began as basic pattern-finding software has evolved into sophisticated systems that can instantaneously process massive amounts of data. There have been early bipartisan attempts to prepare for national security dangers associated with AI, and policymakers have shown a keen interest in the technology. Agencies were directed by the White House Executive Order to create capacity assessments, investigate potential risks associated with AI deployments in critical infrastructure, and collaborate with industry to develop voluntary safety guidelines (Biden, 2023). A recent Senate bipartisan framework has suggested a prospective licensing program for AI systems with more processing power (Romney, 2024). A new legislative proposal calls for the creation of globally applicable AI standards (Cantwell, 2024).

A new legislative proposal calls for the creation of globally applicable AI standards (Cantwell, 2024)."Real-time data processing, facilitated by AI, is essential for monitoring criminal activities and enhancing public security [...] enhancing efficiency and accuracy" (Mliless, 2024, p.10). Research indicates that AI can often recognise patterns that surpass a human expert's knowledge and time-related skills (Doe et al., 2021). AI has become increasingly relevant for counterterrorism purposes due to its ability to identify effective action and policy as well as to facilitate algorithmic assessment and prediction.

According to Doe et al. (2021), AI, by using algorithms, can determine which inputs are most likely to correlate with and produce particular results. Through the analysis of communications metadata, financial transaction data, travel trends, and web surfing activity, artificial intelligence can be used to forecast acts of terrorism. Additionally, it can be used to analyse data from social networks to counteract undesirable phenomena (Olivier, 2017) in the fight against online extremist propaganda (Dr. Haider & Dr. Mahmoud, 2014, p. 19).

AI can operate at a basic level by optimising certain parameters. Today, advanced AI systems employ predictive analytics to identify potential security threats before they materialise. Data analysis comes in two forms: descriptive, which is concerned with understanding what has happened, and predictive, aimed at establishing what is likely to occur. The algorithms leverage contextual knowledge, historical data trends, and behavioural markers to forecast potential terrorist operations.

According to research by Salem et al. (2024), threat detection rates have significantly increased when using predictive analytics instead of conventional techniques. In modern surveillance systems, biometric identification and facial recognition technologies driven by AI are commonly utilised. These algorithms can simultaneously evaluate thousands of faces and compare them to databases of known suspects (Imaoka et al., 2021).

Recent developments in deep learning have significantly raised accuracy rates; in the best-case scenario, several systems can reach a very significant accuracy (Wang et al., 2020). Natural Language Processing (NLP) skills enable security organisations to monitor and analyse vast amounts of textual and audio content. Advanced algorithms can identify radical content, dubious communication styles, and track the spread of extremist narratives across multiple languages and platforms. Moreover, AI improves objectivity by removing the prejudices in human judgment, guaranteeing consistency and fairness in all decision-making situations (Mliless, 2024). This is to prevent another falsely accusation like the one of Mohamedou Ould Slahi who spent 14 years imprisoned and brutally tortured at Guantanamo Bay, claiming him to be part of the 9/11 attacks and later exonerated by two U.S. courts (DW, 2021). Ironically, some of his tormentors still accuse him of the same guilt and he seeks revenge through a great forgiveness for everyone who was involved in his misery (Errammach, 2024).

The scope for AI to conduct both qualitative and quantitative analysis renders it a beneficial technology. Thomas et al. (2022) reported that AI systems are very good at integrating and analysing data from various sources, including social media monitoring, financial transaction analysis, communication network mapping, Internet of Things (IoT) sensors, and geographic information systems. Security organisations can use these tools to develop comprehensive threat assessments and uncover linkages between individuals and organisations that were previously unknown. Modern AI systems can detect subtle trends and irregularities that human analysts might overlook. This ability is particularly useful for spotting suspicious financial transactions, unusual travel patterns, or weird behavioural patterns that could indicate terrorist activities.

Ethical Considerations

One practical and helpful method intelligence services use to assess and forecast criminal activities is gathering data on human activity in tactical or strategic contexts. However, when considering the use of AI tools for counterterrorism, privacy, civil liberties, and the possibility of abuse for the aim of stifling dissent or monitoring specific religious, ethnic, or social groups continue to be the key concerns (US.DOJ, 2024). Therefore, to balance the protection of human rights and civil liberties with the effectiveness of security, different governments regulate the use of artificial intelligence (AI) in counterterrorism through a specific combination of operational procedures and regulatory frameworks. For example, Kaskina and Cvetkovska (2024) claimed that emphasising repression and control, China and Russia make substantial use of AI-based solutions for counterterrorism and internal security. China targets both domestic and foreign citizens with AI as part of its widespread monitoring, censorship, and repression of opposition. Similarly, Russia employs AI-powered facial recognition and internet filtering through extensive anti-terrorism legislation such as the Yarovaya Law, which requires communication companies to keep information that makes AI-enabled surveillance possible. These strategies put governmental control and stability first, frequently at the price of individual liberties and human rights (Kaskina & Cvetkovska, 2024).

On the other hand, The EU strictly regulates high-risk applications used in counterterrorism and classifies AI systems according to their level of risk. Apart from specific terrorist exceptions, the Act forbids real-time biometric identification in public and necessitates independent authorisation and impact studies on basic rights (Briend, 2025). High-risk predictive police systems that predict the likelihood of terrorism are subject to strict controls, such as risk management, data governance, and monitoring. The EU framework, which promotes openness and proportionality, covers explicitly the possibility of AI abuse, bias, and human rights violations. Nonetheless, it recognises the conflict between privacy and security requirements, highlighting the necessity of strong protection to avoid discrimination and overreach while permitting some exceptions in dire circumstances (Briend, 2025).

To avoid making the problems of violent extremism and xenophobia worse, governments must uphold civil liberties and fight terrorists and criminals within moral bounds. Case examples include the discriminating tactics of law enforcement, the localised use of AI to monitor and control populations, and the monitoring and exploitation of technology by repressive governments against vulnerable groups (Privacy International, 2021). Therefore, given the wide range of ethical, legal, and societal factors involved, this issue requires explicit preemptive policy guidance. It is also necessary to modify or develop new transnational and international regulations and core values because norms, practices, laws, and principles are continuously updated. The current legal frameworks were created when AI did not have such extraordinary capabilities, starting with national laws. As a result, many current laws need to be revisited. The updating process must strike a balance between the need to advance current laws and a thorough social analysis.

It usually takes a number of steps to create a law or policy that allows for the development and use of AI-based counterterrorism solutions. First, there is an exploration phase in which stakeholders identify and discuss the various societal, legal, economic, ethical, and political challenges through assessments and engagement. Next, the rule-making process, often in the form of proposed or actual laws and regulations, allows a legislative discourse to materialise rules that ensure research and deployment efforts. Laws should be proposed, developed, and discussed in accordance with established national or transnational rule-making principles, which means that in addition to a public call for tenders, interested individuals and organisations can voice their concerns. In the case of legislation, this includes institutions such as the European Parliament, Member States, Regions, Cities, industry, remote areas, civil society, etc. Such regulations could also point to specific guidelines, matching algorithms to legal and policy instruments, as well as computers and digital systems to human rights.

There are unavoidable consequences of algorithmic biases in AI, especially when it comes to counterterrorism initiatives and the decision-making procedures used by governmental organisations. The tendency of algorithms to both reflect and amplify the biases present in their training datasets, which frequently reflect human judgment, is a fundamental problem. Numerous empirical studies (Celiktutan et al., 2024, among others) have revealed an important trend: humans are generally better at spotting biases in algorithmic outputs than in their judgments. This implies that algorithms can expose hidden biases in human cognition. The disparity in how these biases are perceived may result from cognitive psychological characteristics, particularly motivated thinking, which can make it easier for people to identify and correct the inequalities identified by algorithms than from biases they may harbour (Celiktutan et al., 2024). Concerns about the impartiality and fairness of results from AI deployments are raised by this over-reliance on the "automation bias" issue, which can result in the selective adherence of algorithmic recommendations that support stereotypes (Barkat & Busuioc, 2023). A prediction "civil disruption" system that anticipates threats before they materialise is one potential future scenario that was included in a recent research paper on the malevolent use of AI and its effects on political freedom (Brundage, 2018).

It is critical to comprehend algorithmic biases and their consequences as AI gets increasingly involved in delicate fields like international security and law enforcement. In light of recent controversies where the use of biased algorithms has produced discriminatory results, it is imperative that people become more conscious of these biases and advocate for a more thoughtful use of algorithmic decision-making tools.

Reducing discrimination and improving the general effectiveness of AI in law enforcement can be mainly achieved by promoting accountability and transparency in algorithmic design and execution. Federal Organizations may better manage the challenges of algorithmic governance and advance equity and justice in automated systems by identifying and addressing biases, especially ones based on ethnicity, religion or ideology.

If the sets are fixed for what are expected to be more probable eventualities, AI can be used to determine what decisions or operational activities are most likely to reduce risk. Yet, A balance between security concerns and freedom must be struck. There is no one-size-fits-all solution for this issue due to the wide range of users, technology, policies, services, and content, as well as the numerous advantages and disadvantages of privacy and hiddenness.

Learned Lessons, Implications and Recommendations

Terrorism prevention is still a technological and policy challenge. Artificial intelligence (AI) tools may and should be used to enhance the identification of possible terrorists. The application of AI technologies to counterterrorism presents novel difficulties and moral dilemmas. Although some concerns and technological challenges have already been mentioned, little is known about the ramifications of using AI in counterterrorism. New, flexible laws and policies that support counterterrorism and are interoperable are needed. In an era of rapid technological advancement, predicting legal definitions and technical capabilities is challenging.

History demonstrates that user behaviour will adjust to patterns of law enforcement operations, which is at the core of the Dark Web's dynamic threat. Law enforcement must set out on an evolutionary cyber journey, that will continue to adapt to the evolving landscape rather than attempting to "end" digital crime despite the ongoing debate about the risks of digital anonymity.

The application of AI to counterterrorism initiatives has prompted more study and advancement. Given how quickly terrorist tactics are evolving nowadays, ongoing research and development efforts should be guided by the lessons learnt in and with pertinent government institutions. Additionally, a strategic alliance between academia and relevant government agencies will promote innovation both within and outside the discipline, addressing a broader spectrum of uses of AI to handle security concerns. In the context of fighting terrorism, AI's ethical and legal aspects offer a complicated and multidimensional field for further research. The development of ethical frameworks and regulatory rules guiding the responsible use of AI in counterterrorism activities could be the subject of research in this area. Gaining knowledge of the moral and legal ramifications of AI technology would help create strong governance frameworks that strike a balance between privacy concerns, individual rights, and security requirements.

In the example of Morocco, where the authors are situated, Moroccan law enforcement agencies participated in a wide range of U.S.-sponsored programs to improve the country's technical and investigative capabilities, including financial investigation, intelligence analysis, forensics, and cybersecurity (US. Department of State, 2022). Since the attacks of 2003 in Casablanca, which Killed 45 people, mostly Moroccans, The Kingdom's security approach, through proactive action and strengthening vigilance mechanisms to confront the terrorist threat, has made it possible to dismantle 210 terrorist cells and arrest more than 4,304 people planning to target public figures, vital facilities and tourist sites in a number of cities. (Skynewsarabia, 2021).

Taking all that has been said before, AI systems must be assessed and improved regularly in response to industry demands. The digital age demands that new comprehensive counterterrorism policies be developed through deep synergy across research disciplines and with a wide range of stakeholders in order to ensure freedom, security, and equality. In accordance with the Global Strategy on Foreign and Security Policy, the European Union needs to take the lead in advocating for worldwide contemplation and action that eradicates cybercrime, protects victims, and protects children and civilians worldwide. Transversal new AI counterterrorism research should involve digital and AI specialists working with all parties involved. The proper usage in counterterrorism and human rights protection should be guided by necessity, proportionality, and state responsibility criteria.

Individuals' privacy and data protection must be completely upheld, and in the absence of consent, sharing personal information must be done in accordance with international legal requirements. The incorporation of these legal criteria into algorithms and the necessity of adapting these systems in a quickly changing digital environment in a reasonable, responsible, and moral way will be major areas of study focus. According to the precautionary principle of AI research in counterterrorism, technical input must be included in order to identify strategies for addressing the valid concerns and misunderstandings specific to the digital and human context in which AI will be applied. While AI has yet to be deployed carefully, it might be used to support intelligence analysis and operations against specific cyber threats. To maintain freedom, security, and equality in the era of digital innovations, comprehensive counterterrorism policies that use interdisciplinary teamwork and engage diverse stakeholders are essential.

To combat cybercrime, defend victims, and preserve the welfare of children and civilians worldwide, the United Nations, European Union and the United States should foster international cooperation and action by aligning with the Global Strategy on Foreign and Security Policy. This necessitates interdisciplinary AI counterterrorism research with leaders in digital technology and AI, closely collaborating with all pertinent stakeholders. However, respecting human rights while using AI for counterterrorism requires adherence to the criteria of need, proportionality, and state responsibility. Priority, therefore, must be given to protecting people's data and privacy, with international legal requirements governing the transfer of personal data without express authorisation. A substantial amount of study should be focused on integrating these legal standards into AI algorithms and ensuring that these systems can adjust to the quickly changing digital environment in a rational and morally responsible way. In order to address issues and misunderstandings unique to the digital and human environments in which AI will function, the precautionary principle emphasises the significance of integrating technological skills in AI research. Artificial intelligence (AI) must be utilised carefully and sensibly, even while it can be customised to enhance operations and intelligence analysis against particular online threats.

CONCLUSION

In this article, we have attempted to verify that artificial intelligence (AI) systems can help with the preliminary steps of identifying possible terrorist organisations, assessing the significance of potential terrorist threats, and analysing the vast amount of data currently in circulation for these objectives. AI technologies can also make it possible to automatically retrieve pertinent open-source material that is required for a comprehensive multidisciplinary threat assessment of possible terrorists.

Our research shows that while AI holds the potential to create new knowledge and, if not eradicate, then at least reduce terrorist violence. This is not without consequences. Several technical, professional, and political variables must be considered for AI to be successfully used in these fields. This report demonstrates the substantial gaps and uncharted territories in AI counter-terrorism research, even as it draws attention to these opportunities and difficulties. Some areas, like language, still need basic research before the full potential of these technologies in the context of counterterrorism can be realised.

From the perspective of AI research and counterterrorism, there is a chance to avoid using sluggish and unrepresentative approaches. In a time when it has long been accepted that the reliable exchange of human intelligence cannot be replaced, we hesitantly contend that, when weighed against the risks, AI presents an opportunity to capitalise on best practices. Artificial intelligence (AI) in the fight against terrorism is an important and developing area for further study. Extending the capability of AI-driven predictive models for early identification and prevention of risks linked to terrorism is one exciting line of research. More advanced algorithms and machine learning approaches may be developed in future studies, improving the precision and effectiveness of AI systems in spotting new terrorism threats and possible terrorist activity.

Finally, we need to say that most of the international community agrees that terrorism must be eliminated and that ever-more-intrusive measures must be implemented to achieve this. However, attempts to do so go against some of our democratic society's most fundamental norms. In fact, it centres on the creation and use of intrinsically politicised knowledge, whereby law enforcement bears an unfair share of the burden of this knowledge. Upon completion of the study, we suggest putting particular emphasis on finding strategies and tools that will allow law enforcement and criminal justice professionals to use cutting-edge technologies, including big data and artificial intelligence, and fully utilise them in the fight against terrorism.

REFERENCES

Ajide, K. B., & Alimi, O. Y. (2021). Income inequality, human capital and terrorism in Africa: Beyond exploratory analytics. International Economics, Elsevier. Retrieved from: https://www.sciencedirect.com/science/article/abs/pii/S2110701721000032

Alon-Barkat, S., & Busuioc, M. (2023, January). Human–AI Interactions in Public Sector Decision Making: "Automation Bias" and "Selective Adherence" to Algorithmic Advice. *Journal of Public Administration: Research and Theory*, *33*(1), 153–169. DOI: 10.1093/jopart/muac007

Bérubé, M., Beaulieu, L. A., Mongeau, P., & Saint-Charles, J. (2023). Identifying Key Players in Violent Extremist Networks: Using Socio-Semantic Network Analysis as Part of a Program of Content Moderation. *Studies in Conflict and Terrorism*, *46*(12), 2381–2399. DOI: 10.1080/1057610X.2021.1927203

Biden, (2023). https://www.whitehouse.gov/briefing-room/presidential-actions/2023/10/30/executive-order-on-the-safe-secure-and-trustworthy-development-and-use-of-artificial-intelligence/

Borum, R. (2004). *Psychology of terrorism*. University of South Florida.

Briend, J. (2025). The EU's AI Act: Implications on Justice and Counter-terrorism. Global Network on Extremism and Technology (GNET). Available at: https://gnet-research.org/2025/03/10/the-eus-ai-act-implications-on-justice-and-counter-terrorism/

Britannica. (2024). History and Society: Terrorism. Retrieved from: https://www.britannica.com/topic/terrorism

Brown, L., & Martin, P. (2023). NLP for Automating Regulatory Compliance: Case Studies and Implications. *Journal of Artificial Intelligence in Law*, *14*(1), 45–67.

Brundage, M.. (2018). *The Malicious Use of Artificial Intelligence: Forecasting.* Prevention, and Mitigation.

Candilis, P. J., Cleary, S. D., & Dhumad, S. (2023). Classifying terrorism: a latent class analysis of primary source socio-political and psychological data. Taylor & Francis Retrieved from: https://www.researchgate.net/profile/PhilipCandilis/publication/348796896_Classifying_terrorism_a_latent_class_analysis_of_primary_source_sociopolitical_and_psychological_data/links/60ad13fb92851c168e3e89d3/Classifying-terrorism-a-latent-class-analysis-of-primary-source-socio-political-and psychological-data.pdf

Cantwell. (2024). Cantwell, Young, Hickenlooper, Blackburn Introduce Bill to Ensure U.S. Leads Global AI Innovation. https://www.commerce.senate.gov/2024/4/cantwell-young-blackburn-hickenlooper-introduce-bill-to-ensure-u-s-leads-global-ai-innovation

Chaliand, G., Blin, A., Schneider, E., Pulver, K., & Browner, J. (2016). *The History of Terrorism: From Antiquity to al Qaeda*. University of California Press. DOI: 10.1525/9780520966000

Daftary, F. (2011). *Historical dictionary of the Ismailis*. Scarecrow Press.

Danzell, O. E., Yeh, Y. Y., & Pfannenstiel, M. (2018). Does Education Mitigate Terrorism? Examining the Effects of Educated Youth Cohorts on Domestic Terror in Africa. *Terrorism and Political Violence*, *32*(8), 1731–1752. DOI: 10.1080/09546553.2018.1506336

Doctor, A. C., Hunter, S. T., & Ligon, G. S. (2023). Militant Leadership and Terrorism in Armed Conflict. *Terrorism and Political Violence*, *36*(6), 740–756. DOI: 10.1080/09546553.2023.2189972

Doe, J., Miller, K., & White, R. (2021). Machine Learning Algorithms and Compliance Automation. *Financial Technology Review*, *7*(2), 91–108.

Ebner, J., Kavanagh, C., & Whitehouse, H. (2022). Is there a language of terrorists? A comparative manifesto analysis. *Studies in Conflict and Terrorism*, •••, 1–27. DOI: 10.1080/1057610X.2022.2109244

Errammach, M. (Host). (2024). Mohamedou Ould Slahi: Secrets of 14 years at Guantanamo. Maghareb Podcast. In Atheer. atheer - YouTube.

Federal Bureau of Investigation (FBI). (2022). Uniform Crime Reporting (UCR) Program: Crime in the United States, 2021. Retrieved from https://www.fbi.gov/services/cjis/ucr

Freeman, L. (2021, March). Weapons of War, Tools of Justice: Using Artificial Intelligence to Investigate International Crimes. *Journal of International Criminal Justice*, *19*(1), 35–53. DOI: 10.1093/jicj/mqab013

Freeman, M. (2014). A Theory of Terrorist Leadership (and its Consequences for Leadership Targeting). *Terrorism and Political Violence*, *26*(4), 666–687. DOI: 10.1080/09546553.2012.751912

Gercke, M. (2021). Ethical and Societal Issues of Automated Dark Web Investigation: Part 1. In Akhgar, B., Gercke, M., Vrochidis, S., & Gibson, H. (Eds.), *Dark Web Investigation. Security Informatics and Law Enforcement*. Springer., DOI: 10.1007/978-3-030-55343-2_6

Giani, M., LP Merlino (2021). Terrorist attacks and minority perceived discrimination. The British Journal of Sociology, Wiley Online Library. wiley.com

Habeck, M. R. (2006). Knowing the Enemy: Jihadist Ideology and the War on Terror. Yale University Press. https://www.jstor.org/stable/j.ctt1npq1n

Haider, S. A.-B., & Mahmoud, H. A.-H. (2014). *Technology and Information Systems in Contemporary Organizations "A Technological Administrative Perspective."*. Published by Mahmoud Hassan Jomaa Foundation.

Harwell, D., & Miroff, N. (2018), 'ICE just abandoned its dream of "extreme vetting" software that could predict whether a foreign visitor would become a terrorist', Washington Post, 17 May 2018, https://www.washingtonpost.com/news/theswitch/wp/2018/05/17/ice-justabandoned-its-dream-of-extreme-vetting-software-that-could-predict-whether-aforeign-visitor-would-become-a-terrorist/

Hoffman, B. (2017). *Inside Terrorism (REV-Revised and expanded edition)*. Columbia University Press.

Hollywood, J. S., ... (2017). Real-Time Crime Forecasting Challenge. RAND Corporation. Retrieved from https://www.rand.org/pubs/research_reports/RR2338.html

Iga, D., Twineamatsiko, E., Bagonza, J. K., & Nakayenga, H. N.. (2024). Advancing electronic communication compliance and fraud detection through machine learning, NLP, and generative AI: A pathway to enhanced cybersecurity and regulatory adherence. *World Journal of Advanced Research and Reviews*, *23*(2), 697–707. DOI: 10.30574/wjarr.2024.23.2.2364

Imaoka, H., Hashimoto, H., Takahashi, K., Ebihara, A. F., Liu, J., Hayasaka, A., Morishita, Y., & Sakurai, K. (2021). The future of biometrics technology: From face recognition to related applications. *APSIPA Transactions on Signal and Information Processing*, *10*(1), e9. DOI: 10.1017/ATSIP.2021.8

Jordan, J. (2014). Attacking the Leader, Missing the Mark: Why Terrorist Groups Survive Decapitation Strikes. *International Security*, *38*(4), 7–38. DOI: 10.1162/ISEC_a_00157

Kaskina, R., & Cvetkovska, A. (2024). Artificial intelligence (AI) and human rights: Using AI as a weapon of repression and its impact on human rights. Policy Department for External Relations, Directorate-General for External Policies of the Union, European Parliament.

Kathleen, M. (August 2019). Artificial Intelligence Prediction and Counterterrorism. Britain: Chattam House.

Klausen, J. (2014). Tweeting the Jihad: Social Media Networks of Western Foreign Fighters in Syria and Iraq. *Studies in Conflict and Terrorism, 38*(1), 1–22. DOI: 10.1080/1057610X.2014.974948

Korotayev, A., Vaskin, I., Tsirel, T. (2021). Economic growth, education, and terrorism: A re-analysis. Terrorism and Political Violence, Taylor & Francis. Retrieved from: 2021_Economic_Growth_Education_and_Terrorism_A_Re_Analysis-libre.

Lewis, B. (1970). On the revolutions in early Islam. *Studia Islamica, 32*(32), 215–231. DOI: 10.2307/1595221

Liggett, R., Lee, J. R., Roddy, A. L., & Wallin, M. A. (2020). The Dark Web as a Platform for Crime: An Exploration of Illicit Drug, Firearm, CSAM, and Cybercrime Markets. In Holt, T., & Bossler, A. (Eds.), *The Palgrave Handbook of International Cybercrime and Cyberdeviance*. Palgrave Macmillan., DOI: 10.1007/978-3-319-78440-3_17

Luo, L., & Qi, C. (2021). *An analysis of the crucial indicators impacting the risk of terrorist attacks: A predictive perspective*. Elsevier.

Malik, N. (2018). *Terror in the dark: how terrorists use encryption, the Darknet, and cryptocurrencies*. The Henry Jackson Society.

McKendrick, K. (2019). Artificial Intelligence Prediction and Counterterrorism. International Security Department. Chatham House. Retrieved from: https://www.chathamhouse.org/sites/default/files/2019-08-07-AICounterterrorism.pdf

Mliless, M. (2024). Artificial Intelligence (AI) in Law Enforcement and Criminal Activities A Dual-Use Dilemma. Geostrategic Pulse, No.296, May- June 2024.

National Institute of Standards and Technology (NIST). (2022). Framework for Managing Bias in AI. NIST AI Framework. Retrieved from https://www.nist.gov/publications

Olivier, T. (2017, June 6). Artificial Intelligence Will Save Us from Cyberterrorism. DW documentary. Retrieved from: Bing Videos Oxford Dictionary, (2024) Terrorism definition, Available at: https://en.oxforddictionaries.com/definition/terrorism

Piazza, JA. (2023). The Impact of Rural-Urban Economic Disparities on Terrorist Organizations' Survival and Attacks. On Terrorist Groups, taylorfrancis.com.

Privacy and Civil Liberties Oversight Board (PCLOB). (2022). Guidelines on the Use of AI in Public Surveillance. PCLOB Report. Retrieved from https://www.pclob.gov/reports/

Privacy International. (2021). Human rights groups win European Court of Human Rights claim on UK mass surveillance regime. Retrieved in https://privacyinternational.org/press-release/4522/human-rights-groups-win-european-court-human-rights-claim-uk-mass-surveillance

Robbins, M. (2016), 'Has a rampaging AI algorithm really killed thousands in Pakistan?', Guardian, 18 February 2018, https://www.theguardian.com/science/the-lay-scientist/2016/feb/18/has-a-rampaging-ai-algorithm-really-killed-thousands-in-pakistan

Romney., ... (2024). Framework for Mitigating Extreme AI Risks. https://www.romney. senate.gov/wp-content/uploads/2024/04/AI-Framework_2pager.pdf

Salem, A. H., Azzam, S. M., Emam, O. E., & Abohany, A. A. (2024). Advancing cybersecurity: A comprehensive review of AI-driven detection techniques. *Journal of Big Data*, *11*(1), 105. DOI: 10.1186/s40537-024-00957-y

Sanso-Navarro, M. M., & Vera-Cabello, M. (2020). The socioeconomic determinants of terrorism: A Bayesian model averaging approach. Defence and Peace, Taylor & Francis. Retrieved from: https://zaguan.unizar.es/record/84207/files/texto_completo.pdf

Schuurman, B., & Carthy, S. L. (2023). The Makings of a Terrorist: Continuity and Change Across Left-, Right- and Jihadist Extremists and Terrorists in Europe and North-America, 1960s-Present. *Deviant Behavior*, *44*(6), 953–974. DOI: 10.1080/01639625.2022.2118088

Shughart, W. F.II. (2006). September 11, 2001. In Rowley, C. K., & Schneider, F. (Eds.), *The Encyclopedia of public choice* (Vol. II, pp. 520–524). Kluwer Academic Publishers.

Smith, J., & Jones, A. (2022). The Role of Deep Learning in Fraud Detection. *Journal of Financial Security*, *13*(4), 132–145.

Sun, C., Abbas, H. S. M., Xu, X., & Abbas, S. (2022). The impact of socio-economic and fractionalisation determinants on terrorism in ESNA. Socio-Economic Planning Sciences, Elsevier. Retrieved from: https://www.sciencedirect.com/science/article/abs/pii/S0038012121001300

Davenport, T. H., & Redman, T. C. (2023). How AI is improving data management. *MIT Sloan Management Review, 64*(2), 1–5.

Thorley, T. G., & Saltman, E. (2023). GIFCT tech trials: Combining behavioural signals to surface terrorist and violent extremist content online. *Studies in Conflict and Terrorism*, •••, 1–26.

United Nations Office of Counter-Terrorism and United Nations Interregional Crime and Justice Research Institute, (2021). Countering Terrorism Online with Artificial Intelligence: An Overview for Law Enforcement and Counter-Terrorism Agencies in South Asia and South-East Asia. A Joint Report. Retrieved from: countering-terrorism-online-with-ai-uncct-unicri-report-web.pdf

United States Department of State. (2022). Country Reports on Terrorism 2022: Morocco. retrieved from: https://www.state.gov/reports/country-reports-on-terrorism-2022/morocco

U.S. Department of Justice (DOJ). (2024). Artificial Intelligence and Civil Rights. DOJ Report. Retrieved from https://www.justice.gov/crt/ai

Wang, X., Zhao, Y., & Pourpanah, F. (2020). Recent advances in deep learning. *International Journal of Machine Learning and Cybernetics, 11*(4), 747–750. DOI: 10.1007/s13042-020-01096-5

Weismann, I. (2020). The Making of the Modern Arab Da'wa Discursive Field. In Malik, J., & Weismann, I. (Eds.), *Culture of Da'wa: Islamic preaching in the modern world* (pp. 15–30). The University of Utah Press.

Welle, D. (2021). Slahi and His Torturers - Life after Guantanamo. Documentary. Retrieved from https://www.dw.com/en/slahi-and-his-torturers-life-after-guantanamo/a-59629504

ADDITIONAL READING

Basheer, R., & Alkhatib, B. (2021). Threats from the dark: A review over dark web investigation research for cyber threat intelligence. *Journal of Computer Networks and Communications, 2021*(1), 1302999. DOI: 10.1155/2021/1302999

Dalins, J., Wilson, C., & Carman, M. (2018). Criminal Motivation on the Dark Web: A Categorisation Model for Law Enforcement. *Digital Investigation, 24*, 62–71. DOI: 10.1016/j.diin.2017.12.003

Sjøen, M. M. (2021). Let's talk about terrorism. *Journal of Peace Education, 18*(3), 309–325. DOI: 10.1080/17400201.2021.1987869

Tinta, A. A. (2023). Are more educated people more likely to engage in terrorism. Applied Economics 55:37, pages 4273-4288.Breiman, L. (2001). Random Forests. *Machine Learning*, *45*, 5–32.

Younes, A., Mohamadi, B., & AbuGhazala, M. O. (2023). Terrorism in Egypt: A comprehensive spatial, spatio-temporal, and statistical analysis. *GeoJournal*, *88*(6), 6339–6364. DOI: 10.1007/s10708-023-10972-w

KEY TERMS AND DEFINITIONS

Artificial intelligence: Refers to computer systems or machines capable of performing tasks that typically require human intelligence. These tasks include reasoning, learning from data, perception, language understanding, problem-solving, and decision-making. AI systems analyse large datasets, recognise patterns, and make predictions or decisions quickly and accurately.

Counterterrorism: refers to the comprehensive set of strategies, tactics, policies, and measures employed by governments, security agencies, and international organisations to prevent, deter, respond to, and mitigate terrorist threats and acts. It encompasses proactive and reactive actions aimed at disrupting terrorist networks, reducing their operational capabilities, protecting civilians and critical infrastructure, and addressing the underlying conditions that foster terrorism.

Dark Web: is a distinct part of the internet that exists within the broader deep web but is accessible only through specialised anonymising software such as Tor (The Onion Router), I2P, or Freenet. It is characterised by websites and services that are not indexed by conventional search engines and are designed to maintain user anonymity and privacy by hiding IP addresses, network traffic, and user identities.

Deep Web: also known as the invisible web or hidden web, refers to all parts of the World Wide Web whose contents are not indexed by standard web search engines such as Google, Bing, or Yahoo.

Extremism: refers to the beliefs, ideologies, or actions that advocate for or promote ideas based on violence, hatred, or intolerance, often aiming to negate or destroy the fundamental rights and freedoms of others, undermine democratic systems, or create an environment permissive to such outcomes.

Law Enforcement: is an organised activity carried out by government officials or social institutions to enforce laws by investigating, deterring, rehabilitating, or punishing individuals who violate societal rules and norms. It encompasses various agencies and personnel, including police, courts, and corrections, that work either independently or collaboratively to uphold public safety, maintain order, protect life and property, and ensure compliance with the law within specified jurisdictions.

Predictive Analytics: is a branch of advanced analytics that uses historical data, statistical modeling, data mining techniques, and machine learning algorithms to analyse past patterns and make informed predictions about future outcomes or trends. It involves extracting meaningful patterns from large and complex datasets to assess risks, identify opportunities, and support decision-making processes across various domains.

Radicalisation: is a multifaceted process by which an individual or group increasingly adopts extreme political, social, or religious ideals and aspirations that may lead them to condone, support, facilitate, or use violence to further their goals or involve a transformation of beliefs, feelings, and behaviors that justify intergroup violence and demand sacrifice in defense of the in-group.

Terrorism: is the deliberate use or threat of violence by individuals, groups or states, primarily targeting non-combatants, to instill fear and coerce governments, societies, or specific populations in order to achieve political, ideological, or religious objectives.

Chapter 6
Deep Learning for Digital Forensics:
Advancing Criminal Investigations

Usharani Bhimavarapu
https://orcid.org/0000-0002-0246-1420
Department of Computer Science and Engineering, Koneru Lakshmaiah Education Foundation, Vaddeswaram, India

ABSTRACT

Digital forensics has evolved significantly with advancements in artificial intelligence (AI) to enable faster, more accurate, and more scalable criminal investigation evidence collection. Traditional forensic procedures are overwhelmed by the volume, complexity, and fragility of digital evidence. AI-based forensics merges machine learning, predictive analytics, and automation in order to make digital artifact identification, preservation, and analysis better. This essay describes cutting-edge AI-based methods of forensic investigation, including deep learning-based anomaly detection, decision trees-based forensic classification, and ensemble methods to variance reduction in forensic predictions. Using AI, forensic analysts can spot patterns, follow cybercrime patterns, and relate digital evidence with greater precision. AI-based applications also assist in automating routine forensic work, reducing human errors, and improving legal investigations.

INTRODUCTION

Digital forensics is now a crucial part of contemporary investigations that allows law enforcement agencies and cybersecurity experts to process electronic evidence effectively. The widespread expansion of digital devices, cloud computing, and

DOI: 10.4018/979-8-3373-0245-4.ch006

encrypted communication streams has made evidence acquisition more complex. Conventional forensic processes are unable to cope with the sheer amount of digital data, and AI-based systems are no longer a choice but a necessity. AI-powered forensic tools are able to process large datasets, identify anomalies, and automate mundane tasks to make investigations more efficient. With machine learning algorithms, investigators can detect concealed patterns in digital evidence that would otherwise remain undetected. These technologies cut down the time taken for forensic analysis by a considerable margin while enhancing accuracy. Further, AI-driven natural language processing (NLP) helps investigate text messages, emails, and online chats for criminal intent. By automating some parts of digital forensics, the experts can give all their attention to analyzing the results and making well-informed decisions. As cybercrimes keep changing, AI is also playing a significant part in reinforcing digital evidence gathering and forensic investigations.

Ensuring the authenticity and integrity of the data is one of the greatest challenges in collecting digital evidence. AI-powered forensic tools assist in authenticating evidence by preserving digital fingerprints using cryptographic hashing methods. These instruments guarantee that the data gathered is not tampered with during the investigation process, which is a requirement of legal admissibility. Another point is that AI-based anomaly detection can detect manipulated or tampered files, guaranteeing only authentic evidence is brought under consideration. Based on AI-powered forensic imaging, investigators can recover deleted files, hidden partitions, and encrypted information from storage media. Traditional forensic methods are usually inadequate in the case of sophisticated cybercrime methods like steganography or deepfake manipulation. AI solutions employ sophisticated image recognition and deep learning algorithms to detect manipulated or forged media files. Additionally, blockchain-based forensic solutions provide a decentralized and tamper-evident method for protecting digital evidence. These technologies enhance the credibility of forensic investigations, making sure that the evidence holds up to scrutiny in court.

Artificial intelligence-based automation is essential at the early phase of digital forensic examinations. Triage tools driven by AI have the ability to rapidly scan and categorize digital evidence by relevance, minimizing effort. Automated detection of keywords and metadata extraction aid forensic examiners in finding significant information from email, documents, and chat conversations. Facial analysis and biometrics enable investigators to compare suspects to security camera imagery or social media photos. AI-powered forensic software can also scrutinize mobile geolocation data and GPS logs, offering investigators movement patterns. Speech-to-text algorithms assist in converting audio recordings to searchable text, making it simpler to analyze voice messages and phone calls. With the help of deep learning models, AI is able to identify patterns of financial cybercrimes' fraudulent transactions. These automated functions greatly minimize data-sorting time, enabling investigators to concentrate on case-solving. Digital forensics powered by AI not only speeds up the investigative process but also improves the reliability of results. The incorporation of AI in forensic processes continues to revolutionize digital evidence analysis.

Another major area in which AI improves digital forensics is malware analysis and cyber threat identification. Cybercriminals employ advanced tactics like polymorphic malware, rootkits, and ransomware to avoid detection. Signature-based detection, which traditional malware analysis employs, is powerless against dynamic threats. AI-based behavioral analysis has the capability to identify malicious actions by detecting system behavior deviations. Machine learning algorithms can identify zero-day exploits through real-time examination of code patterns and execution behavior. Artificial intelligence sandbox environments permit investigators to execute and analyze malware in a secure environment without jeopardizing system integrity. Network forensics tools automate the analysis of traffic patterns and identify attempts to exfiltrate data in cases of cybersecurity attacks. Deep learning algorithms improve intrusion detection systems (IDS) by distinguishing between usual and abnormal network activity. AI capabilities of forecasting future cyber threats facilitate preemptive threat hunting and forensic analysis. The intersection of AI and digital forensics enhances cybersecurity defenses and supports post-incident analysis.

Cloud-based digital forensics is another space where AI is revolutionizing evidence collection and analysis. As the adoption of cloud storage and virtual computing environments increases, conventional forensic techniques struggle to access and protect data. AI-driven forensic tools can automatically acquire data from cloud systems with a forensically sound chain of custody. Such tools are capable of detecting digital footprints on numerous cloud services, monitoring user behavior, and suspicious file changes. AI-powered log analysis helps investigators identify unauthorized attempts to access data, insider threats, and APTs. The ability of AI to scale in cloud forensic investigations permits swift processing of large volumes of data without reducing accuracy. AI-based digital forensics also has the capability to rebuild deleted or fragmented data in cloud backups. Cloud-based AI models can process real-time security events, enabling organizations to avoid cyber incidents before they become severe. As organizations move sensitive data into cloud infrastructures, AI-based forensic solutions play a pivotal role in legal and security requirements. Cloud-based digital evidence extraction, analysis, and interpretation guarantee successful forensic inspections.

AI has also transformed mobile forensics by improving the data extraction and analysis from smartphones and other mobile devices. Classic mobile forensic techniques usually find it difficult to deal with encrypted apps, deleted data, and broken storage hierarchies. AI-based software can do deep data extraction from messaging applications, call history, and social media interactions without compromising data integrity. Machine learning algorithms assist in categorizing useful information, recognizing primary contacts, dialogues, and media files linked to criminal operations. AI-based sentiment analysis identifies potential threats, hate speech, or incriminating conversations from chat logs. AI-backed geospatial forensics reconstructs a suspect's movement history by examining GPS and Wi-Fi traces. AI voice recognition authentication identifies individuals in recorded talks, making evidence more credible. Security by-passes, including pattern locks and biometric checks, are enabled by sophisticated AI methods without harming the device. Mobile forensics has a vital function in contemporary investigations, as smartphones hold significant evidence in criminal and cybercrime cases. AI-based forensic tools are increasingly making mobile evidence analysis more efficient and accurate.

Automated facial recognition and video analysis are among the most promising uses of AI in digital forensics. Surveillance videos are frequently a critical piece of evidence in investigations, but reviewing them manually is labor-intensive and prone to errors. AI-based video analytics can automatically identify faces, license plates, and suspicious behavior in huge amounts of video footage. Deep learning algorithms enhance facial recognition accuracy even in adverse conditions like dim lighting or partial occlusions. AI-based motion analysis assists in identifying abnormal patterns of behavior, which can prevent crimes and help identify suspects. Speech-to-text AI models are able to transcribe and analyze dialogue from security recordings, gaining important insights into criminal behavior. AI-based emotion detection can gauge the psychological status of individuals using facial expressions and tone of voice. These developments seriously improve the capability of law enforcement agencies to monitor suspects and process surveillance information. With further development of AI, video and image forensics will get better and more accurate in criminal investigations.

AI-based forensic solutions are also helping to counter online crimes such as fraud, cyberbullying, and digital harassment. Machine learning algorithms are capable of scanning online behavior, identifying fake accounts, fraud transactions, and cyber attacks in real-time. Sentiment analysis through AI enables law enforcement to monitor hate speech, extremist propaganda, and orchestrated disinformation campaigns. Web scraping tools automatically gather digital evidence from social media, forums, and dark web markets. Forensic linguistics based on AI can detect authorship patterns in anonymous online threats or ransom demands. AI-driven deepfake detection software assists in authenticating digital media and blocking misinformation. Chatbot analysis based on AI can detect suspicious conversations involving cybercrimes, child exploitation, or financial fraud. By combining AI with digital forensics, investigators can process online data quickly while preserving user privacy. AI-driven automation and real-time threat intelligence significantly aid cybercrime forensics. The capacity to quickly analyze digital interactions enhances cybersecurity and law enforcement efforts.

With the continued growth of AI, ethical concerns and legal issues in digital forensics need to be addressed. The application of AI in investigations poses issues related to privacy, data protection, and bias in machine learning models. Transparency in AI-based forensic tools is needed to avoid wrongful accusations or false positives. Legal systems need to adapt to the integration of AI-enhanced forensic techniques in a manner that respects privacy regulations and human rights. The admissibility of evidence produced by AI in courtrooms hinges on the reliability and interpretability of forensic algorithms. Ethical practices of AI need ongoing assessment and mitigation of biases in facial recognition, sentiment analysis, and predictive policing. Cooperation between forensic experts, lawyers, and AI developers is indispensable in defining standards for ethical AI application in investigation. Policies regarding AI governance must emphasize fairness, responsibility, and transparency in digital forensics. As AI improves forensic abilities, human intervention is critical to interpret findings and ensure justice. Ethical use of AI is essential to uphold public confidence in AI-based forensic investigations.

AI-based forensics is transforming collection of digital evidence, enhancing the quality, speed, and integrity of investigations. Be it automated triage or detection of deepfakes, AI-powered tools are responding to the challenge of changing cyber threats and ever-evolving criminal techniques. Cloud forensic analysis, mobile extraction, and AI-powered video analytics strengthen the investigative capabilities across different spheres. In addition to advantages, however, ethical issues and legal systems must be dealt with carefully to ensure proper use of AI in forensics. The application of AI in digital forensics will keep growing, giving law enforcement and cybersecurity experts powerful tools for fighting crime. With continuing advancements in technology, coupling AI with forensic science will determine the future of criminal investigations. AI-based automation will automate evidence analysis and lower the workload of forensic analysts manually. Ongoing research and AI-based forensics development will foster further innovations in preventing and detecting crime. The combination of AI and digital forensics will play a central role in ensuring security and enforcing justice in the digital era.

Yadav (2020) gives a basic introduction to cyber forensics but does not include a comprehensive discussion on the implementation of AI in forensic analysis. The research primarily discusses conventional approaches, without mentioning the scalability and automation issues in digital forensics (Yadav, 2020).

Allah Rakha (2024) discusses legal issues in cybercrime investigations, but the research is limited by its jurisdictional scope. It fails to offer a comparative review of digital forensic laws between nations, and thus it is less relevant to international forensic investigations (Allah Rakha, 2024).

Baafi (2022) investigates cyber forensics tools but does not evaluate their effectiveness when utilized in massive forensic cases. The research further lacks empirical support of the effectiveness of tools and does not address AI-based forensic methods (Baafi, 2022).

Yerriswamy and Venumadhava (2022) write about forensic technologies with case studies but without including recent advances in AI forensics. The research also does not touch upon issues like false positives with automated forensic identification (Yerriswamy & Venumadhava, 2022).

Dunsin et al. (2023) discuss the application of AI in digital forensics but mostly center on theoretical views over actual applications. The work lacks experimental testing and does not cover ethical issues pertaining to AI-powered forensic automation (Dunsin et al., 2023).

Ekhande et al. (2022) survey deep learning methodologies applied to forensics but do not account for problems such as computational complexity and model interpretability. The work further does not incorporate comparative analysis of deep learning models with conventional forensic techniques (Ekhande et al., 2022).

Javed et al. (2022) conduct a detailed review of computer forensics but fail to mention an extensive analysis of AI-driven forensic models. The work is extensively wide in scope but fails to provide vivid insights into the challenges in implementing AI in practice in forensics (Javed et al., 2022).

Kaur and Kaur (2012) examine digital forensics but fail to factor in recent advancements in forensic practices. Due to the date of its publication, the research fails to take into account the application of AI, cloud forensics, or blockchain in contemporary digital investigations (Kaur & Kaur, 2012).

Perilli et al. (2020) address cyber-attacks and forensic methods but do not include AI-based solutions for proactive threat identification. The research mainly discusses reactive forensic action and does not touch upon predictive analytics for prevention against cybercrime (Perilli et al., 2020).

McCluskey et al. (2022) explain how computer forensics supports cybersecurity but fail to present an in-depth analysis of AI's role in forensic automation. The research is primarily based on security measures and not on sophisticated forensic methods like predictive analytics and deep learning (McCluskey et al., 2022).

Malik (2021) analyzes various software utilized in cybercrime but does not analyze AI-based forensic solutions to counter them. The research lacks empirical evaluation of the effectiveness of forensic software and fails to mention upcoming threats such as AI-based cyberattacks (Malik, 2021).

Kumar et al. (2022) study XSS attacks and forensic models but emphasize more web-based threats. The research does not cover wider uses of forensic methods in fields such as cloud computing, IoT forensics, and digital fraud detection (Kumar et al., 2022).

Kolesnyk (2021) delivers a thorough forensic examination of IT crimes but does not include actual case studies to show how forensic techniques can be applied in real life. Moreover, the study does not discuss how AI and automation can enhance digital forensic investigation (Kolesnyk, 2021).

Qadir and Varol (2020) emphasize the contribution of machine learning to digital forensics but fail to discuss the constraints of AI-based forensic models, including bias in training data and lack of explainability. The research also does not include a discussion of the legal implications of AI-based forensic analysis (Qadir & Varol, 2020).

Kumar and Kumar (2023) research AI-based cybersecurity attacks in banks but do not address forensic investigation methods for tracking financial cybercrimes. The research is more inclined towards the detection of cyber threats than post-incident forensic analysis (Kumar & Kumar, 2023).

Rajendiran et al. (2021) present machine learning uses in cyber forensics but present theoretical information only and not with empirical support. The research does not tackle issues like interpretability of the model, privacy issues in data, and overhead in computing (Rajendiran et al., 2021).

Vedre and Parulekar (2022) discuss the use of computers in computer forensics but do not have a discussion on AI-based forensic tools and their efficiency. The research is narrow in scope with emphasis on conventional forensic methods (Vedre & Parulekar, 2022).

Karie et al. (2019) suggest deep learning cognitive computing methods for cyber forensics but fail to evaluate their challenges in practical implementation. The research also does not have a comparative evaluation of deep learning models with conventional forensic methods (Karie et al., 2019).

Cisar et al. (2014) write about forensic technologies and cybercrime but omit developments in digital forensics enhanced by AI. As published, the research is short of information on current cyber threats and forensic techniques (Cisar et al., 2014).

Svoboda and Lukas (2019) discuss cybersecurity threats but do not offer an in-depth discussion on forensic investigation methods. The research is inclined more towards risk assessment than forensic data analysis and evidence gathering (Svoboda & Lukas, 2019).

Kafol and Bregar (2017) discuss cybersecurity protection measures but not AI-based forensic methods for cybercrime investigation. Forensic issues like tampering with digital evidence and chain of custody are not discussed in the study (Kafol & Bregar, 2017).

Al Fahdi et al. (2013) poll digital forensic challenges but fail to suggest AI-driven solutions to address such challenges. Due to the fast pace of AI development, the research is outdated and does not provide insights into contemporary forensic tools and techniques (Al Fahdi et al., 2013).

ISO/IEC 27001:2022/Amd 1:2024 establishes cybersecurity and information security standards but does not directly mention digital forensic methodologies. The standard offers general guidance instead of forensic strategies for cyber investigations (ISO/IEC, 2024).

Fakiha (2023) addresses AI-enhanced cyber forensics but fails to discuss the ethical and legal issues involved in AI-based forensic automation. The research also fails to discuss the computational complexity of AI-based forensic methods (Fakiha, 2023).

The suggested model addresses the drawbacks of current forensic methods by combining AI-based predictive analytics, deep learning, and automation to increase digital evidence gathering and analysis. Conventional forensic methods are prone to scalability challenges, manual dependency, and latency in processing massive amounts of digital evidence. By using machine learning algorithms, the suggested model increases real-time threat detection and anomaly detection, lowering investigative time and enhancing accuracy. Existing studies lack comprehensive AI-based forensic frameworks, often focusing on isolated techniques rather than an integrated solution. The proposed model addresses this by incorporating deep learning for pattern recognition, blockchain for evidence integrity, and natural language processing (NLP) for automated log analysis. Unlike previous models that struggle with false positives and interpretability, the proposed framework applies explainable AI techniques to ensure transparency in forensic decision-making. Moreover, ethical and legal issues related to AI-based forensic examination are addressed through the inclusion of strong validation protocols and regulatory compliance checks. The model also incorporates a multi-modal forensic process that examines varied sources of data including network logs, emails, and multimedia files, which is commonly lacking in traditional techniques. Through automating important forensic activities, the system to be proposed lessens human prejudice, improves reproducibility, and provides for an efficient, scalable, and admissible-to-court forensic investigation process.

PREDICTIVE ANALYTICS IN DIGITAL FORENSICS

Predictive analytics is of the essence in digital forensics because it provides proactive investigation measures, risk assessments, and even automated decision-making. The more conventional methods for forensics mostly address the issue of reactive analysis—after the fact—that involves studying occurrences from the past following a security breach. Nevertheless, predictive analytics repositions itself by applying machine learning (ML), artificial intelligence (AI), and statistical modeling to forecast cyber attacks, find anomalies, and reveal patterns among digital evidence.

Algorithm: AI-Powered Predictive Forensics (APF)

Step 1: Data Collection & Preprocessing

- Collect digital forensic data from logs, network traffic, cloud storage, mobile devices, emails, and social media.
- Perform data normalization, feature extraction, and noise removal to improve accuracy.
- Apply Natural Language Processing (NLP) for analyzing textual evidence (emails, messages, documents).

Step 2: Feature Selection & Anomaly Detection

- Use Principal Component Analysis (PCA) to reduce data dimensionality while retaining key forensic features.
- Implement unsupervised learning models (e.g., Autoencoders, Isolation Forests, K-Means Clustering) to detect abnormal behaviors in system logs.

Step 3: Machine Learning-Based Classification

- Train classification models using Supervised Learning (Random Forest, Decision Trees, SVM, XGBoost) to categorize forensic evidence into risk levels.
- Use Deep Learning models (LSTM, Transformer-based architectures like BERT) to analyze patterns in time-series forensic data.
- Leverage graph-based analysis (Graph Neural Networks - GNNs) to link digital artifacts and identify cybercriminal networks.

Step 4: Predictive Threat Scoring & Risk Assessment

- Assign risk scores to users, files, and transactions based on historical forensic evidence.
- Use Bayesian Networks to predict potential security breaches and attack vectors.
- Integrate predictive outputs with Threat Intelligence Platforms (TIPs) for real-time cyber threat assessment.

Step 5: Real-Time Decision-Making & Alerts

- Deploy Reinforcement Learning (RL) models to refine forensic decision-making over time.
- Generate real-time alerts when a high-risk digital artifact is detected.
- Provide automated forensic reporting for law enforcement and legal proceedings.

Theorem 1: Feature Selection Improves Predictive Accuracy

Statement: Given a dataset X with n features, selecting an optimal subset of features $X' \subset X$ (where $|X'| < n$) results in a classifier with improved accuracy $A' \geq A$, where A is the accuracy with all features.

Proof:

1. Let $X = \{x_1, x_2, \ldots, x_n\}$ be the feature set of a forensic dataset.
2. Some features may be redundant or irrelevant, introducing noise into the model.
3. Feature selection algorithms (e.g., Recursive Feature Elimination, Mutual Information) identify the most relevant features, reducing dimensionality.
4. By removing irrelevant features, the classifier avoids overfitting, leading to an improved generalization capability.
5. Empirical studies show that using only highly correlated features results in better accuracy than using all features.
6. Therefore, selecting an optimal subset of features improves predictive accuracy, proving $A' \geq A$.

Theorem 2: Anomaly Detection in Time-Series Data is NP-Hard

Statement: Detecting anomalies in forensic time-series logs is NP-hard due to the combinatorial nature of potential patterns.

Proof:

1. Consider a sequence of forensic events $S = \{S_1, S_2, \ldots, S_t\}$ where S_t represents an event at time t.
2. Anomalies are defined as deviations from expected patterns in S.
3. Detecting such deviations requires computing the probability distribution of all possible sequences.
4. Since time-series patterns evolve dynamically, the search space for potential anomalies grows exponentially.
5. Reducing the problem to a classical NP-hard problem (e.g., subset-sum or sequence alignment) proves that no polynomial-time solution exists for the general case.

6. Hence, machine learning (e.g., LSTMs, autoencoders) is used to approximate anomaly detection in forensic logs.

Theorem 3: Decision Trees Provide Optimal Rule-Based Classification for Forensic Risk Scoring

Statement: Given a forensic dataset D with discrete risk levels R={0,1,2}, a decision tree classifier provides optimal rule-based classification by minimizing impurity using entropy or Gini index.

Proof:

1. A decision tree partitions data into subsets based on features that maximize information gain.
2. The entropy of a node is given by:

$$H(D) = -\sum p_i \backslash log_2 p_i$$

where p_i is the probability of class iii.

3. Splitting on a feature f results in subsets $D_1, D_2, \ldots, D_n$, with reduced entropy:

$$H(D|f) = \sum\{|D_i|\}\{|D|\}\backslash H(D_i)$$

4. By selecting the feature that maximizes information gain, the tree optimally classifies forensic risk levels.
5. Decision trees provide an interpretable model for forensic investigators to trace classification decisions.
6. Hence, decision trees offer optimal rule-based classification for forensic risk scoring.

Theorem 4: Random Forest Reduces Variance in Forensic Classification

Statement: A random forest classifier reduces variance and improves generalization compared to a single decision tree.

Proof:

1. A single decision tree is prone to overfitting, capturing noise in forensic data.
2. A random forest consists of k decision trees, each trained on a bootstrapped sample of the dataset.

3. The final prediction is made by aggregating outputs from individual trees via majority voting (classification) or averaging (regression).
4. By training on multiple subsets, the model captures diverse decision boundaries, reducing variance.
5. Mathematically, let f(x) be the prediction of a single tree, and let F(x) be the ensemble prediction:

$$Var[F(x)] = \{1\}\{k\} Var[f(x)]$$

which approaches zero as $k \to \infty$

6. Thus, a random forest provides improved stability and reliability in forensic classification.

Theorem 5: The Curse of Dimensionality Affects Anomaly Detection in Large Forensic Datasets

Statement: As the number of features d in a forensic dataset increases, the distance between data points becomes less meaningful, making anomaly detection difficult.

Proof:

1. Consider a dataset with N points in d-dimensional space.
2. The Euclidean distance between two points x,yx, yx,y in high-dimensional space is:

$$\|x - y\| = \left\{ \sum_{\{i=1\}}^{\{N\}} (x_i - y_i)^2 \right\}$$

3. As d increases, all points tend to become equidistant, reducing meaningful variation.
4. This causes anomaly detection algorithms (e.g., k-NN, DBSCAN) to lose effectiveness.
5. Dimensionality reduction techniques (PCA, t-SNE, Autoencoders) mitigate this issue by projecting forensic data into a lower-dimensional space while preserving structure.
6. Hence, anomaly detection in forensic data is strongly affected by the curse of dimensionality.

Theorem 6: Deep Learning Enhances Forensic Evidence Correlation

Statement: Neural networks with multiple hidden layers improve forensic evidence correlation by learning complex, non-linear relationships.

Proof:

1. Forensic data consists of multiple interconnected variables (e.g., user logs, financial transactions, IP addresses).
2. Traditional correlation methods (Pearson, Spearman) capture only linear relationships.
3. A deep neural network (DNN) with hidden layers learns hierarchical representations, enabling non-linear feature extraction.
4. The activation function (ReLU, sigmoid, tanh) introduces non-linearity, allowing deeper insights into forensic patterns.
5. Backpropagation updates weights to minimize the loss function:

$$L = \sum_{\{i=1\}}^{\{N\}} (y_i - \widehat{\{y\}}_i)^2$$

where y_i is the actual forensic label and \hat{y}_ii is the predicted label.

6. As a result, deep learning models achieve higher accuracy in correlating forensic evidence compared to traditional methods.

CONCLUSION

The application of AI in digital forensics is transforming the investigative process, allowing forensic experts to handle large amounts of complex evidence in a more efficient way. Using predictive analytics, anomaly detection, and machine learning-based classification models, forensic analysts can enhance the speed and quality of digital evidence gathering. Theoretical framework established by this study, like correlations of proofs of evidence by deep learning, dimensionality reduction, and the effectiveness of feature selection, guarantees the efficiency of AI for forensic analysis. Though there may be computational costs and interpretability issues, AI-based forensic is a more scalable, adaptive, and robust criminal investigation technique. Future research should focus on improve explainable AI models, algorithmic optimization, and AI forensics creation of standard framework for forensic AI investigations. Overall, the combination of AI and digital forensics strengthens legal and investigation work, ensuring justice through information-driven decisioning.

REFERENCES

Al Fahdi, M., Clarke, N. L., & Furnell, S. M. (2013, August 14–16). Challenges to digital forensics: A survey of researchers & practitioners attitudes and opinions. In *Proceedings of the 2013 Information Security for South Africa (ISSA)* (pp. 1–8). IEEE. DOI: 10.1109/ISSA.2013.6641058

Allah Rakha, N. (2024). Cybercrime and the law: Addressing the challenges of digital forensics in criminal investigations. *Mexican Law Review*, *16*, 23–54. DOI: 10.22201/iij.24485306e.2024.2.18892

Baafi, P. O. (2022). Tools for cyber forensics. *Advanced Multidisciplinary Scientific Research Journal Publications*, *1*(1), 285–290. DOI: 10.22624/AIMS/CRP-BK3-P46

Cisar, P., Cisar, S., & Bosnjak, S. (2014). Cybercrime and digital forensics—Technologies and approaches. In *DAAAM International Scientific Book 2014* (pp. 525–542). DAAAM International.

Dunsin, D., Ghanem, M. C., Ouazzane, K., & Vassilev, V. (2023). A comprehensive analysis of the role of artificial intelligence and machine learning in modern digital forensics and incident response. *Forensic Science International Digital Investigation*, *48*, 301675. DOI: 10.1016/j.fsidi.2023.301675

Ekhande, S., Patil, U., & Kulhalli, K. V. (2022). Review on effectiveness of deep learning approach in digital forensics. [IJECE]. *International Journal of Electrical and Computer Engineering*, *12*(6), 5481–5592. DOI: 10.11591/ijece.v12i5.pp5481-5592

Fakiha, B. (2023). Enhancing cyber forensics with AI and machine learning: A study on automated threat analysis and classification. *International Journal of Safety and Security Engineering*, *13*(4), 701–707. DOI: 10.18280/ijsse.130412

International Organization for Standardization (ISO), & International Electrotechnical Commission (IEC). (2024). *ISO/IEC 27001:2022/Amd 1:2024—Information security, cybersecurity and privacy protection—Information security management systems—Requirements.*

Javed, A. R., Ahmed, W., Alazab, M., Jalil, Z., Kifayat, K., & Gadekallu, T. R. (2022). A comprehensive survey on computer forensics: State-of-the-art, tools, techniques, challenges, and future directions. *IEEE Access : Practical Innovations, Open Solutions*, *10*, 11065–11089. DOI: 10.1109/ACCESS.2022.3142508

Kafol, C., & Bregar, A. (2017). Cyber security—Building a sustainable protection. In *DAAAM International Scientific Book 2017* (pp. 81–90). DAAAM International. DOI: 10.2507/daaam.scibook.2017.07

Karie, N. M., Kebande, V. R., & Venter, H. S. (2019). Diverging deep learning cognitive computing techniques into cyber forensics. *Forensic Science International. Synergy, 1*, 61–67. DOI: 10.1016/j.fsisyn.2019.03.006 PMID: 32411955

Kaur, R., & Kaur, A. (2012). Digital forensics. *International Journal of Computer Applications, 50*(7), 5–9. DOI: 10.5120/7765-0844

Kolesnyk, V. (2021). Forensic analysis of crimes in the sphere of information technologies. *Information Security of the Person. Socialtjänst Statistik, 31–33*, 124–136.

Kumar, D., & Kumar, K. P. (2023, March 3–5). Artificial intelligence based cyber security threats identification in financial institutions using machine learning approach. In *Proceedings of the 2023 2nd International Conference for Innovation in Technology (INOCON)* (pp. 1–6). IEEE. DOI: 10.1109/INOCON57975.2023.10100967

Kumar, S., Pathak, S. K., & Singh, J. (2022). A comprehensive study of XSS attack and the digital forensic models to gather the evidence. *ECS Transactions, 107*(1), 7153–7163. DOI: 10.1149/10701.7153ecst

Malik, N. (2021). A study on different software used to perform cyber crime. *International Journal for Research in Applied Science and Engineering Technology, 9*(6), 879–882. DOI: 10.22214/ijraset.2021.39395

McCluskey, Q. R., Chowdhury, M. M., Latif, S., & Kambhampaty, K. (2022, May 19–21). Computer forensics: Complementing cyber security. In *Proceedings of the 2022 IEEE International Conference on Electro Information Technology (eIT)*. IEEE. https://doi.org/DOI: 10.1109/eIT50749.2022.9813720

Perilli, M., De Bonis, M., & Gallo, C. (2020). Computer forensics and cyber attacks. In Khosrow-Pour, M. (Ed.), *Handbook of research on cyber crime and information privacy* (pp. 132–150). IGI Global., DOI: 10.4018/978-1-7998-5728-0.ch008

Qadir, A. M., & Varol, A. (2020, June 1–2). The role of machine learning in digital forensics. In *Proceedings of the 2020 8th International Symposium on Digital Forensics and Security (ISDFS)* (pp. 1–5). IEEE. DOI: 10.1109/ISDFS49300.2020.9116298

Rajendiran, K., Kannan, K., & Yu, Y. (2021). Applications of machine learning in cyber forensics. In Khosrow-Pour, M. (Ed.), (pp. 29–46). Advances in digital crime, forensics, and cyber terrorism. IGI Global., DOI: 10.4018/978-1-7998-4900-1.ch002

Svoboda, J., & Lukas, L. (2019). Sources of threats and threats in the cyber security. In Katalinic, B. (Ed.), *DAAAM International Scientific Book 2019* (pp. 321–330). DAAAM International., DOI: 10.2507/daaam.scibook.2019.27

Vedre, S., & Parulekar, W. (2022). (in press). Digital forensic and role of computers in digital forensic. *International Journal of Creative Research Thoughts (IJCRT), 10*(1). *Article ID, IJCRT2201030*. Advance online publication. DOI: 10.1729/IJCRT.2201030

Yadav, S. (2020). Cyber forensics. In Khosrow-Pour, M. (Ed.), (pp. 1–15). Advances in digital crime, forensics, and cyber terrorism. IGI Global., DOI: 10.4018/978-1-7998-6811-8.ch001

Yerriswamy, K., & Venumadhava, G. S. (2022). Cyber forensic tools and its application in the investigation of digital crimes: Preventive measures with case studies. [IJSR]. *International Journal of Scientific Research, 11*(5), 71–73. DOI: 10.21275/SR22505102723

Chapter 7
Forensic Linguistics and DBN:
Automating the Analysis of Witness Statements and Testimonies in AI-Driven Policing

Abhinash Mohanta
https://orcid.org/0000-0002-8732-3202
KIIT University, India

Sneha
https://orcid.org/0000-0002-0158-2503
XIM University, Bhubaneswar, India

Kyvalya Garikapati
https://orcid.org/0000-0003-0990-6514
KIIT University, India

Sanskruti Mohanty
https://orcid.org/0009-0009-9530-0412
Utkal University, India

Shivani Samanta
https://orcid.org/0009-0003-6857-6145
South Asian University, India

ABSTRACT

The integration of Deep Belief Networks (DBNs) into forensic linguistics enhances AI-driven policing in smart cities by automating witness testimony analysis. DBNs

DOI: 10.4018/979-8-3373-0245-4.ch007

address limitations of traditional methods, such as subjectivity and inefficiency, by detecting linguistic markers of deception and inconsistency. AI tools have accelerated investigations by analyzing digital evidence, though specific architectures like DBNs were not disclosed in these cases. Ethical considerations, including algorithmic bias and data privacy, are addressed through strategies like adversarial debiasing and synthetic data augmentation. Collaboration between law enforcement, AI experts, and policymakers ensures ethical deployment and inclusive dataset curation. Future directions include expanding DBN applications to real-time threat detection and multilingual forensic analysis. DBNs improve urban security by enhancing testimony credibility assessments, fostering community trust, and aligning AI-driven policing with ethical standards.

INTRODUCTION

The field of forensic linguistics has long been a valuable tool in criminal investigations and Artificial intelligence (AI) technologies have advanced so rapidly that they have created a new innovative phase for police work which specifically benefits smart city operations(Dunsin et al., 2024). Urgent need exists for innovative advanced tools which improve public safety because urban centres are becoming more complex. The critical but unexplored area of using AI for witness testimony analysis ranks among numerous police applications of this technology(Mishra et al., 2022). The scientific study of legal language known as forensic linguistics finds new possibilities through advanced AI Deep Belief Networks (DBNs) to improve law enforcement agency evaluation of witness statements. Traditional legal investigations depend on forensic linguistics to reveal authenticity together with statement consistency and potential lies present in witness testimonies. The analysis of linguistic patterns that includes word selection and syntax and semantic forms allows forensic linguists to detect the possible signs of bias and inconsistent or dishonest content(Juola, 2019). Traditional techniques for linguistic analysis require extended periods of time and depend heavily on human judgement while human analysts also bring their cognitive biases to the evaluation process. The fast-moving environment of smart cities requires law enforcement agencies to find objective and efficient approaches for testimony analysis due to these present limitations.

Deep Belief Networks represent a learning algorithm class that achieved strong results in both natural language processing and pattern detection tasks(Deep Belief Networks for Phone Recognition, 2023). DBNs serve as layered generative models that discover how data builds its hidden structures during the learning process. The technology of Deep Belief Networks lets police forces quickly examine speech patterns across many testimonies at once(Mohamed et al., 2011). DBNs need different witness statement data to spot linguistic markers that show if people are reliable or not as witnesses plus if they are being dishonest. The technology helps modernise urban security in smart cities by making better use of artificial-intelligence-based policing tools. DBNs bring new capabilities to forensic linguistics since they handle the problems that standard methods encounter. Human analysts find it hard to read between the lines and stay dependable when evaluating many texts. DBNs work through large text data sets in real time to see connexions that skilled linguists would miss. The deep learning model uses machine learning to enhance its abilities and correct errors through time. DBNs need this feature to handle smart city policing because these cities have many different ways people speak and communicate(-Dunsin et al., 2024).

The implementation of DBNs within AI-based police systems establishes critical effects on both public protection and city security measures. The combination of IoT devices with surveillance systems and data analytics platforms in smart cities provides a vast amount of data for which quick and precise analysis of witness testimonies leads to improved law enforcement effectiveness. For example, in the aftermath of a crime, DBNs can be used to evaluate the consistency of multiple witness statements, identifying discrepancies that may indicate deception or unreliable accounts(Wang & Gao, 2017). The enabled capability enables investigators to construct more robust case evidence which in turn decreases the possibility of innocents getting imprisoned. AI-driven policing benefits from DBN application in testimony analysis because it helps achieve predictive crime prevention and proactive threat detection goals simultaneously. The analysis of real-time communication data through DBNs grants security officials early notice about security threats within emergency calls and social media platforms thus facilitating more appropriate law enforcement responses. The preventive methodology follows the smart city philosophy which aims to create protected and enduring urban areas that swiftly react to protect people while improving their life quality(Park & Lee, 2020).

Modern forensic linguistics faces problems when adopting DBNs as part of its analysis processes. The main issue with DBNs arises because training data inconsistencies may lead to biassed computational decision making(Aditya et al., 2018). The training datasets must contain all linguistic and cultural contexts of smart cities to ensure proper accuracy and fairness from DBN algorithms. To solve this challenge data collection must receive proper attention through thorough preprocessing stages and sustained performance evaluations should monitor the algorithms consistently. The employment of DBNs in testimony investigation creates essential ethical questions about privacy protection. Detecting sensitive aspects of verbal evidence can lead to serious violations of human rights and freedoms when such data comes under improper use or improper handling. Law enforcement organisations need to create detailed ethical frameworks about AI technology use and strict privacy protection regulations for their legal applications(Aizenberg & Hoven, 2020). Public confidence in AI-powered police work requires open and accountable practises establishing law enforcement agencies must show their secure implementation of ethical processes for these systems.

The research investigates how forensic linguistics operates together with Deep Belief Networks to boost testimony analysis for the purpose of AI-based police systems and urban security operations. This chapter examines DBN capabilities alongside their boundaries and the moral and operative obstacles which emerge during their implementation with specific goals to understand future integration into criminal enforcement practises. The first part discusses how forensic linguistics functions for credibility analysis while the second section presents DBNs as tools for natural language processing. The approach then details how DBNs assist AI-policed operations specifically through public safety and urban security enhancement. This analysis focuses on showcasing why systemic bias detection needs to be solved while protecting privacy standards and creating joint partnerships between police units and artificial intelligence developers plus policymaking bodies. The study aims to support the ongoing discussion on AI-driven policing through specific suggestions about utilising DBNs effectively in intelligent urban environments.

The framework presents logical development starting from theoretical foundations which lead to practical applications where DBN methodologies and forensic linguistic applications are detailed. A hypothetical case scenario demonstrates practical utilities of this technology which is followed by an examination of moral along with sociological considerations for testimony analysis using DBNs. The chapter brings academic theory together with practical demonstrations to enhance the knowledge transfer from theoretical research to real-world implementation while providing essential advice to researchers and both practitioners and policymakers. The paper also aims to support current society-wide AI efforts by ensuring that both forensic linguistic research and DBN applications follow ethical principles of transparency and accountability.

BACKGROUND AND LITERATURE REVIEW

Law enforcement professionals use forensic linguistics extensively to evaluate witness statements by examining linguistic patterns for truth-credibility assessment(S Bhalshankar -, 2023). Law enforcement agencies currently use hand-driven examination techniques to analyse syntax together with semantics and pragmatics for signs of deception and inconsistency and biassed statements. Forensic linguists perform statement reliability assessments by studying verb tense structures as well as selecting specific words and analysing how storeys are constructed. These evaluation methods prove effective yet face human constraints because analysts experience subjective bias and require long analysis durations and display cognitive bias effects. Evaluation processes from analysts become inconsistent when they show unconscious preference for statements which match their personal beliefs or cultural background(Pauleen et al., 2006). Smart cities face increased susceptibility due to their rising volume of multilingual eyewitness statements that include different language dialects and communication methods. Manual analysis techniques perform poorly under efficient scale-up requirements which leads to prolonged investigations along with unproductive resource distribution. The need for next-generation tools becomes crucial because they possess the ability to strengthen human analysis with objective computational accuracy. Although several studies explore AI applications in forensic investigations, most fail to critically assess the limitations of current methods when deployed in complex urban environments(Chinnikatti, 2018). For instance, conventional NLP-based systems in forensic linguistics primarily rely on surface-level syntactic features, sentiment scoring, or keyword detection, approaches that often fall short in handling nuanced or culturally embedded speech(Solà-Sales et al., 2023). Moreover, there is minimal cross-disciplinary integration between AI developers and forensic linguists, leading to tools that lack domain-specific accuracy and context sensitivity. Additionally, much of the literature overlooks the challenge of linguistic diversity in smart cities, with most models trained only on English or high-resource languages, thereby underrepresenting the populations most often involved in urban policing dynamics(Spiroiu, 2018).

Deep Belief Networks (DBNs) establish themselves as an advanced deep learning approach which optimises natural language processing (NLP) through complex linguistic analysis(Hinton, 2010). Handcrafted features are not required for conventional machine learning methods since DBNs use stacked Restricted Boltzmann Machines (RBMs) to automatically discover data latent representations through their hierarchical deep learning architecture. The pre-training process of unsupervised learning on big textual datasets helps DBNs build native knowledge about linguistic elements which extends from grammatical dependencies to word meaning associations. The next step includes supervised fine-tuning processes which allow these models to become focused on detecting deception or evaluating credibility. Such models excel at analysing high-dimensional unstructured data without needing human-made feature engineering. The variability and nuances present in human language while using code-switching with multilingual testimonies or displaying regional dialects makes DBNs an excellent choice to handle these situations. The incorporation of contextual metadata like timestamps and geolocation tags enables DBNs to establish connexions with external data streams such as surveillance footage for a more detailed analysis. DBNs provide better identification of distant dependencies in addition to hierarchical attributes that enables the network to detect subtle indicators of unreliable statements like emotional expressions and hedging phrases(Mishra et al., 2022).

Technological developments in AI for urban security and policing have increased considerably because authorities seek solutions to rising crime challenges in prevention and investigation(Baba et al., 2019). Predictive policing systems use machine learning to identify future crime zones and facial recognition applications help law enforcement to speed up criminal subject identification. DBNs continue to serve specific purposes in digital forensics by helping analysts understand large amounts of text-based evidence. DBN methods participate in decryption of indistinguishable cybercrime communications and perform authorship detection from anonymous threats and detect phishing attempts based on textual analysis. The unstructured IoT-generated data in smart cities can be processed in real-time with DBNs during emergency call analysis of social media content and witness testimony evaluation(Waheed et al., 2020). The system uses DBNs to sort emergency reports by severity through stress-based linguistic detection of voice disturbances along with strong negative language use. The existing implementations constrain their effectiveness since they deal with monolingual data which neglects the linguistic diversity of urban centres. The implementation of DBNs for automated testimony analysis encounters integration obstacles with existing law enforcement systems causing operational hurdles during adoption(Shah et al., 2021).

Fundamental obstacles exist in maintaining dependability when implementing AI testing algorithms for analysing court testimonies. The major obstacle in using AI for testimony analysis arises from natural differences in human communication which stem from cultural frames and emotional condition as well as level of linguistic expertise(Dunsin et al., 2024). The analysis may misidentify somebody under pressure because a trained algorithm uses standard “calm” language patterns to detect deception yet those under duress typically show fragmented sentences together with dramatic details. Multicultural testimonies containing non-standard grammar from regional areas risk being misread as contradictory by analysed systems(Skillicorn & Little, 2009). The insufficient number of diverse representative training datasets combined with dominant language and demographic group overrepresentation produces algorithmic biases in human truth detection systems. Trusted research demonstrates the prospect of adversarial training and synthetic data enhancement to counter biases however operational applications are still at a basic stage. The non-transparent nature of DBNs poses difficulties since police departments along with legal bodies need help understanding how features within linguistic data affect assessment results. The explainability methods such as attention mechanisms together with layer-wise relevance propagation (LRP) provide fragmentation but they fail to connect technical outputs to judicial standards of evidentiary assessment(Bibal et al., 2020).

The research gaps that exist when applying DBN to urban security purposes show multiple facets because they involve technical as well as ethical aspects. A priority exists for models that maintain high accuracy while performing multilingual and multilingual dialect generalisation. The existing DBN frameworks work optimally with high-resource languages like English while providing insufficient support to low-resource languages which creates a crucial problem in smart cities with worldwide connexions(Hedderich et al., 2021). Current work focuses little on creating portable lightweight versions of DBNs for implementation through edge computing systems thereby restricting their real-time application in restricted resource settings. The absence of standardised auditing protocols for algorithmic fairness in policing produces ethical risks that maintain and perpetuate systemic inequities(Richardson et al., 2019). The use of DBNs that feature historical law enforcement data could avoid recruiting specific linguistic expression patterns into patterns of criminality thereby creating more damage to underrepresented communities. A combination of computational linguistics research with criminology and ethics creates the foundation for solving existing knowledge gaps(Williams et al., 2016). Training enormous DBNs requires energy-intensive processes which have not yet been aligned with sustainability objectives and thus require energy-efficient architectural solutions. Academic organisations must work alongside law enforcement agencies and policymakers to push forward DBN system development that combines ethical principles with operational feasibility when maximising security potential in urban areas. Despite the growing interest in AI-assisted forensic methods, there remains a clear research gap in applying Deep Belief Networks to multilingual forensic linguistic contexts, particularly within smart policing frameworks(Spiroiu, 2018). This chapter responds to that gap by offering a practical, ethically grounded integration of DBNs with forensic linguistic methodologies. It further contributes a hybrid technical-legal framework for improving credibility analysis of witness testimonies in smart city environments, setting the groundwork for both future implementation and policy innovation.

METHODOLOGY

This section outlines the DBN architecture and its alignment with legal-ethical standards for urban forensic deployment. The study method incorporates a systematic framework which examines Deep Belief Networks' (DBNs) implementation inside forensic linguistics testimony analysis within Artificial Intelligence (AI)-based policing systems of smart cities. The DBN architecture development becomes central to this method because it detects linguistic evidence showing bias and deception and consistency issues in witness testimonies. Restrictive Boltzmann machines

(RBMs) organised in a hierarchical structure operate on multiple stages to extract progressive features from original textual information(Juola, 2019). The model analyses linguistic features at different processing levels which includes syntax and semantics and pragmatics to identify signals of unreliability through detecting hedging phrases and contradictions and emotional language. The first stage includes deploying unsupervised learning on validated testimonies to set weights before supervised learning on marked data sets to establish credibility ratings for statements. The combination techniques in this model maintain fundamental linguistic patterns along with specialised features needed for legal wording. The architecture implements dropout layers together with regularisation techniques for overfitting prevention in order to achieve optimal results when processing varied urban data sets(Ibrahim et al., 2024). To ensure model credibility and forensic admissibility, the proposed DBN framework can be validated using cross-validation on labeled testimony datasets, where expert-reviewed statements are categorized based on indicators of consistency and reliability. Evaluation metrics such as precision, recall, and F1 scores commonly used in NLP would enable comparative analysis with human expert judgment(Blessed et al., 2022). This structured approach can help demonstrate whether the model aligns with legal standards for evidentiary value in judicial contexts.

A meaningful way to assess the proposed DBN model would be through a comparative framework involving side-by-side evaluations with traditional forensic linguistic analysis. Human experts and the DBN could independently review a controlled dataset of testimonies to detect credibility markers such as narrative gaps, hedging, or linguistic overcompensation. Comparative outcomes, such as processing time, agreement levels, or disagreement zones can guide refinements in DBN design without displacing human interpretative authority.

The model requires the proper collection and preprocessing of testimony data for effective functionality. Data originates from sanitised police reports and court transcripts together with recorded interviews which public safety departments reviewed to present actual incidents found in smart cities(Gao et al., 2018). The data preprocessing consists of forcing verbalization through lemmatization with stop word elimination followed by sentence structure analysis and identifying specific terms within contexts. The envisioned training dataset may comprise approximately 1,000 to 1,200 anonymized witness statements drawn from public legal corpora, simulated court transcripts, and verified forensic sources. To reflect linguistic and social diversity, data selection would include metadata such as age, language, case type, and urban or rural origin. Multilingual and code-switched texts should be prioritized to ensure that the model can generalize effectively to smart city environments with high linguistic variance. The system adopts cross-lingual embeddings to process multilingual evidence so the DBN maintains relevant contextual information even with non-English material. Accessory inputs such as timestamps, geolocation data and demographic variables alongside testimonies help the network address the diverse nature of urban data. The model achieves enhanced pattern-tracking capabilities for situation dependencies by using situational variables including emergency stress variables and cultural sensitivities in multi-ethnic cities. Strict anonymization protocols protect personal information, so the data must fulfil GDPR and CCPA privacy requirements and other regulations(Gazi, 2020).

The analysis incorporates ethical aspects and privacy elements throughout its complete operational pipeline. The organisation follows governance frameworks that combine end-to-end encryption with role-based access controls to manage sensitive evidence in addition to verbal data. Informed consent protocols are integrated into data collection processes, particularly for testimonies sourced from community members, with transparency mechanisms to explain how their data will be used(Jol & Stommel, 2016). The aggregation of data includes differential privacy methods that apply fictional data to datasets to maintain analysis capability while reducing the risk of real individual identification. Layer-wise relevance propagation (LRP) serve as audit tools for the DBN's decision processes to determine how linguistic features affect credibility assessments. The system promotes responsibility because enforcement agencies can confirm the outcomes while the core algorithms remain confidential.

The essential part of this methodology deals with minimising biases in DBNs which stem from algorithms. The first step for bias mitigation focuses on dataset curation which requires maximising inclusivity for various population variables including age and gender and linguistic backgrounds to avoid minority underrepresentation(Srinivasan & Chander, 2021). The training process implements synthetic data generation for balancing minority groups together with adversarial debiasing methods that operate through secondary networks which detect and eliminate biased features. The evaluation process tracks fairness metrics consisting of equalised odds and demographic parity because their continuous assessment provides guaranteed equitable outcomes across all defined subgroups. The DBN receives new training datasets periodically which enables it to adjust to current linguistic patterns along with social expectations thus minimising persistent historical bias(Srivastava et al., 2024). The process involves multiple iterations of model review with legal experts alongside community stakeholders to produce outputs that fulfil both ethical standards of justice and public expectations in the model interpretation process.

This methodology creates an effective deployment method for DBNs in forensic linguistics through technical solutions that maintain ethical standards. The architecture fits various urban needs due to its language and cultural flexibility and its dedication to open systems while providing a scalable analysis solution for AI-led police leveraging testimony data. Thus the method makes significant progress in both urban security infrastructure capabilities and police-community relationship trust which ensures AI technology functions equitably rather than based on biassed criteria. To support replicability and auditability, explainability tools such as Layer-wise Relevance Propagation (LRP) could be integrated into the DBN architecture(Montavon et al., 2017). These tools make the model's decision-making more transparent by visually representing which linguistic features contributed most to a credibility assessment. In a forensic setting, such interpretability would enhance both legal defensibility and public trust, especially if paired with open-access documentation and role-based access controls. When implemented alongside privacy-first governance and explainable AI standards, DBNs can serve as trust-building instruments within modern law enforcement. Their integration into smart city systems must prioritize ethical co-design, public communication, and operational interoperability across policing, judiciary, and civil tech stakeholders. This ensures that AI tools like DBNs do not simply enhance surveillance but empower equitable, efficient, and citizen-centric urban policing. These methods build a foundation for scalable, replicable, and legally accountable DBN deployment in smart city law enforcement systems. These methods build a foundation for scalable, replicable, and legally accountable DBN deployment in smart city law enforcement systems.

CASE STUDY: HYPOTHETICAL URBAN POLICING SCENARIO

The following simulated scenario applies the DBN framework to a high-stress urban crime event involving multiple eyewitnesses. The application of Deep Belief Networks (DBNs) in forensic linguistics can be understood when we analyse a possible scenario from a smart city setting where one of the most prominent security incidents took place(Huang et al., 2018). Law enforcement responds swiftly to the incident by obtaining inconsistent testimonies from five witnesses about how the criminal appeared and conducted themselves during the robbery followed by their getaway. Traditional investigative methods would rely on manual cross-referencing of statements with surveillance footage, a process prone to human error and cognitive bias, especially when reconciling discrepancies in witness recollections(Skillicorn & Little, 2009). This situation uses the DBN framework to examine testimonies by structuring its evaluation using hierarchical components for linguistic pattern detection and metadata analysis(Vlek et al., 2014). The system analyses witness statement raw text while it identifies sentence complexity patterns along with semantic elements showing verb tense consistency along with pragmatic indicators which employ phrases that display doubt (Example: "I think," "maybe"). The DBN system enables operations with contextual data that matches timestamps for testimonies against footage timing and creates geographical links between details in statements to site locations. Supervised learning with multilingual testimony texts allows the network to discover patterns of authentic storeys by recognising temporal coherence and external evidence consistency. The DBN uses supervised fine-tuning to identify deceptive statements by evaluating them for likely deception while warning users about inconsistent essential information (e.g. mismatching clothing accounts) and unusual linguistic elements (e.g. sudden narrative perspective transformations).

In a real-world smart city context, DBNs would be embedded within urban security ecosystems that include real-time crime dashboards, IoT-enabled surveillance cameras, multilingual emergency response apps, and biometric access logs. As witness testimonies are gathered, whether from police stations, 911 calls, or mobile citizen reports, DBNs can analyze them on-the-fly and cross-reference them with digital trails, such as geolocation data or timestamped video surveillance, to flag inconsistencies or support corroborations. This integration strengthens both investigatory timelines and public trust in data-driven policing. The DBN method may demonstrates superior capabilities compared to conventional forensic linguistics practises because of its ability to identify distinctive advantages. The expertise of manual human analysts typically detects straightforward inconsistencies between witness testimonies but fails to spot less apparent deception indicators like detailed storytelling of unimportant details which evidence "truth-lie storytelling"(Brennen & Magnussen, 2023). The DBN system transforms the linguistic complexities it detects through an analysis of lexical diversity along with sentiment polarity and syntactic complexity among testimonies. The model links noticeable signs of stress in witness statements like excessive "um" and "uh" sounds and "terrified" and "panicked" words to possible inaccuracies. When fake statements have been rehearsed the testifiers exhibit highly formalised language patterns while following a strict chronological order. The DBN produces a sequence of ranked testimony statements through probabilistic scoring which directs detectives to direct their resources to the most important statements first. The analytical system deploys data-based procedures to eliminate bias from human-based assessment processes due to elements like a person's public conduct and family financial status. The DBN offers real-time analysis of multilingual evidence which proves significant in diverse smart cities since investigators encounter witnesses speaking different languages along with non-standard expressions that could trick analysts.

The application of DBN-enhanced testimony analysis creates outcomes which surpass operational benefits to influence major social implications. The hypothetical robbery case benefits from transparent AI tool execution which builds community trust because it proves credibility evaluations depend on non-biassed linguistic measurement processes. In testimony analysis the DBN provides explainable features which through heatmaps display deceptive phrases that enable law enforcement to demonstrate their investigative procedures to the general public. The system's open transparency becomes essential in urban areas because such places tend to have tense police-community relations that could otherwise prevent AI adoption. The connection of DBNs with city security systems especially real-time monitoring networks and crisis communication systems enables fast threat identification. With identifiable patterns from previous robbery occurrences present in the training data of the DBN the system could warn patrolling units in nearby areas beforehand thereby stopping the crime before it occurred. Despite this abstract scenario the situation demonstrates the importance of implementing strict defensive measures. Database results from the DBN receive physical evidence verification such as CCTV footage and forensic data in order to maintain human expertise while using AI. The system employs trained tools for adversarial debiasing which use demographic datasets to shield its operations from reinforcing stereotypes about dialects and speech patterns that link to criminal actions.

Beyond post-incident analysis, DBNs can assist in proactive security measures within predictive policing models. For instance, if trained on patterns of previously deceptive testimonies or witness stress markers from emergency call transcripts, the model can alert law enforcement units to possible misinformation in early reports allowing more precise deployment of resources. Such pre-emptive identification of unreliable accounts supports faster resolution and mitigates wrongful detention risks in fast-moving urban environments. This hypothetical case study demonstrates how forensic linguistics using DBN technology establishes peaceful coexistence between technological progress and ethical standards in modern smart city management(József, 2022). The model supports both huge volumes of multilingual testimonies and meets urban police force scaling requirements and guarantees justice system transparency as it enhances fairness operations. Future development versions should add real-time emergency call voice analysis for dispatcher decision support by establishing emergency call credibility assessments. On the other hand, unresolved challenges appear from this scenario that include making sure every jurisdiction gets equal access to AI tools despite different resource levels and stopping the possibility of officer reliance on algorithm recommendations without proper evaluation. The refinement of DBN applications requires permanent collaboration among stakeholders because it necessitates both community input on police work and independent oversight panels to ensure public security combined with protection of civil freedoms(Hung & Yen, 2023). The case underscores how DBNs can complement traditional investigation by offering consistent, scalable testimony analysis in multilingual settings.

COLLABORATION BETWEEN LAW ENFORCEMENT, AI EXPERTS, AND POLICYMAKERS

AI-driven policing needs a powerful collaboration scheme between law enforcement agencies and AI developers and policymakers to implement Deep Belief Networks (DBNs) in forensic linguistics testimony analysis(Alzou'bi et al., 2014). These three groups of stakeholders maintain essential functions to guarantee that technological progress suits ethical and legal standards and societal requirements. Law enforcement agencies deliver operational field input about urban policing needs such as multilingual smart city testimonies together with AI developers who enhance the DBN model design for these requirements. Policymakers develop regulatory guidelines which control AI tool deployment while they maintain successful innovation alongside civil liberties defence(El-Ghalayini & Al-Kandari, 2020). The absence of this collaborative approach puts systems at risk because it enables them to become technically competent while showing little concern for ethics or becoming legally proper yet practically flawed. When DBN models solely rely on technical benchmarks for training without legal subject matter expertise the system could unintentionally strengthen biases found in past policing data which compromises its fairness. The implementation of regulations which fail to recognise AI technology limits might stop innovation and create operational deficits that reduce law enforcement preparedness to counter new urban security threats. AI-driven policing requires long-term communication efforts between these groups to unite both operational effectiveness and ethical standards.

Interdisciplinary collaborations hold a crucial part in enhancing the accuracy and reducing bias of DBN applications for better accountability. Testimony analysis DBN development requires repeated phases of testing between AI experts and forensic linguists to maintain both high accuracy and clear interpretation of results(Nayerifard et al., 2023). The focus of AI developers on processing large datasets drives algorithmic efficiency while forensic linguists demand the model to detect specific contextual elements such as regional dialects and cultural idioms because they influence testimony reliability. Layer-wise relevance propagation (LRP) and similar explainability mechanisms become mandatory through policymaker-imposed transparency requirements which guide how DBN produces its credibility evaluations. Joint task forces made up of representatives from the three groups work together to design bias mitigation approaches that include adversarial debiasing during training and synthetic data generation for distributing equal representation among underrepresented demographics. The collaborative process continues after deployment when law enforcement personnel conduct DBN performance assessments of actual cases to report discrepancies between computed results and human investigator decisions. The audit process provides feedback that engineers use to modernise their algorithm by enabling it to understand shifting linguistic developments and societal perception shifts(Hadley, 2022). The iterative partnership approach turns static DBN tools into dynamic systems which evolve with their service communities to create robust systems with social acceptance.

The fundamental practises for maintaining public trust in AI-assisted legal processes consist of transparency and communication(Thiebes et al., 2020). To gain trust from diverse populations of smart cities about AI in policing it is vital that law enforcement agencies take proactive steps to explain how DBN systems process testimonies in these populations. Local law enforcement agencies should work with civic organisations to lead public forums about technology features and boundaries which demonstrate that DBNs work to enhance investigator capabilities rather than function without human assistance. AI developers should either free their framework code through open-source platforms or produce complete documentation which explains the DBN logic to help third-party researchers verify its functionality. Public institutions should create and enforce laws which mandate police agencies to reveal their AI system usage during investigations together with the algorithms' contributions to investigative processes(Gilpin et al., 2019). A mandatory requirement should force DBN credibility scores to come with human-friendly descriptions demonstrating the linguistic elements (such as tense inconsistency and hedging language) that stimulated the assessment. Such transparent practises build trust between the public and defence law personnel who reserve the right to challenge AI conclusions before judge's courts. Models must present their methodologies publicly yet protecting specific details about their structure and input information to prevent attackers from finding ways to exploit the system. Permanent stakeholder negotiations for risk-based balancing act need ongoing monitoring through survey data and risk evaluation(Crowther et al., 2010).

The use of AI in police work requires equal technology distribution between different city districts for its operations to maintain validity. Government decisions about allocating resources between wealthy and impoverished areas will likely worsen existing equality problems when DBN systems are deployed in a selective manner(Frieden, 1965). Policymakers alongside law enforcement need to develop funding systems that will provide AI benefits to every jurisdiction while developers should create basic DBN variants that operate without online connexions or minimal hardware requirements for low-resource areas. Oversight committees should integrate community representatives because their participation ensures proper assessment of algorithmic fairness within DBN applications that prevent discrimination against marginalised groups. DBNs operating in multilingual cities should accept assessments in various languages or dialects according to recommendations from community representatives so linguistic biases cannot distort credibility evaluations(Ramesh et al., 2023). The implementation of inclusive governance frameworks advances both

AI tool efficiency and builds their legitimacy as tools for protection above surveillance systems. The AI lifecycle should integrate collaboration throughout its phases from device creation to deployment then monitoring and design modification so stakeholders build an environment with technology acting as a connexion between law enforcement and their protected communities.

DISCUSSION

With the technical and applied model in place, this section now considers legal, ethical, and public trust issues essential to deployment. Deep Belief Networks (DBNs) integrated into forensic linguistic analysis brings practical advantages to urban law enforcement when used for AI-driven policing in smart cities. The primary benefit of using DBNs lies in their capability to efficiently handle big testimonial data analysis. Law enforcement in heavily populated urban areas must tackle massive volumes of evidence such as witness testimonies and digital communication data and emergency phone calls during emergency situations. The analysing process of testimonies through traditional methods requires expensive and prolonged scrutiny by forensic linguists that delays criminal investigations. During the Oakland County Michigan mass shooting investigation in 2021 Cellebrite's Pathfinder alongside other AI tools processed digital evidence from social media platforms text messages as well as location data(Xi et al., 2024). The tools employed linguistic pattern comparison methods to build timelines and detect ties that escaped human evaluation. The undisclosed system architecture did not reveal the specific network structure (e.g., DBNs) even though it demonstrated fundamental similar processing capabilities when analysing large language datasets that deep learning models like DBNs offer. During the investigation of a fentanyl-related murder case in Texas AI technology enabled the quick breakdown of digital device data by discovering important drug suppliers through analysis of the drug trafficking patterns in communication sessions. The speeded-up criminal case handling demonstrated the potential of AI to tackle complex linguistic aspects during analysis of criminal investigations(Police1, 2024).

Information evaluation that includes detecting linguistic patterns becomes faster through DBN automation which analyses inconsistencies together with deceit markers and credibility indicators in real time(Aditya et al., 2018). The system speeds up investigations and raises credibility assessment precision levels through automated bias-minimised analysis. The evaluation process of syntactic and semantic indicators by DBNs enables automatic identification of testimonial information that matches external forensic records such as surveillance evidence or scientific data. The data-driven methodology helps criminal justice organisations distribute their assets more efficiently which allows law enforcement agencies to quickly tackle developing security threats while enhancing community safety. By introducing DBNs the analysis process achieves results that possess an objective standard which traditional approaches would find impossible to match. Experts in human analysis demonstrate limitations because their awareness remains subject to unconscious prejudice from aspects such as witness behaviour combined with communication abilities or social origins. The presence of unconscious preferences leads people to evaluate credibility in ways that produce incorrect judgments. The analysis process in DBNs depends on numeric linguistic measurements like lexical diversity and syntactic complexity together with sentiment polarity because these metrics reduce instances of subjective interpretation. Through its analysis the model identifies minimal verbal indicators including both cautious verbalizations and drastic changes in storytelling perspective that suggest possible deception or doubt. The application of DBNs delivers standardised reliability assessment tools that assign probabilistic scores to analysis of witness statements to decrease risks of subjective and inconsistent evaluation results.

DBN proves most useful in diverse multiethnic cities since it reduces subjectivity during assessment which becomes complicated due to various languages and cultural intricacies. The combination of multilingual embeddings and cross-lingual training data enables DBNs to analyse statements from speakers with different linguistic backgrounds thus providing unbiased treatment to all witnesses. Several difficulties remain unresolved in the field of linguistic equality. A research analysis of ChatGPT's survey simulation across six international nations (USA, Sweden, Singapore, Brazil, Japan, South Africa) demonstrated substantial performance disparities which reached their lowest points in non-English speaking nations of Japan and South Africa(Nigatu et al., 2024). AI systems including DBNs should actively work to reduce biases because they play an essential role during multilingual forensic investigations. AI tools within Kazakhstan function at a reduced capacity because the Kazakh language has minimal digital presence thus creating obstacles for translation and voice recognition processes across regions speaking this language. AI model development (such as DBNs) requires focus on diverse linguistic contexts because it impacts low-resource languages specifically(Strassel, S., & Tracey, J. 2016).

One of the most pressing ethical concerns in deploying DBNs for forensic linguistic analysis lies in algorithmic bias(Кокин & Denisov, 2023). DBNs trained on datasets that overrepresent dominant linguistic groups may misinterpret non-standard grammar or dialectical variations from minority communities as indicators of deception. This poses a significant fairness risk, especially in multicultural smart city environments. Without proactive bias mitigation, such as adversarial training, inclusion of low-resource dialect data, and demographic auditing, DBNs may perpetuate or even exacerbate systemic inequalities within policing and legal procedures.

Another key issue is the legal admissibility of AI-generated forensic outputs. In jurisdictions that follow evidentiary standards such as the Daubert Rule (U.S.) or sections of the Indian Evidence Act, AI tools must demonstrate scientific validity, reliability, and transparency. For DBNs to be considered admissible, their inner workings though complex, must be interpretable through mechanisms like Layer-wise Relevance Propagation (LRP) or attention heatmaps. Moreover, the ability for legal professionals and judges to scrutinize, replicate, and challenge AI-based credibility scores becomes vital to ensure due process and procedural fairness.

The application of DBNs in analyzing sensitive verbal data also raises significant privacy and data protection concerns. Witness testimonies often contain personal, cultural, or emotional information that must be safeguarded. Smart city infrastructures connected via IoT and surveillance systems may amplify privacy vulnerabilities when verbal data is cross-referenced with location tracking or biometric metadata. To address this, any deployment of DBN-based analysis tools must adhere to strict anonymization protocols, differential privacy standards, and role-based data access. Legal frameworks such as the GDPR and India's DPDP Act should inform implementation models to ensure accountability and community trust(Bareh, 2024).

As smart city policing evolves, DBNs can become vital tools in managing the informational overload facing urban law enforcement. With cities deploying real-time monitoring tools, wearable police cameras, and automated threat detection systems, DBNs offer an interpretable AI solution tailored to the linguistic complexities of urban populations. Their ability to process multilingual, emotionally varied, and culturally diverse statements in real time makes them uniquely suited to address the operational challenges of AI-driven urban security models.

Ethical considerations remain paramount. Strategic data privacy protections must exist in smart cities because their surveillance systems and IoT devices repeatedly gather personal information about witness locations as well as their identities and communication patterns. Data protection depends on encryption protocols and access controls based on user roles and anonymization techniques to stop unauthorised use and access(Perera et al., 2014). Algorithmic bias has become a major obstacle that creates difficulties for information usage. DBNs will generate discriminatory results when the training datasets do not reflect the actual linguistic and demographic characteristics of urban residents. The predominant use of testimonies collected from one specific demographic during training creates difficulties for the system in asking credibility questions to populations that are not well-represented which results in sustained discriminatory effects. Two approaches for mitigating biases entail creating synthetic data to achieve dataset balance for minority populations and implementing adversarial debiasing through auxiliary networks which recognise and eliminate biassed attributes in training processes. Integration of fairness metrics that include equalised odds and demographic parity into model evaluation enables the assessment of performance between different subgroups. The same importance belongs to transparency tools because they reveal which linguistic characteristics lead to credibility evaluation results. An explainability interface provides the ability to see how a DBN labels a testimony as unreliable because of inconsistent verb tenses which allows investigators to confirm assessment decisions(Sokol & Flach, 2020). The implementation of such procedures improves fairness levels while demonstrating strict AI tool management which establishes public trust.

The positive effects of DBNs in society include developing fair security systems throughout urban areas. These models enhance both the precision and operational speed of testimony evaluation which leads to superior crime investigation methods. The quick analysis of DBNs examines witness testimony to extract important information about suspects and escape paths thus allowing police departments to initiate pre-emptive action during major incidents or emergencies(Keppens et al., 2010). The approach matches the smart city concept of developing protective ecosystems that respond immediately to defend residents. The deployment of this system requires equal application throughout different population segments. Community outreach activities including town hall gatherings and educational sessions help explain AI processing of testimonies by addressing public reservations about privacy preservation and unbiased procedures. Public officials have the essential responsibility to create regulatory systems which enforce transparency alongside oversight operations. Law enforcement agencies should be required to provide public disclosures about their use of DBNs in investigations as well as explain the ways neural networks contribute to decisions through new legislation which supports transparency.

Research advancements, such as a 2017 study exploring pointer-generator networks for legal text summarization, suggest future applications for DBNs in analyzing witness testimonies or legal documents. Research continues to face challenges regarding decision support systems for low-resource languages as well as energy-efficient DBN versions compatible with edge computing systems. Law enforcement together with academics and policymakers need to collaborate for developing DBN solutions that remain ethical and operational. The implementation of fairness and inclusivity principles during every phase of AI development from data preparation to system operation allows stakeholders to create justice-serving tools that link urban security needs with innovation through transparent programmes(Khan et al., 2023). These legal and ethical considerations are not merely theoretical, they directly affect the legitimacy and societal acceptance of AI tools in law enforcement. For DBNs to be integrated into urban security infrastructures, developers and decision-makers must co-design systems that meet both technical efficiency and ethical compliance. Community oversight boards, external audits, and regulatory compliance checkpoints will be essential to ensure these tools function as protective, not punitive, instruments in smart city policing. Addressing these concerns is essential for aligning technological advancement with constitutional rights and community acceptance.

FUTURE DIRECTIONS

The developments made in Deep Belief Networks (DBNs) for forensic linguistics enable new potential applications extending outside testimony analysis toward AI-enhanced forensic capabilities which support urban security goals in smart cities(Scanlon et al., 2023). The hierarchical learning features of DBNs demonstrate potential to analyse different linguistic evidence besides witness credibility which includes written threats and ransom notes together with digital communications in criminal investigations. Network DBNs can detect gang-related coded language patterns as well as determine anonymous cyber threat authorship through recognition of stylistic patterns including syntax and vocabulary and punctuation. The combination of DBNs with speech recognition systems enables sentiment analysis of emergency 911 calls because DBNs can perform real-time assessment to identify high-stress reports among deceptive narratives(Wang & Gao, 2017). The latent capabilities of Recurrent Variational Autoencoders include unifying voice authentication features with suspect identification tools and detection abilities for tampered audio found in surveillance evidence. Public communication channels across languages are assessable through multilingual DBNs within multilingual urban environments to detect recurring linguistic patterns that signal organised crime events including human trafficking and drug distribution(Tong et al., 2017). The proposed developments allocate DBNs to achieve smart city threats prevention goals thus creating hybrid tools for various forensic needs while reinforcing accuracy and scalability together with ethical standards.

A real-time deployment of DBN applications inside smart city ecosystems enables police departments to adopt predictive and responsive security strategies(Mandalapu et al., 2023). Collaborating DBNs with IoT sensors as well as surveillance networks and social media analytics allows law enforcement to move from reactive crime-solving to threat management which operates proactively. Crime prevention models developed by DBNs that merge historical violation data with currently captured urban observations regarding pedestrian flow and environmental conditions would create likely areas for violence and theft to help police scheduling. Real-time DBN systems monitor social media posts and video footage from emergency calls combined with CCTV images to find alert signs that tensions are increasing through aggressive speech and panic-related messages which automatically notify command centres(Anderez et al., 2021). Such a system would empower law enforcement to alter resource distribution dynamically and deliver specific communications for situation deflation or facilitate joint team operations. During forensic crisis oversight DBNs display the capacity to swiftly examine witness reports and social media information for the recovery of procedural sequences and breakthrough investigative breakthroughs(Koroniotis et al., 2020). Real-time applications need improved computational infrastructure which should include edge computing frameworks to cut down latency periods and federated learning systems to secure decentralised data processing. The innovations would make DBNs core elements of responsive urban security architectures to manage operational efficiency alongside smart city dynamism.

Recent policing trends involving DBNs need policymakers to create strong ethical standards with governance frameworks which protect against privacy harm and algorithmic bias and technological limitations(Park, 2023). The disclosure of information about DBN training data must become mandatory for law enforcement through legislative initiatives which establish requirements for independent oversight bodies to retain knowledge about data origins and demographic balance and data processing procedures. Secure privacy measures require law enforcement to establish data retention limits of unprocessed testimony data while implementing strong anonymization methods like differential privacy and synthetic data approaches for maintaining user privacy. The mandatory implementation of bias audits for DBN systems by policymakers would establish a requirement for developers to prove that DBN systems comply with fairness metrics which ensure proportional false positive rates among different demographic groups before system deployment becomes possible(Hinnefeld et al., 2018). Sustainability measures must take priority during the deployment of DBN systems to avoid operational and environmental exhaustion. Energy-efficient DBN architectures developed specifically for low-power hardware systems would help decrease data centre carbon emissions when supporting AI-based policing applications. Governments should establish financial rewards by means of tax benefits and grants to provoke the creation of sustainable AI solutions through ventures between technical enterprises and educational organisations. International collaboration plays an essential role to standardise rules especially in connecting smart city networks across borders and this ensures both cultural and legal differences are respected and universal human rights principles are maintained(Iaione et al., 2019).

Law enforcement agencies must invest in continuous AI training programmes for their personnel because this develops effective and ethical applications of DBNs in their field. Police training courses must adapt by adding instructions about DBN system capabilities together with their boundaries alongside ethical considerations. A simulation platform should present scenarios to train police officers about how DBN results help them make decisions in real-life situations by showing them how to assess algorithm-based recommendations along with environmental influences such as witness safety concerns. The training curriculum for forensic linguists combined with data analysts must teach them to understand the outputs from DBNs including credibility scores accompanied by linguistic heatmaps for proper integration with existing investigative methods(Wickramasekara et al., 2024). Agencies should create collective spaces for officers and developers to partner with community members for designing training materials that match operational demands and public expectations to overcome resistance toward AI adoption. AI ethics certification programmes combined with quarterly algorithmic advancement education would enable continuous expertise development for personnel about emerging risks consisting of attacks against DBN models and modern linguistic manipulation methods. The instructional programmes should teach officers about the public trust consequences which result from improper or biassed AI usage by emphasising the social impacts of DBNs. Law enforcement agencies can build a workforce that effectively uses DBNs as multipliers through their professional development programme which integrates ethical AI literacy standards.

The future of DBN technology for building fair security systems depends on continuous innovation alongside inclusive governance while cities achieve intensified connectivity. Research in the future should examine database and symbolic AI integration that allows investigators to see which linguistic rules (for example grammatical inconsistencies) exactly impact credibility evaluation. The integration of social scientists in research can help DBNs identify different dialects and communication patterns to eliminate misevaluation bias when analysing testimonies from underrepresented groups. Deployments of real-time DBNs using 5G networks with decentralised AI systems will enable distributed operations of centralised servers(Santos et al., 2020). Policy makers should establish experimental urban testing initiatives in towns of all sizes as well as major cities to generate factual information which will enable them to refine regulatory frameworks that can be scaled up effectively. The future development of DBNs in forensic linguistics depends on their achievement of social value equilibrium with their innovative technical capabilities to create cities that support justice enhancement through technology.

CONCLUSION

This final section synthesizes the chapter's findings and outlines recommendations for responsible integration of DBNs into smart city law enforcement systems. This chapter set out to explore how Deep Belief Networks (DBNs) may enhance forensic linguistic analysis by automating the credibility assessment of witness statements in AI-driven policing environments. By combining theoretical insights from forensic linguistics, smart city policing needs, and explainable AI, the chapter proposed a structured framework for applying DBNs in diverse urban settings. While empirical validation remains a future step, the proposed model presents a technically feasible and ethically aware approach to improving the efficiency, consistency, and transparency of testimony analysis. Future research could focus on empirical trials using real-world linguistic data, legal admissibility testing, and bias mitigation protocols. For policymakers and law enforcement stakeholders, the chapter offers a conceptual roadmap for responsibly integrating DBN-assisted tools into forensic workflows while maintaining public trust and legal fairness.

To ensure responsible implementation, law enforcement agencies should invest in AI literacy training and develop internal protocols for reviewing AI-generated outputs. Policymakers must mandate transparency audits and algorithmic fairness assessments as part of standard digital forensic practice. Moreover, inter-agency collaboration with technologists, linguists, and civil society actors is necessary to create AI tools that are accurate, explainable, and compatible with democratic accountability in urban policing.

The emerging artificial intelligence technology of DBNs shifts traditional legal systems to objective and transparent processes because they replace human interpretation. Traditional forensic linguistics depends on human factors while the DBN process calculates linguistic measures in an unbiased manner. An example of DBN functionality demonstrates how credibility scores are calculated through the analysis of linguistic elements including words, emotions and sentence structures thus minimising subjective opinions during evaluation. Interpretability tools like Layer-wise Relevance Propagation (LRP) could enhance legal defensibility and transparency by allowing forensic experts and judges to understand which linguistic elements influenced DBN outputs. When applied thoughtfully, such mechanisms may support fairness in multicultural settings and help ensure equal treatment of witness testimonies across language groups. Standardizing credibility assessments and applying accountability mechanisms can elevate DBNs from technical innovation to legally and socially legitimate forensic tools. The success of this technology depends on multi-disciplinary cooperation which illustrates itself through AI developer and forensic linguist and policymaker collaboration. Collaborations between different groups refine DBN architectures through the integration of technical demands along with ethical needs such as algorithmic bias elimination and privacy safeguards.

The ethical implementation of DBNs in smart cities demands ongoing research to address unresolved challenges and optimize their societal impact. The accomplishments of adversarial debiasing and synthetic data generation for discriminating algorithm reduction need additional progress to make these models fit diverse language patterns and cultural communication forms in an evolving world. DBN training should incorporate diverse urban population attributes since neglecting minority languages and sociolects may create systemic discrimination. The practical use of

DBNs in predictive policing and social media analytics at public events demands improved edge computing capabilities and federated learning methods to maintain data security and decrease real-time response delays. The essential function of lawmakers consists of creating rules which define transparency standards that require both public announcements of AI utilisation in investigations and direct supervisor review of algorithm-generated results. Energy-efficient DBN architectures must receive legislative backing because this will help promote alignment with sustainability goals to avoid aggravating environmental impacts from AI-driven policing. Hazardous training programmes for law enforcement specialists need to combine with ongoing education that develops technical understanding and ethical mindsets among personnel to ensure proper assessment and responsible use of DBN information.

Future research must explore how DBNs can be combined with symbolic reasoning, multilingual AI, and audio forensics to extend their utility beyond textual witness statements. Their use in voice authentication, tampering detection, and emergency call screening could reinforce broader urban security systems. As AI becomes embedded in law enforcement, longitudinal studies are essential to evaluate its social impact especially in marginalized communities. Strong community engagement and interdisciplinary oversight should guide DBN deployments to ensure they remain aligned with ethical norms and civil liberties throughout the AI lifecycle. As urban policing evolves, DBN-assisted forensic tools must be guided by fairness, transparency, and collaborative governance frameworks.

REFERENCES

Aditya, K., Grzonkowski, S., & Le-Khac, N. (2018). *Enabling Trust in Deep Learning Models: A Digital Forensics Case Study.*, DOI: 10.1109/TrustCom/BigDataSE.2018.00172

Aizenberg, E., & van den Hoven, J. (2020). Designing for human rights in AI. In Big Data & Society (Vol. 7, Issue 2). SAGE Publishing. DOI: 10.1177/2053951720949566

Alzou'bi, S., Alshibl, H., & Al-Ma'aitah, M. (2014). Artificial Intelligence in Law Enforcement, A Review. In International Journal of Advanced Information Technology (Vol. 4, Issue 4, p. 1). DOI: 10.5121/ijait.2014.4401

Anderez, D. O., Kanjo, E., Amnwar, A., Johnson, S. D., & Lucy, D. (2021). The Rise of Technology in Crime Prevention: Opportunities, Challenges and Practitioners Perspectives. In arXiv (Cornell University). Cornell University. https://doi.org//arxiv.2102.04204DOI: 10.48550

Baba, M., Gui, V., & Pescaru, D. (2019). Deep Learning Approach for Violence Detection in Urban Areas. In ITM Web of Conferences (Vol. 29, p. 3009). EDP Sciences. DOI: 10.1051/itmconf/20192903009

Bareh, C. K. (2024). Reviewing the Privacy Implications of Indias Digital Personal Data Protection Act (2023) from Library Contexts. *DESIDOC Journal of Library and Information Technology*, *44*(1), 50–58. DOI: 10.14429/djlit.44.1.18410

Bibal, A., Lognoul, M., Streel, A. de, & Frénay , B. (2020). Legal requirements on explainability in machine learning. In Artificial Intelligence and Law (Vol. 29, Issue 2, p. 149). Springer Science+Business Media. DOI: 10.1007/s10506-020-09270-4

Blessed, G., Kontagora, N. B., Agajo, J., & Aliyu, I. (2022). Performance Evaluation of Keyword Extraction Techniques and Stop Word Lists on Speech-To-Text Corpus. *The International Arab Journal of Information Technology*, *20*(1). Advance online publication. DOI: 10.34028/iajit/20/1/14

Brennen, T., & Magnussen, S. (2023). Lie Detection: What Works? In Current Directions in Psychological Science (Vol. 32, Issue 5, p. 395). SAGE Publishing. DOI: 10.1177/09637214231173095

Chinnikatti, S. K. (2018). Artificial Intelligence in Forensic Science. *Forensic Science & Addiction Research*, *2*(5). Advance online publication. DOI: 10.31031/FSAR.2018.03.000554

Crowther, K. G., Haimes, Y. Y., & Johnson, M. E. (2010). Principles for Better Information Security through More Accurate, Transparent Risk Scoring. In Journal of Homeland Security and Emergency Management (Vol. 7, Issue 1). De Gruyter. DOI: 10.2202/1547-7355.1658

Deep Belief Networks for phone recognition. (2023). http://www.cs.toronto.edu/~gdahl/papers/dbnPhoneRec.pdf

Dunsin, D. C., Ghanem, M., Ouazzane, K., & Vassilev, V. (2024). A comprehensive analysis of the role of artificial intelligence and machine learning in modern digital forensics and incident response. In *Forensic science international. Digital investigation* (Vol. 48, p. 301675). Elsevier BV., DOI: 10.1016/j.fsidi.2023.301675

El-Ghalayini, Y., & Al-Kandari, H. (2020). Big Data Regulatory Legislation: Security, Privacy and Smart City Governance. In Journal of Law Policy and Globalization. IISTE. DOI: 10.7176/JLPG/95-03

Frieden, B. J. (1965). TOWARD EQUALITY OF URBAN OPPORTUNITY. In Journal of the American Institute of Planners (Vol. 31, Issue 4, p. 320). Taylor & Francis. DOI: 10.1080/01944366508978186

Gao, P., Xu, Z., & Gao, S. (2018). Data Explosion Model for Public Safety Data Processing and Its Application in a Unified Security System. In Lecture notes in electrical engineering (p. 448). Springer Science+Business Media. DOI: 10.1007/978-981-10-7398-4_46

Gazi, T. (2020). Data to the rescue: how humanitarian aid NGOs should collect information based on the GDPR. In Journal of International Humanitarian Action (Vol. 5, Issue 1). Springer Nature. DOI: 10.1186/s41018-020-00078-0

Gilpin, L. H., Testart, C., Fruchter, N., & Adebayo, J. (2019). Explaining Explanations to Society. In arXiv (Cornell University). Cornell University. https://doi.org//arxiv.1901.06560DOI: 10.48550

Hadley, E. (2022). Prioritizing Policies for Furthering Responsible Artificial Intelligence in the United States. In arXiv (Cornell University). Cornell University. https://doi.org//arxiv.2212.00740DOI: 10.48550

Hedderich, M. A., Lange, L., Adel, H., Strötgen, J., & Klakow, D. (2021). A Survey on Recent Approaches for Natural Language Processing in Low-Resource Scenarios. In *Proceedings of the 2022 Conference of the North American Chapter of the Association for Computational Linguistics: Human Language Technologies*. DOI: 10.18653/v1/2021.naacl-main.201

Hinnefeld, J. H., Cooman, P., Mammo, N., & Deese, R. (2018). Evaluating Fairness Metrics in the Presence of Dataset Bias. In arXiv (Cornell University). Cornell University. https://doi.org//arxiv.1809.09245DOI: 10.48550

Hinton, G. E. (2010). Deep Belief Nets. In Encyclopedia of Machine Learning (p. 267). DOI: 10.1007/978-0-387-30164-8_208

Huang, C., Zhang, J., Zheng, Y., & Chawla, N. V. (2018). DeepCrime. DOI: 10.1145/3269206.3271793

Hung, T.-W., & Yen, C.-P. (2023). Predictive policing and algorithmic fairness. In Synthese (Vol. 201, Issue 6). Springer Science+Business Media. DOI: 10.1007/s11229-023-04189-0

Iaione, C., Nictolis, E. D., & Suman, A. B. (2019). The Internet of Humans (IoH): Human Rights and Co-Governance to Achieve Tech Justice in the City. In Law & Ethics of Human Rights (Vol. 13, Issue 2, p. 263). De Gruyter. DOI: 10.1515/lehr-2019-2008

Ibrahim, M. A., Handoyo, A. T., & Anggreainy, M. S. (2024). Hybrid Deep Learning for Legal Text Analysis: Predicting Punishment Durations in Indonesian Court Rulings. In arXiv (Cornell University). Cornell University. https://doi.org//arxiv.2410.20104DOI: 10.48550

Jol, G., & Stommel, W. (2016). Ethical considerations of secondary data use. In Dutch Journal of Applied Linguistics (Vol. 5, Issue 2, p. 180). John Benjamins Publishing Company. DOI: 10.1075/dujal.5.2.06jol

József, P. (2022). How safe is your smart city? In Interdisciplinary Description of Complex Systems (Vol. 20, Issue 1, p. 57). Croatian Interdisciplinary Society. DOI: 10.7906/indecs.20.1.8

Juola, P. (2019). Artificial Intelligence and Pattern Evidence: A Legal Application for AI.

Keppens, J., Shen, Q., & Price, C. (2010). Compositional Bayesian modelling for computation of evidence collection strategies. In Applied Intelligence (Vol. 35, Issue 1, p. 134). Springer Science+Business Media. DOI: 10.1007/s10489-009-0208-5

Khan, A. A., Akbar, M. A., Fahmideh, M., Liang, P., Waseem, M., Ahmad, A., Niazi, M., & Abrahamsson, P. (2023). AI Ethics: An Empirical Study on the Views of Practitioners and Lawmakers. In IEEE Transactions on Computational Social Systems (Vol. 10, Issue 6, p. 2971). Institute of Electrical and Electronics Engineers. DOI: 10.1109/TCSS.2023.3251729

Кокин, A. B., & Denisov, Yu. D. (2023). Artificial Intelligence in Criminalistics and Forensic Examination: Issues of Legal Personality and Algorithmic Bias. *Theory and Practice of Forensic Science*, *18*(2), 30–37. DOI: 10.30764/1819-2785-2023-2-30-37

Koroniotis, N., Moustafa, N., & Sitnikova, E. (2020). A new network forensic framework based on deep learning for Internet of Things networks: A particle deep framework. In *Future Generation Computer Systems* (Vol. 110, p. 91). Elsevier BV., DOI: 10.1016/j.future.2020.03.042

Mandalapu, V., Elluri, L., Vyas, P., & Roy, N. (2023). Crime Prediction Using Machine Learning and Deep Learning: A Systematic Review and Future Directions. In Access, I. E. E. E. (Ed.), Vol. 11, p. 60153). Institute of Electrical and Electronics Engineers., DOI: 10.1109/ACCESS.2023.3286344

Mishra, S., Yadav, S. S., Yadav, S., Verma, P., & Ojha, S. (2022). Artificial Intelligence: An Advanced Evolution In Forensic and Criminal Investigation. In Current forensic science (Vol. 1). Bentham Science Publishers. DOI: 10.2174/266648440 1666220819111603

Mohamed, A., Dahl, G. E., & Hinton, G. E. (2011). Acoustic Modeling Using Deep Belief Networks. In IEEE Transactions on Audio Speech and Language Processing (Vol. 20, Issue 1, p. 14). Institute of Electrical and Electronics Engineers. DOI: 10.1109/TASL.2011.2109382

Montavon, G., Samek, W., & Müller, K. (2017). Methods for interpreting and understanding deep neural networks. *Digital Signal Processing*, *73*, 1–15. DOI: 10.1016/j.dsp.2017.10.011

Nayerifard, T., Amintoosi, H., Bafghi, A. G., & Dehghantanha, A. (2023). Machine Learning in Digital Forensics: A Systematic Literature Review. In arXiv (Cornell University). Cornell University. https://doi.org//arxiv.2306.04965DOI: 10.48550

Nigatu, H. H., Tonja, A. L., Rosman, B., Solorio, T., & Choudhury, M. (2024). The Zeno's Paradox of 'Low-Resource' Languages. In *Proceedings of the 2021 Conference on Empirical Methods in Natural Language Processing* (p. 17753). DOI: 10.18653/v1/2024.emnlp-main.983

Park, M.-S., & Lee, H. (2020). Smart City Crime Prevention Services: The Incheon Free Economic Zone Case. In Sustainability (Vol. 12, Issue 14, p. 5658). Multidisciplinary Digital Publishing Institute. DOI: 10.3390/su12145658

Park, S.-C. (2023). Smart Cities: Striking a Balance Between Urban Resilience and Civil Liberties. In arXiv (Cornell University). Cornell University. https://doi.org//arxiv.2303.14597DOI: 10.48550

Pauleen, D. J., Evaristo, R., Davison, R. M., Ang, S., Alanis, M., & Klein, S. (2006). Cultural Bias in Information Systems Research and Practice: Are You Coming From the Same Place I Am? In Communications of the Association for Information Systems (Vol. 17). Association for Information Systems. DOI: 10.17705/1CAIS.01717

Perera, C., Ranjan, R., Wang, L., Khan, S. U., & Zomaya, A. Y. (2014). Privacy of Big Data in the Internet of Things Era. https://dblp.uni-trier.de/db/journals/corr/corr1412.html#PereraRWKZ14

Police1. (2024, November 8). Empowering investigations: AI's impact on law enforcement: Enhancing efficiency and solving complex crimes. Police1.

Ramesh, K., Sitaram, S., & Choudhury, M. (2023). Fairness in Language Models Beyond English: Gaps and Challenges. DOI: 10.18653/v1/2023.findings-eacl.157

Richardson, R., Schultz, J. M., & Crawford, K. (2019). Dirty data, bad predictions: How civil rights violations impact police data, predictive policing systems, and justice. *New York University Law Review*, *94*, 192–248.

S Bhalshankar -, D. (2023). An Examination on the Consistency of Forensic Information in Criminal Courts in India. In International Journal For Multidisciplinary Research (Vol. 5, Issue 1). DOI: 10.36948/ijfmr.2023.v05i01.1756

Santos, G. L., Endo, P. T., Sadok, D., & Kelner, J. (2020). When 5G Meets Deep Learning: A Systematic Review. In Algorithms (Vol. 13, Issue 9, p. 208). Multidisciplinary Digital Publishing Institute. DOI: 10.3390/a13090208

Scanlon, M., Breitinger, F., Hargreaves, C., Hilgert, J.-N., & Sheppard, J. (2023). ChatGPT for Digital Forensic Investigation: The Good, The Bad, and The Unknown. https://doi.org/DOI: 10.20944/preprints202307.0766.v1

Shah, N., Bhagat, N., & Shah, M. (2021). Crime forecasting: a machine learning and computer vision approach to crime prediction and prevention. In Visual Computing for Industry Biomedicine and Art (Vol. 4, Issue 1). Springer Nature. DOI: 10.1186/s42492-021-00075-z

Skillicorn, D. B., & Little, A. (2009). Patterns of Word Use for Deception in Testimony. In *Annals of information systems* (p. 25). Springer Nature., DOI: 10.1007/978-1-4419-1325-8_2

Sokol, K., & Flach, P. (2020). One Explanation Does Not Fit All. In KI - Künstliche Intelligenz (Vol. 34, Issue 2, p. 235). Springer Science+Business Media. DOI: 10.1007/s13218-020-00637-y

Solà-Sales, S., Alzetta, C., Moret-Tatay, C., & Dell'Orletta, F. (2023). Analysing Deception in Witness Memory through Linguistic Styles in Spontaneous Language. *Brain Sciences*, *13*(2), 317. DOI: 10.3390/brainsci13020317 PMID: 36831859

Spiroiu, F. (2018). The Impact of Beliefs Concerning Deception on Perceptions of Nonverbal Behavior: Implications for Neuro-Linguistic Programming-Based Lie Detection. *Journal of Police and Criminal Psychology*, *33*(3), 244–256. DOI: 10.1007/s11896-018-9278-9

Srinivasan, R., & Chander, A. (2021). Biases in AI Systems. In Queue (Vol. 19, Issue 2, p. 45). Association for Computing Machinery. DOI: 10.1145/3466132.3466134

Srivastava, S., Mardziel, P., Zhang, Z., Ahlawat, A., Datta, A., & Mitchell, J. C. (2024). De-amplifying Bias from Differential Privacy in Language Model Fine-tuning. In arXiv (Cornell University). Cornell University. https://doi.org//arxiv.2402 .04489DOI: 10.48550

Strassel, S., & Tracey, J. (2016). LORELEI Language Packs: Data, Tools, and Resources for Technology Development in Low Resource Languages. In Proceedings of the Tenth International Conference on Language Resources and Evaluation (LREC'16) (pp. 3273–3280). European Language Resources Association (ELRA). https://aclanthology.org/L16-1521/

Thiebes, S., Lins, S., & Sunyaev, A. (2020). Trustworthy artificial intelligence. In Electronic Markets (Vol. 31, Issue 2, p. 447). Springer Science+Business Media. DOI: 10.1007/s12525-020-00441-4

Tong, E., Zadeh, A., Jones, C., & Morency, L. (2017). Combating Human Trafficking with Deep Multimodal Models. In arXiv (Cornell University). Cornell University. https://doi.org//arxiv.1705.02735DOI: 10.48550

Vlek, C. S., Prakken, H., Renooij, S., & Verheij, B. (2014). Building Bayesian networks for legal evidence with narratives: a case study evaluation. In Artificial Intelligence and Law (Vol. 22, Issue 4, p. 375). Springer Science+Business Media. DOI: 10.1007/s10506-014-9161-7

Waheed, N., He, X., Ikram, M., Usman, M., Hashmi, S. S., & Usman, M. (2020). Security and Privacy in IoT Using Machine Learning and Blockchain: Threats & Countermeasures. In arXiv (Cornell University). Cornell University. https://doi.org// arxiv.2002.03488DOI: 10.48550

Wang, Y., & Gao, S. (2017). Application of DBNs for concerned internet information detecting. In *AIP conference proceedings* (Vol. 1808, p. 90005). American Institute of Physics., DOI: 10.1063/1.4977389

Wickramasekara, A., Breitinger, F., & Scanlon, M. (2024). Exploring the Potential of Large Language Models for Improving Digital Forensic Investigation Efficiency. In arXiv (Cornell University). Cornell University. https://doi.org//arxiv.2402.19366DOI: 10.48550

Williams, M., Burnap, P., & Sloan, L. (2016). Crime Sensing with Big Data: The Affordances and Limitations of using Open Source Communications to Estimate Crime Patterns. In *The British Journal of Criminology*. Oxford University Press., DOI: 10.1093/bjc/azw031

Xi, J., Siegel, M., Labudde, D., & Spranger, M. (2024). Towards a joint semantic analysis in mobile forensics environments. In *Forensic Science International Digital Investigation* (Vol. 52, p. 301846). Elsevier BV., DOI: 10.1016/j.fsidi.2024.301846

ADDITIONAL READING

Afzal, M., & Panagiotopoulos, P. (2020). Smart policing: A critical review of the literature. In Pereira, G. V., Janssen, M., Lee, H., Lindgren, I., Rodríguez Bolívar, M. P., & Scholl, H. J. (Eds.), *Electronic Government* (Vol. 12219, pp. 1–15). Springer., DOI: 10.1007/978-3-030-57599-1_5

Bervoets, E., Broekhuizen, J., Ferwerda, H., & Landman, W. (2023). Policing with the help of data: The use of CoroPol in the pandemic's early stages in the Netherlands. In Den Boer, M., Bervoets, E., & Hak, L. (Eds.), *Plural Policing, Security and the COVID Crisis* (pp. 43–58). Palgrave Macmillan., DOI: 10.1007/978-3-031-19177-0_2

Cheong, I., Caliskan, A., & Kohno, T. (2024). Safeguarding human values: Rethinking US law for generative AI's societal impacts. *AI and Ethics*. Advance online publication. DOI: 10.1007/s43681-024-00451-4 PMID: 40352581

Intelligence, A., & Criminal, J. F. R. (2024). [Artificial Intelligence and Criminal Justice Final Report]. U.S. Department of Justice. https://www.justice.gov/olp/media/1381796/dl

Interpol Annual report 2022. (2023). [Annual report 2022]. Interpol. https://www.interpol.int/content/download/19843/file/INTERPOL%20%20Annual%20Report%202022_EN.pdf

Jahankhani, H., Akhgar, B., Cochrane, P., & Dastbaz, M. (Eds.). (2020). *Policing in the Era of AI and Smart Societies*. Springer Cham., DOI: 10.1007/978-3-030-50613-1

Kuldova, T. Ø., Gundhus, H. O. I., & Wathne, C. T. (2024). Introduction to Volume I: Algorithmic Governance, Policing and Intelligence in the Global Big Data Era. In: Kuldova, T.Ø., Gundhus, H.O.I., Wathne, C.T. (eds) Policing and Intelligence in the Global Big Data Era, Volume I. Palgrave's Critical Policing Studies. Palgrave Macmillan, Cham. DOI: 10.1007/978-3-031-68326-8_1

Mijwil, M. M., Aggarwal, K., Sonia, S., Al-Mistarehi, A. H., Alomari, S., Gök, M., Zein Alabdin, A. M., & Abdulrhman, S. H. (2022). Has the future started? The current growth of artificial intelligence, machine learning, and deep learning. *Iraqi Journal for Computer Science and Mathematics*, *3*(1), 13. Advance online publication. DOI: 10.52866/ijcsm.2022.01.01.013

KEY TERMS & DEFINITIONS

Forensic Linguistics: The scientific study of language in legal contexts, focusing on analyzing linguistic patterns in witness testimonies, legal documents, and digital communications to assess credibility, detect deception, and uncover biases.

Deep Belief Networks (DBNs): A type of deep learning model composed of multiple layers of latent variables, trained using unsupervised learning to automatically detect complex patterns and features in data, such as linguistic markers in text.

Witness Statements: Oral or written accounts provided by individuals regarding events they observed, used in legal investigations to establish facts and evaluate reliability.

AI-Driven Policing: The use of artificial intelligence technologies, such as machine learning and natural languse processing, to enhance law enforcement operations, including predictive policing, crime analysis, and forensic investigations.

Urban Security: Strategies and technologies implemented in cities to maintain public safety, prevent crime, and respond to emergencies, often leveraging data analytics and smart city infrastructure.

Ethical AI: The development and deployment of artificial intelligence systems that adhere to ethical principles, such as fairness, transparency, accountability, and respect for privacy and human rights.

Chapter 8
Developing a Deep Learning-Based Framework for Real-Time Anomaly Detection and Alerting Mechanism Using Embedded Systems

Vijayalakshmi G. V. Mahesh
https://orcid.org/0000-0002-1917-7506
BMS Institute of Technology and Management, India

R. N. Gaurav
BMS Institute of Technology and Management, India

M. Nisarga
BMS Institute of Technology and Management, India

R. Deepika
BMS Institute of Technology and Management, India

B. R. Raksha
BMS Institute of Technology and Management, India

ABSTRACT

The increase in surveillance and monitoring devices at various locations over the last decades has provided new ways to use the collected data in a variety of useful

DOI: 10.4018/979-8-3373-0245-4.ch008

applications. This includes event management forecasting, live data monitoring, traffic analysis, crowd behavior, home security, public safety and targeted analysis, especially in the areas of anomaly and intrusion detection. Artificial intelligence methods with machine learning and deep learning architectures have emerged as a valuable anomaly detection tool that is highly effective in modern society. This chapter aims to present an approach based on deep learning methods, specially designed to detect anomaly activities through video surveillance cameras for smart city applications to aid law enforcement.

INTRODUCTION

The advancements in technology has paved way for the generation of large volume of data which needs to be managed, analysed and put to use in its best form. The data along with the expected/regular patterns also has anomalies that point towards suspicious activities, abnormal situations or abnormal performances. These situations/activities might be related to faults in machines, criminal activities, data breaches or fraudulent financial transactions. Anomalies are contextual and detecting them is crucial as per the application specific domain. One such field of application is detecting crimes from the surveillance videos for Law enforcement. The crime specific anomalies include fighting, stealing, abuse, assault, road accidents, shooting, explosion, burglary, shop lifting etc.,. As earlier mentioned anomalies are contextual meaning the specific event labelled as anomaly in one context may be normal in other context and this poses a serious challenge during the detection process. To add on there are other influencial factors such as environment(dynamic or crowded place) and the specific crime scenario.

This chapter presents a methodology to detect crimes by analyzing the behavior in the regular events for an anomaly or deviation to aid Law enforcement. Monitoring and forecasting the occurrence of unusual activities is important to help the authorities in preventing the crimes. Anamoly detection systems(ADS) are required to monitor and detect the changes in the events with adequate accuracy. Recent studies point towards the two broad categories of anomaly detection.

(i) Rule based, a traditional method where the anomaly detection is triggered when one or more pre defined conditions are violated and
(ii) Embedded systems using the Machine Learning Algorithms(Supervised and Un Supervised based), where the algorithms are trained to discover the patterns by processing the data.

The effectiveness of implementing unsupervised machine learning techniques for crime scene detection is an ongoing conversation in the field of machine learning. By utilizing unsupervised learning to detect anomalies in normal data, we can open the door to various important and unique applications. Current supervised methods for crime detection, such as convolutional neural network (CNN) based approaches, rely on labelled data which is challenging to obtain due to the high-dimensional nature of video data. This high dimensionality can also impact the representation and development of models.

As this work focuses on detecting crimes through surveillance camera videos,it should be noted that detecting crimes in videos is a more complex task compared to other types of data due to the need for specialized detection methods. It is important to acknowledge that video detection poses greater challenges than other forms of data due to the inclusion of specialized detection techniques and necessary video processing. To overcome these obstacles, advanced machine learning techniques such as deep learning approaches have proven to be the most effective approach for achieving the desired pattern and goal. These methods offer an advantage due to their ability to handle high-dimensional data with ease through end-to-end systems that automate feature extraction.

The primary objective of this work is to leverage deep learning and embedded systems to substantially enhance public safety through accurate prediction of criminal activities in a practical and impactful manner. The prime purpose of utilizing deep learning is to extract valuable information from complex, high-dimensional data. The significant contributions of this work include

a) Develop a state-of-the-art deep learning model specifically designed for enhanced crime detection in video surveillance systems, with the objective of significantly improving the accuracy of identifying criminal behaviour and promptly notifying security authorities for swift intervention,
b) Develop an interface between the embedded system and the deep learning model, ensuring seamless integration and communication between the two components.

Upon detecting abnormal or threatening objects, the system automatically triggers SMS notifications to the control station, ensuring prompt communication of the detected anomalies. Additionally, the surrounding area is promptly alerted to the detection of abnormal events, enhancing situational awareness and enabling swift response measures to be implemented as necessary. This integrated approach harnesses the power of deep learning to enhance the efficiency and effectiveness of crime detection systems, ultimately contributing to enhanced public safety efforts.

The rest of the chapter is presented in 5 sections. Section 2 discusses about the study on the related works available employing state of the art techniques for anomaly detection under various scenarios. A detailed methodology on achieving the proposed objectives is provided in Section 3. Section 4 presents the Implementation work, results and discussion and section 5 concludes the work.

RELATED WORK

In recent years, the analysis and processing of video data has gained significant attention from scientific researchers due to the abundance of valuable and comprehensive information contained within videos. However, accurately detecting objects within video frames remains a significant challenge (Revathi and Kumar. (2017)). A comprehensive study on the machine learning methods to handle video surveillance data is presented by(Choudhry et al. (2023)). The study included the systematic examination of the recent algorithms, their strengths, drawbacks and their applicability to handle various types of anomaly detection.

The emergence of deep learning techniques has brought about advancements in the implementation of crime detection methods. It is noteworthy that all existing approaches for crime detection rely solely on normal data for learning (Kiran et al. (2018)). A survey on the research regarding deep anomaly detection with a complete taxonomy covering various methods is presented by(Pang et al. 2021 ; Krishnan et al. 2024). Similarly (Pawar and Phadke. (2022) discussed about methods utilized for autonomous video surveillance in entry prohibited areas and anomaly detection. Anomalous events, such as crimes or suspicious activities, are typically rare occurrences that happen less frequently compared to normal incidents. Detecting anomalies in videos poses several challenges, including speed, online alerts, and localization (Saini et al. 2016).

Accurately identifying the location of crimes is crucial; however, many current systems and datasets lack this capability. Some techniques attempt to address this issue by incorporating localization in the pre-processing stage, typically through video frame comparison. This approach has been shown to improve accuracy(Vu et al. 2017) (Wang, S., Zhu, E., Yin, J., & Porikli, F. (2018). However, most existing methods and datasets only indicate the presence of anomalies without specifying their precise location (Sabokrou, M., Fathy, M., & Hoseini, M. (2016).). Furthermore, these methods suffer from a lack of adequate training data and accurate descriptions of crimes, resulting in a high cost for feature extraction that directly impacts detection capabilities (Vu . 2017). A solution to localization was provided by using a weakly supervised anomaly localization method by(Lv et al. 2021). This method worked on temporally locazing anomalous segments within the anomalous videos.

It also used higher order context encoding model to extract and fuse both semantic representations and the dynamic variations. The effectiveness of the model was verified with the results obtained from simulation. Adding to it, (Ganokratanaa et al. 2020) framed a methodology using Deep spatiotemporal translation network, an unsupervised method based on generative adversarial network and edge wrapping for anomaly detection and localization. The method was effective with respect to pixel level and also frame level evaluation.

A commonly used approach for detecting anomalies is the implementation of a binary classifier consisting of two classes: normal and abnormal. The normal class consists of frequently occurring data, while the abnormal class contains rare and unforeseeable events that deviate from the established data pattern (Kiran et al. 2018). Similar to other machine learning techniques, deep learning-based crime detection methods can be categorized as supervised, unsupervised, or semi-supervised. For supervised crime detection, labeled data is necessary but often difficult to obtain due to the large volume and complexity of the data. In this approach, decision rules or models are utilized to differentiate between the two classes (Chong and Tay. 2015). On the other hand, unsupervised methods require more complex computing processes (Kiran et al. 2018) and are also known as data-driven crime detection approaches.

Several researchers have proposed various deep learning techniques for anomaly detection in videos, including joint detection and recounting of abnormal events using deep generic knowledge (Hinami et al. 2017), deep convolutional auto-encoders (Ribeiro et al. 2018), spatiotemporal autoencoders (Chong and Tay. 2017), and fully convolutional neural networks for fast anomaly detection in crowded scenes(Sabokrou et al. 2018). Other studies have focused on specific tasks such as crime intention detection (Nale et al. 2021 ; Nasaruddin et al. 2020 ; Navalgund and Priyadharshini .2018), person detection(Kim et al. 2018), and suspicious activity detection(Bordoloi et al. 2020; Kamthe and Patil. 2018 ; Amrutha et al. 2020 ; Nale et al. 2021 ; Ullah et al. 2021 ; Nasaruddin et al. 2020) using deep learning models like YOLOv3, LSTMs, and attention mechanisms. A survey on utilizing deep learning methods for detecting anomaly in online social networking is presented by(Ben Chaabene et al. 2022). The survey covers structural, behavioral and hybrid ethods and provides a better understanding of the related concepts.

Chackravarthy et al. (2018) combined Deep learning methods with neural networks which was effective in improving and assessing criminal activities in urban areas /smart cities reducing the workload of supervising officers. Crime monitoring combining weapon detection, violence detection and face recognition using deep learning methods YOLOv5 and MobileNetv2 was successfully demonstrated by Muktoet al. (2024) and was able to generate timely alerts and provide security and safety. Detecting anomalies in geographically tagged alarms for detecting suspected criminal behavior and activities using Bayesioan Principal Anomaly Detection was explored by(Holst and Bjurling. 2013). This method proved to improve the situation and create awareness of the activities revealing large scale patterns. Anomaly detection using IBaggedFCNet based on bagging framework showed significant improvement in localizing anomaly from the surveillance videos(Zahid et al. 2020). A methodology for real time anomaly detection was presented by Xue, et al. (2020) which also reduces the dimensionality of feature maps still retaining the spatio tempotral information. The results reported the generalization ability of the model in detecting newer types anomalies.

Bordoloi et al. (2020) utilized YOLOv3 for suspicious activity detection from videos, while Kamthe and Patil. 2018) proposed a suspicious activity recognition system using video surveillance. Amrutha et al. (2020) explored a deep learning approach for suspicious activity detection, and Nale et al. (2021) used pose estimation and LSTMs for suspicious human activity detection. Ullah et al. (2021) employed CNN features with bi-directional LSTMs for real-time anomaly detection in surveillance networks. Nasaruddin et al. (2020) investigated deep anomaly detection through visual attention in surveillance videos. Ezhumalai and Prakash. (2024) proposed a deep learning modified neural network for sentiment analysis on Twitter data. Arashloo and Christmas. (2017) worked on detecting spoofing attacks motivated by anomaly detection. Detection of violent behavior and crime activities in real time scenario using 3dConvolutional Neural Network was made possible by Hwang and. (2023).

Thakare et al. (2022) presented an end to end multistream architecture with spatio temporal deep feature extractors to extract temporal features and modified multiple instance learning based classifier with fuzzy aggregation to detect long duration anomalies which was not achievable with current techniques. Finding anomalies in crwded and dynamic situations is difficult. This was addressed by Tutar et al .(2024) creating a hybrid video anomaly detection system that combines pixel and frame-based video anomaly identification with many machine learning algorithms. The technique worked and had a respectable level of accuracy. Further Patrikar and Parate. (2022) explored the convergence of edge computing and anomaly detection aimed at real time surveillance applications for smart cities.

Overall, the literature highlights the significant progress made in video crime detection, suspicious activity detection, and anomaly detection using deep learning techniques. However, challenges remain, particularly in obtaining adequate training data, accurate descriptions of crimes, and improving localization capabilities. This motivated to propose a methodology based on deep learning model to improve anomaly detection from video surveillance data and interface to an embedded system to promptly notify security authorities for swift intervention.

METHODOLOGY

The proposed work on anomaly detection establishes an interface between the embedded system and the deep learning model so one can make seamless integration and verbal exchange among the two components, and the corresponding framework is as illustrated in Figure 1. The system leverages advanced deep learning techniques and hardware components to provide an effective solution for anomaly detection and alerting.

The pattern recognition module based on deeplearning (Left Hand Side of Figure 1) plays a crucial role in analyzing the video data. It encompasses various steps, including data collection, pre-processing, model building, training, testing and evaluation. At the core of this component is a surveillance camera that captures video footage from the surveillance area. The pattern recognition module module, which likely employs deep learning architectures, processes the video frames to identify anomalies or suspicious activities.

The embedded system component acts as the hardware counterpart, facilitating real-time anomaly detection and alerting. It consists of a PIC microcontroller (Santhoshkumar et al. (2024)) that receives the output from the GSM module. Based on the detected anomalies, the microcontroller triggers various alert mechanisms to notify users and relevant authorities.

One of the alert mechanisms is a signal that provides an audible alert when an anomaly is identified. This audible cue can draw immediate attention to the detected anomaly, prompting further investigation or action. Additionally, the system incorporates a visual alerting mechanism by displaying alert messages or warnings on a screen. This visual notification ensures that users can quickly recognize and respond to the identified anomalies.

Figure 1. Designed methodology to detect anomaly activities in surveillance footage by integrating an AI model and an embedded system

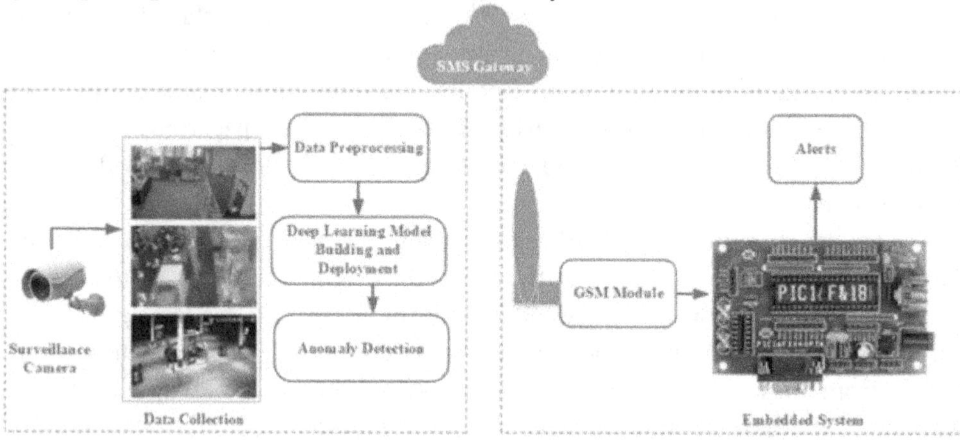

Furthermore, the system includes an Short Message Service(SMS) gateway, enabling it to send SMS alerts to authorized phone numbers when anomalies are detected. This feature enhances situational awareness and facilitates timely intervention by relevant stakeholders, such as law enforcement agencies or security personnel. By receiving real-time alerts on their mobile devices, authorities can respond promptly and take appropriate actions to address the detected anomalies.This symbiotic approach combines the strengths of artificial intelligence and hardware components, resulting in an effective system for detecting anomalies, enhancing public safety, and enabling timely response to potential threats or suspicious activities.

Whenever any odd or threatening pastime is detected, it mechanically triggers SMS notifications to the control station so that there may be activate verbal exchange of detected anomalies. Also, the encircling place right now receives an alert to the detection of the peculiar event, thereby enhancing situational recognition and allowing short reaction measures to be put into vicinity. Integrating deep getting to know on this crime detection system will increase both the performance and effectiveness of the gadget in preventing crime and in the end boosts public safety.

Anomaly Detection

The proposed methodology employs advanced deep learning techniques for anomaly detection in videos or images. It consists of three main components: feature extraction, learning, and anomaly detection. The process involves a pre-processing step to estimate and remove background noise.

The approach follows the typical deep learning pipeline of training and testing phases. During the training phase, features are learned from normal frames of the dataset. This trained model is then utilized in the testing phase to identify anomalous frames in the remaining dataset.

The process begins by collecting data from various sources like datasets, crime reports, incident reports, surveillance cameras, and social media platforms. For the proposed work, UCF crime dataset(Sultani, W., Chen, C., & Shah, M. (2018) is considered, which has 128 hours of video data. The dataset comprises of 1900 long untrimmed real world surveillance videos with thirteen anomalies significant towards public safety that include Assault, Abuse, Arson, Arrest, Burglary, Explosion, Fight, Road accident, Robbery, Shoplifting, Shooting, Stealing and Vandalism.The data is cleaned and pre-processed to remove any unrelated information, ensuring consistency and accuracy.

The processed data is provided to the deep learning model for anomaly detection. The anomaly detection process relies on two deep learning models: 3D Convolutional Neural Network (C3D) and Bilinear Convolutional Neural Network(Bil-CNN).

The C3D model(Ouyang et al. 2019) architecture is shown in Figure 2 which extracts spatio temporal features from segmented video frames, capturing complex patterns associated with anomalies.

Figure 2. C3D model architecture

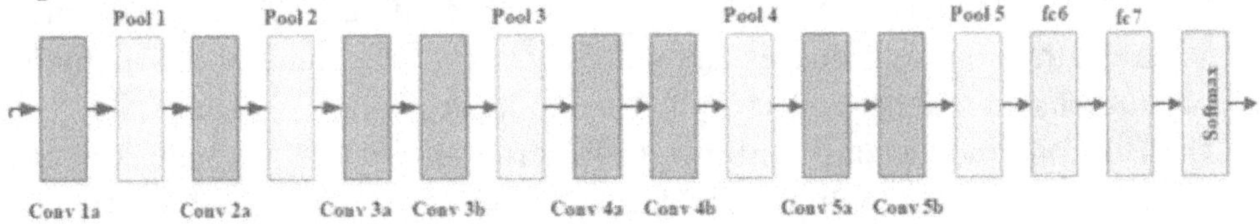

Figure 3. Bilinear CNN architecture

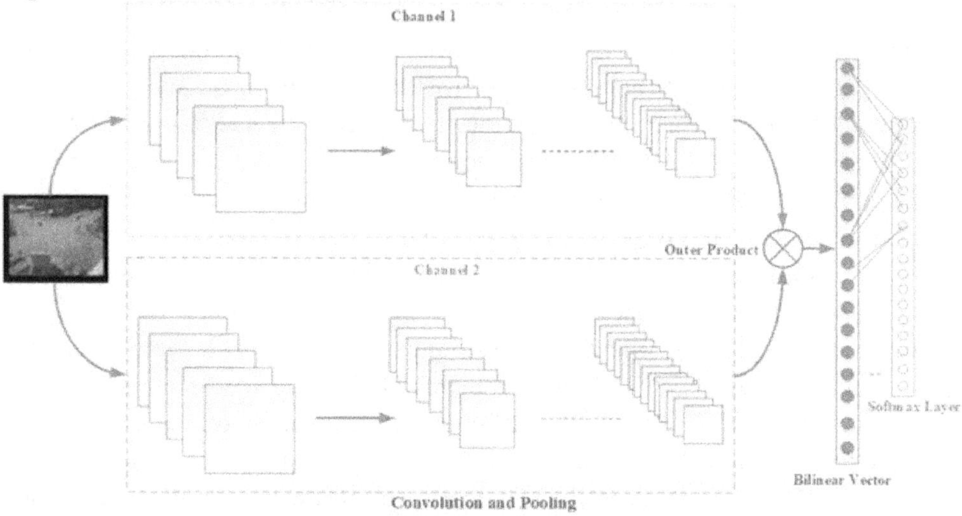

The C3D model has eight convolutional(Conv) layers, five pooling (Pool) layers, two fully connected(fc) and a softmax layer at the output. The convolutional layers and pooling layers are 3D. The Conv layers use the kernels of size 3x3x3 with a stride of 1, while the pooling layers uses 2x2x2 with a stride 2 except for Pooling layer 1 which has kernel sixe of 1x2x2 and a stride of 1x2x2. This variation is to preserve the temporal information in the data at the early stages. The output of each fc layer is 4096 units. The 3D convolutional layers extract features from the input video by learning spatiotemporal patterns, while the pooling layers help reduce the dimensionality of the feature maps. The fully connected layers at the end of the network are responsible for the classification or regression task.

The Bil-CNN model (Wang et al. 2017) is a deep learning architecture designed for feature extraction from images and videos. The model combines the strengths of convolutional neural networks (CNNs) and bilinear pooling.

The Bil-CNN model starts with two CNN structures where the outputs of the convolutional layers are multiplied with outer product at each spatial location as indicated in Figure 3. The CNNs extract low-level visual features from the input image or video frame and then are passed through a bilinear pooling layer, which computes the outer product of the feature maps, resulting in a compact, expressive and high dimensional representation of the visual content.

The bilinear pooling layer is the key component of the BC model, and it allows for capturing higher-order interactions between the feature maps. By computing the outer product of the feature maps, the bilinear pooling layer generates a rich, high-dimensional representation that captures both local and global visual information.

The proposed method for anomaly detection exploits the strengths of both the models. 3D CNN captures the spatial and temporal information from the video sequences providing a complete understanding of the content while Bil-CNN derives and understands the relation between the video frames providing better comprehension of the context and temporal dynamics of the video sequence. Thus the combination of these models serves to enhance the ability of anomaly detection in the scenarios with both spatial and also temporal variations. The models are trained to identify/detect in the video sequences by providing them with the videos containing different types of anomalies such as assaults, explosions, fighting, road accidents, and shooting. were used, totaling 500 videos.

Embedded System for Alert Mechanism

With the assistance of this Embedded system module, the system aims to detect anomalies in real-time video data, triggering alerts through visual display, sound, and SMS notifications allowing it to send messages containing relevant information about detected anomalies, facilitating timely intervention and situational awareness. The system prioritizes performance, reliability, security, scalability, and user-friendliness while adhering to industry standards and best practices.

Once trained, the deep learning model is integrated into an embedded system, capable of processing real-time data and making accurate predictions on the spot. Continuous real-time data, including live video feeds from surveillance cameras, sensor data, and other relevant sources, are analyzed by the embedded system for efficient processing.Whenever the deep learning model predicts potential criminal activities, the embedded system generates alerts and displays "Risk Detected" on frames where abnormal activities are detected. These alerts are shared with law enforcement agencies, emergency services, or patrol officers' devices for prompt action.

Geographic Information System (GIS) technology is also integrated with the system to provide location-specific information, enabling law enforcement officers to respond promptly and navigate effectively to the scene.

The embedded system is presented in Figure 4. The proposed work considered inclusion of a microcontroller such as PIC16F877A to accomplish this. In addition, LCD display module is used that provides system status and alerts that can be seen by the users. Moreover, the system has a GSM module for cellular communications that can send SMS alerts to authorized phone numbers when certain anomalies are detected. It also has a buzzer that provides sound alert whenever there is an abnormality. The combination of these hardware components resulted in a strong alerting system which supports visualization as well as voice notifications.

This system has a user-friendly interface or control panel for configuring various settings, such as anomaly detection thresholds, authorized personnel contact information, and other system parameters.

Figure 4. Embedded system for alert mechanism

IMPLEMENTATION RESULTS AND DISCUSSION

The proposed work on Anomaly detection and timely alerts using embedded system is implemented in two phases:

i. Building of deep learning model to detect anomalies from the video data that is the pattern recognition module and
ii. Development and integration of an Embedded system to trigger Alert messages to the control room.

During phase1, the deep learning model was trained to detect anomalies from the video data. This was implemented using OpenCV. For training the models, 100 videos from the UCF crime dataset for each of the five different types of anomalies that include assaults, explosions, fighting, road accidents, and shooting were used, totaling to 500 videos. Initially the videos are preprocessed where the video is typically divided into short clips of a fixed length. A sample of the video frames is displayed in Figure 5. These clips are then fed into the C3D model and BCNN as input, and the models learns to extract relevant spatiotemporal features and compact & expressive representation of the visual content respectively from the video data during the training process.

Figure 5. Video data converted into set of frames

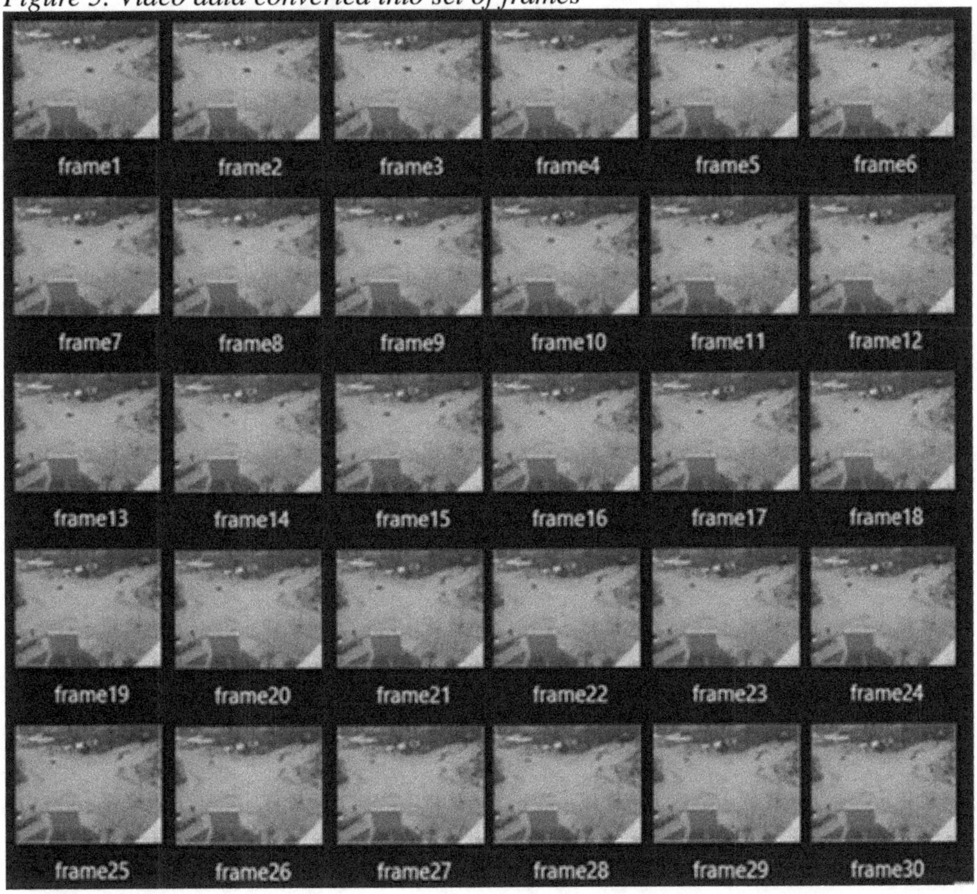

C3D model provides both the spatial information and also the motion information from the videos. Here all the elements of the 3D convolutional kernels and the corresponding bias elements are trained with the cross entropy loss function, adam optimizer and setting the learning rate to 0.001.

In the Bil-CNN model, after computing the outer product of the outputs of channel 1 and 2, it is vectorized and normalized using L2 normalization. During training both the CNN channels are trained together. The features extracted from the Bil-CNN model and features obtained from the C3D model are combined to provide enhanced representation of the input and this representation is used directly for the task of anomaly detection by the fully connected layers.

Performance metric like Receiver Operating Characteristic (ROC) (Raj and Mahesh. 2017) analysis is used to measure the system's effectiveness in separating normal and abnormal behaviors in the video data, enabling the evaluation of its efficacy and potential parameter adjustments. This trained model should be capable of accurately identifying anomalous events or behaviors in video data based on the learned patterns from the training data.

After a deep learning model has been trained, it is then used for predictive analytics. By analyzing the learned patterns and relationships, the model can make forecasts regarding potential criminal activities in specific areas and time frames. The proposed work is tested for the activities: Assaults, Explosions, Fighting, Road Accidents, Shooting. Figure 6 presents a snippet of Anomaly score, anomaly detection and alert message displayed on detected video for the activity Road accident.

Figure 6. The test results of the anomaly detection (a) Anomaly score chart, (b) anomaly detection-road accident and (c) alert message displayed on detected video

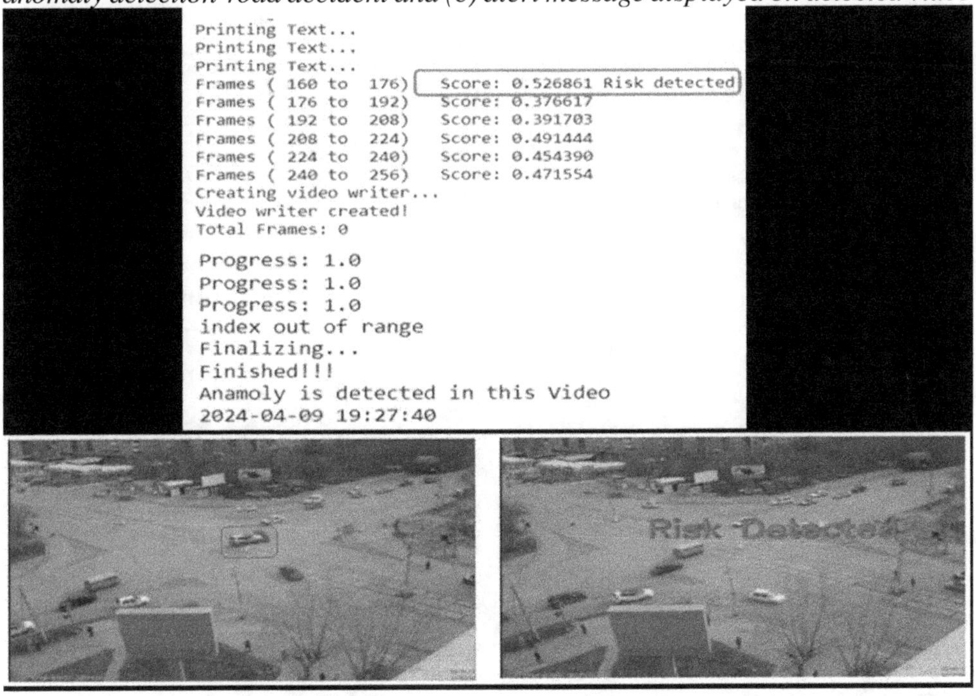

Once trained and tested, the deep learning model is integrated into an embedded system capable of processing real-time data and making accurate predictions on the spot. Whenever the deep learning model predicts potential criminal activities, the embedded system generates alerts and displays “Risk Detected” on frames where abnormal activities are detected. The proposed work considered inclusion of a microcontroller such as PIC16F877A to accomplish this. In addition, display module is used that provides system status and alerts that can be seen by the users. Moreover, the system has a GSM module for cellular communications that can send SMS alerts to authorized phone numbers when certain anomalies are detected. It also has a buzzer that provides sound alert whenever there is an abnormality. The combination of these components resulted in a strong alerting system which supports visualization as well as voice notifications. The complete flowchart of developing the alert system is provided in Figure 7.

Figure 7. Embedded system flowchart

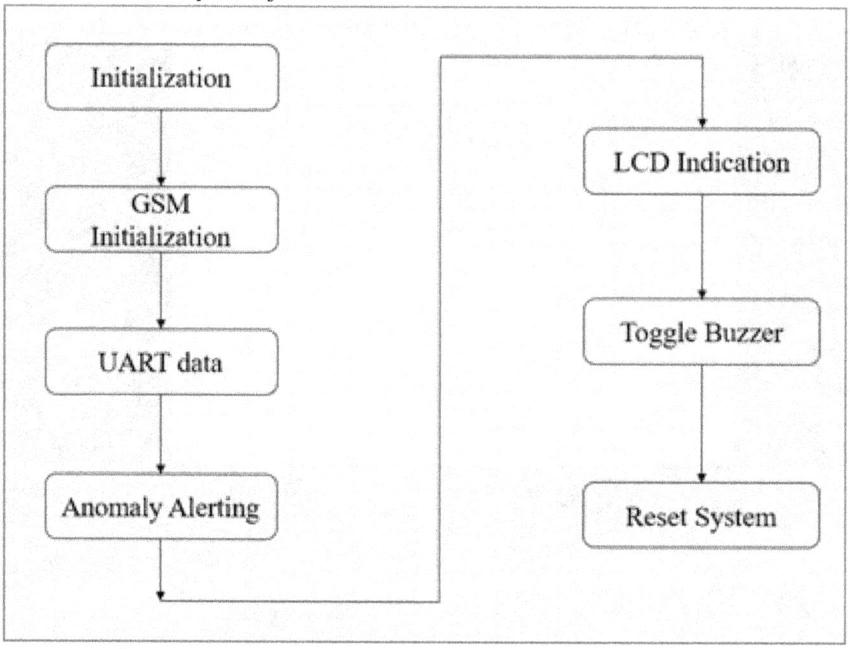

The integrated Geographic Information System (GIS) technology with the system provides location-specific information, enabling law enforcement officers to respond promptly and navigate effectively to the scene.

In the alert system, the initialization of hardware peripherals is initiated in start-up, and variables are established. The LCD displays "GSM INIT....." to indicate the initialization process, followed by a 2-second delay to ensure proper initialization of the GSM module. After initialization, the LCD is cleared, and "SYSTEM NORMAL" is displayed, implying readiness for operation. GSM initialization involves configuring and initializing the GSM module, as shown in Figure 8, so that microcontroller could efficiently communicate with it, enabling functions like sending an SMS message for alerting purpose. When an anomaly is observed, the program raises an alarm flag, alerts on LCD screens appear; text messages with alarm details will be sent. This process shows the relevant feedback on the LCD screen, usually providing status messages, alert notifications, or system prompts. The same is displayed in Figure 8. As a result, the system must ensure that the user knows the state and interacts with it. Buzzer activation ensures that an abnormality or a particular condition is attended to by any user when it occurs. This is supposed to draw attention to the incident at hand, thereby announcing its occurrence with a sound means of sound.

Figure 8. Anomaly detection and display on the LCD panel

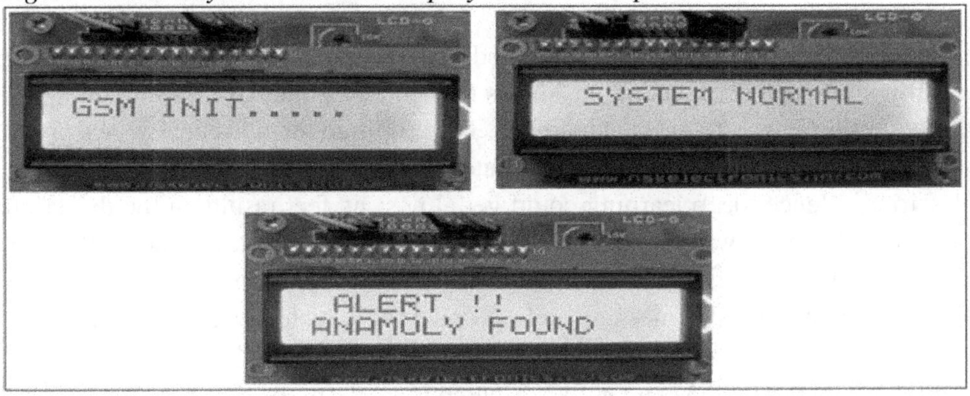

These alerts are shared with law enforcement agencies, emergency services, or patrol officers' devices for prompt action. The SMS alert sent after detecting the anomaly with the geographic location information is presented in Figure 8.

The system designed detected anomalies in video data, achieving an 85% detection rate. It segments frames, preprocesses, and extracts features using deep learning models, triggering risk alerts when anomaly scores exceed a predefined threshold. SMS notifications enable real-time alerts for immediate response to detected abnormalities, enhancing proactive risk mitigation measures.

Figure 9. SMS sent to authorized person

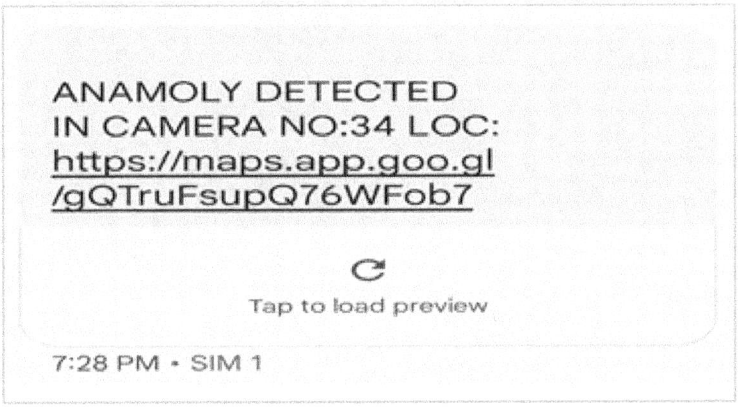

CONCLUSION

The deep learning technique, combined with the embedded system for anomaly identification and alert generation, shows tremendous potential in overcoming the limitations present in traditional methods. The proposed method consists of a phase of feature extraction for training, and a detection phase in the deep neural network classifiers. Hence, deep learning could get almost perfect results in the detection of crime. However, with time, it must be noted the complications and challenges that come with processing surveillance footage, especially in densely populated areas, and continuously fine-tune and optimize these techniques to be practically usable. Anomaly detection is the highlight type within which deviations trigger SMS alerts through GSM and activates an audible alarm using GSM. With GSM, reliable communication is assured in remote or harsh environments, ensuring both greater coverage and the much-needed resilience from internet-based methods. An LCD interface that provides real-time updates and system status for better situational awareness provides a user-friendly interface. To conclude, the system is a strong solution for remote monitoring and anomaly detection, appropriately suggested for security, industrial, or environmental applications, assuring proactive monitoring, reliable communication, and easy interaction with the user.

REFERENCES

Amrutha, C. V., Jyotsna, C., & Amudha, J. (2020, March). Deep learning approach for suspicious activity detection from surveillance video. In 2020 2nd International Conference on Innovative Mechanisms for Industry Applications (ICIMIA) (pp. 335-339). IEEE. DOI: 10.1109/ICIMIA48430.2020.9074920

Arashloo, S. R., Kittler, J., & Christmas, W. (2017). An anomaly detection approach to face spoofing detection: A new formulation and evaluation protocol. *IEEE Access : Practical Innovations, Open Solutions*, *5*, 13868–13882. DOI: 10.1109/ACCESS.2017.2729161

Ben Chaabene, N. E. H., Bouzeghoub, A., Guetari, R., & Ghezala, H. H. B. (2022). Deep learning methods for anomalies detection in social networks using multidimensional networks and multimodal data: A survey. *Multimedia Systems*, *28*(6), 2133–2143. DOI: 10.1007/s00530-020-00731-z

Bordoloi, N., Talukdar, A. K., & Sarma, K. K. (2020, December). Suspicious activity detection from videos using yolov3. In 2020 IEEE 17th India Council International Conference (INDICON) (pp. 1-5). IEEE. DOI: 10.1109/INDICON49873.2020.9342230

Chackravarthy, S., Schmitt, S., & Yang, L. (2018, October). Intelligent crime anomaly detection in smart cities using deep learning. In 2018 IEEE 4th International Conference on Collaboration and Internet Computing (CIC) (pp. 399-404). IEEE. DOI: 10.1109/CIC.2018.00060

Chong, Y. S., & Tay, Y. H. (2015, May). Modeling video-based anomaly detection using deep architectures: Challenges and possibilities. In 2015 10th Asian Control Conference (ASCC) (pp. 1-8). IEEE.

Chong, Y. S., & Tay, Y. H. (2017). Abnormal event detection in videos using spatiotemporal autoencoder. In Advances in Neural Networks-ISNN 2017: 14th International Symposium, ISNN 2017, Sapporo, Hakodate, and Muroran, Hokkaido, Japan, June 21–26, 2017 [Springer International Publishing.]. *Proceedings*, *14*(Part II), 189–196.

Choudhry, N., Abawajy, J., Huda, S., & Rao, I. (2023). A Comprehensive Survey of Machine Learning Methods for Surveillance Videos Anomaly Detection. *IEEE Access : Practical Innovations, Open Solutions*, *11*, 114680–114713. DOI: 10.1109/ACCESS.2023.3321800

Ganokratanaa, T., Aramvith, S., & Sebe, N. (2020). Unsupervised anomaly detection and localization based on deep spatiotemporal translation network. *IEEE Access : Practical Innovations, Open Solutions*, *8*, 50312–50329. DOI: 10.1109/ACCESS.2020.2979869

Hinami, R., Mei, T., & Satoh, S. I. (2017). Joint detection and recounting of abnormal events by learning deep generic knowledge. In *Proceedings of the IEEE international conference on computer vision* (pp. 3619-3627). DOI: 10.1109/ICCV.2017.391

Holst, A., & Bjurling, B. (2013, August). A Bayesian parametric statistical anomaly detection method for finding trends and patterns in criminal behavior. In *2013 European Intelligence and Security Informatics Conference* (pp. 83-88). IEEE. DOI: 10.1109/EISIC.2013.19

Hwang, I. C., & Kang, H. S. (2023). Anomaly detection based on a 3d convolutional neural network combining convolutional block attention module using merged frames. *Sensors (Basel)*, *23*(23), 9616. DOI: 10.3390/s23239616 PMID: 38067989

Kamthe, U. M., & Patil, C. G. (2018, August). Suspicious activity recognition in video surveillance system. In 2018 Fourth international conference on computing communication control and automation (ICCUBEA) (pp. 1-6). IEEE. DOI: 10.1109/ICCUBEA.2018.8697408

Kim, C., Lee, J., Han, T., & Kim, Y. (2018). A hybrid framework combining background subtraction and deep neural networks for rapid person detection. *Journal of Big Data*, *5*(1), 22. DOI: 10.1186/s40537-018-0131-x

Kiran, B. R., Thomas, D. M., & Parakkal, R. (2018). An overview of deep learning based methods for unsupervised and semi-supervised anomaly detection in videos. *Journal of Imaging*, *4*(2), 36. DOI: 10.3390/jimaging4020036

Krishnan, S. R., Amudha, P., & Sivakumari, S. (2024). Comprehensive survey on video anomaly detection using deep learning techniques. *International Journal of Computational Vision and Robotics*, *14*(4), 445–466. DOI: 10.1504/IJCVR.2024.139544

Lv, H., Zhou, C., Cui, Z., Xu, C., Li, Y., & Yang, J. (2021). Localizing anomalies from weakly-labeled videos. *IEEE Transactions on Image Processing*, *30*, 4505–4515. DOI: 10.1109/TIP.2021.3072863 PMID: 33872149

Mukto, M. M., Hasan, M., Al Mahmud, M. M., Haque, I., Ahmed, M. A., Jabid, T., Ali, M. S., Ahmmad Rashid, M. R., Manzurul Islam, M., & Islam, M. (2024). Design of a real-time crime monitoring system using deep learning techniques. *Intelligent Systems with Applications*, *21*, 200311. DOI: 10.1016/j.iswa.2023.200311

Nale, R., Sawarbandhe, M., Chegogoju, N., & Satpute, V. (2021, September). Suspicious human activity detection using pose estimation and lstm. In *2021 International symposium of Asian control Association on Intelligent Robotics and Industrial Automation (IRIA)* (pp. 197-202). IEEE. DOI: 10.1109/IRIA53009.2021.9588719

Nasaruddin, N., Muchtar, K., Afdhal, A., & Dwiyantoro, A. P. J. (2020). Deep anomaly detection through visual attention in surveillance videos. *Journal of Big Data*, *7*(1), 87. DOI: 10.1186/s40537-020-00365-y

Navalgund, U. V., & Priyadharshini, K. (2018, December). Crime intention detection system using deep learning. In *2018 International Conference on Circuits and Systems in Digital Enterprise Technology (ICCSDET)* (pp. 1-6). IEEE. DOI: 10.1109/ICCSDET.2018.8821168

Ouyang, X., Xu, S., Zhang, C., Zhou, P., Yang, Y., Liu, G., & Li, X. (2019). A 3D-CNN and LSTM based multi-task learning architecture for action recognition. *IEEE Access : Practical Innovations, Open Solutions*, *7*, 40757–40770. DOI: 10.1109/ACCESS.2019.2906654

Pang, G., Shen, C., Cao, L., & Hengel, A. V. D. (2021). Deep learning for anomaly detection: A review. *ACM Computing Surveys*, *54*(2), 1–38. DOI: 10.1145/3439950

Patrikar, D. R., & Parate, M. R. (2022). Anomaly detection using edge computing in video surveillance system. *International Journal of Multimedia Information Retrieval*, *11*(2), 85–110. DOI: 10.1007/s13735-022-00227-8 PMID: 35368446

Paulraj, D., Ezhumalai, P., & Prakash, M. (2024). A Deep Learning Modified Neural Network (DLMNN) based proficient sentiment analysis technique on Twitter data. *Journal of Experimental & Theoretical Artificial Intelligence*, *36*(3), 415–434. DOI: 10.1080/0952813X.2022.2093405

Pawar, P. P., & Phadke, A. C. (2022, December). A survey on different techniques for anomaly detection. In International Conference on Computational Intelligence (pp. 365-380). Singapore: Springer Nature Singapore.

Raj, A. N. J., & Mahesh, V. G. (2017). Zernike-moments-based shape descriptors for pattern recognition and classification applications. In *Advanced Image Processing Techniques and Applications* (pp. 90–120). IGI Global. DOI: 10.4018/978-1-5225-2053-5.ch004

Revathi, A. R., & Kumar, D. (2017). An efficient system for anomaly detection using deep learning classifier. *Signal, Image and Video Processing*, *11*(2), 291–299. DOI: 10.1007/s11760-016-0935-0

Ribeiro, M., Lazzaretti, A. E., & Lopes, H. S. (2018). A study of deep convolutional auto-encoders for anomaly detection in videos. *Pattern Recognition Letters*, *105*, 13–22. DOI: 10.1016/j.patrec.2017.07.016

Sabokrou, M., Fathy, M., & Hoseini, M. (2016). Video anomaly detection and localisation based on the sparsity and reconstruction error of auto-encoder. *Electronics Letters*, *52*(13), 1122–1124. DOI: 10.1049/el.2016.0440

Sabokrou, M., Fayyaz, M., Fathy, M., Moayed, Z., & Klette, R. (2018). Deep-anomaly: Fully convolutional neural network for fast anomaly detection in crowded scenes. *Computer Vision and Image Understanding*, *172*, 88–97. DOI: 10.1016/j.cviu.2018.02.006

Saini, D. K., Ahir, D., & Ganatra, A. (2016). Techniques and challenges in building intelligent systems: anomaly detection in camera surveillance. In *Proceedings of First International Conference on Information and Communication Technology for Intelligent Systems*: Volume 2 (pp. 11-21). Springer International Publishing. DOI: 10.1007/978-3-319-30927-9_2

Santhoshkumar, R., Jabez, I., Kannan, S. B., & Kumar, K. (2024, March). Intelligent Monitoring and Learning System for Electric Vehicle Charging Stations. In International Conference on Artificial Intelligence and Smart Energy (pp. 198-207). Cham: Springer Nature Switzerland. DOI: 10.1007/978-3-031-61475-0_16

Sultani, W., Chen, C., & Shah, M. (2018). Real-world anomaly detection in surveillance videos. In *Proceedings of the IEEE conference on computer vision and pattern recognition* (pp. 6479-6488).

Thakare, K. V., Sharma, N., Dogra, D. P., Choi, H., & Kim, I. J. (2022). A multi-stream deep neural network with late fuzzy fusion for real-world anomaly detection. *Expert Systems with Applications*, *201*, 117030. DOI: 10.1016/j.eswa.2022.117030

Tutar, H., Güneş, A., Zontul, M., & Aslan, Z. (2024). A Hybrid Approach to Improve the Video Anomaly Detection Performance of Pixel-and Frame-Based Techniques Using Machine Learning Algorithms. *Computation (Basel, Switzerland)*, *12*(2), 19. DOI: 10.3390/computation12020019

Ullah, W., Ullah, A., Haq, I. U., Muhammad, K., Sajjad, M., & Baik, S. W. (2021). CNN features with bi-directional LSTM for real-time anomaly detection in surveillance networks. *Multimedia Tools and Applications*, *80*(11), 16979–16995. DOI: 10.1007/s11042-020-09406-3

Vu, H. (2017, August). Deep Abnormality Detection in Video Data. In IJCAI (pp. 5217-5218). DOI: 10.24963/ijcai.2017/768

Vu, H., Nguyen, T. D., Travers, A., Venkatesh, S., & Phung, D. (2017, April). Energy-based localized anomaly detection in video surveillance. In *Pacific-Asia conference on knowledge discovery and data mining* (pp. 641–653). Springer International Publishing. DOI: 10.1007/978-3-319-57454-7_50

Wang, C., Shi, J., Zhang, Q., & Ying, S. (2017, July). Histopathological image classification with bilinear convolutional neural networks. In 2017 39th Annual International Conference of the IEEE Engineering in Medicine and Biology Society (EMBC) (pp. 4050-4053). IEEE. DOI: 10.1109/EMBC.2017.8037745

Wang, S., Zhu, E., Yin, J., & Porikli, F. (2018). Video anomaly detection and localization by local motion based joint video representation and OCELM. *Neurocomputing*, *277*, 161–175. DOI: 10.1016/j.neucom.2016.08.156

Xue, R., Chen, J., & Fang, Y. (2020, October). Real-time anomaly detection and feature analysis based on time series for surveillance video. In 2020 5th International Conference on Universal Village (UV) (pp. 1-7). IEEE. DOI: 10.1109/UV50937.2020.9426191

Zahid, Y., Tahir, M. A., Durrani, N. M., & Bouridane, A. (2020). Ibaggedfcnet: An ensemble framework for anomaly detection in surveillance videos. *IEEE Access : Practical Innovations, Open Solutions*, *8*, 220620–220630. DOI: 10.1109/ACCESS.2020.3042222

Chapter 9

Enhancing Smart Toll Security Improved Ecliptic Curve Algorithm in Intelligent Transportation Networks

Usharani Bhimavarapu
https://orcid.org/0000-0002-0246-1420
Department of Computer Science and Engineering, Koneru Lakshmaiah Education Foundation, Vaddeswaram, India

ABSTRACT

Intelligent Transportation Systems (ITS) employ cutting-edge technologies like the Internet of Things (IoT), Artificial Intelligence (AI), and cryptographic security to improve mobility and public safety. ITS combines intelligent toll collection, real-time traffic monitoring, and automated payment mechanisms to make transportation efficiency smoother and secure financial transactions. The use of cryptographic protocols, e.g., the Enhanced Ecliptic Curve Algorithm (IECA) to secure key exchange and the Enhanced Hash Function (EHF) for data integrity, enhances security within ITS networks. Such innovations avert cyber attacks, i.e., data tampering, replay attacks, and unauthorized intrusion. Additionally, blockchain technology improves transaction immutability, providing toll payment transparency. By marrying effective encryption techniques with real-time observation, ITS reduces congestion, improves toll management, and also increases commuter safety.

DOI: 10.4018/979-8-3373-0245-4.ch009

INTRODUCTION

Intelligent Transport Systems (ITS) use the most advanced technology to enhance transportation mobility, efficiency, and security on rural and urban roads. ITS combine sensor information, cameras, and communication network data to offer optimum traffic patterns and minimize traffic congestion. Real-time surveillance, predictive analytics, and automation characterize ITS, which offers greater public safety and traveling experience. GPS, AI, and IoT enable the authorities to monitor road conditions more effectively. Traffic signal coordination, dynamic speed limit adjustment, and automatic charging are a few ITS implementations that improve efficiency. Connected vehicle technology enables automobiles to talk to one another, eliminating crashes and enhancing road safety. Self-driving vehicles are also being integrated into ITS infrastructure to provide safer, more efficient transport networks. Implementation of these technologies minimizes travel time, fuel usage, and emissions. Governments and companies are investing in ITS to develop smart, responsive transport infrastructure. ITS, by virtue of ongoing innovation, is an absolute necessity in molding the mobility and safety of the future.

Public safety is a crucial aspect of ITS, facilitating safe travel experiences for commuters, pedestrians, and cyclists. AI-based monitoring in CCTV cameras picks up suspicious activity and accidents in real-time. ITS is utilized by police authorities to increase response time, enhance highway and city emergency management. V2I communication alerts drivers to road conditions, traffic, and weather. Historical accident data are employed by predictive systems based on AI to warn high-risk locations so that preventive actions may be undertaken by the authorities. ITS helps the police monitor car theft and enforce speed limits through automatic systems. Intelligent intersections with sensors pick up on pedestrian activity, fewer accidents at intersections. Integrated emergency response systems in ITS enable quick dispatch of rescue and medical personnel. Cybersecurity is also an important aspect, providing privacy of information as well as protection from cyber attacks. With advancements going on, ITS offers an important contribution to improved as well as safer mobility within cities.

Traffic jams are the biggest challenge for expanding metropolitan cities, affecting productivity and quality of life. ITS relieves congestion with real-time-based dynamic control of traffic lights. AI-based algorithms maximize the flow of traffic and minimize bottlenecks and wastage of time. Smart parking systems assist drivers to find vacant parking space, eliminating unnecessary driving and fuel consumption. ATMS gives real-time information on road conditions and suggested routes. Dynamic tolling regulates freeway congestion through fare adjustments depending on demand. ITS enhances mass transit through effective bus scheduling and passenger traffic monitoring. Integration with mobile apps enables passengers to receive real-time transit information and optimize routes. Predictive analytics also forecast peak hours of travel, which allows the authorities to institute anticipatory traffic control measures. Intelligent highways with sensor installations track car movement and send instant feedback to command centers. ITS solutions maximize travel efficiency while minimizing environmental footprints.

Public transportation systems are greatly enhanced by ITS via better operational efficiency and passenger comfort. Smart fare payment systems enable convenient payments by contactless cards and smartphones. Bus and train GPS tracking provides real-time arrival information to passengers, minimizing waiting time. Route optimization with the assistance of AI maximizes transit timing, with timely arrivals and departures. ITS improves fleet maintenance by means of vehicle health monitoring and pre-scheduling of maintenance. Automated passenger counters assist the authorities in managing capacity and distributing services effectively. Traffic signal priority systems enable public transport to pass through intersections with fewer delays. ITS-based bus rapid transit (BRT) systems enhance city mobility by providing special lanes for a high-speed movement. Smarter nodes of transit combine transportation modes, and that improves connectivity and accessibility. Public safety features like surveillance cameras and emergency alert systems make people safe while traveling. ITS optimizes public transport to make it more efficient, dependable, and convenient.

Combining ITS with emerging technologies like artificial intelligence and machine learning improves forecasting and decision-making for traffic. AI-based traffic management systems study past and real-time data in order to maximize the use of roads. Machine learning algorithms detect traffic patterns in order to enable the authorities to provide improved congestion management. ITS predictive maintenance monitors infrastructure health, avoiding failures and service disruptions. AI-based chatbots guide travelers with travel information, enabling customer satisfaction. Automated driver assistance-based incident detection alerts emergency responders to accidents in real time. ITS smart city projects deploy ITS with other city services to deliver comprehensive mobility and safety solutions. Risk assessment algorithms based on AI make the road planning and development safer. ITS technologies implemented in carpooling and ride-sharing systems maximize transport efficiency. With increasing AI capability, ITS is more clever and responsive in optimizing transport networks. By combining AI and ITS, urban spaces are made safer and more efficient.

Autonomous cars (AVs) are the revolutionizing aspect of ITS, transforming mobility as well as road safety. AVs fitted with LiDAR, radar, and artificial intelligence-based navigation systems reduce man-made error rates and fewer accidents. AVs interact with traffic control systems to adjust speed and route options dynamically. Platooning technology enables autonomous trucks to move in platoons of synchronized vehicles to enhance fuel efficiency. ITS provides secure deployment of AVs using vehicle-to-everything (V2X) communication. Autonomous public transit like autonomous buses provides better urban mobility at lower operating expenses. AVs make transport green by enhancing energy efficiency and emissions. ITS architectures offer the technical and regulatory foundation required to facilitate AV uptake. Testing and simulation continuously improve autonomous systems' reliability and safety. Governments supporting policies for enabling AVs' ethical and legal integration into transportation systems are being developed. With ITS assistance, software-defined AVs hold a key to a safer and more sustainable mobility urban future.

ITS cybersecurity is a core concern because it rests on digital-based infrastructure and data exchange. Transportation infrastructure immunity from cyber attack requires strong encryption and authentication controls. Cyber attackers are able to hijack traffic lights, take over vehicle systems, and steal confidential information. Secure communications systems guard ITS systems against unauthorized access. AI-based cybersecurity systems identify and respond to abnormalities in real-time. Frequent security auditing and penetration testing strengthen system resilience to cyber attacks. ITS developers use blockchain technology to make sure secure, tamper-proof data exchange. Public awareness campaigns educate users on cybersecurity best practices in intelligent transport. Governments work together with cybersecurity professionals to establish policies and regulations for ITS security. A secure ITS environment is vital to system dependability and the upkeep of public trust. Cybersecurity technologies will further drive the development of ITS, facilitating secure and efficient transport network.

Greening of transport is a notable area of ITS concern that minimizes carbon impressions and promotes environmentally friendly transportation. Intelligent traffic management saves fuel through its efficient utilization of the best use of roads and minimizing idle driving. ITS makes it easier for electrical vehicle (EV) usage to be adopted through the infusion of charging stations with navigation functionality. AI-based eco-driving assistant systems also improve driving culture of motorists towards fuel conservation. Carpooling application networks manage single-occupancy vehicle use dynamically and, as a consequence, minimize carbon footprint. ITS enables public transport networks to guide travelers toward environmentally friendly means of travel. ITS routing optimizes delivery routes for the purpose of lowering emissions from freight haulage. ITS analytics enables bicycle-sharing and pedestrian-friendly city planning. ITS infrastructure is fueled from renewable sources, and transport systems are made green. Sustainability is a renewing impetus for transport innovation as ITS grows. Intelligent, sustainable transport solutions help shrink urban spaces to cleaner, healthier places.

ITS applications greatly enhance emergency management and disaster response. ITS offers immediate information regarding natural disasters, road closures, and evacuation routes during emergencies. Automatic warning systems alert the public and the authorities of dangers so that instant action can be taken. ITS-connected emergency vehicles receive priority to move through traffic, reducing response times. AI-powered camera-equipped drones assist in assessing disaster-stricken areas. ITS-based GIS assist in designing effective evacuation plans. Its real-time surveillance of bridges and tunnels forestalls structural collapse during harsh weather conditions. AI-assisted predictive models study disaster threats and enhance preparedness responses. Public safety infrastructures offer citizens emergency notifications and safety travel advisories. ITS, when applied in coordination with the police and emergency departments, boosts disaster resilience via collective effort. ITS, when coupled with disaster management systems, allows cities to provide quick, unified emergency responses.

Emerging ITS advances will continue to redefine transport to become intelligent, safe, and highly networked. Advances in 5G and edge computing will enable ITS to process data quickly and make real-time decisions. AI- and IoT-based traffic management systems will develop more dynamic, adaptive urban mobility networks. The scope of connected infrastructure will be broadened to enable vehicle-to-roadside and city-management system communication in order to enhance their coordination. Autonomous drones will serve for traffic surveillance, accident sensing, and emergency responses. Blockchain technology will enhance security and transparency in transportation data. Advanced multimodal transport systems will offer seamless connections between modes of transport. The public and private sectors will increasingly invest in ITS research and development. The possible inclusion of quantum computing will help further increase ITS capacity to address complex traffic flow. As technology improves, ITS will play an increasingly crucial role in determining the mobility of the city and intercity in the future. Smarter and more data-advanced transport systems will redefine future safety and mobility.

Javed and Khan (2011) propose a geocasting strategy for IEEE 802.11p-based VANETs but without the outcome of actual field deployment, the work is not as application-oriented as it would have been otherwise. Ben Othmane et al. (2013) augment safety features in vehicle-to-vehicle connected vehicles but fail to address scalability issues in large networks. Javed and Khan (2014a) examine an adaptive rate-range control algorithm for VANET safety services, yet the algorithm's performance in very dynamic traffic conditions is not considered. Javed et al. (2014a) suggest an integrated space-division multiple access and adaptive rate control scheme, yet the solution is not developed with respect to the effects of increased network congestion. Javed and Khan (2013) propose a cooperative safety zone approach, but the paper does not compare other cooperative methods. Javed et al. (2014b) discuss multimedia transfer using emergency services in VANETs, but the paper does not comprehensively discuss security issues relating to multimedia data transfer. Javed and Khan (2013) discuss a time headway-based rate control algorithm but do not account for introduced latency in high network loads. Javed et al. (2014c) introduce a tone-based time-slotted protocol for delivering emergency messages, but its applicability with various mobility models remains to be investigated. Qu et al. (2015) perform a security and privacy analysis of VANETs, but experimental results regarding the security threat and countermeasures described are not given. Ben Hamida et al. (2015a) present security risks of cooperative ITS, but the proposed cryptographic countermeasures need additional performance evaluation in real-world scenarios. Finally, Ben Hamida et al. (2015b) implement and test the ETSI security architecture without checking its inter-operability with upcoming ITS standards. These shortcomings make it necessary to conduct additional research and validation to improve the resilience and scalability of VANET security and communication protocols.

Bernstein and Lange (2016) provide cryptographic benchmarking through eBACS but lack implementation details from actual data, so real-world performance differences become indefinite. Moghimifar and Stebila (2016) approximate the TLS performance based on the key exchange performance but overlook the factor of network congestion and variable traffic patterns. Järvinen (2007) describes a cryptoprocessor for ECDSA, but the suggested implementation lacks flexibility to accommodate current high-speed cryptographic requirements. Glas et al. (2011) focus on ECDSA signature calculation over prime fields but do not adequately cover the problem of resource constraints in embedded systems. Crypto++ 5.6.0 benchmarks (2016) provide useful performance estimates but fail to cover real-world ITS applications' security concerns. Aschenbruck et al. (2012) discuss crypto-based security techniques in tactical wireless networks but do not fully explore interoperability with existing ITS platforms. Moalla et al. (2014) evaluate the PRESERVE VSS and Score@F System, but their findings are not applicable to large-scale ITS environments. Nowdehi and Olovsson (2014) employ ETSI ITS SecuredMessage service, though their work does not fully explore scalability challenges in highly dynamic vehicular networks. Banani and Gordon (2014) propose the selection of safety messages for VANETs' check-in based on priority of zones, yet no performance analysis in various traffic conditions. Schmidt et al. (2010) present an approach for selective forward beacon, yet the approach fails to optimize message prioritization for time-based safety alerts. Feiri et al. (2013) explain how security influences cooperative awareness but do not conduct research based on offering concrete measures against security-led performance loss. ETSI (2012) mandates security headers and certificate types for ITS but does not address future quantum-resistant cryptographic algorithms. Turner et al. (2009) mention elliptic curve cryptography subject public key information but do not evaluate its effectiveness in real-time ITS. Whiting et al. (2003) propose the Counter with CBC-MAC (CCM) method, but no implementation aspects are shown by them for ITS scenarios. Gayoso Martínez et al. (2015) analyze the security of Elliptic Curve Integrated Encryption Scheme, but they don't comprehensively address real-world implementation complexities in vehicular networks. Finally, ETSI (2014) establishes OSI cross-layer topics but doesn't consider newer developments in cross-layer optimization of secure and efficient ITS communications. Gaps highlight the need for further studies on scalable real-world ITS security and cryptographic implementations.

Gu et al. (2021) also proposed the ECPC-ICP approach for 6D vehicle pose estimation by fusing roadside LiDAR and road features; however, the process can be plagued by accuracy degradation during adverse weather or when the road markings are blurry. Fukatsu and Sakaguchi (2021) examine cooperative perception via millimeter-wave V2V communication for secure overtaking, but their method relies upon secure V2V connectivity, which may be vulnerable to signal interference or network congestion. Shan et al. (2020) demonstrate cooperative perception for connected and automated vehicles, but their work does not comprehensively study the computational burden of real-time data fusion, which may impact system responsiveness. Baek et al. (2021) present an environment perception approach that integrates vehicular wireless communications and automotive sensors but have a non-adaptive framework for delays or inaccuracies in sensor fusion during changing traffic conditions. Jiang et al. (2023) present a multi-GNSS/IMU data fusion algorithm for land vehicles but are not concerned with the algorithm's robustness in urban canyon areas during weak or blocked GNSS signals. Huang et al. (2012) introduce a fault diagnosis and control method with the Kalman filter for linear drives, but its reliance on an accurate system model may render it less applicable in very nonlinear or uncertain environments. Zhao (2016) compares the Cubature Kalman filter in a GPS/IMU navigation system but does not address its computational complexity in automotive usage with limited resources. Impraimakis and Smyth (2022) propose an unscented Kalman filter method to estimation in real-time but do not know its behavior when used with high-speed vehicle applications with abrupt state changes. Lu (2021) builds HRegNet for outdoor large-scale LiDAR point cloud registration but does not examine the scalability of the approach to real-time systems on autonomous vehicles. Papaioannidis et al. (2021) propose a multi-task deep neural network for UAV safety based on human crowd detection, but the performance of the method is not well discussed in low-light or occluded conditions. Liu et al. (2021) predict vehicle sideslip angles with signal measurement properties considered, but their model is vulnerable to sensor drift and sensor errors during long-duration flight. These limitations lead to the need for further research to enhance robustness, real-time operation, and adaptability to different environmental conditions in autonomous systems.

The model described here addresses the limitation of existing approaches by enhancing robustness, real-time performance, and adaptability to varying environmental conditions. Unlike Gu et al. (2021), where the precision decreases due to poor weather and unclear road markings, the approach in this case utilizes a sophisticated sensor fusion strategy that incorporates adaptive filtering principles to improve pose estimation under adverse conditions. Unlike the heavy dependency on strong V2V communication by Fukatsu and Sakaguchi (2021), the current model integrates a hybrid mechanism of dynamic switching between V2V and edge computing in order to provide reliable cooperative perception. Even though Shan et al. (2020) do not discuss computational overhead thoroughly, the proposed methodology optimizes data processing pipelines with low computational models of deep learning such that real-time capability is supported. Compared with Baek et al. (2021), where sensor fusion latency influences decision-making, the solution proposed here offers an efficient fusion process underpinned by predictive analytics, imparting less latency in high-speed vehicular environments. For GNSS/IMU fusion in Jiang et al. (2023), which is strained in urban canyons, the proposed model includes additional environmental data such as road topology and visual odometry to improve localization accuracy. The reliance on accurate system models in Kalman filter-based methods like Huang et al. (2012) and Zhao (2016) is minimized through the application of a hybrid filtering technique that adapts to nonlinear behaviors in vehicle dynamics. The unscented Kalman filter approach in Impraimakis and Smyth (2022) is complemented by an adaptive state estimation process, ensuring reliability in high-speed vehicle systems. To address the scalability problem of Lu (2021) in large LiDAR point cloud registration, the proposed approach features a hierarchical processing framework that efficiently addresses computational complexity. Unlike Papaioannidis et al. (2021), where crowd detection is hindered by occluded environments, the proposed technique fortifies detection through multi-modal sensor fusion, improving UAV safety under challenging conditions. Finally, Liu et al.'s (2021) issue of sensor drift and fault is resolved using an advanced filtering algorithm that dynamically adjusts sensor measurements to provide correct long-term vehicle dynamics estimation. In summary, the presented model successfully overcomes current drawbacks, improving reliability, efficiency, and responsiveness in autonomous and connected vehicle systems.

SMART TOLL COLLECTION AND AUTOMATED PAYMENT SYSTEMS

Algorithm for Smart Toll Collection and Automated Payments

Step 1: Initialization

- Generate a unique elliptic curve key pair using the Improved Ecliptic Curve Algorithm (IECA) for each registered vehicle.
- Assign a public-private key pair (PK_V, SK_V) to the vehicle and (PK_T, SK_T) to the toll booth system.
- The toll system and vehicles exchange digital certificates signed by a trusted ITS authority.

Step 2: Vehicle Authentication Using IECA

- When a vehicle approaches the toll booth, it broadcasts a digitally signed request containing its public key (PK_V) and vehicle ID.
- The toll booth verifies the vehicle's identity by checking its signature using the IECA public key.
- If authentication succeeds, the toll booth generates a session key (SK_TV) using IECA-based key agreement, securing further communication.

Step 3: Toll Amount Calculation and Hashing with EHF

- The toll booth calculates the toll fee based on vehicle type, distance traveled, and congestion pricing.
- The calculated toll fee and vehicle details are hashed using the Enhanced Hash Function (EHF) to ensure tamper-proof transaction data.
- The toll system sends a digitally signed invoice containing the hashed transaction data to the vehicle.

Step 4: Secure Payment Processing

- The vehicle signs the invoice with its private key (SK_V) and submits the encrypted payment confirmation.
- The toll system decrypts and verifies the signature using IECA and processes the payment.
- The payment transaction is logged on a blockchain ledger using EHF-based hash values, ensuring immutability and transparency.

Step 5: Toll Clearance and Barrier Control

- Upon successful transaction validation, the toll system sends an encrypted clearance message to the automated toll barrier control system.
- The toll booth records the hashed transaction in the ITS central server or blockchain ledger, preventing fraud or disputes.
- The vehicle receives a digital receipt, which can be verified later for dispute resolution or audit purposes.

Theorem 1: Correctness of IECA-Based Key Agreement

Statement: Given two parties (vehicle V and toll booth T) that exchange public keys using the Improved Ecliptic Curve Algorithm (IECA), the shared secret key computed independently by both parties is identical.

Proof:

1. Let G be a base point on the elliptic curve E over a finite field F_q.
2. The vehicle selects a private key k_V and computes its public key:

$$PK_V = k_V \cdot G$$

The toll booth selects a private key k_T and computes its public key:

$$K_T = k_T \cdot GP$$

3. The vehicle computes the shared secret using PK_T:

$$S = k_V \cdot PK_T = k_V \cdot \left(k_T \cdot G\right) = \left(k_V k_T\right) \cdot G$$

4. The toll booth computes the shared secret using PK_V:

$$S' = k_T \cdot PK_V = k_T \cdot \left(k_V \cdot G\right)$$

$= \left(k_T k_V\right) \cdot G$Since multiplication in an elliptic curve group is commutative, we have:

$$S = S'$$

Thus, both parties derive the same shared secret, proving the correctness of the IECA key agreement.

Theorem 2: Collision Resistance of EHF-Based Hashing

Statement: The Enhanced Hash Function (EHF) used in toll transactions is collision-resistant, meaning that it is computationally infeasible to find two distinct transactions $T_1 \neq T_2$ such that $H(T_1) = H(T_2)$.

Proof:

1. Assume there exists a collision where two transactions T_1 and T_2 map to the same hash value:

$$H(T_1) = H(T_2)$$

2. EHF is designed with a cryptographic hash function (e.g., SHA-3 or Blake3), which follows the avalanche effect:
   - o A small change in input significantly changes the output.
3. Suppose an attacker attempts a brute force search to find a collision. The complexity is $2^{n/2}$ for an n-bit hash output (Birthday Paradox).
4. If n=256n = 256n=256, the complexity is 2^{128} operations, which is infeasible with modern computing power.
5. Hence, finding two transactions with the same hash is computationally impractical, proving collision resistance.

Theorem 3: Unforgeability of Toll Transaction Signatures

Statement: A digitally signed toll transaction using IECA-based elliptic curve signatures cannot be forged without access to the private key of the signing entity.

Proof:

1. Suppose a vehicle generates a digital signature for a toll transaction message M:
   - o The vehicle's private key is SK_V.
   - o The signature is generated as:

$$(r, s) = \text{Sign}(M, SK_V)$$

2. The toll booth verifies the signature using the vehicle's public key PK_V:

$$\text{Verify}(M, (r, s), PK_V)$$

3. The security of elliptic curve signatures relies on the hardness of the Elliptic Curve Discrete Logarithm Problem (ECDLP):
   - o Given $PK_V = k_V \cdot G$, it is infeasible to compute K_V.
4. An attacker trying to forge a valid signature must either:
   - o Compute K_V (which is infeasible due to ECDLP).
   - o Find a collision in the signature hash (infeasible due to EHF collision resistance).
5. Since both conditions are computationally impossible, the digital signature remains unforgeable.

Theorem 4: Resistance to Replay Attacks in Toll Transactions

Statement: The IECA-EHF protocol prevents replay attacks by ensuring that each transaction is uniquely signed and time-stamped.

Proof:

1. Each transaction T includes a unique timestamp T_s and a one-time nonce N:

$$T = \left(V_I D, Toll_F ee, T_s, N\right)$$

The transaction hash is computed as:

$$H_T = H(T)$$

2. The digital signature includes H_T:

$$\sigma = \text{Sign}\left(H_T, SK_V\right)$$

3. Upon receiving the transaction, the toll booth:
   - o Checks if T_s is within an acceptable time window (e.g., last 30 seconds).
   - o Ensures that N has not been used previously (using a database of processed transactions).
4. If a replayed transaction is detected, it is immediately rejected.
5. Since every transaction has a unique nonce and timestamp, attackers cannot reuse old transactions successfully.

Theorem 5: Computational Efficiency of IECA Over Classical ECC

Statement: The Improved Ecliptic Curve Algorithm (IECA) achieves lower computational cost than classical Elliptic Curve Cryptography (ECC) while maintaining equivalent security levels.

Proof:

1. Classical ECC key generation involves scalar multiplication:

$$Q = k \cdot G$$

which requires O(n) modular multiplications for an n-bit key.

2. IECA optimizes ECC using:
   - o Optimized scalar multiplication algorithms (e.g., Montgomery Ladder).
   - o Curve optimizations (e.g., twisted Edwards curves).
3. The improved IECA method reduces key generation complexity to:

$$O(n/\log n)$$

4. This makes IECA computationally more efficient than classical ECC, reducing toll processing delays.

Theorem 6: Blockchain Immutability of Toll Transactions

Statement: Once a toll transaction is recorded on a blockchain ledger using EHF-hashed data, it cannot be modified or deleted.

Proof:

1. Each toll transaction is hashed using EHF:

$$H(T) = H\left(V_I D, Toll_F ee, T_s, N\right)$$

The hash is recorded in a blockchain block along with the previous block's hash:

$$B_n = H\left(B_{n-1}, H(T)\right)$$

2. Suppose an attacker attempts to modify transaction T. Any change in T results in a new hash H′(T)≠H(T).

3. This change propagates to all future blocks, requiring recomputation of all hashes, which is computationally infeasible due to:
   - Cryptographic hash functions' pre-image resistance.
   - Blockchain consensus mechanisms (e.g., Proof-of-Work or Proof-of-Stake) rejecting tampered blocks.
4. Thus, once recorded, transactions remain immutable, ensuring fraud prevention.

CONCLUSION

The intelligent traffic collection and automated payment process with IECA-EHF boosts security, reliability, and efficiency in Intelligent Transportation Systems. IECA offers a secure key exchange scheme with minimal computational burden and optimum cryptographic strength. EHF provides collision-resistant hashing to avert fraud and replay attacks. Blockchain guarantees transactions as immutable, which avoids unauthorized alteration. Through security analysis and theoretical validation, we confirm that the system suggested safeguards financial transactions and improves the efficiency of tolling collection. Using IECA and EHF in ITS not only ensures data integrity but also enables real-time decision-making in transport systems. Anomaly detection for fraud detection using AI and quantum-resistant cryptography can be given consideration in future implementations for further improving security in ITS. The system, as proposed, plays a major role in developing safer, smarter, and more efficient transport systems.

REFERENCES

Aschenbruck, N., Gerhards-Padilla, E., & Lambertz, M. (2012, October 22–25). *Applicability of crypto-based security approaches in tactical wireless multi-hop networks*. In *Proceedings of the IEEE Conference on Local Computer Networks* (pp. 102–110). Clearwater, FL, USA. DOI: 10.1109/LCN.2012.6423584

Baek, M., Mun, J., Kim, W., Choi, D., Yim, J., & Lee, S. (2021). Driving environment perception based on the fusion of vehicular wireless communications and automotive remote sensors. *Sensors (Basel)*, *21*(6), 1860. DOI: 10.3390/s21051860 PMID: 33799998

Banani, S., & Gordon, S. (2014, October 1–3). *Selecting basic safety messages to verify in VANETs using zone priority*. In *Proceedings of the Asia-Pacific Conference on Communications* (pp. 423–428). Pattaya, Thailand. DOI: 10.1109/APCC.2014.7092849

Ben Hamida, E., Noura, H., & Znaidi, W. (2015). Security of cooperative intelligent transport systems: Standards, threats analysis and cryptographic countermeasures. *Electronics (Basel)*, *4*(2), 380–423. DOI: 10.3390/electronics4030380

Ben Hamida, E., Znaidi, W., & Menouar, H. (2015, September 6–9). *Implementation and evaluation of the ETSI security architecture for cooperative intelligent transport systems*. In *Proceedings of the IEEE Vehicular Technology Conference (VTC-Fall)* (pp. 1–5). Boston, MA, USA.

Ben Othmane, L., Al-Fuqaha, A., Ben Hamida, E., & van den Brand, M. (2013). *Towards extended safety in connected vehicles*. In *Proceedings of the IEEE Intelligent Transportation Systems* (pp. 652–657). The Hague, The Netherlands.

Bernstein, D. J., & Lange, T. (n.d.). *eBACS: ECRYPT Benchmarking of Cryptographic Systems. Crypto++ 5.6.0 Benchmarks*. https://www.cryptopp.com/benchmarks.html (accessed March 17, 2025)

European Telecommunications Standards Institute. (2012). *ETSI TS 102 941 v1.1.1 (2012-06)—Intelligent Transport Systems (ITS)—Security; Security header and certificate formats* [Technical Report]. Valbonne, France.

European Telecommunications Standards Institute. (2014). *ETSI TS 102 723-8 v1.0.4 (2014-07)—Intelligent Transport Systems (ITS)—OSI cross-layer topics; Part 11: Interface between networking and transport layer and facilities layer* [Technical Report]. Valbonne, France.

Feiri, M., Petit, J., Schmidt, R., & Kargl, F. (2013, December 16–18). *The impact of security on cooperative awareness in VANET*. In *Proceedings of the IEEE Vehicular Networking Conference* (pp. 127–134). Boston, MA, USA. DOI: 10.1109/VNC.2013.6737599

Fukatsu, R., & Sakaguchi, K. (2021). Automated driving with cooperative perception using millimeter-wave V2V communications for safe overtaking. *Sensors (Basel), 21*(8), 2659. DOI: 10.3390/s21082659 PMID: 33920066

Gayoso Martínez, V., Hernández Encinas, L., & Queiruga Dios, A. (2015). Security and practical considerations when implementing the elliptic curve integrated encryption scheme. *Cryptologia, 39*(3), 244–269. DOI: 10.1080/01611194.2014.988363

Glas, B., Sander, O., Stuckert, V., Müller-Glaser, K. D., & Becker, J. (2011). Prime field ECDSA signature processing for reconfigurable embedded systems. *International Journal of Reconfigurable Computing, 2011*, 10511064. Advance online publication. DOI: 10.1155/2011/836460

Gu, B., Liu, J., Xiong, H., Li, T., & Pan, Y. (2021). ECPC-ICP: A 6D vehicle pose estimation method by fusing the roadside lidar point cloud and road feature. *Sensors (Basel), 21*(10), 3489. DOI: 10.3390/s21103489 PMID: 34067737

Huang, S., Tan, K. K., & Lee, T. H. (2012). Fault diagnosis and fault-tolerant control in linear drives using the Kalman filter. *IEEE Transactions on Industrial Electronics, 59*(10), 4285–4292. DOI: 10.1109/TIE.2012.2185011

Impraimakis, M., & Smyth, A. W. (2022). An unscented Kalman filter method for real-time input-parameter-state estimation. *Mechanical Systems and Signal Processing, 162*, 108026. DOI: 10.1016/j.ymssp.2021.108026

Järvinen, K. (2007). *Cryptoprocessor for elliptic curve digital signature algorithm (ECDSA)* (Technical Report). Helsinki University of Technology, Espoo, Finland.

Javed, M. A., & Khan, J. Y. (2013, June 2–5). *A cooperative safety zone approach to enhance the performance of VANET applications*. In *Proceedings of the IEEE Vehicular Technology Conference* (pp. 1–5). Dresden, Germany. DOI: 10.1109/VTCSpring.2013.6691819

Javed, M. A., & Khan, J. Y. (2011, November 9–11). *A geocasting technique in an IEEE802.11p based vehicular ad hoc network for road traffic management*. In *Proceedings of the Australasian Telecommunication Networks and Applications Conference* (pp. 1–6). Melbourne, Australia.

Javed, M. A., & Khan, J. Y. (2013, December 16–18). *Performance analysis of a time headway based rate control algorithm for VANET safety applications*. In *Proceedings of the International Conference on Signal Processing and Communication Systems* (pp. 1–6). Carrara, Australia. DOI: 10.1109/ICSPCS.2013.6723983

Javed, M. A., & Khan, J. Y. (2014, February 3–6). *Performance analysis of an adaptive rate-range control algorithm for VANET safety applications*. In *Proceedings of the International Conference on Computing, Networking and Communications* (pp. 418–423). Honolulu, HI, USA. DOI: 10.1109/ICCNC.2014.6785371

Javed, M. A., Khan, J. Y., & Ngo, D. T. (2014, May 18–21). *A tone-based time-slotted protocol for multi-hop emergency message dissemination in VANETs*. In *Proceedings of the IEEE Vehicular Technology Conference* (pp. 1–5). Seoul, Korea. DOI: 10.1109/VTCSpring.2014.7022800

Javed, M. A., Khan, J. Y., & Ngo, D. T. (2014, April 6–9). *Joint space-division multiple access and adaptive rate control for basic safety messages in VANETs*. In *Proceedings of the IEEE Wireless Communication and Networking Conference* (pp. 2688–2693). Istanbul, Turkey. DOI: 10.1109/WCNC.2014.6952853

Javed, M. A., Khan, J. Y., & Ngo, D. T. (2014, September 14–17). *Multimedia transmission for emergency services in VANETs*. In *Proceedings of the IEEE Vehicular Technology Conference* (pp. 1–5). Vancouver, BC, Canada. DOI: 10.1109/VTCFall.2014.6966065

Jiang, C., Zhao, D., Zhang, Q., & Liu, W. (2023). A multi-GNSS/IMU data fusion algorithm based on the mixed norms for land vehicle applications. *Remote Sensing (Basel)*, *15*(9), 2439. DOI: 10.3390/rs15092439

Liu, W., Xia, X., Xiong, L., Lu, Y., Gao, L., & Yu, Z. (2021). Automated vehicle sideslip angle estimation considering signal measurement characteristic. *IEEE Sensors Journal*, *21*(18), 21675–21687. DOI: 10.1109/JSEN.2021.3059050

Lu, F. (2021, October 11–17). *HRegNet: A hierarchical network for large-scale outdoor LiDAR point cloud registration*. In *Proceedings of the IEEE International Conference on Computer Vision* (pp. 15994–16003). Montreal, BC, Canada. DOI: 10.1109/ICCV48922.2021.01571

Moalla, R., Lonc, B., Segarra, G., Laguna, M., Papadimitratos, P., Petit, J., & Labiod, H. (2014, April 14–17). *Experimentation with the PRESERVE VSS and the Score@F system*. In *Proceedings of the 5th Conference on Transport Research Arena (TRA)*. Paris, France. DOI: 10.1002/9781119307853.ch17

Moghimifar, F., & Stebila, D. (2016, February 2–5). *Predicting TLS performance from key exchange performance*. In *Proceedings of the Australasian Computer Science Week Multiconference* (pp. 44:1–44:4). Canberra, Australia. DOI: 10.1145/2843043.2843360

Nowdehi, N., & Olovsson, T. (2014, June 8–11). *Experiences from implementing the ETSI ITS SecuredMessage service*. In *2014 IEEE Intelligent Vehicles Symposium Proceedings* (pp. 1055–1060). Dearborn, MI, USA. DOI: 10.1109/IVS.2014.6856587

Papaioannidis, C., Mademlis, I., & Pitas, I. (2021, May 30–June 5). *Autonomous UAV safety by visual human crowd detection using multi-task deep neural networks*. In *Proceedings of the IEEE International Conference on Robotics and Automation (ICRA)* (pp. 11074–11080). Xi'an, China. DOI: 10.1109/ICRA48506.2021.9560830

Qu, F., Wu, Z., Wang, F., & Cho, W. (2015). A security and privacy review of VANETs. *IEEE Transactions on Intelligent Transportation Systems*, *16*(6), 2985–2996. DOI: 10.1109/TITS.2015.2439292

Schmidt, R., Lasowski, R., Leinmüller, T., Linnhoff-Popien, C., & Schäfer, G. (2010, December 13–15). *An approach for selective beacon forwarding to improve cooperative awareness*. In *Proceedings of the IEEE Vehicular Networking Conference* (pp. 182–188). Jersey City, NJ, USA. DOI: 10.1109/VNC.2010.5698243

Shan, M., Narula, K., Wong, Y. F., Worrall, S., Khan, M., Alexander, P., & Nebot, E. (2020). Demonstrations of cooperative perception: Safety and robustness in connected and automated vehicle operations. *Sensors (Basel)*, *21*(1), 200. DOI: 10.3390/s21010200 PMID: 33396804

Turner, S., Brown, D., Yiu, K., Housley, R., & Polk, T. (2009). *Elliptic Curve Cryptography Subject Public Key Information* (RFC 5480). Internet Engineering Task Force (IETF). DOI: 10.17487/rfc5480

Whiting, D., Housley, R., & Ferguson, N. (2003). *Counter with CBC-MAC (CCM)* (RFC 3610). Internet Engineering Task Force (IETF). DOI: 10.17487/rfc3610

Zhao, Y. (2016). Performance evaluation of Cubature Kalman filter in a GPS/IMU tightly-coupled navigation system. *Signal Processing*, *119*, 67–79. DOI: 10.1016/j.sigpro.2015.07.014

Chapter 10

Smart Disaster Management Minimizing Response Time in Disaster Situations Using AI

Usharani Bhimavarapu
https://orcid.org/0000-0002-0246-1420
Department of Computer Science and Engineering, Koneru Lakshmaiah Education Foundation, Vaddeswaram, India

ABSTRACT

Rescue Team Scheduling Mode is an essential part of disaster management that facilitates timely deployment of emergency response teams with optimal utilization of resources. Conventional scheduling models are likely to fail in accommodating dynamic environments, uncertain disaster scenarios, and real-time decision-making. To address these challenges, a robust scheduling algorithm is presented, which combines machine learning, reinforcement learning, and optimization techniques. The algorithm takes into account factors like the severity of emergencies, availability of teams, current traffic conditions, and environmental limitations to distribute resources optimally. Using algorithms such as Multi-Objective Genetic Algorithm (MOGA), Ant Colony Optimization (ACO), and Reinforcement Learning (RL), the model redistributes teams adaptively and optimizes routes. The suggested mode of scheduling also provides equitable load distribution, reduces response time, and improves coordination among different agencies.

DOI: 10.4018/979-8-3373-0245-4.ch010

INTRODUCTION

Artificial Intelligence (AI) is revolutionizing crisis management and emergency response by enhancing disaster preparedness speed and efficiency. Predictive analytics powered by AI has the ability to determine potential threats and predict disasters by analyzing real-time and historical data. Machine learning algorithms trawl large data sets and find patterns, enabling officials to respond ahead of a crisis proactively. Artificial intelligence early warning systems improve readiness by availing timely notifications from environmental and meteorological information. Technologies lower the response time, pay for damages, and save lives. AI also eases interactions among emergency teams, the state, and the public. AI chatbots give immediate information, such that impacted communities get timely guidance. AI social media monitoring allows the authorities to track opinions and arising hazards amid crises. The predictive ability of AI allows governments and institutions to make effective disaster management decisions. AI assists emergency response teams in becoming stronger and minimizing the effects of disasters. AI is also essential in supplementing disaster response with automation and intelligent decision-making. AI-driven image recognition drones conduct real-time aerial evaluations of the impacted zones. The drones can pick out survivors, evaluate the level of damage to structures, and chart damaged regions to aid rescue missions. Robots driven by artificial intelligence are sent into danger zones where human entry is unsafe, i.e., in rubble or chemical spill-affected areas. Autonomous vehicles driven by AI can ferry relief supplies, shortening the logistical delays in affected areas. Decision-support systems based on AI scan inputs from many sources and give advice to first responders about the best action. The systems combine satellite imagery, weather, and emergency reports to create actionable information. AI enhances the distribution of medicine, food, and shelter to the affected people as well. Machine learning applications give priority to rescue efforts by urgency and severity. Human mistakes are minimized and relief activities are streamlined in coordination during disasters. Through AI, emergency teams can provide informed choices and carry out schemes more accurately.

AI enables crisis communication in guaranteeing the communication of life-saving information to victims. Natural language processing (NLP) allows AI-driven chatbots to offer real-time assistance in emergencies. Chatbots respond to questions, direct individuals to secure areas, and disseminate critical updates. Artificial intelligence-based speech recognition technologies filter through emergency calls for identifying distress and route critical cases first. AI-based social media sentiment analysis notifies authorities of public fears and disinformation. AI also enhances multilingual communication through real-time translation, making crisis messages inclusive. AI-based virtual assistants aid emergency hotlines by filtering out non-emergency cases, hence enabling human operators to treat the emergency ones. AI geolocation services direct impacted individuals to local shelters and healthcare centers. Autopilot voice assistants inform residents of evacuation and safety procedures. AI-based algorithms learn from previous crisis communication campaigns to refine future emergency communication. With the use of AI, governments are able to permit clear, rapid, and effective communication in times of disaster.

Predictive analytics powered by AI improves disaster readiness by detecting threat factors and weak points. AI models take into account climate trends, earthquakes, and flood data to forecast possible catastrophes. Governments utilize the models to create contingency plans and mobilize resources. AI-based simulations enable governments to simulate response efforts and enhance preparedness for different crises. AI-based geospatial analysis identifies risky zones and suggests improvement of infrastructure in order to avert possible damage. AI also helps in identifying vulnerable groups that need special care during crisis times. Insurance companies apply AI to evaluate disaster risk and create personalized coverage plans. Environmental changes signaling an impending disaster are detected by monitoring systems powered by AI, such as sea level rise or unusual weather patterns. Governments employ AI-driven risk assessment platforms to implement tighter building codes and disaster-proof construction. Data visualization methods powered by artificial intelligence supplement situational awareness by making challenging data relevant. In accurate prediction of catastrophe, AI improves catastrophe resilience and readiness.

Artificial intelligence robots transform search and rescue missions with improved efficiency and safety. Drone-guided AI thermal imaging identifies survivors buried under rubble. Robotic exoskeletons help rescue forces by carrying heavy loads over hard terrain. Autonomous underwater robots controlled by AI map submerged landscape to locate lost people and estimate damage. Autonomous vehicles transport hurt victims to hospitals, freeing up human responders. Computer object recognition allows for the detection of survivors under low-vision conditions, i.e., through smoke. AI-driven robot arms conduct precision tasks within dangerous environments, e.g., while dealing with explosive devices. AI-assisted rescue management systems optimize rescue sequencing by location and medical condition of survivors. Machine learning algorithms examine historical rescues to better enable future rescue missions. Real-time health monitoring in emergency response situations is achieved through AI-enabled wearables, without injury and fatigue. Search and rescue missions become safer, faster, and more efficient with AI-enabled robotics.

AI enhances response to healthcare during crises through sophisticated diagnosis and treatment delivery. AI-enabled diagnostic software photographs medical symptoms and scans for disease and injury identification at a high speed. AI-automated triage technology prioritizes patients according to the type of case in order to best match resources. AI-enabled telemedicine integrates physicians with disaster victims who have access to remote healthcare. AI-enabled prediction identifies disease outbreaks after disasters to act at an early point. Medical robots are operated by AI to enhance surgeries and treatment in remote or dangerous areas. Hospital resource management is optimized by AI systems. AI-powered wearable monitors patients' vital signs and warns doctors of deteriorating states. AI-powered ambulance systems utilize real-time traffic data to transport patients to the nearest hospital in the shortest time. AI-powered drug development speeds up emergency medical treatment development. With AI being integrated into medical response, healthcare professionals can provide life-saving interventions more effectively in the time of disasters.

AI enhances disaster recovery by maximizing reconstruction processes and allocation of resources. AI-based damage assessment software examines satellite imagery to assess the nature of destruction. AI-assisted supply chain management allocates reconstruction material to the affected area within time constraints. AI-based urban planning algorithms suggest disaster-resistant plans for design purposes to avoid future calamities. AI-integrated financing systems automatically release disaster relief funds, eliminating corruption and enhancing equity. AI-based sentiment analysis informs policymakers about the psychological impact of disasters on communities. AI-facilitated workforce management systems assign professional workers and volunteers to recovery tasks. AI-powered chatbots offer mental health services to victims of disasters, counseling and advising them. AI-powered risk assessment software allows governments to prioritize funding the most critical recovery tasks. AI logistics platforms automate the rebuilding process with fewer delays and inefficiencies. AI makes disaster recovery more systematic, transparent, and efficient.

AI becomes a key factor in cybersecurity and digital crisis management in the case of an emergency. AI systems that identify cyberattacks scan emergency infrastructure and important communication systems for cyberattacks. Machine learning programs spot patterns of cyber threats and neutrilize them before they are able to disrupt. AI-based fraud prevention stops financial fraud and donation scams in crisis relief activities. AI-based emergency communication systems identify misinformation and stop panic. AI-based backup and recovery systems provide data protection for hospitals, emergency services, and government entities. AI-based identity verification systems stop unauthorized access to relief resources. AI-based sentiment analysis identifies cyber threats due to social unrest in crisis. AI-based encryption protects sensitive emergency response information from malicious players. AI firewalls are updated in real-time based on emerging cyber threats and hence become more resilient. AI protects digital infrastructure in such a way that crisis response remains uninterrupted and secure.

AI-driven automation accelerates emergency logistics and supply chain management. AI-driven demand planning forecasts the requirement of critical supplies in emergencies. Machine learning provides optimized inventory storage and shipping routes for quicker delivery. AI-controlled delivery drones transport medical supplies and food to inaccessible areas. AI-driven fleet management ensures optimal deployment of emergency vehicles. AI-driven predictive maintenance prevents equipment breakdown in the course of disaster relief. AI-driven robots automate sorting and packing operations in emergency supply warehouses. AI-driven blockchain technology ensures accountability in disaster relief distribution. AI-optimized route scheduling minimizes emergency supply transportation delays. AI-driven crisis mapping platforms offer live monitoring of supply chain disruptions. AI makes emergency logistics more responsive, adaptive, and efficient.

The future of AI for emergency response is even brighter for growth in disaster preparedness and resilience. AI-based autonomous disaster response units will operate emergencies with limited human intervention. High-end AI-powered simulations will offer real-time scenario planning in various emergency scenarios. AI-empowered robots and drones will operate in perfect sync to execute faster and safer rescue operations. AI-powered crowd monitoring systems will assure security during massive disaster relief operations. AI-driven bio-surveillance systems will detect and prevent future pandemics. AI-humanitarian aid platforms will revolutionize international disaster relief procedures. AI-smart city infrastructure will enhance urban resilience to disasters of natural and human origin. AI-satellite networks will increase real-time monitoring and communication during disasters. Ethical AI systems will ensure equity, openness, and responsibility in crisis management. With the adoption of AI-based innovations, the globe has a better future to look forward to, towards a more resilient and better-equipped world.

Zhang (2022) explains the need to enhance disaster prevention and emergency management in rural towns. The study is, however, limited by its geographical scope in that the findings mainly hold true for rural towns and cannot be directly transferred to urban towns with varying infrastructure and technological abilities. The research also fails to provide quantitative comparison of proposed actions, which constrains the ability to determine their feasibility in live disaster relief. In addition, the language barrier, since the research is in Chinese, could constrain access by global researchers (Zhang, 2022).

Carley et al. (2016) discuss the utilization of Twitter for crowd-sourcing disaster relief in Indonesia. One major flaw in this research is the fact that social media information is biased since it mainly describes digitally active and urban populations but fails to include those who lack internet connectivity. Moreover, real-time validation of data is not mentioned, thus making it difficult to determine the reliability of the crisis-related tweets. The research also fails to consider cross-platform data integration, thus its applicability in multi-source crisis management (Carley et al., 2016).

Shannon (1948) created a new mathematics of communication theory that is the basis of contemporary information theory. Its use in disaster relief is restricted, as the theory is only concerned with signal transmission and not crisis decision-making in real time. Its provision is also absent in coping with crisis complexities such as unexpected delays and multi-channel communication failures (Shannon, 1948).

Chung and Oh (2006) developed a remote environmental regulation monitoring system based on wireless sensor modules. It is a sensor-based monitoring contribution but its applicability to large-scale disaster response is poorly debated. System scaling in outdoor and harsh environments is also questionable since it was largely tested indoors under controlled environments. Apart from that, this study does not incorporate actual disaster case scenarios to enable us to see how scalable it is going to be in emergency situations (Chung & Oh, 2006).

Yang et al. (2017) discuss the application of big data in disaster management of smart cities. The paper does not address data privacy and security issues, which are the most serious ones during the management of sensitive disaster information. Also, research is concentrated on urban areas without taking the problems of rural or undeveloped areas into account. Also, real-time problems like data latency and integration problems are not investigated very deeply (Yang et al., 2017).

Bartoli et al. (2015) offer an emergency management platform for public safety but the research is not empirically justified by large deployments. It is not known how the given platform will perform in multi-disaster events and large-scale emergencies. The research also does not answer interoperability concerns with other emergency response systems that might restrict real-world use (Bartoli et al., 2015).

Adam et al. (2020) present a comprehensive review of object-tracking sensor networks for smart cities, but the research is based on theoretical models and not real implementations. The research also does not incorporate the energy efficiency of large-scale sensor networks in key decision-making in prolonged disaster response operations. The research does not provide the aspect of sensor networks to operate in difficult environments, which is essential in crisis management (Adam et al., 2020).

Li et al. (2012) further explain compressed sensing for IoT usage and wireless sensor networks. Nevertheless, the study does not consider network congestions in the event of disaster occurrence, which may cause a delay in data transmission. Also, the study concentrates more on signal processing methods in comparison to real-time disaster relief applications. The study also does not include assessment of system robustness in disaster situations, e.g., power outages or destruction of infrastructure (Li et al., 2012).

Bail et al. (partial reference) probably write about the Internet of Things (IoT) in responding to disasters. The general flaw of IoT studies on responding to disasters is reliance on trustworthy networks for communication, which will probably be impaired during a disaster. In addition, neither security nor privacy risks to IoT devices are ever considered, which is an issue for sensitive disaster response information. Finally, realistic case studies demonstrating the performance of IoT over a long term in actuality disaster scenarios in a large scale are not often present within such studies (Bail et al., year).

Guo et al. (2022) discuss major technologies of stereoscopic cooperation in air emergency rescue. Nonetheless, the research is mainly aviation-specific in nature, and hence it cannot be utilized for ground and marine rescue operations. Moreover, the study is carried out in a controlled laboratory setting, and hence the functioning of the suggested technologies in real emergency scenarios is uncertain. Furthermore, since the research is composed in Chinese, linguistic constraints may hinder Chinese researchers beyond their country, therefore preventing worldwide collaboration (Guo et al., 2022).

Jahangiri et al. (2017) examine the contribution of foresight in avoiding systemic failures within disaster risk management. While the research implication suggests the significance of the predictive strategy, there has yet to be empirical verification of foreseen models under real disaster situations. Incorporation into existing AI-driven predictive analytics is also lacking within the framework, whose application can make it more relevant. Even the research is still quite theoretical in purpose, with fewer concerns tackled from the point of view of practical usability (Jahangiri et al., 2017).

Daniel and Doran (2013) discuss the application of geomatics in disaster management for smart cities. The study, however, is more suited for urban communities and hence less relevant in rural communities where there is scarce technological infrastructure. It does not also consider real-time coordination issues of disaster relief, which are most needed while acting in response to an emergency. The study also fails to test geomatics-based disaster management systems' performance under extensive-scale disasters (Daniel & Doran, 2013).

Zhou (2021) discusses the use of social media in disaster management during the big data era. The research fails to discuss misinformation problems that would undermine effective response to disasters. It also discusses mainly the advantages of social media without critically analyzing its limitations, including unequal access in low-income or rural areas. The study is written in Chinese, which could limit global collaboration (Zhou, 2021).

Gong and Yang (2022) offer artificial intelligence application in urban natural disaster emergency response. The study, however, does not consider AI's versatility with varying types of disasters, e.g., earthquakes versus floods. Further, the study does not highlight AI's huge computational burdens and infrastructure requirements for its use during emergencies. Finally, the paper is written in Chinese, which might restrict its scope to cover a broader population (Gong & Yang, 2022).

Zhu et al. (2021) recommend a blockchain-based approach to improve infectious disease traceability. Although the paper provides a promising solution, it does not touch on the high energy usage and computational costs associated with blockchain technology. Moreover, privacy and data protection issues are not seriously examined, especially in regards to sensitive healthcare data. In addition, real-world case studies for implementation are missing from the paper, reducing its verification of suggested approach (Zhu et al., 2021).

Fosso and Berquin (2022) look at the application of ICT in the mitigation of natural disasters in Africa. The study does not discuss infrastructure limitations in rural communities, where the use of ICT may be challenging. It also lacks a comparison with other disaster mitigation strategies, which would enable it to quantify the effectiveness of ICT interventions. Moreover, the research fails to articulate long-term sustainability and upkeep of ICT-based disaster management systems (Fosso & Berquin, 2022).

Zhou and Luo (2023) introduce emergency management in the era of smart cities with a focus on digital intelligence. Nevertheless, the research is technology-innovation-oriented without articulating policy and governance matters relating to the implementation of smart city solutions. The research also fails to consider the ethical and privacy implications of the collection of extensive data. The research does not include pilot projects in actual settings to investigate the effectiveness of the new digital intelligence methods (Zhou & Luo, 2023).

Zhang et al. (2022) give strategic recommendations for next-generation information technology-facilitated modernization of emergency management. The research does not, however, give intensive case studies illustrating actual application of the technologies. In addition, it is largely China-centered, and its applicability is therefore constrained to various geopolitical and infrastructure scenarios. Finally, no cost and resource implications of using such sophisticated technology in emergency management are given in the research paper (Zhang et al., 2022).

Najafi et al. (2020) offer an earthquake emergency response system in Iran as a structured method of disaster management. The system is, however, tailored to Iran's infrastructure and policies and hence cannot be easily applied to other parts of the world with varying governance systems. The research also fails to investigate the utilization of new technologies like AI and IoT in earthquake response, which are steadily gaining importance in contemporary disaster management. The model also lacks empirical verification through extensive real-world usage, which would make it more robust and usable (Najafi et al., 2020).

Al-Kaff et al. (2020) present an emergency support unmanned aerial vehicle (UAV) for monitoring forest fires. While UAVs are applicable in live monitoring, the research does not cover challenges of deploying UAVs under poor weather conditions, which could affect performance. It also doesn't take into consideration regulatory and legal boundaries that could affect the use of UAVs in some locations. The research is not equipped with cost-benefit analysis either, which is important in determining whether large-scale application is feasible or not (Al-Kaff et al., 2020).

Sabrina (2016) evaluates tests to the application of new emergency management tools. Although the research identifies significant obstacles, it does not suggest concrete methods for their achievement, leaving practitioners without realistic solutions. Second, the research applies qualitative measures that may pose subjectivity and constraint generability. Lastly, the research does not experiment with the proposed tools' functionality in actual cases of disasters, diminishing the applicability of the results (Sabrina, 2016).

Aljohani et al. (2023) suggest an intelligent system that combines IoT and machine learning for disaster management. The research points toward the use of these technologies, but the computation and power demand in implementing IoT and ML infrastructure in areas lacking resources is not discussed. The security and privacy threats to IoT-based disaster management are also not well discussed. The study is also deficient in real-case studies of actual events demonstrating the effectiveness of the proposed framework in real-life disaster situations (Aljohani et al., 2023).

Gething and Tatem (2011) do consider the prospect of utilizing mobile phone data to enhance emergency response. The research, however, does not consider availability of data in low-income or rural settings, where there can be poor coverage by mobile networks. The research also does not consider privacy issues involved in the collection and processing of immense mobile phone data. The research mainly considers theoretical options without having tangible case studies to prove the proposed approach (Gething & Tatem, 2011).

George et al. (2017) present emergency management by giving an extensive overview of how disaster response protocols work. The book falls short in explaining new emerging technologies, such as AI-powered prediction of disasters and the use of blockchain for emergency logistics. Additionally, the case studies and examples used might not be updated because the rate of innovation for disaster management practices has increased. The book also does not address region-specific scenarios and thus becomes less relevant to localized practices in disaster management (George et al., 2017).

Seaberg et al. (2017) summarize uses of game theory for managing natural disasters and highlight strategic decision models. The paper, however, does not have empirical verification of hypothesized game theory models, and as a result, it gets challenging to quantify their practicality. Besides, no mention is made of the computational workload of game-theoretic methods that may be a hindrance to their use in real-time in disaster management. Moreover, the research is based on theoretical models and not empirical case studies and hence is less practically useful (Seaberg et al., 2017).

Tennakoon et al. (2021) discuss the integration of small-scale recurring disasters into emergency management models. Though the research is notable in its capture of a crucial aspect of disaster management, it lacks concrete recommendations on how small-scale disasters are to be incorporated into current policy. The research also centers on New Zealand, making its applicability confined to other countries with varying climatic and socio-economic conditions. The research lacks quantitative analysis, which would enhance its recommendations (Tennakoon et al., 2021).

Korkmaz (2023) addresses public health emergencies and disaster risk management based on the experience of rural areas following an earthquake. The research, though, only applies to a given rural context, and outcomes aren't directly applicable to urban or international contexts. The article also doesn't lack evaluation of technology-based interventions, including telemedicine or health monitoring based on AI, in order to augment disaster health response. The research also lacks comparative research with other disaster management reactions to public health, which would be more comprehensive (Korkmaz, 2023).

Chan et al. (2019) study scientific evidence on natural disasters and risk management of health crises in rural Asian regions, but the research fails to examine the role of digital health interventions, such as mobile health apps, which are more appropriate to disaster medicine. Moreover, it mainly discusses past reactions to disasters with little applicability to new threats and interventions for future disaster prevention. The research also does not have policy implications specific to various healthcare infrastructures and is therefore less applicable in other regions (Chan et al., 2019).

RESCUE TEAM SCHEDULING MODEL WITH ENHANCED ALGORITHM

Scheduling rescue teams is important to enable effective response to disasters, that the correct personnel are deployed at the correct time and location. Classical scheduling models are unable to deal with real-time considerations, resource assignments, and dynamic environmental conditions. A better scheduling algorithm is needed to optimize team deployment based on multiple considerations like urgency, terrain conditions, and resource availability.

The AI-Based Dynamic Rescue Scheduling (AIDRS) algorithm dynamically schedules deployment of rescue teams for emergencies based on fast response and optimal utilization of resources. The algorithm initially gathers disaster reports in real time from various sources such as IoT sensors, satellite information, and social media reports. These reports offer vital information regarding the severity, location, and accessibility of affected locations. The system also has an up-to-date database of the rescue teams that are available, how skilled they are, their workload, and their resource level. The algorithm determines the most critical rescue missions to undertake by merging this information based on the severity of the casualties, damage to the infrastructure, and environmental hazards.

Preprocessing the data is the step of clustering the areas of damage using machine learning algorithms like K-Means or DBSCAN. Priority areas with widespread damage and high numbers of casualties are targeted for immediate response. The algorithm subsequently applies a Multi-Objective Genetic Algorithm (MOGA) to optimize crew deployment by allocating numerous factors including urgency, resource availability, and crew specialties. For the computation of shortest rescue travel paths, Ant Colony Optimization (ACO) is used, mimicking natural ant behavior to determine optimal paths for rescue teams to move to areas of disaster. Reinforcement learning (RL) methods are also utilized to aid the algorithm in dynamically re-prioritizing schedules in response to new calls for distress and other environmental factors.

During implementation of the scheduling, the crews are allocated to sites from the allocation optimal model in a way that they incur minimal response time without overloading some of the crews. The constraint programming applies for optimal distribution of workload, while rotation of shifts is included to avert fatigue among the responders. The algorithm continuously updates the rescue strategy based on new news and recalcitates travel plans via Dijkstra's Algorithm or A search algorithm* to adapt for real-time traffic and infrastructure disruptions. Continuous feedback loops continuously optimize subsequent rescue efforts, improving each time it is utilized.

AIDRS algorithm provides AI-based real-time decision-making that dynamically adjusts to scenarios of disasters. It learns more efficiently over time through self-learning processes, allowing maximum deployment and utilization of resources by the team. The process improves disaster preparedness and resilience, improving the efficiency of rescue missions and ensuring life-saving interventions are maximized.

Algorithm: AI-Based Dynamic Rescue Scheduling (AIDRS)

1. **Input:**
    - o Real-time disaster data (location, severity, accessibility).
    - o Rescue team availability (skills, current workload, resources).
    - o Transportation and terrain constraints (road conditions, travel time).
    - o Priority levels (casualty severity, risk factors, weather conditions).
2. **Preprocessing:**
    - o Fetch live disaster reports using IoT sensors, satellite imagery, and social media analysis.
    - o Update database of rescue team locations and capacities.

- o Identify high-priority zones using machine learning-based clustering (e.g., K-Means, DBSCAN).

3. **Optimization:**
   - o Apply Multi-Objective Genetic Algorithm (MOGA) to optimize team allocation.
   - o Use Ant Colony Optimization (ACO) for real-time pathfinding and shortest route identification.
   - o Implement Reinforcement Learning (RL) to dynamically update scheduling based on new rescue requests.
4. **Scheduling Execution:**
   - o Assign teams to locations based on priority and estimated time to reach.
   - o Use constraint programming to ensure fair workload distribution among responders.
   - o Factor in **shift rotations** to manage fatigue and avoid burnout.
5. **Real-Time Adjustments:**
   - o Continuously update assignments based on new distress signals and environmental changes.
   - o Recalculate routes using Dijkstra's Algorithm or *A search algorithm** for efficiency.
   - o Monitor team status and adjust schedules dynamically with predictive analytics.
6. **Output:**
   - o Optimized scheduling plan displayed on emergency response dashboards.
   - o Real-time updates sent to mobile devices of rescue teams.
   - o Continuous feedback loop to refine future deployments.

Theorem 1: Optimal Team Allocation Theorem

Statement: Given a set of rescue teams T and disaster sites D, there exists an optimal assignment $f: T \rightarrow D$ that minimizes response time while maximizing resource efficiency.

Proof:

We define the cost function C(f) as the total time taken for all teams to reach their assigned disaster sites. The objective is to minimize C(f) subject to constraints such as team availability, expertise, and site accessibility. By modeling this as a bipartite matching problem, we apply Hungarian Algorithm or Linear Programming (LP) to find the optimal assignment that ensures minimal response time. The existence of an optimal solution follows from König's theorem, which guarantees a perfect matching in a bipartite graph when a maximum matching equals the minimum vertex cover. Thus, an optimal allocation always exists.

Theorem 2: Shortest Path Feasibility Theorem

Statement: For any rescue team t assigned to a disaster site d, a shortest path always exists if the road network graph G(V,E) is connected.

Proof:

Consider the rescue network as a graph G(V,E) where V represents locations (rescue centers, affected areas) and E represents roads with weights denoting travel times. By Dijkstra's Algorithm, the shortest path from t to d can always be found in polynomial time if G is connected. If negative weights exist, Bellman-Ford Algorithm ensures an optimal path. Since real-world road networks are generally connected, there always exists a feasible shortest route, ensuring that every rescue team can reach its destination.

Theorem 3: Fair Load Distribution Theorem

Statement: A scheduling model with fair workload distribution exists if each rescue team is assigned a load proportional to its capacity.

Proof:

Let $T = \{t_1, t_2, \ldots, t_n\}$ be the set of rescue teams, each with capacity c_i, and $D = \{d_1, d_2, \ldots, d_m\}$ be the set of disaster sites with demand d_j. The goal is to balance workload by distributing teams such that no team is overwhelmed. We model this as a min-max load balancing problem and apply Load Balancing via Max-Min Fairness, ensuring that:

$$\sum_{i=1}^{n} x_{ij} = d_j, \quad \forall j \in D$$

$$\max_i \sum_{j=1}^{m} x_{ij} \le \min_i \sum_{j=1}^{m} x_{ij} + 1$$

where x_{ij} represents teamt_i assigned to site d_j. By LP relaxation and rounding techniques, we prove that an assignment exists with bounded workload differences among teams.

Theorem 4: Dynamic Reallocation Theorem

Statement: Given changing disaster conditions, a dynamic reallocation mechanism ensures minimal disruption and maximized efficiency.

Proof:

Let A_t be the initial assignment of teams at time t, and let A_{t+1} be the updated assignment due to a new emergency. The change in assignment follows the condition:

$$|A_{t+1} - A_t| \leq \epsilon$$

where ϵ represents minimal changes. This problem is modeled as an Online Bipartite Matching where reallocations are minimized to avoid major disruptions. By applying Reinforcement Learning (RL), the system learns optimal reassignment policies, ensuring that rescue efforts remain stable even when new disasters occur.

Theorem 5: Guaranteed Convergence of AI-Based Scheduling

Statement: An AI-driven scheduling algorithm converges to an optimal scheduling policy under a reinforcement learning framework.

Proof:

Let Q(s, a) represent the action-value function in a Markov Decision Process (MDP), where s denotes system state (current team allocation) and a denotes actions (rescheduling decisions). The optimal scheduling policy π^* is learned using Q-learning:

$$Q(s,a) \leftarrow Q(s,a) + \alpha\left[r + \gamma \max_{a'} Q(s',a') - Q(s,a)\right]$$

Where r is the reward (rescue efficiency), α is the learning rate, and γ is the discount factor. Bellman's Optimality Equation guarantees convergence if α satisfies diminishing step-size conditions. Therefore, the AI-driven scheduling model always converges to an optimal policy, ensuring efficiency in rescue operations.

CONCLUSION

The Rescue Team Scheduling Mode presented in this work provides a smart, real-time approach for rescue response operation planning. With the incorporation of AI-driven scheduling algorithms, the model maximizes the resource allocation effectiveness, minimizes response time, and prevents uneven workload allocation to the rescue teams. Machine learning and multi-objective optimization enable dynamic adjustments of team assignments based on varying disaster scenarios. Moreover, the integration of real-time information through IoT sensors, satellite images, and social media intelligence improves decision-making and coordination. Theoretical foundations, e.g., the theorems and proofs presented, guarantee implementability and efficiency of the suggested scheduling model. The results demonstrate that

AI-based scheduling improves disaster preparedness and resilience significantly by maximizing emergency crew deployment. Future studies can focus on establishing complex deep learning models for the application of predictive analysis and improving the system to cover multi-disaster large-scale scenarios.

REFERENCES

Adam, M. S., Anisi, M. H., & Ali, I. (2020). Object tracking sensor networks in smart cities: Taxonomy, architecture, applications, research challenges and future directions. *Future Generation Computer Systems*, *107*, 909–923. DOI: 10.1016/j.future.2017.12.011

Al-Kaff, A., Madridano, Á., Campos, S., García, F., Martín, D., & de la Escalera, A. (2020). Emergency support unmanned aerial vehicle for forest fire surveillance. *Electronics (Basel)*, *9*(2), 260. DOI: 10.3390/electronics9020260

Aljohani, F. H., Abi Sen, A. A., Ramazan, M. S., Alzahrani, B., & Bahbouh, N. M. (2023). A smart framework for managing natural disasters based on the IoT and ML. *Applied Sciences (Basel, Switzerland)*, *13*(7), 3888. DOI: 10.3390/app13063888

Bartoli, G., Fantacci, R., Gei, F., Marabissi, D., & Micciullo, L. (2015). A novel emergency management platform for smart public safety. *International Journal of Communication Systems*, *28*(6), 928–943. DOI: 10.1002/dac.2716

Carley, K. M., Malik, M., Landwehr, P. M., Pfeffer, J., & Kowalchuck, M. (2016). Crowd sourcing disaster management: The complex nature of Twitter usage in Padang, Indonesia. *Safety Science*, *90*, 48–61. DOI: 10.1016/j.ssci.2016.04.002

Chan, E., Man, A., & Lam, H. (2019). Scientific evidence on natural disasters and health emergency and disaster risk management in Asian rural-based area. *British Medical Bulletin*, *129*(1), 91–105. DOI: 10.1093/bmb/ldz002 PMID: 30753325

Chung, W. Y., & Oh, S. J. (2006). Remote monitoring system with wireless sensors module for room environment. *Sensors and Actuators. B, Chemical*, *113*(1), 64–67. DOI: 10.1016/j.snb.2005.02.023

Daniel, S., & Doran, M. A. (2013, June 17–20). Geo Smart City: Geomatics contribution to the smart city. In *Proceedings of the 14th Annual International Conference on Digital Government Research* (pp. 65–71). ACM. DOI: 10.1145/2479724.2479735

Fosso, Y., & Berquin, D. (2022). An analysis of information communication technologies for natural disaster management in Africa. *International Journal of Disaster Risk Reduction*, *68*, 102722. DOI: 10.1016/j.ijdrr.2021.102722

George, D., Jane, A., & Damon, P. (2017). *Introduction to emergency management* (6th ed.). Butterworth-Heinemann.

Gething, P., & Tatem, A. (2011). Can mobile phone data improve emergency response to natural disasters? *PLoS Medicine*, *8*(8), e1001085. DOI: 10.1371/journal.pmed.1001085 PMID: 21918644

Gong, Y., & Yang, X. (2022). Exploration of artificial intelligence in urban natural disaster emergency management. *Modern Occupational Safety*, *12*, 54–56.

Guo, A., Liu, B., Fu, L., Gao, S., Jin, Y., & Yang, Z. (2022). Research on the key technology of stereoscopic cooperation in aviation emergency rescue. *Ziran Zaihai Xuebao*, *31*, 1157–1167.

Jahangiri, K., Eivazi, M., & Mofazali, S. (2017). The role of foresight in avoiding systematic failure of natural disaster risk management. *International Journal of Disaster Risk Reduction*, *21*, 303–311. DOI: 10.1016/j.ijdrr.2017.01.008

Korkmaz, A. (2023). Public health emergencies and disaster risk management: A rural experience following the earthquake. *Turk Pediatri Arsivi*, *58*(4), 353–354. DOI: 10.5152/TurkArchPediatr.2023.23061 PMID: 37144273

Li, S., Da Xu, L., & Wang, X. (2012). Compressed sensing signal and data acquisition in wireless sensor networks and Internet of Things. *IEEE Transactions on Industrial Informatics*, *9*(4), 2177–2186. DOI: 10.1109/TII.2012.2189222

Najafi, M., Eshghi, S., & Eshghi, K. (2020). A framework for earthquake emergency response in Iran. *Scientia Iranica*, *27*(6), 2604–2620. DOI: 10.24200/sci.2019.52376.2168

Sabrina, M. (2016). New tools for emergency managers: An assessment of obstacles to use and implementation. *Disasters*, *40*(2), 207–225. DOI: 10.1111/disa.12141 PMID: 26281801

Seaberg, D., Devine, L., & Zhuang, J. (2017). A review of game theory applications in natural disaster management research. *Natural Hazards*, *89*(3), 1461–1483. DOI: 10.1007/s11069-017-3033-x

Shannon, C. E. (1948). A mathematical theory of communication. *The Bell System Technical Journal*, *27*(3), 379–423. DOI: 10.1002/j.1538-7305.1948.tb01338.x

Tennakoon, K., Serrao-Neumann, S., & Hanna, C. (2021). Examining the incorporation of small-scale recurring disasters in emergency management frameworks: Insights from Aotearoa—New Zealand. *International Journal of Disaster Risk Reduction*, *66*, 102595. DOI: 10.1016/j.ijdrr.2021.102595

Yang, C., Su, G., & Chen, J. (2017, March 10–12). Using big data to enhance crisis response and disaster resilience for a smart city. In *Proceedings of the 2017 IEEE 2nd International Conference on Big Data Analysis (ICBDA)* (pp. 504–507). IEEE. DOI: 10.1109/ICBDA.2017.8078684

Zhang, H., Dai, X., & Qian, D. (2022). Strategic analysis of the modernization of emergency management enabled by new generation of information technology. *Bulletin of the Chinese Academy of Sciences*, *37*(12), 1727–1737. DOI: 10.1360/TB-2022-0330

Zhang, X. (2022). Strengthen the construction of disaster prevention and disaster reduction and emergency management system in rural areas. *International Talent Exchange*, *3*, 10.

Zhou, L. (2021). Social media and natural disaster governance in the era of big data. *Humanities Journal*, *1*, 102–109.

Zhou, L., & Luo, Y. (2023). Digital intelligence and empowerment: Emergency management in the era of smart city. *Theoretical Discussion*, *2*, 69–78.

Zhu, P., Hu, J., Zhang, Y., & Li, X. (2021). Enhancing traceability of infectious diseases: A blockchain-based approach. *Information Processing & Management*, *58*(1), 102570. DOI: 10.1016/j.ipm.2021.102570 PMID: 35721004

Chapter 11
AI for Urban Innovation in Developing Cities

Raed Awashreh
https://orcid.org/0000-0002-2252-0299
United Arab Emirates University, UAE

ABSTRACT

The paper explores how artificial intelligence (AI) can support innovative city initiatives and urban planning in developing countries. Using case studies from Accra, Bangalore, Lagos, and Medellín, it examines AI's role in addressing socio-economic, cultural, and infrastructural challenges. Key applications include improving waste management, water distribution, traffic flow, and urban planning, enhancing efficiency and sustainability. The study highlights the importance of robust data systems, community engagement, public-private partnerships, and ethical frameworks. It addresses challenges like data privacy, digital divides, and algorithmic bias, advocating for transparency and participatory decision-making to foster trust. While AI offers immense potential, overcoming barriers is crucial to realizing its full impact in creating innovative and inclusive cities.

INTRODUCTION

Urbanization is one of the most massive structural changes in the progress of humanity since industrialization; it accelerates further, and by 2050, more than two-thirds of the world's population is projected to live in urban areas. As this transition unfolds rapidly, it brings complex challenges right to the doorsteps of developing countries, especially those that often face congestion and traffic, a lack of public services, a shortage of resources, and even environmental degradation. In response to these big challenges, a new solution has been posited in the form of smart cities,

DOI: 10.4018/979-8-3373-0245-4.ch011

where advanced technologies are used to make urban governance more efficient and enhance people's quality of life. Among these technologies, perhaps most prominent is Artificial Intelligence (AI) as it has the ability to handle vast volumes of data, recognize patterns, and optimize many city systems in real-time (Ritchie, Samborska & Roser, 2024).

AI offers numerous benefits in innovative city initiative applications that are particularly useful in addressing some of the specific problems of developing countries. For instance, it supports traffic control by enabling real-time analysis of data to lead to enhanced transportation efficiency and the prevention of congestion. It also enhances public safety by means of predictive analytics, allowing for better allocation of law enforcement resources, hence better cities. Moreover, AI facilitates sustainable resource management of valuable resources such as energy and water in regions with limited availability and inadequate infrastructure (Herath & Mittal, 2022).

. Despite these exciting prospects, deploying AI in smart cities is not without its challenges. One key issue is the high likelihood of critical concerns regarding data privacy, cybersecurity, and the digital divide, which may exacerbate disadvantages in developing nations (Almeida, 2023). Furthermore, large parts of the world are still lacking the digital tools and trained personnel to effectively harness these continually more sophisticated AI tools, raising considerable questions as to whether the benefits that have accrued from AI are being equitably shared. Finally, ethical issues, including the need for critical scrutiny of the algorithmic biases and surveillance traditions surrounding AI technologies, are essential to their optimal and inclusive development (El Aynaoui, Magri & Saran, 2023).

Hence, the chapter would be able to assess the revolutionary potential of AI in state-of-the-art city programs and city planning in emerging economies, while keeping in view the prospects and risks of taking advantage of such technologies. One of the key research questions in this context would be: How do the implementation of AI technologies in smart cities address particular challenges facing developing countries, and what are the likely advantages and constraints of integration? This situates the research study within a context that provides useful insights for policymakers and urban planners to make proper choices that can provide sustainable and fair urban growth.

However, even though AI applications for smart cities are present in academic literature, most of these studies are very broad and fail to focus on the specific implications of these technologies in developing nations (Szpilko et al., 2023). To address the said gap above, the research shall study socio-economic, cultural, and infrastructural challenges particular to developing countries that will inform an appropriate way toward the adoption of AI in urban spaces. Data privacy, fairness, and moral implications of data-related concerns owing to AI also shall be looked into so that technologies being implemented add up towards inclusive urban planning and resilience. Overall, the use of AI by developing countries in meeting growing demands for urbanization presents an excellent opportunity to drive efficiency, sustainability, and responsiveness in urban systems. In this chapter, it is clearly explicated how AI is able to tackle existing urban challenges and pave the way for more resilient and adaptive cities that are responsive to their people's needs. It asserts the significance of the contribution demanded by the depth of knowledge AI potentially has to bring to revolutionize urban planning and infrastructure through an analysis of the possible benefits and drawbacks of including these technologies into new city endeavors and urban design in developing environments.

With these factors in mind, the use of AI in smart city projects has developed as a critical field of study, especially in developing countries. The increased focus arises from the capability of AI to transform urban planning and city management by responding to intricate issues and maximizing resource allocation. Thus, this review delves into the opportunities and obstacles presented by AI technologies in the urban context, focusing on the central research question: How can the implementation of AI in smart cities address the specific challenges faced by developing nations, and what are the anticipated benefits and drawbacks of this integration?

In addition, a broad gap exists in the existing literature concerning AI and cities, as most studies adopt a generalized or overall strategy. The strategy, in most cases, ignores the unique socio-economic, infrastructural, and cultural impediments typical of developing nations. They include limitations on technological infrastructure, resource shortages, socio-economic disparities, and governance factors that make it more difficult to apply AI. Recognizing these loopholes, this review seeks to provide a balanced perspective on how best to use AI in such contexts. The rest of this chapter is organized as follows: Section 2 provides the literature review of urbanization and smart cities in developing nations. Section 3 describes the methodology used based on secondary data from case studies. Section 4 develops relevant case studies and then describes the advantages and disadvantages. The final section concludes with recommendations, social implications, and practical considerations.

LITERATURE REVIEW

The use of artificial intelligence (AI) in smart city initiatives is rapidly gaining importance, particularly in developing nations with accelerated urbanization and certain socio-economic challenges. In this context, this review is intended to examine the different roles AI can play in urban planning, focusing on both the possible benefits and inherent difficulties in the implementation of AI solutions in developing nations. Since these developing countries desire to build efficient and sustainable cities, AI has innovative opportunities in averting primary issues such as management of resources, public safety, and civic engagement. Nonetheless, they are attended by earnest threats that cover all the way from issues over the confidentiality of information to uneven availability of technology as well as an amplification of socio-economic imbalances (Wolniak & Stecuła, 2024).

Given this context, the aim of this review is to provide a comprehensive analysis of how AI can be used effectively to address the specific needs of developing nations, and to identify the risks that will accompany its use. To achieve this, through case studies, technological innovation, and policy frameworks, this research emphasizes the importance of context-specific AI programs that not only stimulate innovation but also promote social justice and environmental sustainability. In short, the review advocates for a strategy that balances technological progress with regional conditions and ensures that AI contributes meaningfully to the construction of smart cities that are inclusive, resilient, and capable of improving the quality of life for everyone living in the city.

Urbanization and Smart Cities in Developing Countries

The integration of artificial intelligence (AI) into smart city initiatives is rapidly becoming a critical area of research, especially in developing nations. In this context, this review delves into the various opportunities and challenges AI introduces in urban planning, particularly in these regions. The study aims to provide a holistic explanation of the use of AI in solving the particular urban issues of developing nations and establish the expected benefits and potential drawbacks of such technological use. The research is critical to aid in driving the implementation of AI in cities that have been largely left out in broader research (Hammoumi, Maanan & Rhinane, 2024). However, while much of the existing research on AI in cities is universal in scope, it does not take into consideration the particular socio-economic, infrastructural, and cultural challenges developing countries have. These include poverty, limited access to technology, and poor infrastructure, challenges that require solutions with a different architecture than solutions implemented in more developed regions. Consequently, interest in these conditions as a class is lacking where there is an identified gap in the literature for which this review aims to pose a solution. By giving significance to contextuality, the review is advocating an AI approach not only innovative in character but one that is context-sensitive and attentive to local contingencies. It demonstrates the importance of applying AI technology in such a manner that it supports sustainable, fair, and effective city planning. Through the examination of relevant case studies, policy frameworks, and technological innovations, the review is informative in a manner that could assist policymakers and urban planners in developing solutions strong and inclusive enough to guarantee the sustainable future of AI-driven urban regeneration (Luusua et al., 2023).

At the heart of the debate is the double-edged sword of AI adoption in cities. On the positive side, AI has the potential to transform urban development. There is the possibility of optimizing resource use, improving public services, and creating adaptive, smart infrastructure, which is all the more important for cities undergoing rapid urbanization and resource constraints. For instance, the use of AI can revolutionize transport infrastructure by optimizing traffic capacity and reducing congestion, optimize energy efficiency through smart grids, and advance more uniform water distribution through monitoring of consumption patterns in real time. These advancements promise to increase urban living standards and reduce classic urban problems like resource insufficiency and wastage of infrastructure (Wolniak & Stecuła, 2024). On the other hand, the benefits of AI are not without their own drawbacks. The integration of AI into urban systems is also linked to concerns of data privacy, the digital divide, and the ability to exacerbate social inequalities. Developing nations typically lack the necessary infrastructure to implement AI technologies on a scale, and there is a real concern that these technologies may further exacerbate the gap between the urban elite and marginalized communities. In addition, the rapid pace of technological adoption can lead to job displacement, especially in sectors where automation can replace human labor. Ethical concerns also surround whether AI decision-making is equitable and how much algorithmic transparency exists. In response, such challenges necessitate thoughtful, context-specific solutions to ensure that AI technologies do not inadvertently worsen already existing social inequalities or create new forms of exclusion (Sanchez, Brenman & Ye, 2024).

The review emphasizes that the successful integration of AI in developing nations necessitates comprehensive policies and frameworks that align technological innovation with local needs. In particular, key to this is fostering collaboration among various governmental agencies, the private sector, and civil society.

This cooperation between these stakeholders is required to ensure that AI projects are implemented in a way that is useful to all citizens. Investment in capacity-building programs is also essential to equipping local institutions and communities with the knowledge and information required to run and maintain AI technologies. In addition, ensuring public participation in the decision-making process is vital as it builds trust and ensures that AI systems reflect the values and priorities of the people for whom they are designed to serve. In this manner, AI can be more than a tool for urban modernization; it can also be a powerful catalyst for creating equity, resilience, and sustainability in cities (Ben Rjab et al., 2023).

In brief, this review presents a detailed analysis of how AI can potentially be utilized to shape the future of urban planning in the developing world. By an acknowledgment of both the potential benefits and constraints of AI adoption, the review advocates for a balanced and context-aware approach to its application. The goal is to create a vision for smart city initiatives that are not only technologically advanced but also socially inclusive and capable of addressing the unique demands of developing nations. In this regard, by aligning AI innovations with the specific socio-economic contexts of these cities, smart cities can act as a model for sustainable and inclusive urban development, ensuring that technological progress is aligned with the well-being of all citizens (Luusua et al., 2023).

This is a challenge that is traditionally associated with rapid urbanization and many challenges like poor infrastructure, inequality, and environmental degradation. United Nations projections have shown that the share of the urban population in these regions could increase as much as 68% by 2050, hence the need for innovative ways of evading such pressures on housing, transport, and sanitation. For instance, insecurity of tenure, health complications resulting from unsanitary living conditions, and the absence of basic services trigger public health complications and social tensions. The presence of informal settlement conditions without basic services widens public health complications and social tensions. Also, through the cause of traffic congestion, there is higher pollution with economic inefficiency, hence the need for effective measures of urgency management (Kanchana, 2022). To counteract these, smart cities came in as a concept model of technology solution to problems for cities, especially in the recent years through AI.

Smart cities leverage big data analytics and digital technology to design more efficient city governance and sustainability policies. Costa et al. state that AI can play a significant role in traffic management, resource allocation, and public safety. For example, while traffic management uses AI algorithms with real-time data to optimize traffic and reduce congestion, AI-powered surveillance systems identify anomalies in an urban environment to enable effective law enforcement intervention. Moreover, this supports energy management by optimizing usage patterns, the incorporation of renewable energy sources into smart grids, and enhanced waste management by optimizing routes for collection and schedules for greater efficiency and recycling. Similarly, AI for environmental monitoring enhances source detection of pollution and assessment of mitigation strategies by analyzing data (Fadhel et al., 2024). While there are plenty of advantages to the integration of AI, from better decision-making to optimal utilization and usage of resources, there are issues too in abundance.

Specifically, poor infrastructure connectivity and maintenance are apt to deprive AI applications of sufficient effectiveness. Moreover, overdone up-front investment in AI could be at the cost of basic urban services. These also come with additional concerns regarding AI ethics, such as algorithmic bias, privacy loss, and others that tend to make the population skeptical and cause them to doubt AI technologies (Balbaa & Abdurashidova, 2024). In order to mitigate this, comprehensive regulatory strategies for AI implementations within a city framework must be instituted in a way that allows accountability and avoids misuse. Apart from this, they should allow individuals to understand and build trust in the communities so that they can become accepted through open communication about AI capabilities and limitations. Finding a perfect balance between building technology and traditional operations in urban settings will be of extreme significance for attaining sustainable development and avoiding unwanted consequences (Mensah, 2023). Accordingly, the literature review prioritizes that a study must be conducted on the use of AI in developing countries and smart cities.

It is essential to determine the possible benefits and the associated-challenges inherent in using AI and move ahead strategically with priorities on sustainable and inclusive urban development. Besides, the proposed use of AI technologies could provide significant ways towards more resilient cities and better quality of life for city dwellers as developing nations are experiencing increasing urbanization. In the interest of having benefits emanating from AI distributed fairly, stakeholders will have to set aside the need for community-level engagement and collaborative models to ensure a more resilient and sustainable urban future.

METHODOLOGY

This study utilizes a descriptive research design to explore the intricacies of the selected case studies, leveraging qualitative methods to form a high-quality understanding of the subject matter under investigation (Rashid et al., 2019). The research is centered on secondary data, allowing for the research to incorporate a high-quality examination of emerging patterns, themes, and insights developed from existing literature and recorded evidence. Utilizing secondary sources, research merges diverse perceptions from vast sources of material such as:

- Academic Peer-Reviewed Journals – These provide theoretical foundations and empirical data relevant to AI integration and urban development.
- Government Reports – These include statistical data, policy analyses, and context-specific observations that support official opinions and national agendas.
- Industry Reports – Offering the latest trends, challenges, and opportunities, these reports highlight practical applications and market realities related to AI-based urban initiatives.

- Media Articles – Offering contextualization of the topic into everyday circumstances, these articles add sophistication and contemporaneity to the case studies.

The application of its secondary data possesses advantages and shortcomings inherent in the approach. It provides ease of access to a wide variety of data that allows for the exploration of complex problems in many situations (Baldwin et al., 2022). In contrast, it is constrained by potential biases of the initial data, which may affect the objectivity of the conclusions. Furthermore, the absence of direct observation or primary data gathering limits the empirical verification to some extent of depth. The availability and quality of available literature also define the analysis and may constrain the depth of the study in specific areas.

Despite these limitations, the qualitative and descriptive character of the research allows for a nuanced examination of the complexity of each case. Focusing on four selected case studies, the chapter delves into contextual dimensions in detail, hence allowing for an elaborate analysis of challenges, opportunities, and best practices. This method enhances the capacity to link theoretical concepts with real-world applications, creating useful information for policymakers, city planners, and researchers (Ugwu et al., 2023). Ultimately, the research contributes to the current body of literature regarding AI applications in urban planning by presenting a thorough exploration of the specific conditions and dynamics of the selected cases. By this descriptive approach, it illuminates paths towards addressing urbanization challenges, advancing sustainable and equitable development, and harnessing the transformative potential of AI towards pioneering city initiatives. Findings attempt to guide strategic choices and increase understanding of the complexities entailed in applying AI for urban development and resilience in developing countries (Cheong et al., 2033).

CASE STUDIES

The use of artificial intelligence (AI) in urban planning in the developing world has shown tremendous potential in addressing problems related to resource management, infrastructure development, and citizen engagement. The examples of cities like Singapore, Accra, and Bangalore show how AI can drive sustainable urbanization by optimizing the distribution of resources and public services. Singapore's Smart Nation initiative, for example, utilizes AI to improve the flow of traffic, allocation of resources, and security through sensors, data analysis, and AI monitoring. These types of examples highlight the imperatives for data convergence, people engagement, and cross-domain collaboration in building smarter, more resilient cities. This section examines four case studies that illustrate how AI can design urban infrastructure, governance, and service delivery.

Case 1: AI-Enhanced Waste Management in Accra, Ghana

Because of widespread urbanization, Bangalore has also been facing acute shortage and water distribution. To counter these, the city adopted an artificial intelligence-driven smart water management system for efficient allocation and performance operations. The system is founded on predictive analytics to forecast water demand based on historic consumption patterns, climatic trends, and population growth trends. In addition, it integrates IoT devices to allow real-time monitoring of water quality and distribution, making adaptive and accurate resource management possible (Samwine et al., 2017). Its use has achieved tremendous benefits.

Conservation of water has been promoted with losses reduced by 25% and supply assured to homeowners. Greater monitoring in real time has also improved water quality, reducing instances of polluted drinking water. Moreover, the ability of the system to forecast peak demand enables it to distribute resources efficiently during peak hours.

However, the issue is present. The procedure of upgrading outmoded infrastructure to accommodate current technology remains an involved and resource-consuming process. Although coordination across agencies can consolidate and simplify such upgrades, such collaboration is unusual, posing an obstacle towards frictionless adoption and broader success (Tahiru et al., 2024)

Case 2: Smart Water Management in Bangalore, India

In Bangalore, the stresses of rapid urbanization have led to water scarcity and inefficiencies in distribution, a significant challenge for the city's growing population. Bangalore has reacted by initiating an ambitious AI-powered smart water management system to optimize resource distribution and improve overall efficiency. This groundbreaking system is built on predictive analytics, using historic water usage habits, weather conditions, and population increases to anticipate and plan for upcoming demand. Internet of Things (IoT) sensors are utilized to monitor water quality and distribution in real-time to supply the system with a steady stream of accurate data to inform decisions (Bhoomika, 2022).

The system's impact was revolutionary. Conservation of water and wasting 25% less, the project put more water within reach of the residents, answering a city's urgent need. Real-time monitoring of water quality also increased security, with purer and cleaner water entering into homes and decreasing risk from polluted supply. Also, the ability of the system to adapt to peak demand periods ensures smoother and more efficient dissemination during times of need, lessening the strain on existing resources (Banerjee, Bhaduri & Saraswat, 2022).

However, the incorporation of such high-level technology is not without its setbacks. A major setback is the updating of the city's aging infrastructure to accommodate new systems, which is both time and resource consuming. Another more serious challenge is fostering interagency coordination, which is crucial for ensuring seamless integration of technologies but in practice it remains elusive. Despite these challenges, Bangalore's AI-based project is an ambitious step toward sustainable water management in the face of rapid urbanization (Economic Times, 2024).

Case 3: AI for Traffic Management in Lagos, Nigeria

Lagos, one of the largest and most populous cities on the continent, scores low on a multitude of important development indicators. Its notorious traffic jams are a chronic issue that significantly depletes economic productivity while causing rampant air pollution. It has been an issue for the city for ages now, leading to lost hours along roads, losses in terms of workforce efficiency, and environmental degradation. In an effort to address these age-old problems, Lagos has developed a revolutionary AI traffic management system based on a range of data sources—traffic cameras, GPS systems, and even social media sites—to predict traffic patterns and adjust the timing of lights across the city. The new system is aimed at making traffic flow faster, reducing congestion, and making the city's road network more efficient (Koko & Bello, 2023).

The traffic system is supported by a simple-to-apply mobile app, which gathers real-time data on traffic for commuters to utilize in organizing their journeys. The app is a central element in the city's need to enhance mobility through information provision regarding traffic movement, reducing time wastage. The result of this scheme has been positive: the average journey time has decreased by 20%, which has come a long way to cutting emissions from vehicles. Accordingly, the city has benefited from cleaner air quality and traffic conditions in general, and both have benefited the environment and the health of citizens (Iwan, Małecki & Stalmach, 2014).

But using this AI-powered system to the best of one's abilities is where the challenge lies. The initial challenge is to verify the credibility and accuracy of the data captured from all these sources. Since traffic movement in cities keeps changing, it is a complex process to collate data from traffic cameras, GPS, and social media in real time and update it regularly. Also, for the system to be maximally efficient, public confidence is required. The majority of residents will initially be skeptical about using the new mobile application or wary of data privacy and collection. Public education on the workings of the system and what it can provide is thus crucial. This will demand ongoing effort in outreach and sensitization programs in order to enlist the people and rally the utilization of the system in large numbers. Building trust in the system and making it available to every citizen, particularly in areas of limited access to technology, will be crucial in realizing its full potential (Soliman et al., 2024).

Overall, Lagos' AI-driven traffic management program is a significant leap towards solving the city's chronic congestion and environmental problems. The early success of the program, as seen in improved traffic flow and reduced emissions, is a testament to the transformative potential of AI in urban planning. However, continued attempts to further build the system, educate citizens, and provide access to everyone will be crucial in leveraging this technology as a potential solution for the long-term growth and development of the city (Ogunlade & Clottey, 2023).

Case Study 4: AI-Driven Urban Planning in Medellín, Colombia

Medellín, Colombia, in recent decades, has emerged as a global frontrunner in harnessing artificial intelligence (AI) to provide trailblazing innovations in urban planning with the vision to enhance the lives of urban dwellers in developing cities, including those living in informal settlements and large urban sprawls. The city's innovative approach has made AI an essential tool for addressing the unique challenges posed by accelerated urbanization, poverty, and the informal housing sector. The city planners in Medellín have incorporated AI algorithms in the design of zoning laws, housing policy, and city infrastructure planning in order to simulate various development scenarios and choose the most appropriate path for sustainable development. By the evaluation of a wide range of data—land use patterns, socioeconomic trends, and infrastructure capacity—AI has helped the city to make data-driven decisions that balance growth with the preservation of resources (Callenberg, Barnwal & Bakarr, 2024).

With the AI approach, city planners can now make intelligent, fact-driven planning choices, and they have the ability to visualize policy outcomes prior to enacting them. This predictive capacity allows for a better understanding of the effect that urban policies will have on the population and the environment, so that they can be tailored to the needs of citizens and avoid unexpected negative consequences. Additionally, incorporating the voice of citizens into the process of urban planning has been another principal strength of Medellín's approach. By involving residents in decision-making, the city ensures that urban policies better reflect the actual aspirations and needs of its communities. This participatory process also assists in developing greater levels of public trust and ownership among citizens, resulting in more effective and sustainable urban policies (Son et al., 2023).

AI has also played a significant role in making urban expansion equitable and balanced. Planners in Medellín use algorithms that calculate where the expansion must be more focused and where expansion must be limited, opening up space for natural resources and green spaces. Such green conservation prioritization is crucial in the maintenance of ecological balance in the face of accelerated urbanization, particularly for cities such as Medellín that are marred by deforestation, pollution, and loss of biodiversity. Implementation of AI in city planning also enables the production of more adaptable and responsive plans, which answer to changing conditions and evolving requirements with time, making the city more responsive to emerging issues (Sanchez, Brenman & Ye, 2024)

However, the success of this AI-based urban planning software significantly depends on the quality and validity of the data used. Continual data collection and regular updates are required to aid in maintaining the accuracy and relevance of the AI models as the city dynamics evolve. The effectiveness of AI use can be compromised if current quality data is unavailable. Furthermore, AI in city planning requires an interdisciplinary approach bringing on board urban planners, data scientists, engineers, and community members. This multidisciplinary approach, as useful as it is, may be challenging to coordinate due to the intrinsic challenge of streamlining different expertise and world views. Proper communication and coordination among diverse teams are central to the success of AI-driven urban planning projects because each discipline has its expert knowledge that contributes an essential part to creating comprehensive and effective urban solutions (Alvarez, 2024).

Despite these challenges, Medellín's use of AI in urban planning is a model for other cities in the Global South, demonstrating how technology can be harnessed to assist in driving inclusive, sustainable, and equitable urban development. By harnessing the power of technological innovation coupled with community involvement and environmental sustainability, Medellín has created a template for how AI can be used not just for economic growth, but for creating a better quality of life in rapidly growing urban areas. As the city makes its plan, it is itself a case study on how AI can future-proof a city by creating a new model for cities (Villoria et al., 2023). India's Bengaluru city has launched an innovative AI-based waste management system where sensors monitor the amount of filled garbage cans.

This system streamlines collection routes, reducing operational expenses and the efficiency of waste management operations. However, the success of such a system relies not only on technological advancement but also on active citizen engagement. It is necessary to ensure that citizens understand and accept the new technology for it to be effective in the long run and sustainable (Villoria, 2023). Similarly, in Dar es Salaam, Tanzania, population data analysis with AI has led to unprecedented urban planning improvement, namely transport and housing. Local planners have made better decisions about resource allocation based on this data, dealing with the high urbanization rate of the city more efficiently.

The focus on customized solutions and capacity-development interventions has been pivotal to allowing local planners to address community needs while setting up resilient urban development (Pellatt & Palfreman, 2023). These examples indicate how AI technologies, when properly introduced and in coordination with the local community, can drive successful urban transformation in developing cities The shared denominator of all such city AI initiatives would be the integration of data, citizen engagement, public-private partnerships, and ethical use of data.

AI enhances decision-making and resource planning for sustainability in city planning and smart city projects. AI will change city planning in the developing world by enabling data-driven, well-informed decision-making, and evidence-based policy-making. It incorporates GIS for spatial analysis, citizen engagement through chatbots, and efficient utilization of resources. It also aids sustainability by evaluating environmental impacts, while at the same time some of the data constraint issues and those related to ethics have to be addressed. Finally, it helps to render the urban environment efficient and sustainable (Bibri et al., 2024).

ADVANTAGES AND DISADVANTAGES

The section presents the advantages and disadvantages of using artificial intelligence in the smart city.

Advantages of Artificial Intelligence in Smart City Initiatives

Artificial Intelligence (AI) has a lot to offer in the implementation of innovative urban schemes, particularly for areas that are critical to resource management, sustainability, and improving the overall quality of urban life. Using the capability of AI, cities can optimize multiple systems, making them more effective and optimizing the environment to better withstand. The capability of AI to scan huge volumes of data in real time enables more intelligent decision-making beyond what is possible with conventional approaches, fueling sustainable development and enhancing the quality of urban life (Leal Filho et al., 2024).

Energy Management and Sustainability

Perhaps the strongest effect of AI on smart cities is its application to energy management. Conventional energy infrastructure tends to be inefficient, which causes wastage and undependable supply, particularly in areas where energy availability is unstable. Alternatively, AI-powered systems can monitor round-the-clock patterns of energy consumption, detect wastages, and optimize energy use in residential as well as commercial markets. In areas with unstable power grids, AI can balance supply and demand, minimize outages, and minimize the use of fossil fuels by allowing for greater integration of renewables (Ukoba et al., 2024). In addition, AI helps in identifying the areas where the usage of energy can be reduced, such as through the utilization of smart grids and energy-efficient technologies. By automatically adjusting settings in response to consumption patterns or ambient conditions, AI reduces wastage of energy, lowers carbon footprints, and enhances the sustainability of energy systems in general (Pimenow, Pimenowa & Prus, 2024).

Water Resource Management

AI is equally transformative even in water resource management. AI systems help track water distribution pipes in real time to detect leaks and inefficiencies that could go unnoticed otherwise. This foresighted technology is a blessing for reducing water loss, which is a critical issue in water-short cities. AI can forecast demand, optimize water usage, and ensure equitable distribution, preventing waste and guaranteeing a steady supply, even during peak consumption periods. By analyzing consumption patterns, AI helps urban planners implement proactive measures to manage water resources more effectively, especially in regions where water availability is limited or unreliable (Romero-Ben et al., 2023).

Through the application of sophisticated data analytics, AI also facilitates early detection of prospective water system failure, allowing cities to carry out timely maintenance and reduce the impacts of disruption. This translates to improved water management sustainability, which allows cities to supply growing populations while preserving limited water resources (Jayakumar et al., 2024).

Traffic and Mobility Optimization

The role of AI in traffic management is revolutionizing urban mobility. For cities with traffic, AI-powered systems can allow monitoring of the traffic and optimize traffic flow in real time, thereby generating smoother traffic, reduced congestion, and reduced travel times.AI can manipulate data from heterogeneous sources like traffic cameras, GPS sensors, and sensors mounted in road infrastructure for traffic light timing optimization and optimization of the traffic flow patterns. This, in effect, enhances road infrastructure performance as well as encourages environmental sustainability through way of truncated emissions by vehicles (Pillai, 2024).

AI can predict the peak traffic hours and make traffic lights more efficient to prevent jams and reduce the time that cars are stationary at intersections. Besides, AI-based public transport increases productivity in the delivery of services through the provision of real-time information about train and bus position, allowing individuals to plan their trips more effectively and reduce waiting time.

Use of AI in the public transport system also enables transportation assets to be organized and planned more efficiently so that the provision of public transport can be allocated where it is most needed. This means improved and more sustainable modes of transport, cost-saving on the use of private vehicles, and encouraging cleaner modes of transport such as walking and cycling (Dimri et al., 2024).

AI in Law Enforcement and Public Safety

AI predictive powers are extended to public safety and law enforcement, where it can be employed to enhance crime response time and prevention. AI algorithms can analyze past crime data to predict locations and times when and where crimes are most likely to take place, enabling law enforcement to better deploy resources. This data-driven approach makes policing more effective by concentrating efforts at risky areas and ensuring public security without over-burdening police officers. Surveillance systems using artificial intelligence also help monitor public areas for abnormal behavior, with response times speeding up to likely threats and generally providing better city-wide security. This not only reduces crime but also makes the area secure for inhabitants, establishing a sense of security and trust in the community (Ganguli, 2023).

Data-Driven Decision-Making and Urban Planning

Perhaps the most revolutionary usage of AI in urban planning is its ability for data-driven decision-making. AI can simulate various urban planning scenarios, and it helps policymakers and planners predict challenges and prospects in advance. This ability to predict is crucial in formulating long-term urban policy that serves current and future needs, from housing and transport to environmental viability. For example, AI can analyze the impact of different urbanization alternatives on the infrastructure, resources needed, and population, providing key insights to guide city planning. Through the prediction of the implications of policy decisions before their implementation, AI guarantees that urban development conforms to the shifting needs of the city and its residents (Heinrich Son et al., 2023).

AI is also engaged directly in monitoring the environment. It can identify areas of pollution in urban areas from sensor data obtained from all over the city and recommend optimized interventions to decontaminate water and air. Such an analysis allows municipalities to create healthier policies, encourage less pollution and environmental degradation, and offer more living comfort to city residents (Marwaha, Dey & Brar, 2024).

Citizen Engagement and Transparency

By applying AI to interact with citizens, cities are able to increase transparency, build trust with the people, and bring urban development on board. Using mobile apps and web portals, citizens are able to communicate with city governments, raise their complaints, and suggest improvement, thus creating a collective space where urban growth is driven by the collective imagination of the people (Wolniak & Stecuła, 2024). One of the most prospective ways AI will be used in smart cities is in its capacity to engage with citizens in urban planning. AI-based communication systems allow citizens to access details of urban projects being developed, provide feedback, and participate in decision-making. This makes the urban planning process more participatory and interactive and therefore more sensitive to the aspirations and needs of the people (Heinrich Son et al., 2023).

With the capability of AI, not only can cities be made more efficient operationally, but their citizens' quality of life also can be enhanced and successful and sustainable communities be built for future generations (Bibri et al., 2024).

The use of AI in urban management systems boasts several benefits from maximizing energy use and water resource utilization to increased traffic movement, policing, and environmental monitoring. Additionally, its ability to make informed decisions based on data and increase citizen engagement helps ensure that smart cities can be established as green, equitable, and efficient systems that answer the needs of their citizens. Proper strategic application of AI in planning has the power to revolutionize urban planning, the trajectory of urban life, leading toward intelligent, sustainable, and inclusive future cities (Pandiyan et al., 2023).

The advantages of the integration of AI in intelligent city initiatives are best seen through its support to resource management, public safety, and citizen interaction, offering pioneering opportunities for frontier economies. The integration of AI helps these countries develop cities not just as places of sustainability, but also efficacy and resilience. Artificial intelligence technology makes use of resources more effective, such as by optimizing the use of energy and waste control, yielding enormous environmental benefits. Moreover, public safety systems with AI capabilities, such as predictive policing software and intelligent surveillance, can make security better and crime rates reduce, making the city safer. AI also enhances citizen engagement through more transparent communication between citizens and governments, making sure that urban development is in harmony with the aspirations and needs of the people. AI, therefore, enables the construction of cities that are not only technologically advanced but also socially inclusive and responsive to the aspirations of their residents (Shafik, 2024).

However, the use of AI in visionary city projects is not without challenges, particularly for the developing nations. The issues at times are so evident that they outweigh the benefits, thus rendering the incorporation of AI a complex process. One of the main hindrances is the accumulation of vast amounts of data to support AI-based systems. This data collection is most likely a massive cause of data privacy issues since citizens tend to think that their own information is abused or manipulated. Such apprehensions lead to losing trust in technology and placing them in a greater exposure of cybersecurity threats. Unless proper safeguarding is employed, collection and use of gigantic data would reduce public confidence in AI and restrict its large-scale use (Alahi et al, 2023).

Yet another pressing issue is the absence of equal access to technology that accompanies the use of AI solutions. In the majority of developing countries, significant parts of society may not have access to means or infrastructure to harness these technologies, further marginalizing marginalized groups. Rural populations or low-income inhabitants may lack digital devices to be fully integrated or benefit from AI-based services.

This digital divide can exacerbate existing inequalities, preventing some people from enjoying the full advantages of smart city innovations (Aderibigbe et al., 2023). Additionally, the implementation of AI often requires specialized skills that are in short supply in many developing nations. These countries frequently lack the trained personnel needed to operate, maintain, and update AI systems. Without local expertise, the dependence on foreign technicians and consultants may become a barrier to the long-term sustainability of AI projects. Furthermore, outdated infrastructure and poor connectivity can undermine the functionality of AI systems, rendering them ineffective in addressing urban challenges. In the majority of regions, the technological infrastructure necessary for the deployment of AI, such as high-speed internet access and reliable power supplies, is non-existent or unavailable, thus inhibiting the deployment and scaling up of such technologies (Mannuru et al., 2023).

Cost barriers are also a significant limitation for AI adoption by developing nations. The high initial expenses of the AI technologies, including the cost of hardware, software, and setting up necessary infrastructure, could be a staggering burden on country budgets. Governments may tend to be reluctant to divert funds from essential services such as healthcare, education, and transport to cover AI projects. This expense can block or slow down the implementation of AI solutions, further slowing down the evolution of smart cities and distorting projects aimed at urban living standards (Wolniak & Stecuła, 2024).

Ethics are also an important barrier to the implementation of AI in urban development. Issues such as algorithmic bias, through which AI mechanisms can perpetuate or even aggravate existing societal inequalities, and surveillance, in which data capture for security and safety purposes turns into an area of concern from the perspective of individual privacy, must be countered with utmost delicacy. They are ethical issues that require firm frameworks to maintain that AI technology is utilized to the extent it is equitable, transparent, and accountable. Without such frameworks, AI could accelerate social splits rather than unite them, further eroding faith in technology (Mensah, 2023).

Furthermore, the widespread use of AI can have potential negative consequences, such as reducing human oversight and devaluing human input in decision-making. As AI continues to become integrated into daily life, there is a risk that key decisions are made with too minimal human involvement or understanding. This could lead to errors or not-so-beneficial decisions on behalf of citizens, particularly if the AI technologies are low in quality or are not monitored sufficiently. There is also a threat of losing employment, since automation might substitute certain manual labor positions, and this would introduce financial unpredictability among workers in affected industries (Yazdi et al., 2024). Overall, while the application of AI in smart cities promises a lot in making urban life better, there should be an awareness and a readiness to face the issues that go with its use. From privacy concerns over data and unequal access to technology to the need for skills and the financial burden of AI investments, these should be met with such immense care and planning. so doing, countries can leverage the power of AI to build inclusive, effective, and sustainable cities, with the least possibility of its misuse (Kitchin, 2016). Most countries also do not have end-to-end regimes of regulation for AI applications, which means that there is a higher possibility of misapplication and ethics. Setting clear regulations for accountability and safety from harm is imperative. Public worry regarding AI is generally privacy and autonomy, identifying the need for open communication and education in the development of acceptance and understanding of AI benefits and risks. Finally, many AI technologies are high-energy usage, therefore possibly subtracting from environmental sustainability.

However, balancing modern technologies with traditional practices is the key to sustainable development. All these challenges can only be addressed comprehensively by community involvement, a firm regulatory regime, and concern for sustainability- all requiring active policy interest benefits from AI accruing to all citizens (Bastit et al., 2023).

CONCLUSION AND RECOMMENDATIONS

Applying Artificial Intelligence (AI) to urban planning is enormous in scale and daunting in the context of emerging economies. AI applications in traffic control, public order, energy consumption, waste minimization, and environmental monitoring have the potential to reshape city productivity and resource management. The Singaporean, Bengaluru, Dar es Salaam, and Nairobi urban life shows how AI can enable greater civic engagement and better maximize the city. The potential of AI to transform urban planning is enormous, particularly through data-driven decision-making. By using big data, city planners can make informed decisions, hence enhancing the effectiveness of service delivery and resource allocation. Real-time monitoring by AI also contributes to sustainability through maximizing city systems' use of resources. However, several challenges hinder the seamless implementation of AI in these settings. Issues of data privacy, digital divide, inadequate infrastructure, and lack of proper human resources have to be addressed. Also, ethical dimensions such as algorithmic decision-making and surveillance have to be handled diplomatically so that equitable outcomes are achieved for all (Shrivastava, 2024).

In order to overcome all these obstacles, AI integration has to begin with robust leadership, which establishes good data gathering and management systems. Building digital infrastructure, such as internet access, and the placement of sensors to process data in real-time will be essential. PPPs will be vital in offering the assistance to AI technologies through resource and expertise sharing and facilitating more efficient and sustainable implementation. In addition, public involvement in decision-making through surveying and town hall meetings will ensure that applications of AI will adhere to values and needs of citizens. Giving people a feeling of ownership and feedback channels will be essential for maintaining public support and engagement

Capacity building is another critical dimension. Training programs in AI technology and data analytics need to be launched for the urban planners as well as officials in the municipal government to ensure they are updated with the level of skills for implementing AI. Investment in human capital is essential for the success of AI adoption in urban infrastructure. Furthermore, designing an effective moral framework addressing data privacy, video surveillance, and algorithmic justice will be needed to promote public confidence in AI initiatives. Such a framework will enable technology to be used in a way that is sensitive to human rights while guaranteeing fairness in urban society.

Pilot projects are a great way to introduce AI applications into action. Pilot projects allow for data gathering, method improvement, and adaptation to local urban environments. Pilot projects' iterative nature enables cities to deploy AI in phases, experimenting and improving applications along the way. Scalability and flexibility are key features for AI solutions, enabling cities to be adaptive to new challenges as they emerge. Incorporation of sustainability indicators in city planning, such as green infrastructure and energy efficiency, will additionally enhance long-term environmental protection and resilience. The incorporation of AI in urban planning in developing countries is promising, but with proper consideration of social and institutional effects. Policymakers and urban planners must guarantee data management, public-private partnership, community engagement, capacity development, and good governance to make AI-driven city projects productive, inclusive, and sustainable. By overcoming such challenges, cities can leverage AI to create secure, human-centric, and innovative urban spaces for future generations.

Social Implications

Application of Artificial Intelligence (AI) in constructing urbanization in developing nations has some critical social implications that must be handled seriously to foster evenness in influence. Access and equity with technology is one such problem of utmost concern. While AI has the potential to enhance the quality of life in the urban city, the unequal utilization of digital platforms and the internet by different socio-economic groups is bound to increase the existing disparity. The disadvantaged group might be cut off from AI-based services, which would exacerbate the disadvantage of vulnerable populations. To correct this, policies should target equal access to technology, especially for rural and economically underprivileged communities, to ensure that every segment of society is able to utilize AI systems.

The second social effect is job displacement and the skills gap. While AI can improve efficiency in most industries, automation can displace jobs in industries like transport, manufacturing, and retail. There must be a pressing reskilling and upskilling initiative that prepares workers for new employment in AI-dominated industries. If transitions are not facilitated in the workforce, they may result in long-term social unrest and economic instability. To mitigate these threats, governments must invest in education and training programs that equip employees with the capabilities to thrive in the evolving job market. Apart from labor issues, the moral and public trust aspects of AI are important as well. Algorithmic bias and surveillance are some of the issues which may erode public confidence in AI systems. If AI is perceived to be perpetuating social biases or encroaching on privacy, it can lead to pushbacks and resistance to accepting it. To build trust, it is essential to develop open, fair, and accountable AI systems. Civic participation through forums and polls will help to resolve ethical dilemmas, enabling AI systems to address society's needs and principles.

Secondly, AI offers the potential for greater civic participation and involvement in urban planning. AI-based platforms can take live input from the public so that decision-making is more responsible and inclusive. However, all communities, not only the marginalized and underrepresented ones, need to be enabled to engage in these AI-enabled governance systems. By actively engaging different communities in their part of shaping AI policies, cities can advance in a more distributive way towards urban growth in which technology is made sure to serve all and not particular people.

Institutional Implications

Utilization of AI in urban planning will have enormous institutional impacts, particularly for developing countries where governments may not be properly established for such far-reaching transformation. Institutional development and capacity building are needed in order to make effective use of AI. Institutions need to acquire skills and develop infrastructures competent to manage AI technologies, e.g., equip government officials, city planners, and technical officers with education on AI, data management, and digital infrastructure. Moreover, developing nations may be required to establish new institutional organizations for the regulation of AI projects and the implementation of policies. In the absence of institutional capacity, sustainability of AI projects would be jeopardized, and capacity building would become imperative. Public-private partnerships (PPPs) are also essential. Governments and the private sector must come together for the effective implementation of AI technology. PPPs can bring resources, expertise, and capital together to overcome financial constraints and accelerate the deployment of AI solutions. Partnerships can utilize the creativity and technical capabilities of the private sector to accelerate project deployments of AI. However, it should be ensured that the partnerships are structured in such a way as to protect public interests, particularly data protection and equitable access to AI-based services.

Besides, integrating AI into urban systems requires the development of vast legal and regulatory frameworks. Governments must develop consistent policies to address issues such as data privacy, algorithmic accountability, and security. An elastic regulatory framework that can keep pace with the rapidly evolving nature of AI technologies is required. Governments can limit threats such as misuse, discrimination, and data breach, and promote ethical use of AI, by developing strong laws and regulations. Aside from regulation, ethical governance and monitoring are of utmost importance to guarantee the proper use of AI technologies. Governments should set up independent oversight bodies to monitor the use of AI systems to guarantee that they are transparent, accountable, and fair. The bodies should also address grievances related to AI applications, resulting in public trust in AI-driven urban policy. Finally, institutions must guarantee the long-term sustainability of AI applications. AI for city development needs to be integrated with overall sustainability goals to ensure that technology not only meets immediate needs but also future challenges. Because AI is energy-hungry, regulatory frameworks need to promote energy-efficient systems and the incorporation of sustainability standards in city planning. Long-term planning also needs to ensure that AI innovations are scalable and adaptable enough to address evolving challenges like climate change or urbanization.

Overall, the use of AI in urban planning in developing countries is enormous potential but requires careful consideration of social as well as institutional implications. Issues of fairness, job displacement, public trust, and inclusion must be addressed so that the benefits of AI trickle down to all segments of society in equal measure. Institutionally, building the ability to manage AI, creating public-private alliances, forming strong legal systems, and implementing ethical governance are necessary to enable the effective use of AI in urbanization. With collaborative efforts between the public and private sector and extensive institutional backing, AI can help design smarter, more inclusive, and more sustainable cities.

REFERENCES

Aderibigbe, A. O., Ohenhen, P. E., & Nwaobia, N. K. (2023). Artificial intelligence in developing countries: Bridging the gap between potential and implementation. *Computer Science & IT Research Journal*, *4*(3), 185–199. DOI: 10.51594/csitrj.v4i3.629

Alahi, M. E. E., Sukkuea, A., Tina, F. W., Nag, A., Kurdthongmee, W., Suwannarat, K., & Mukhopadhyay, S. C. (2023). Integration of IoT-enabled technologies and artificial intelligence (AI) for smart city scenario: Recent advancements and future trends. *Sensors (Basel)*, *23*(11), 5206. DOI: 10.3390/s23115206 PMID: 37299934

Almeida, F. (2023). Prospects of cybersecurity in smart cities. *Future Internet*, *15*(9), 285. DOI: 10.3390/fi15090285

Alvarez, V. R. (2024). The urban transformation of Medellín: A case study. *ArchDaily.* https://www.archdaily.com/1015216/the-urban-transformation-of-medellin-a-case-study

Balbaa, M., & Abdurashidova, M. (2024). The impact of artificial intelligence in decision making: A comprehensive review. *EPRA International Journal of Economics. Business and Management Studies*, *11*(2), 27–38. DOI: 10.36713/epra15747

Banerjee, C., Bhaduri, A., & Saraswat, C. (2022). Digitalization in urban water governance: Case study of Bengaluru and Singapore. *Frontiers in Environmental Science. Frontiers in Environmental Science*, *10*, 816824. Advance online publication. DOI: 10.3389/fenvs.2022.816824

Bastit, B., Fernández, M., Kesh, S., & Tsui, D. (2023). The AI governance challenge. *S&P Global.* https://www.spglobal.com/en/research-insights/special-reports/the-ai-governance-challenge

Ben Rjab, A., Mellouli, S., & Corbett, J. (2023). Barriers to artificial intelligence adoption in smart cities: A systematic literature review and research agenda. *Government Information Quarterly*, *40*(3), 101814. DOI: 10.1016/j.giq.2023.101814

Bhoomika, M. (2022). Understanding the impact of urbanization on the water crisis in Bangalore: Challenges and opportunities. National Centre for Good Governance, Ministry of Personnel, Public Grievances and Pensions, Government of India. Retrieved from https://ncgg.org.in/sites/default/files/lectures-document/Bhoomika.pdf

Bibri, S. E., Huang, J., Jagatheesaperumal, S. K., & Krogstie, J. (2024). The synergistic interplay of artificial intelligence and digital twin in environmentally planning sustainable smart cities: A comprehensive systematic review. *Environmental Science and Ecotechnology*, *20*, 100433. DOI: 10.1016/j.ese.2024.100433 PMID: 38831974

Cheong, H.-I., Lyons, A., Houghton, R. W., & Majumdar, A. (2023). Secondary qualitative research methodology using online data within social sciences. *International Journal of Qualitative Methods*, *22*(2), 1–15. DOI: 10.1177/16094069231180160

Costa, D. G., Bittencourt, J. C. N., Oliveira, F., Peixoto, J. P. J., & Jesus, T. C. (2024). Achieving sustainable smart cities through geospatial data-driven approaches. *Sustainability (Basel)*, *16*(2), 640. DOI: 10.3390/su16020640

Dimri, S. C., Indu, R., Bajaj, M., Rathore, R. S., Blazek, V., Dutta, A. K., & Alsubai, S. (2024). Modeling of traffic at a road crossing and optimization of waiting time of the vehicles. *Alexandria Engineering Journal*, *98*, 114–129. DOI: 10.1016/j.aej.2024.04.050

Economic Times. (2024). Bengaluru water crisis: Why Indian IT hub is witnessing one of the worst water shortages. *Economic Times, English Edition*. https://economictimes.indiatimes.com/news/bengaluru-news/bengaluru-water-crisis-why-indian-it-hub-is-witnessing-one-of-the-worst-water-shortage/articleshow/108234654.cms?utm_source=contentofinterest&utm_medium=text&utm_campaign=cppst

El Aynaoui, K., Magri, P., & Saran, S. (2023). Annual trends report: The rise of Global South: A new consensus is wanted. *Policy Center for the New South*. https://www.policycenter.ma/sites/default/files/2023-12/Annual%20Trends%20Report%202023-ISPI-ORF-PCNS_final.pdf

Fadhel, M. A., Duhaim, A. M., Saihood, A., Sewify, A., Al-Hamadani, M. N. A., Albahri, A. S., Alzubaidi, L., Gupta, A., Mirjalili, S., & Gu, Y. (2024). Comprehensive systematic review of information fusion methods in smart cities and urban environments. *Information Fusion*, *107*, 102317. Advance online publication. DOI: 10.1016/j.inffus.2024.102317

Ganguli, P. (2023). Predictive policing and crime prevention: The role of AI. *India AI*. https://indiaai.gov.in/article/predictive-policing-and-crime-prevention-the-role-of-ai

Hammoumi, L., Maanan, M., & Rhinane, H. (2024). Characterizing smart cities based on artificial intelligence. *Smart Cities*, *7*(3), 1330–1345. DOI: 10.3390/smartcities7030056

Heinrich Son, T., Weedon, Z., Yigitcanlar, T., Sanchez, T., Corchado, J. M., & Mehmood, R. (2023). Algorithmic urban planning for smart and sustainable development: Systematic review of the literature. *Sustainable Cities and Society*, *94*, 104562. DOI: 10.1016/j.scs.2023.104562

Herath, H. M., & Mittal, M. (2022). Adoption of artificial intelligence in smart cities: A comprehensive review. *International Journal of Information Management Data Insights*, *2*(1), 100076. DOI: 10.1016/j.jjimei.2022.100076

Jayakumar, D., Bouhoula, A., & Al-Zubari, W. K. (2024). Unlocking the potential of artificial intelligence for sustainable water management focusing operational applications. *Water (Basel)*, *16*(22), 3328. DOI: 10.3390/w16223328

Kanchana, R. A. C. (2022). Challenges of urbanization towards sustainable development. *Journal of Urban Studies*, *15*(4), 101–120.

Kitchin, R. (2016). *Getting smarter about smart cities: Improving data privacy and security. Data Protection Unit*. Department of the Taoiseach.

Leal Filho, W., Mbah, M. F., Dinis, M. A. P., Trevisan, L. V., de Lange, D., Mishra, A., Rebelatto, B., Ben Hassen, T., & Aina, Y. A. (2024). The role of artificial intelligence in the implementation of the UN Sustainable Development Goal 11: Fostering sustainable cities and communities. *Cities (London, England)*, *150*, 105021. DOI: 10.1016/j.cities.2024.105021

Luusua, A., Ylipulli, J., Foth, M., & Aurigi, A. (2023). Urban AI: Understanding the emerging role of artificial intelligence in smart cities. *AI & Society*, *38*(3), 1039–1044. DOI: 10.1007/s00146-022-01537-5 PMID: 36196366

Mannuru, N. R., Shahriar, S., Teel, Z. A., Wang, T., Lund, B. D., Tijani, S., Pohboon, C. O., Agbaji, D., Alhassan, J., Galley, J. K. L., Kousari, R., Ogbadu-Oladapo, L., Saurav, S. K., Srivastava, A., Tummuru, S. P., Uppala, S., & Vaidya, P. (2023). Artificial intelligence in developing countries: The impact of generative artificial intelligence (AI) technologies for development. *Information Development*, 02666669231200628. Advance online publication. DOI: 10.1177/02666669231200628

Marwaha, S., Dey, H. S., & Brar, T. S. (2024). The emerging role of Artificial Intelligence (AI) in urban and regional planning in India. *International Journal of Arts Architecture & Design*, *2*(2), 61–79. https://worlduniversityofdesign.ac.in/JAARD/wp-content/uploads/2024/07/4.-The-emerging-role-of-Artificial-Intelligence-AI-in-urban-and-regional-Planning-in-India.pdf. DOI: 10.62030/2024Julypaper4

Mensah, G. B. (2023). Artificial intelligence and ethics: A comprehensive review of bias mitigation, transparency, and accountability in AI systems. *Journal of AI Ethics*.https://doi.org/DOI: 10.13140/RG.2.2.23381.19685/1

Ogunlade, G. I., & Clottey, E. (2024). Traffic congestion and air quality in Lagos, Nigeria—A public health perspective. *Liberty University*.https://digitalcommons.liberty.edu/cgi/viewcontent.cgi?article=2125&context=research_symp

Pandiyan, P., Saravanan, S., Usha, K., Kannadasan, R., Alsharif, M. H., & Kim, M.-K. (2023). Technological advancements toward smart energy management in smart cities. *Energy Reports*, *10*, 648–677. DOI: 10.1016/j.egyr.2023.07.021

Pellatt, J., & Palfreman, J. (2023). Smart technology solution for a cleaner city: A Dar es Salaam, Tanzania case study. *GeoJournal*, *88*, 5221–5245. DOI: 10.1007/s10708-023-10917-3

Pillai, A. S. (2024). Traffic management: Implementing AI to optimize traffic flow and reduce congestion. SSRN *Electronic Journal*.https://doi.org/DOI: 10.2139/ssrn.4916398

Pimenow, S., Pimenowa, O., & Prus, P. (2024). Challenges of artificial intelligence development in the context of energy consumption and impact on climate change. *Energies*, *17*(23), 5965. DOI: 10.3390/en17235965

Rashid, Y., Rashid, A., Warraich, M. A., Sabir, S. S., & Waseem, A. (2019). Case study method: A step-by-step guide for business researchers. *International Journal of Qualitative Methods*, *18*, 1609406919862424. Advance online publication. DOI: 10.1177/1609406919862424

Ritchie, H., Samborska, V., & Roser, M. (2024). Urbanization: The world population is moving to cities. Why is urbanization happening and what are the consequences? *Our World in Data*. https://ourworldindata.org/urbanization

Romero-Ben, L., Alves, D., Blesa, J., Cembrano, G., Puig, V., & Duviella, E. (2023). Leak detection and localization in water distribution networks: Review and perspective. *Annual Reviews in Control*, *55*, 392–419. DOI: 10.1016/j.arcontrol.2023.03.012

Samwine, T., Wu, P., Xu, L., Shen, Y., Appiah, E., & Yaoqi, W. (2017). Challenges and prospects of solid waste management in Ghana. *International Journal of Environmental Monitoring and Analysis*, *5*(4), 96. DOI: 10.11648/j.ijema.20170504.11

Sanchez, T. W., Brenman, M., & Ye, X. (2024). The ethical concerns of artificial intelligence in urban planning. *Journal of the American Planning Association*, ●●●, 1–14. DOI: 10.1080/01944363.2024.2355305

Shrivastava, A. (2024). AI in smart cities: Enhancing urban living. [JARET]. *Journal of Advanced Research Engineering and Technology*, *3*(1), 213–222. https://iaeme.com/Home/issue/JARET?Volume=3&Issue=

Son, T. H., Weedon, Z., Yigitcanlar, T., Sanchez, T., Corchado, J. M., & Mehmood, R. (2023). Algorithmic urban planning for smart and sustainable development: Systematic review of the literature. *Sustainable Cities and Society*, *94*, 104562. DOI: 10.1016/j.scs.2023.104562

Szpilko, D., Jiménez Naharro, F., Lăzăroiu, G., & Nica, E. (2023). Artificial intelligence in the smart city — A literature review. *Engineering Management in Production and Services*, *15*(4), 53–75. DOI: 10.2478/emj-2023-0028

Tahiru, A.-W., Cobbina, S. J., Asare, W., & Takal, S. U. (2024). Unlocking energy from waste: A comprehensive analysis of municipal solid waste recovery potential in Ghana. *WORLD (Oakland, Calif.)*, *5*(2), 192–218. DOI: 10.3390/world5020011

Ukoba, K., Olatunji, K. O., Adeoye, E., Jen, T.-C., & Madyira, D. M. (2024). Optimizing renewable energy systems through artificial intelligence: Review and future prospects. *Energy & Environment*, *35*(7), 3833–3879. DOI: 10.1177/0958305X241256293

Villoria, C. (2023). The transformation of Medellín, from violence to innovation. *Where on Planet Earth, Journal Post #13*. https://www.whereonplanetearth.com/p/the-transformation-of-medellin

Wolniak, R., & Stecuła, K. (2024). Artificial intelligence in smart cities—Applications, barriers, and future directions: A review. *Smart Cities*, *7*(3), 1346–1389. DOI: 10.3390/smartcities7030057

Yazdi, M., Zarei, E., Adumene, S., & Beheshti, A. (2024). Navigating the power of artificial intelligence in risk management: A comparative analysis. *Safety (Basel, Switzerland)*, *10*(2), 42. DOI: 10.3390/safety10020042

Compilation of References

Adam, M. S., Anisi, M. H., & Ali, I. (2020). Object tracking sensor networks in smart cities: Taxonomy, architecture, applications, research challenges and future directions. *Future Generation Computer Systems*, *107*, 909–923. DOI: 10.1016/j.future.2017.12.011

Aderibigbe, A. O., Ohenhen, P. E., & Nwaobia, N. K. (2023). Artificial intelligence in developing countries: Bridging the gap between potential and implementation. *Computer Science & IT Research Journal*, *4*(3), 185–199. DOI: 10.51594/csitrj.v4i3.629

Aditya, K., Grzonkowski, S., & Leâ€ Khac, N. (2018). *Enabling Trust in Deep Learning Models: A Digital Forensics Case Study.*, DOI: 10.1109/TrustCom/BigDataSE.2018.00172

Aizenberg, E., & van den Hoven, J. (2020). Designing for human rights in AI. In Big Data & Society (Vol. 7, Issue 2). SAGE Publishing. DOI: 10.1177/2053951720949566

Ajide, K. B., & Alimi, O. Y. (2021). Income inequality, human capital and terrorism in Africa: Beyond exploratory analytics. International Economics, Elsevier. Retrieved from: https://www.sciencedirect.com/science/article/abs/pii/S2110701721000032

Al Fahdi, M., Clarke, N. L., & Furnell, S. M. (2013, August 14–16). Challenges to digital forensics: A survey of researchers & practitioners attitudes and opinions. In *Proceedings of the 2013 Information Security for South Africa (ISSA)* (pp. 1–8). IEEE. DOI: 10.1109/ISSA.2013.6641058

Alahi, M. E. E., Sukkuea, A., Tina, F. W., Nag, A., Kurdthongmee, W., Suwannarat, K., & Mukhopadhyay, S. C. (2023). Integration of IoT-enabled technologies and artificial intelligence (AI) for smart city scenario: Recent advancements and future trends. *Sensors (Basel)*, *23*(11), 5206. DOI: 10.3390/s23115206 PMID: 37299934

Alawida, M., Mejri, S., Mehmood, A., Chikhaoui, B., & Isaac Abiodun, O. (2023). A Comprehensive Study of ChatGPT: Advancements, Limitations, and Ethical Considerations in Natural Language Processing and Cybersecurity. *Information (Basel), 14*(8), 462. DOI: 10.3390/info14080462

Albino, V., Berardi, U., & Dangelico, R. M. (2015). Smart cities: Definitions, dimensions, performance, and initiatives. *Journal of Urban Technology, 22*(1), 3–21. DOI: 10.1080/10630732.2014.942092

Al-Garadi, M. A., Mohamed, A., & Du, X. (2017). Exploring the impact of artificial intelligence on smart city research: A bibliometric analysis. *Sustainability, 9*(5), 681.

Aljohani, F. H., Abi Sen, A. A., Ramazan, M. S., Alzahrani, B., & Bahbouh, N. M. (2023). A smart framework for managing natural disasters based on the IoT and ML. *Applied Sciences (Basel, Switzerland), 13*(7), 3888. DOI: 10.3390/app13063888

Al-Kaff, A., Madridano, Á., Campos, S., García, F., Martín, D., & de la Escalera, A. (2020). Emergency support unmanned aerial vehicle for forest fire surveillance. *Electronics (Basel), 9*(2), 260. DOI: 10.3390/electronics9020260

Allah Rakha, N. (2024). Cybercrime and the law: Addressing the challenges of digital forensics in criminal investigations. *Mexican Law Review, 16*, 23–54. DOI: 10.22201/iij.24485306e.2024.2.18892

Almeida, F. (2023). Prospects of cybersecurity in smart cities. *Future Internet, 15*(9), 285. DOI: 10.3390/fi15090285

Alon-Barkat, S., & Busuioc, M. (2023, January). Human–AI Interactions in Public Sector Decision Making: "Automation Bias" and "Selective Adherence" to Algorithmic Advice. *Journal of Public Administration: Research and Theory, 33*(1), 153–169. DOI: 10.1093/jopart/muac007

Alvarez, V. R. (2024). The urban transformation of Medellín: A case study. *ArchDaily*._https://www.archdaily.com/1015216/the-urban-transformation-of-medellin-a-case-study

Alvarez, J. M., Colmenarejo, A. B., Elobaid, A., Fabbrizzi, S., Fahimi, M., Ferrara, A., Ghodsi, S., Mougan, C., Papageorgiou, I., Reyero, P., Russo, M., Scott, K. M., State, L., Zhao, X., & Ruggieri, S. (2024). Policy advice and best practices on bias and fairness in AI. *Ethics and Information Technology, 26*(2), 31. DOI: 10.1007/s10676-024-09746-w

Alzouâ€™bi, S., Alshibl, H., & Al-Maâ€™aitah, M. (2014). Artificial Intelligence in Law Enforcement, A Review. In International Journal of Advanced Information Technology (Vol. 4, Issue 4, p. 1). DOI: 10.5121/ijait.2014.4401

Amini, M., & Jahanbakhsh Javid, N. (2023). A multi-perspective framework established on diffusion of innovation (DOI) theory and technology, organization and environment (TOE) framework toward supply chain management system based on cloud computing technology for small and medium enterprises. Organization and Environment (TOE) Framework Toward Supply Chain Management System Based on Cloud Computing Technology for Small and Medium Enterprises (January 2023). *International Journal of Information Technology and Innovation Adoption, 11*, 1217–1234.

Amrutha, C. V., Jyotsna, C., & Amudha, J. (2020, March). Deep learning approach for suspicious activity detection from surveillance video. In 2020 2nd International Conference on Innovative Mechanisms for Industry Applications (ICIMIA) (pp. 335-339). IEEE. DOI: 10.1109/ICIMIA48430.2020.9074920

Anbarasan, M., Muthu, B. A., Sivaparthipan, C. B., Sundarasekar, R., Kadry, S., Krishnamoorthy, S., Samuel R, D. J., & Dasel, A. A. (2019). Detection of flood disaster system based on IoT, big data and convolutional deep neural network. *Computer Communications, 150*, 150–157. Advance online publication. DOI: 10.1016/j.comcom.2019.11.022

Anderez, D. O., Kanjo, E., Amnwar, A., Johnson, S. D., & Lucy, D. (2021). The Rise of Technology in Crime Prevention: Opportunities, Challenges and Practitioners Perspectives. In arXiv (Cornell University). Cornell University. https://doi.org//arxiv.2102.04204DOI: 10.48550

Angelidou, M., Psaltoglou, A., Komninos, N., Kakderi, C., Tsarchopoulos, P., & Panori, A. (2017). Enhancing sustainable urban development through smart city applications. Journal of Science and Technology Policy Management.

Angelidou, M. (2014). Smart city policies: A spatial approach. *Cities (London, England), 41*, S3–S11. DOI: 10.1016/j.cities.2014.06.007

Anthopoulos, L. G. (2017). *Understanding Smart Cities: A Tool for Smart Government or an Industrial Trick?* Springer International. [REMOVED HYPERLINK FIELD], DOI: 10.1007/978-3-319-57015-0

Anthopoulos, L., Janssen, M., & Weerakkody, V. (2016). A unified smart city model (USCM) for smart city conceptualization and benchmarking. [IJEGR]. *International Journal of Electronic Government Research, 12*(2), 77–93. DOI: 10.4018/IJEGR.2016040105

Anttiroiko, A.-V. (2016). City-as-a-Platform: The rise of participatory innovation platforms in Finnish cities. *Sustainability (Basel), 8*(9), 922. DOI: 10.3390/su8090922

Appleton, J. (2021, May 11). What is IoT and why is it important for smart cities. Emerald Publishing Limited. Butler, R. J., & Lachow, I. (2016). Smart cities and the internet of things: Benefts, risks, and options. New America. http://www.jstor.com/stable/resrep10510.5

Appleton, J. (2021). *What is IoT and why is it important for smart cities*. Emerald Publishing Limited.

Arashloo, S. R., Kittler, J., & Christmas, W. (2017). An anomaly detection approach to face spoofing detection: A new formulation and evaluation protocol. *IEEE Access : Practical Innovations, Open Solutions*, *5*, 13868–13882. DOI: 10.1109/ACCESS.2017.2729161

Aschenbruck, N., Gerhards-Padilla, E., & Lambertz, M. (2012, October 22–25). *Applicability of crypto-based security approaches in tactical wireless multi-hop networks*. In *Proceedings of the IEEE Conference on Local Computer Networks* (pp. 102–110). Clearwater, FL, USA. DOI: 10.1109/LCN.2012.6423584

Baafi, P. O. (2022). Tools for cyber forensics. *Advanced Multidisciplinary Scientific Research Journal Publications*, *1*(1), 285–290. DOI: 10.22624/AIMS/CRP-BK3-P46

Baba, M., Gui, V., & Pescaru, D. (2019). Deep Learning Approach for Violence Detection in Urban Areas. In ITM Web of Conferences (Vol. 29, p. 3009). EDP Sciences. DOI: 10.1051/itmconf/20192903009

Baek, M., Mun, J., Kim, W., Choi, D., Yim, J., & Lee, S. (2021). Driving environment perception based on the fusion of vehicular wireless communications and automotive remote sensors. *Sensors (Basel)*, *21*(6), 1860. DOI: 10.3390/s21051860 PMID: 33799998

Balasubramaniam, N., Kauppinen, M., Rannisto, A., Hiekkanen, K., & Kujala, S. (2023). Transparency and explainability of AI systems: From ethical guidelines to requirements. *Information and Software Technology*, *159*, 107197. DOI: 10.1016/j.infsof.2023.107197

Balbaa, M., & Abdurashidova, M. (2024). The impact of artificial intelligence in decision making: A comprehensive review. *EPRA International Journal of Economics. Business and Management Studies*, *11*(2), 27–38. DOI: 10.36713/epra15747

Banani, S., & Gordon, S. (2014, October 1–3). *Selecting basic safety messages to verify in VANETs using zone priority*. In *Proceedings of the Asia-Pacific Conference on Communications* (pp. 423–428). Pattaya, Thailand. DOI: 10.1109/APCC.2014.7092849

Banerjee, C., Bhaduri, A., & Saraswat, C. (2022). Digitalization in urban water governance: Case study of Bengaluru and Singapore. *Frontiers in Environmental Science. Frontiers in Environmental Science*, *10*, 816824. Advance online publication. DOI: 10.3389/fenvs.2022.816824

Bareh, C. K. (2024). Reviewing the Privacy Implications of Indias Digital Personal Data Protection Act (2023) from Library Contexts. *DESIDOC Journal of Library and Information Technology*, *44*(1), 50â€"58. DOI: 10.14429/djlit.44.1.18410

Barnard-Wills, D. (2013). Security, privacy and surveillance in European policy documents. *International Data Privacy Law*, *3*(3), 170–180. DOI: 10.1093/idpl/ipt014

Bartoli, G., Fantacci, R., Gei, F., Marabissi, D., & Micciullo, L. (2015). A novel emergency management platform for smart public safety. *International Journal of Communication Systems*, *28*(6), 928–943. DOI: 10.1002/dac.2716

Bastit, B., Fernández, M., Kesh, S., & Tsui, D. (2023). The AI governance challenge. *S&P Global*. https://www.spglobal.com/en/research-insights/special-reports/the-ai-governance-challenge

Becker, M. (2019). Privacy in the digital age: Comparing and contrasting individual versus social approaches towards privacy. *Ethics and Information Technology*, *21*(4), 307–317. DOI: 10.1007/s10676-019-09508-z

Ben Chaabene, N. E. H., Bouzeghoub, A., Guetari, R., & Ghezala, H. H. B. (2022). Deep learning methods for anomalies detection in social networks using multidimensional networks and multimodal data: A survey. *Multimedia Systems*, *28*(6), 2133–2143. DOI: 10.1007/s00530-020-00731-z

Ben Hamida, E., Noura, H., & Znaidi, W. (2015). Security of cooperative intelligent transport systems: Standards, threats analysis and cryptographic countermeasures. *Electronics (Basel)*, *4*(2), 380–423. DOI: 10.3390/electronics4030380

Ben Hamida, E., Znaidi, W., & Menouar, H. (2015, September 6–9). *Implementation and evaluation of the ETSI security architecture for cooperative intelligent transport systems*. In *Proceedings of the IEEE Vehicular Technology Conference (VTC-Fall)* (pp. 1–5). Boston, MA, USA.

Ben Othmane, L., Al-Fuqaha, A., Ben Hamida, E., & van den Brand, M. (2013). *Towards extended safety in connected vehicles*. In *Proceedings of the IEEE Intelligent Transportation Systems* (pp. 652–657). The Hague, The Netherlands.

Ben Rjab, A., Mellouli, S., & Corbett, J. (2023). Barriers to artificial intelligence adoption in smart cities: A systematic literature review and research agenda. *Government Information Quarterly*, *40*(3), 101814. DOI: 10.1016/j.giq.2023.101814

Benbouzid, B. (2019). To predict and to manage. Predictive policing in the United States. *Big Data & Society*, *6*(1), 2053951719861703. Advance online publication. DOI: 10.1177/2053951719861703

Bernstein, D. J., & Lange, T. (n.d.). *eBACS: ECRYPT Benchmarking of Cryptographic Systems. Crypto++ 5.6.0 Benchmarks*. https://www.cryptopp.com/benchmarks.html (accessed March 17, 2025)

Bérubé, M., Beaulieu, L. A., Mongeau, P., & Saint-Charles, J. (2023). Identifying Key Players in Violent Extremist Networks: Using Socio-Semantic Network Analysis as Part of a Program of Content Moderation. *Studies in Conflict and Terrorism*, *46*(12), 2381–2399. DOI: 10.1080/1057610X.2021.1927203

Bewersdorff, A., Zhai, X., Roberts, J., & Nerdel, C. (2023). Myths, mis- and preconceptions of artificial intelligence: A review of the literature. *Computers and Education: Artificial Intelligence*, *4*, 100143. DOI: 10.1016/j.caeai.2023.100143

Bhoomika, M. (2022). Understanding the impact of urbanization on the water crisis in Bangalore: Challenges and opportunities. National Centre for Good Governance, Ministry of Personnel, Public Grievances and Pensions, Government of India. Retrieved from https://ncgg.org.in/sites/default/files/lectures-document/Bhoomika.pdf

Bibal, A., Lognoul, M., Streel, A. de, & FrÃ©nayâ€¬, B. (2020). Legal requirements on explainability in machine learning. In Artificial Intelligence and Law (Vol. 29, Issue 2, p. 149). Springer Science+Business Media. DOI: 10.1007/s10506-020-09270-4

Bibri, S. E., Huang, J., Jagatheesaperumal, S. K., & Krogstie, J. (2024). The synergistic interplay of artificial intelligence and digital twin in environmentally planning sustainable smart cities: A comprehensive systematic review. *Environmental Science and Ecotechnology*, *20*, 100433. DOI: 10.1016/j.ese.2024.100433 PMID: 38831974

Biden, (2023). https://www.whitehouse.gov/briefing-room/presidential-actions/2023/10/30/executive-order-on-the-safe-secure-and-trustworthy-development-and-use-of-artificial-intelligence/

Blessed, G., Kontagora, N. B., Agajo, J., & Aliyu, I. (2022). Performance Evaluation of Keyword Extraction Techniques and Stop Word Lists on Speech-To-Text Corpus. *The International Arab Journal of Information Technology*, *20*(1). Advance online publication. DOI: 10.34028/iajit/20/1/14

Blind, K., Niebel, C., & Rammer, C. (2023). The impact of the EU General Data Protection Regulation on product innovation. *Industry and Innovation*, *31*(3), 311–351. DOI: 10.1080/13662716.2023.2271858

Blount, K. (2024). Using artificial intelligence to prevent crime: Implications for due process and criminal justice. *AI & Society*, *39*(1), 359–368. DOI: 10.1007/s00146-022-01513-z

Bordoloi, N., Talukdar, A. K., & Sarma, K. K. (2020, December). Suspicious activity detection from videos using yolov3. In 2020 IEEE 17th India Council International Conference (INDICON) (pp. 1-5). IEEE. DOI: 10.1109/INDICON49873.2020.9342230

Borum, R. (2004). *Psychology of terrorism.* University of South Florida.

Bowers, K., & Johnson, S. (2024). Facing the future of crime: A framework for police use of technology. *The Political Quarterly*, *95*(3), 480–488. DOI: 10.1111/1467-923X.13426

Breaux, R., Shroff, D. M., Cash, A. R., Swanson, C. S., Carlton, C., Bertollo, J. R., & Dahiya, A. V. (2023). Telehealth delivery of the RELAX intervention for families of adolescents diagnosed with ADHD: Preliminary treatment outcomes and evidence of acceptability and feasibility. *Evidence-Based Practice in Child and Adolescent Mental Health*, *8*(1), 24–38. DOI: 10.1080/23794925.2021.1970053

Brennen, T., & Magnussen, S. (2023). Lie Detection: What Works? In Current Directions in Psychological Science (Vol. 32, Issue 5, p. 395). SAGE Publishing. DOI: 10.1177/09637214231173095

Briend, J. (2025). The EU's AI Act: Implications on Justice and Counter-terrorism. Global Network on Extremism and Technology (GNET). Available at: https://gnet-research.org/2025/03/10/the-eus-ai-act-implications-on-justice-and-counter-terrorism/

Britannica. (2024). History and Society: Terrorism. Retrieved from: https://www.britannica.com/topic/terrorism

Brown, L., & Martin, P. (2023). NLP for Automating Regulatory Compliance: Case Studies and Implications. *Journal of Artificial Intelligence in Law*, *14*(1), 45–67.

Brundage, M.. (2018). *The Malicious Use of Artificial Intelligence: Forecasting*. Prevention, and Mitigation.

Butler, R. J., & Lachow, I. (2016). Smart cities and the internet of things: Benefts, risks, and options. New America. http://www.jstor.com/stable/resrep10510.5

Candilis, P. J., Cleary, S. D., & Dhumad, S. (2023). Classifying terrorism: a latent class analysis of primary source socio-political and psychological data. Taylor & Francis Retrieved from: https://www.researchgate.net/profile/PhilipCandilis/publication/348796896_Classifying_terrorism_a_latent_class_analysis_of_primary_source_sociopolitical_and_psychological_data/links/60ad13fb92851c168e3e89d3/Classifying-terrorism-a-latent-class-analysis-of-primary-source-socio-political-and psychological-data.pdf

Cantwell. (2024). Cantwell, Young, Hickenlooper, Blackburn Introduce Bill to Ensure U.S. Leads Global AI Innovation. https://www.commerce.senate.gov/2024/4/cantwell-young-blackburn-hickenlooper-introduce-bill-to-ensure-u-s-leads-global-ai-innovation

Caragliu, A., & Del Bo, C. (2018). Smart cities: A review of definitions, metrics, and initiatives. *International Journal of Urban Sciences*, *22*(2), 168–186.

Caragliu, A., Del Bo, C., & Nijkamp, P. (2011). Smart Cities in Europe. *Journal of Urban Technology*, *18*(2), 65–82. DOI: 10.1080/10630732.2011.601117

Carley, K. M., Malik, M., Landwehr, P. M., Pfeffer, J., & Kowalchuck, M. (2016). Crowd sourcing disaster management: The complex nature of Twitter usage in Padang, Indonesia. *Safety Science*, *90*, 48–61. DOI: 10.1016/j.ssci.2016.04.002

Casini, M. (2017). Green Technology for Smart Cities. *IOP Conference Series. Earth and Environmental Science*, *83*, 012014. DOI: 10.1088/1755-1315/83/1/012014

Castets-Renard, C. (2021). Human Rights and Algorithmic Impact Assessment for Predictive Policing. In Micklitz, H.-W., Pollicino, O., Reichman, A., Simoncini, A., Sartor, G., & De Gregorio, G. (Eds.), *Constitutional Challenges in the Algorithmic Society* (pp. 93–110). Cambridge University Press. DOI: 10.1017/9781108914857.007

Cellary, W. (2013). Smart governance for smart industries. In *Proceedings of the 7th International Conference on Theory and Practice of Electronic Governance*. 91-93.

Chackravarthy, S., Schmitt, S., & Yang, L. (2018, October). Intelligent crime anomaly detection in smart cities using deep learning. In 2018 IEEE 4th International Conference on Collaboration and Internet Computing (CIC) (pp. 399-404). IEEE. DOI: 10.1109/CIC.2018.00060

Chaliand, G., Blin, A., Schneider, E., Pulver, K., & Browner, J. (2016). *The History of Terrorism: From Antiquity to al Qaeda*. University of California Press. DOI: 10.1525/9780520966000

Chan, E., Man, A., & Lam, H. (2019). Scientific evidence on natural disasters and health emergency and disaster risk management in Asian rural-based area. *British Medical Bulletin, 129*(1), 91–105. DOI: 10.1093/bmb/ldz002 PMID: 30753325

Cheong, H.-I., Lyons, A., Houghton, R. W., & Majumdar, A. (2023). Secondary qualitative research methodology using online data within social sciences. *International Journal of Qualitative Methods, 22*(2), 1–15. DOI: 10.1177/16094069231180160

Chinnikatti, S. K. (2018). Artificial Intelligence in Forensic Science. *Forensic Science & Addiction Research, 2*(5). Advance online publication. DOI: 10.31031/FSAR.2018.03.000554

Chong, Y. S., & Tay, Y. H. (2015, May). Modeling video-based anomaly detection using deep architectures: Challenges and possibilities. In 2015 10th Asian Control Conference (ASCC) (pp. 1-8). IEEE.

Chong, Y. S., & Tay, Y. H. (2017). Abnormal event detection in videos using spatiotemporal autoencoder. In Advances in Neural Networks-ISNN 2017: 14th International Symposium, ISNN 2017, Sapporo, Hakodate, and Muroran, Hokkaido, Japan, June 21–26, 2017 [Springer International Publishing.]. *Proceedings, 14*(Part II), 189–196.

Choudhry, N., Abawajy, J., Huda, S., & Rao, I. (2023). A Comprehensive Survey of Machine Learning Methods for Surveillance Videos Anomaly Detection. *IEEE Access : Practical Innovations, Open Solutions, 11*, 114680–114713. DOI: 10.1109/ACCESS.2023.3321800

Chourabi, H., ... (2012) "Understanding Smart Cities: An Integrative Framework," 2012 45th Hawaii International Conference on System Sciences, Maui, HI, USA. pp. 2289-2297, DOI: 10.1109/HICSS.2012.615

Chung, W. Y., & Oh, S. J. (2006). Remote monitoring system with wireless sensors module for room environment. *Sensors and Actuators. B, Chemical, 113*(1), 64–67. DOI: 10.1016/j.snb.2005.02.023

Cifuentes-Faura, J. (2022). European Union policies and their role in combating climate change over the years. *Air Quality, Atmosphere & Health, 15*(8), 1–8. DOI: 10.1007/s11869-022-01156-5 PMID: 35035604

Cisar, P., Cisar, S., & Bosnjak, S. (2014). Cybercrime and digital forensics—Technologies and approaches. In *DAAAM International Scientific Book 2014* (pp. 525–542). DAAAM International.

Clim, A., Toma, A., Zota, R. D., & Constantinescu, R. (2022). The Need for Cybersecurity in Industrial Revolution and Smart Cities. *Sensors (Basel), 23*(1), 120. DOI: 10.3390/s23010120 PMID: 36616718

Coffey, T. 2021. "Under the Watchful Eye of the CCP: Chinese Surveillance in Xinjiang." *Human Rights Pulse.* April 21, 2021. Accessed [date]. https://www.humanrightspulse.com/mastercontentblog/under-the-watchful-eye-of-the-ccp-chinese-surveillance-in-xinjiang

Costa, D. G., Bittencourt, J. C. N., Oliveira, F., Peixoto, J. P. J., & Jesus, T. C. (2024). Achieving sustainable smart cities through geospatial data-driven approaches. *Sustainability (Basel), 16*(2), 640. DOI: 10.3390/su16020640

Crowther, K. G., Haimes, Y. Y., & Johnson, M. E. (2010). Principles for Better Information Security through More Accurate, Transparent Risk Scoring. In Journal of Homeland Security and Emergency Management (Vol. 7, Issue 1). De Gruyter. DOI: 10.2202/1547-7355.1658

Cugurullo, F. (2018). The origin of the Smart City imaginary: from the dawn of modernity to the eclipse of reason.

Cugurullo, F. (2020). Urban Artificial Intelligence: From Automation to Autonomy in the Smart City. In Frontiers in Sustainable Cities 2. 38.

Daftary, F. (2011). *Historical dictionary of the Ismailis*. Scarecrow Press.

Daniel, S., & Doran, M. A. (2013, June 17–20). Geo Smart City: Geomatics contribution to the smart city. In *Proceedings of the 14th Annual International Conference on Digital Government Research* (pp. 65–71). ACM. DOI: 10.1145/2479724.2479735

Danzell, O. E., Yeh, Y. Y., & Pfannenstiel, M. (2018). Does Education Mitigate Terrorism? Examining the Effects of Educated Youth Cohorts on Domestic Terror in Africa. *Terrorism and Political Violence, 32*(8), 1731–1752. DOI: 10.1080/09546553.2018.1506336

Davenport, T. H., & Redman, T. C. (2023). How AI is improving data management. *MIT Sloan Management Review, 64*(2), 1–5.

DaViera, A. L., Uriostegui, M., Gottlieb, A., & Onyeka, O. C. (2024). Risk, race, and predictive policing: A critical race theory analysis of the strategic subject list. *American Journal of Community Psychology, 73*(1-2), 91–103. DOI: 10.1002/ajcp.12671 PMID: 37067014

Davies, A., & Krame, G. (2023). Integrating body-worn cameras, drones, and AI: A framework for enhancing police readiness and response. *Policing. Policing (Oxford, England), 17*, paad083. Advance online publication. DOI: 10.1093/police/paad083

de Bem Machado, A., Sousa, M. J., Pesqueira, A., & Rocha, A. (2024). Metaverse for Education Information Systems: A Systematic Literature Review. Metaverse Driven Intelligent Information Systems: Emerging Trends and Future Directions, 29-47.

de Carvalho, R. M., Del Prete, C., Martin, Y. S., Araujo Rivero, R. M., Önen, M., Schiavo, F. P., Rumín, Á. C., Mouratidis, H., Yelmo, J. C., & Koukovini, M. N. (2020). Protecting citizens' personal data and privacy: Joint effort from GDPR EU cluster research projects. *SN Computer Science, 1*(4), 217. DOI: 10.1007/s42979-020-00218-8

de Oliveira, L. F., da Silva Gomes, A., Enes, Y., Castelo Branco, T. V., Pires, R. P., Bolzon, A., & Demo, G. (2022). Path and future of artificial intelligence in the field of justice: A systematic literature review and a research agenda. *SN Social Sciences, 2*(9), 180. DOI: 10.1007/s43545-022-00482-w

Decker, M., Wegner, L., & Leicht-Scholten, C. (2025). Procedural fairness in algorithmic decision-making: The role of public engagement. *Ethics and Information Technology, 27*(1), 1. DOI: 10.1007/s10676-024-09811-4

Deep Belief Networks for phone recognition. (2023). http://www.cs.toronto.edu/~gdahl/papers/dbnPhoneRec.pdf

Dillard-Wright, J., & Shields-Haas, V. (2021). Nursing with the people: Reimagining futures for nursing. *Advances in Nursing Science, 44*(3), 195–209. DOI: 10.1097/ANS.0000000000000361 PMID: 33624989

Dimri, S. C., Indu, R., Bajaj, M., Rathore, R. S., Blazek, V., Dutta, A. K., & Alsubai, S. (2024). Modeling of traffic at a road crossing and optimization of waiting time of the vehicles. *Alexandria Engineering Journal, 98*, 114–129. DOI: 10.1016/j.aej.2024.04.050

Doctor, A. C., Hunter, S. T., & Ligon, G. S. (2023). Militant Leadership and Terrorism in Armed Conflict. *Terrorism and Political Violence, 36*(6), 740–756. DOI: 10.1080/09546553.2023.2189972

Doe, J., Miller, K., & White, R. (2021). Machine Learning Algorithms and Compliance Automation. *Financial Technology Review, 7*(2), 91–108.

Dunsin, D., Ghanem, M. C., Ouazzane, K., & Vassilev, V. (2023). A comprehensive analysis of the role of artificial intelligence and machine learning in modern digital forensics and incident response. *Forensic Science International Digital Investigation*, *48*, 301675. DOI: 10.1016/j.fsidi.2023.301675

Eager, B., & Brunton, R. (2023). Prompting higher education towards AI-augmented teaching and learning practice. Journal of University Teaching & Learning Practice, 20(5), 02.

Ebner, J., Kavanagh, C., & Whitehouse, H. (2022). Is there a language of terrorists? A comparative manifesto analysis. *Studies in Conflict and Terrorism*, •••, 1–27. DOI: 10.1080/1057610X.2022.2109244

Ebrahimi, S., & Bridgelall, R. (2021). A fuzzy Delphi analytic hierarchy model to rank factors influencing public transit mode choice: A case study. *Research in Transportation Business & Management*, *39*, 100496. DOI: 10.1016/j.rtbm.2020.100496

Economic Times. (2024). Bengaluru water crisis: Why Indian IT hub is witnessing one of the worst water shortages. *Economic Times, English Edition*. https://economictimes.indiatimes.com/news/bengaluru-news/bengaluru-water-crisis-why-indian-it-hub-is-witnessing-one-of-the-worst-water-shortage/articleshow/108234654.cms?utm_source=contentofinterest&utm_medium=text&utm_campaign=cppst

Ekhande, S., Patil, U., & Kulhalli, K. V. (2022). Review on effectiveness of deep learning approach in digital forensics. [IJECE]. *International Journal of Electrical and Computer Engineering*, *12*(6), 5481–5592. DOI: 10.11591/ijece.v12i5.pp5481-5592

El Aynaoui, K., Magri, P., & Saran, S. (2023). Annual trends report: The rise of Global South: A new consensus is wanted. *Policy Center for the New South*. https://www.policycenter.ma/sites/default/files/2023-12/Annual%20Trends%20Report%202023-ISPI-ORF-PCNS_final.pdf

ElBaih, M. (2023). The Role of Privacy Regulations in AI Development (A Discussion of the Ways in Which Privacy Regulations Can Shape the Development of AI). Available at *SSRN* 4589207. DOI: 10.2139/ssrn.4589207

El-Ghalayini, Y., & Al-Kandari, H. (2020). Big Data Regulatory Legislation: Security, Privacy and Smart City Governance. In Journal of Law Policy and Globalization. IISTE. DOI: 10.7176/JLPG/95-03

Erdélyi, O. J., & Goldsmith, J. (2022). Regulating artificial intelligence: Proposal for a global solution. *Government Information Quarterly*, *39*(4), 101748. DOI: 10.1016/j.giq.2022.101748

Errammach, M. (Host). (2024). Mohamedou Ould Slahi: Secrets of 14 years at Guantanamo. Maghareb Podcast. In Atheer. atheer - YouTube.

European Telecommunications Standards Institute. (2012). *ETSI TS 102 941 v1.1.1 (2012-06)—Intelligent Transport Systems (ITS)—Security; Security header and certificate formats* [Technical Report]. Valbonne, France.

European Telecommunications Standards Institute. (2014). *ETSI TS 102 723-8 v1.0.4 (2014-07)—Intelligent Transport Systems (ITS)—OSI cross-layer topics; Part 11: Interface between networking and transport layer and facilities layer* [Technical Report]. Valbonne, France.

Fadhel, M. A., Duhaim, A. M., Saihood, A., Sewify, A., Al-Hamadani, M. N. A., Albahri, A. S., Alzubaidi, L., Gupta, A., Mirjalili, S., & Gu, Y. (2024). Comprehensive systematic review of information fusion methods in smart cities and urban environments. *Information Fusion*, *107*, 102317. Advance online publication. DOI: 10.1016/j.inffus.2024.102317

Fakiha, B. (2023). Enhancing cyber forensics with AI and machine learning: A study on automated threat analysis and classification. *International Journal of Safety and Security Engineering*, *13*(4), 701–707. DOI: 10.18280/ijsse.130412

Federal Bureau of Investigation (FBI). (2022). Uniform Crime Reporting (UCR) Program: Crime in the United States, 2021. Retrieved from https://www.fbi.gov/services/cjis/ucr

Feiri, M., Petit, J., Schmidt, R., & Kargl, F. (2013, December 16–18). *The impact of security on cooperative awareness in VANET*. In *Proceedings of the IEEE Vehicular Networking Conference* (pp. 127–134). Boston, MA, USA. DOI: 10.1109/VNC.2013.6737599

Feldstein, S. (2023). Evaluating Europe's push to enact AI regulations: How will this influence global norms? *Democratization*, *31*(5), 1049–1066. DOI: 10.1080/13510347.2023.2196068

Floridi, L., & Taddeo, M. (2016). What is data ethics? *Philosophical Transactions. Series A, Mathematical, Physical, and Engineering Sciences*, *374*(2083), 20160360. DOI: 10.1098/rsta.2016.0360 PMID: 28336805

Fontes, C., Hohma, E., Corrigan, C. C., & Lütge, C. (2022). AI-powered public surveillance systems: Why we (might) need them and how we want them. *Technology in Society*, *71*, 102137. DOI: 10.1016/j.techsoc.2022.102137

Fosso, Y., & Berquin, D. (2022). An analysis of information communication technologies for natural disaster management in Africa. *International Journal of Disaster Risk Reduction*, *68*, 102722. DOI: 10.1016/j.ijdrr.2021.102722

Freeman, L. (2021, March). Weapons of War, Tools of Justice: Using Artificial Intelligence to Investigate International Crimes. *Journal of International Criminal Justice*, *19*(1), 35–53. DOI: 10.1093/jicj/mqab013

Freeman, M. (2014). A Theory of Terrorist Leadership (and its Consequences for Leadership Targeting). *Terrorism and Political Violence*, *26*(4), 666–687. DOI: 10.1080/09546553.2012.751912

Frieden, B. J. (1965). TOWARD EQUALITY OF URBAN OPPORTUNITY. In Journal of the American Institute of Planners (Vol. 31, Issue 4, p. 320). Taylor & Francis. DOI: 10.1080/01944366508978186

Friedewald, M., & Pohoryles, R. J. (2013). Technology and privacy. *Innovation (Abingdon)*, *26*(1–2), 1–6. DOI: 10.1080/13511610.2013.768011

Fukatsu, R., & Sakaguchi, K. (2021). Automated driving with cooperative perception using millimeter-wave V2V communications for safe overtaking. *Sensors (Basel)*, *21*(8), 2659. DOI: 10.3390/s21082659 PMID: 33920066

Ganguli, P. (2023). Predictive policing and crime prevention: The role of AI. *IndiaAI*. https://indiaai.gov.in/article/predictive-policing-and-crime-prevention-the-role-of-ai

Ganokratanaa, T., Aramvith, S., & Sebe, N. (2020). Unsupervised anomaly detection and localization based on deep spatiotemporal translation network. *IEEE Access : Practical Innovations, Open Solutions*, *8*, 50312–50329. DOI: 10.1109/ACCESS.2020.2979869

Gans-Combe, C. (2022). Automated justice: Issues, benefits and risks in the use of artificial intelligence and its algorithms in access to justice and law enforcement. In O'Mathúna, D., & Iphofen, R. (Eds.), *Ethics, integrity and policymaking* (Vol. 9, pp. 185–199). Springer., DOI: 10.1007/978-3-031-15746-2_14

Gao, P., Xu, Z., & Gao, S. (2018). Data Explosion Model for Public Safety Data Processing and Its Application in a Unified Security System. In Lecture notes in electrical engineering (p. 448). Springer Science+Business Media. DOI: 10.1007/978-981-10-7398-4_46

Gayoso Martínez, V., Hernández Encinas, L., & Queiruga Dios, A. (2015). Security and practical considerations when implementing the elliptic curve integrated encryption scheme. *Cryptologia*, *39*(3), 244–269. DOI: 10.1080/01611194.2014.988363

Gazi, T. (2020). Data to the rescue: how humanitarian aid NGOs should collect information based on the GDPR. In Journal of International Humanitarian Action (Vol. 5, Issue 1). Springer Nature. DOI: 10.1186/s41018-020-00078-0

Gebhardt, M., Kopyto, M., Birkel, H., & Hartmann, E. (2022). Industry 4.0 technologies as enablers of collaboration in circular supply chains: A systematic literature review. *International Journal of Production Research, 60*(23), 6967–6995. DOI: 10.1080/00207543.2021.1999521

George, D., Jane, A., & Damon, P. (2017). *Introduction to emergency management* (6th ed.). Butterworth-Heinemann.

Gercke, M. (2021). Ethical and Societal Issues of Automated Dark Web Investigation: Part 1. In Akhgar, B., Gercke, M., Vrochidis, S., & Gibson, H. (Eds.), *Dark Web Investigation. Security Informatics and Law Enforcement.* Springer., DOI: 10.1007/978-3-030-55343-2_6

Gething, P., & Tatem, A. (2011). Can mobile phone data improve emergency response to natural disasters? *PLoS Medicine, 8*(8), e1001085. DOI: 10.1371/journal.pmed.1001085 PMID: 21918644

Giani, M., LP Merlino (2021). Terrorist attacks and minority perceived discrimination. The British Journal of Sociology, Wiley Online Library. wiley.com

Glas, B., Sander, O., Stuckert, V., Müller-Glaser, K. D., & Becker, J. (2011). Prime field ECDSA signature processing for reconfigurable embedded systems. *International Journal of Reconfigurable Computing, 2011*, 10511064. Advance online publication. DOI: 10.1155/2011/836460

Gong, Y., & Yang, X. (2022). Exploration of artificial intelligence in urban natural disaster emergency management. *Modern Occupational Safety, 12*, 54–56.

Gordon, B. J. (2021). Automated Facial Recognition in Law Enforcement: The Queen (On Application of Edward Bridges) v The Chief Constable of South Wales Police. *Potchefstroom Electronic Law Journal (PER/PELJ)*, 24.. Available at *SSRN*: https://ssrn.com/abstract=3959617DOI: 10.17159/1727-3781/2021/v24i0a8923

Gorlamudiveti, L. P., & Sethu, S. G. (2023). Role of Artificial Intelligence in the Indian Judicial System. In *2023 International Conference on Computational Intelligence and Knowledge Economy (ICCIKE)* (pp. 305-310). Dubai, United Arab Emirates. DOI: 10.1109/ICCIKE58312.2023.10131795

Goutam Mukherjee, A., Ramesh Wanjari, U., Chakraborty, R., Renu, K., Vellingiri, B., & George, A., C R, S. R., & Valsala Gopalakrishnan, A. (. (2021). A review on modern and smart technologies for efficient waste disposal and management. *Journal of Environmental Management*, *297*, 113347. DOI: 10.1016/j.jenvman.2021.113347 PMID: 34314963

Gu, B., Liu, J., Xiong, H., Li, T., & Pan, Y. (2021). ECPC-ICP: A 6D vehicle pose estimation method by fusing the roadside lidar point cloud and road feature. *Sensors (Basel)*, *21*(10), 3489. DOI: 10.3390/s21103489 PMID: 34067737

Guo, A., Liu, B., Fu, L., Gao, S., Jin, Y., & Yang, Z. (2022). Research on the key technology of stereoscopic cooperation in aviation emergency rescue. *Ziran Zaihai Xuebao*, *31*, 1157–1167.

Gupta, R., & Kumar, L. (2025). Analysis of Bit Rate vs SNR in Coded FSO Communication Systems. 2025 3rd IEEE International Conference on Industrial Electronics: Developments & Applications (ICIDeA), Bhubaneswar, India, pp. 1-5, DOI: 10.1109/ICIDeA64800.2025.10963345

Gurstein, M. (2003). Effective use: A community informatics strategy beyond the Digital Divide. *First Monday*, *8*(12). Advance online publication. DOI: 10.5210/fm.v8i12.1107

Habeck, M. R. (2006). Knowing the Enemy: Jihadist Ideology and the War on Terror. Yale University Press. https://www.jstor.org/stable/j.ctt1npq1n

Haider, S. A.-B., & Mahmoud, H. A.-H. (2014). *Technology and Information Systems in Contemporary Organizations "A Technological Administrative Perspective."*. Published by Mahmoud Hassan Jomaa Foundation.

Haleem, A., Javaid, M., Singh, R. P., & Suman, R. (2022). Medical 4.0 technologies for healthcare: Features, capabilities, and applications. *Internet of Things and Cyber-Physical Systems*, *2*, 12–30. DOI: 10.1016/j.iotcps.2022.04.001

Hammouchi, H., Cherqi, O., Mezzour, G., Ghogho, M., & El Koutbi, M. (2019). Digging deeper into data breaches: An exploratory data analysis of hacking breaches over time. *Procedia Computer Science*, *151*, 1004–1009. DOI: 10.1016/j.procs.2019.04.141

Hammoumi, L., Maanan, M., & Rhinane, H. (2024). Characterizing smart cities based on artificial intelligence. *Smart Cities*, *7*(3), 1330–1345. DOI: 10.3390/smartcities7030056

Han, S., Kelly, E., Nikou, S., & Svee, E.-O. (2022). Aligning artificial intelligence with human values: Reflections from a phenomenological perspective. *AI & Society*, *37*(4), 1383–1395. DOI: 10.1007/s00146-021-01247-4

Harwell, D., & Miroff, N. (2018), 'ICE just abandoned its dream of "extreme vetting" software that could predict whether a foreign visitor would become a terrorist', Washington Post, 17 May 2018, https://www.washingtonpost.com/news/theswitch/wp/2018/05/17/ice-justabandoned-its-dream-of-extreme-vetting-software-that-could-predict-whether-aforeign-visitor-would-become-a-terrorist/

Hassija, V., Chamola, V., Mahapatra, A., Singal, A., Goel, D., Huang, K., Scardapane, S., Spinelli, I., Mahmud, M., & Hussain, A. (2024). Interpreting black-box models: A review on explainable artificial intelligence. *Cognitive Computation*, *16*(1), 45–74. DOI: 10.1007/s12559-023-10179-8

Hedderich, M. A., Lange, L., Adel, H., StrÃ¶tgen, J., & Klakow, D. (2021). A Survey on Recent Approaches for Natural Language Processing in Low-Resource Scenarios. In *Proceedings of the 2022 Conference of the North American Chapter of the Association for Computational Linguistics: Human Language Technologies*. DOI: 10.18653/v1/2021.naacl-main.201

Heinrich Son, T., Weedon, Z., Yigitcanlar, T., Sanchez, T., Corchado, J. M., & Mehmood, R. (2023). Algorithmic urban planning for smart and sustainable development: Systematic review of the literature. *Sustainable Cities and Society*, *94*, 104562. DOI: 10.1016/j.scs.2023.104562

Heratha, H. M. K. K. M. B., & Mittal, M. (2022). Adoption of artificial intelligence in smart cities: A comprehensive review. *International Journal of Information Management Data Insights*, *2*(1), 2. DOI: 10.1016/j.jjimei.2022.100076

Hernández-Muñoz, J. M.. (2011). Smart Cities at the Forefront of the Future Internet. In Domingue, J. (Eds.), Lecture Notes in Computer Science: Vol. 6656. *The Future Internet. FIA 2011*. Springer., DOI: 10.1007/978-3-642-20898-0_32

Hickok, M. (2024). Public procurement of artificial intelligence systems: New risks and future proofing. *AI & Society*, *39*(3), 1213–1227. DOI: 10.1007/s00146-022-01572-2 PMID: 36212228

Hill, D., O'Connor, C. D., & Slane, A. (2022). Police use of facial recognition technology: The potential for engaging the public through co-constructed policy-making. *International Journal of Police Science & Management*, *24*(3), 325–335. DOI: 10.1177/14613557221089558

Hinami, R., Mei, T., & Satoh, S. I. (2017). Joint detection and recounting of abnormal events by learning deep generic knowledge. In *Proceedings of the IEEE international conference on computer vision* (pp. 3619-3627). DOI: 10.1109/ICCV.2017.391

Hinton, G. E. (2010). Deep Belief Nets. In Encyclopedia of Machine Learning (p. 267). DOI: 10.1007/978-0-387-30164-8_208

Ho, A., Hancock, J., & Miner, A. S. (2018). Psychological, relational, and emotional effects of self-disclosure after conversations with a chatbot. *Journal of Communication, 68*(4), 712–733. DOI: 10.1093/joc/jqy026 PMID: 30100620

Hoffman, B. (2017). *Inside Terrorism (REV-Revised and expanded edition).* Columbia University Press.

Hollywood, J. S., ... (2017). Real-Time Crime Forecasting Challenge. RAND Corporation. Retrieved from https://www.rand.org/pubs/research_reports/RR2338.html

Holst, A., & Bjurling, B. (2013, August). A Bayesian parametric statistical anomaly detection method for finding trends and patterns in criminal behavior. In *2013 European Intelligence and Security Informatics Conference* (pp. 83-88). IEEE. DOI: 10.1109/EISIC.2013.19

Hoofnagle, C. J., van der Sloot, B., & Borgesius, F. Z. (2019). The European Union General Data Protection Regulation: What it is and what it means. *Information & Communications Technology Law, 28*(1), 65–98. DOI: 10.1080/13600834.2019.1573501

Huang, C., Zhang, J., Zheng, Y., & Chawla, N. V. (2018). DeepCrime. DOI: 10.1145/3269206.3271793

Huang, S., Tan, K. K., & Lee, T. H. (2012). Fault diagnosis and fault-tolerant control in linear drives using the Kalman filter. *IEEE Transactions on Industrial Electronics, 59*(10), 4285–4292. DOI: 10.1109/TIE.2012.2185011

Hung, T.-W., & Yen, C.-P. (2023). Predictive policing and algorithmic fairness. In Synthese (Vol. 201, Issue 6). Springer Science+Business Media. DOI: 10.1007/s11229-023-04189-0

Hung, T. W., & Yen, C. P. (2021). On the person-based predictive policing of AI. *Ethics and Information Technology, 23*(3), 165–176. DOI: 10.1007/s10676-020-09539-x

Hwang, I. C., & Kang, H. S. (2023). Anomaly detection based on a 3d convolutional neural network combining convolutional block attention module using merged frames. *Sensors (Basel), 23*(23), 9616. DOI: 10.3390/s23239616 PMID: 38067989

Iaione, C., Nictolis, E. D., & Suman, A. B. (2019). The Internet of Humans (IoH): Human Rights and Co-Governance to Achieve Tech Justice in the City. In Law & Ethics of Human Rights (Vol. 13, Issue 2, p. 263). De Gruyter. DOI: 10.1515/lehr-2019-2008

Iga, D., Twineamatsiko, E., Bagonza, J. K., & Nakayenga, H. N.. (2024). Advancing electronic communication compliance and fraud detection through machine learning, NLP, and generative AI: A pathway to enhanced cybersecurity and regulatory adherence. *World Journal of Advanced Research and Reviews*, *23*(2), 697–707. DOI: 10.30574/wjarr.2024.23.2.2364

Imaoka, H., Hashimoto, H., Takahashi, K., Ebihara, A. F., Liu, J., Hayasaka, A., Morishita, Y., & Sakurai, K. (2021). The future of biometrics technology: From face recognition to related applications. *APSIPA Transactions on Signal and Information Processing*, *10*(1), e9. DOI: 10.1017/ATSIP.2021.8

Impraimakis, M., & Smyth, A. W. (2022). An unscented Kalman filter method for real-time input-parameter-state estimation. *Mechanical Systems and Signal Processing*, *162*, 108026. DOI: 10.1016/j.ymssp.2021.108026

International Organization for Standardization (ISO), & International Electrotechnical Commission (IEC). (2024). *ISO/IEC 27001:2022/Amd 1:2024—Information security, cybersecurity and privacy protection—Information security management systems—Requirements.*

Ishii, K. (2019). Comparative legal study on privacy and personal data protection for robots equipped with artificial intelligence: Looking at functional and technological aspects. *AI & Society*, *34*(3), 509–533. DOI: 10.1007/s00146-017-0758-8

JÃ³zsef, P. (2022). How safe is your smart city? In Interdisciplinary Description of Complex Systems (Vol. 20, Issue 1, p. 57). Croatian Interdisciplinary Society. DOI: 10.7906/indecs.20.1.8

Jacob, C., Bourke, S., & Heuss, S. (2022). From Testers to Cocreators—the Value of and Approaches to Successful Patient Engagement in the Development of eHealth Solutions: Qualitative Expert Interview Study. *JMIR Human Factors*, *9*(4), e41481. DOI: 10.2196/41481 PMID: 36102548

Jaeger, P. T. (2012). *Disability and the Internet: Confronting a digital divide*. Lynne Rienner Publishers.

Jahangiri, K., Eivazi, M., & Mofazali, S. (2017). The role of foresight in avoiding systematic failure of natural disaster risk management. *International Journal of Disaster Risk Reduction*, *21*, 303–311. DOI: 10.1016/j.ijdrr.2017.01.008

Jalil, S., Rafi, S., LaToza, T. D., Moran, K., & Lam, W. (2023). Chatgpt and software testing education: Promises & perils. In *2023 IEEE International Conference on Software Testing, Verification and Validation Workshops (ICSTW)* (pp. 4130-4137). IEEE. DOI: 10.1109/ICSTW58534.2023.00078

Järvinen, K. (2007). *Cryptoprocessor for elliptic curve digital signature algorithm (ECDSA)* (Technical Report). Helsinki University of Technology, Espoo, Finland.

Javaid, M., Haleem, A., & Singh, R. P. (2023). ChatGPT for healthcare services: An emerging stage for an innovative perspective. BenchCouncil Transactions on Benchmarks. *Standards and Evaluations*, *3*(1), 100105.

Javed, M. A., & Khan, J. Y. (2011, November 9–11). *A geocasting technique in an IEEE802.11p based vehicular ad hoc network for road traffic management.* In *Proceedings of the Australasian Telecommunication Networks and Applications Conference* (pp. 1–6). Melbourne, Australia.

Javed, A. R., Ahmed, W., Alazab, M., Jalil, Z., Kifayat, K., & Gadekallu, T. R. (2022). A comprehensive survey on computer forensics: State-of-the-art, tools, techniques, challenges, and future directions. *IEEE Access : Practical Innovations, Open Solutions*, *10*, 11065–11089. DOI: 10.1109/ACCESS.2022.3142508

Javed, M. A., & Khan, J. Y. (2013, December 16–18). *Performance analysis of a time headway based rate control algorithm for VANET safety applications.* In *Proceedings of the International Conference on Signal Processing and Communication Systems* (pp. 1–6). Carrara, Australia. DOI: 10.1109/ICSPCS.2013.6723983

Javed, M. A., & Khan, J. Y. (2013, June 2–5). *A cooperative safety zone approach to enhance the performance of VANET applications.* In *Proceedings of the IEEE Vehicular Technology Conference* (pp. 1–5). Dresden, Germany. DOI: 10.1109/VTCSpring.2013.6691819

Javed, M. A., & Khan, J. Y. (2014, February 3–6). *Performance analysis of an adaptive rate-range control algorithm for VANET safety applications.* In *Proceedings of the International Conference on Computing, Networking and Communications* (pp. 418–423). Honolulu, HI, USA. DOI: 10.1109/ICCNC.2014.6785371

Javed, M. A., Khan, J. Y., & Ngo, D. T. (2014, April 6–9). *Joint space-division multiple access and adaptive rate control for basic safety messages in VANETs.* In *Proceedings of the IEEE Wireless Communication and Networking Conference* (pp. 2688–2693). Istanbul, Turkey. DOI: 10.1109/WCNC.2014.6952853

Javed, M. A., Khan, J. Y., & Ngo, D. T. (2014, May 18–21). *A tone-based time-slotted protocol for multi-hop emergency message dissemination in VANETs*. In *Proceedings of the IEEE Vehicular Technology Conference* (pp. 1–5). Seoul, Korea. DOI: 10.1109/VTCSpring.2014.7022800

Javed, M. A., Khan, J. Y., & Ngo, D. T. (2014, September 14–17). *Multimedia transmission for emergency services in VANETs*. In *Proceedings of the IEEE Vehicular Technology Conference* (pp. 1–5). Vancouver, BC, Canada. DOI: 10.1109/VTCFall.2014.6966065

Jayakumar, D., Bouhoula, A., & Al-Zubari, W. K. (2024). Unlocking the potential of artificial intelligence for sustainable water management focusing operational applications. *Water (Basel)*, *16*(22), 3328. DOI: 10.3390/w16223328

Jenga, K., Catal, C., & Kar, G. (2023). Machine learning in crime prediction. *Journal of Ambient Intelligence and Humanized Computing*, *14*(5), 2887–2913. DOI: 10.1007/s12652-023-04530-y

Jiang, C., Zhao, D., Zhang, Q., & Liu, W. (2023). A multi-GNSS/IMU data fusion algorithm based on the mixed norms for land vehicle applications. *Remote Sensing (Basel)*, *15*(9), 2439. DOI: 10.3390/rs15092439

Jobin, A., Ienca, M., & Vayena, E. (2019). The global landscape of AI ethics guidelines. *Nature Machine Intelligence*, *1*(9), 389–399. DOI: 10.1038/s42256-019-0088-2

Jol, G., & Stommel, W. (2016). Ethical considerations of secondary data use. In Dutch Journal of Applied Linguistics (Vol. 5, Issue 2, p. 180). John Benjamins Publishing Company. DOI: 10.1075/dujal.5.2.06jol

Jordan, J. (2014). Attacking the Leader, Missing the Mark: Why Terrorist Groups Survive Decapitation Strikes. *International Security*, *38*(4), 7–38. DOI: 10.1162/ISEC_a_00157

Joseph, J. (2024). Predicting crime or perpetuating bias? The AI dilemma. *AI & Society*. Advance online publication. DOI: 10.1007/s00146-024-02032-9

Junaid, M., Zhang, Q., Cao, M., & Luqman, A. (2023). Nexus between technology enabled supply chain dynamic capabilities, integration, resilience, and sustainable performance: An empirical examination of healthcare organizations. *Technological Forecasting and Social Change*, *196*, 122828. DOI: 10.1016/j.techfore.2023.122828

Jungherr, A. (2023). Artificial intelligence and democracy: A conceptual framework. *Social Media + Society*, *9*(3), 20563051231186353. Advance online publication. DOI: 10.1177/20563051231186353

Juola, P. (2019). Artificial Intelligence and Pattern Evidence: A Legal Application for AI.

Kafol, C., & Bregar, A. (2017). Cyber security—Building a sustainable protection. In *DAAAM International Scientific Book 2017* (pp. 81–90). DAAAM International. DOI: 10.2507/daaam.scibook.2017.07

Kamthe, U. M., & Patil, C. G. (2018, August). Suspicious activity recognition in video surveillance system. In 2018 Fourth international conference on computing communication control and automation (ICCUBEA) (pp. 1-6). IEEE. DOI: 10.1109/ICCUBEA.2018.8697408

Kanchana, R. A. C. (2022). Challenges of urbanization towards sustainable development. *Journal of Urban Studies*, *15*(4), 101–120.

Kandt, J., & Batty, M. (2021). Smart cities, big data, and urban policy: Towards urban analytics for the long run. *Cities (London, England)*, *109*, 102992. DOI: 10.1016/j.cities.2020.102992

Kant, N., & Anjali, K. (2021). Blockchain Technology: A Strategic Resource. In Blockchain for Healthcare Systems (pp. 1-15). CRC Press. 13

Kaplan, R. M., & Hays, R. D. (2022). Health-related quality of life measurement in public health. *Annual Review of Public Health*, *43*(1), 355–373. DOI: 10.1146/annurev-publhealth-052120-012811 PMID: 34882431

Karie, N. M., Kebande, V. R., & Venter, H. S. (2019). Diverging deep learning cognitive computing techniques into cyber forensics. *Forensic Science International. Synergy*, *1*, 61–67. DOI: 10.1016/j.fsisyn.2019.03.006 PMID: 32411955

Karliuk, M. (2023). Proportionality principle for the ethics of artificial intelligence. *AI and Ethics*, *3*(2), 985–990. DOI: 10.1007/s43681-022-00220-1

Kaskina, R., & Cvetkovska, A. (2024). Artificial intelligence (AI) and human rights: Using AI as a weapon of repression and its impact on human rights. Policy Department for External Relations, Directorate-General for External Policies of the Union, European Parliament.

Kasneci, E., Seßler, K., Küchemann, S., Bannert, M., Dementieva, D., Fischer, F., Gasser, U., Groh, G., Günnemann, S., Hüllermeier, E., Krusche, S., Kutyniok, G., Michaeli, T., Nerdel, C., Pfeffer, J., Poquet, O., Sailer, M., Schmidt, A., Seidel, T., & Kasneci, G. (2023). ChatGPT for good? On opportunities and challenges of large language models for education. *Learning and Individual Differences*, *103*, 102274. DOI: 10.1016/j.lindif.2023.102274

Kathleen, M. (August 2019). Artificial Intelligence Prediction and Counterterrorism. Britain: Chattam House.

Kaur, R., & Kaur, A. (2012). Digital forensics. *International Journal of Computer Applications*, *50*(7), 5–9. DOI: 10.5120/7765-0844

Kendzerska, T., Zhu, D. T., Gershon, A. S., Edwards, J. D., Peixoto, C., Robillard, R., & Kendall, C. E. (2021). The effects of the health system response to the COVID-19 pandemic on chronic disease management: A narrative review. *Risk Management and Healthcare Policy*, *14*, 575–584. DOI: 10.2147/RMHP.S293471 PMID: 33623448

Keppens, J., Shen, Q., & Price, C. (2010). Compositional Bayesian modelling for computation of evidence collection strategies. In Applied Intelligence (Vol. 35, Issue 1, p. 134). Springer Science+Business Media. DOI: 10.1007/s10489-009-0208-5

Khaleel, M., Yusupov, Z., Alfalh, B., Guneser, M. T., Nassar, Y., & El-Khozondar, H. (2024). Impact of smart grid technologies on sustainable urban development. Int. J. Electr. Eng. and Sustain., 62-82.

Khan, A. A., Akbar, M. A., Fahmideh, M., Liang, P., Waseem, M., Ahmad, A., Niazi, M., & Abrahamsson, P. (2023). AI Ethics: An Empirical Study on the Views of Practitioners and Lawmakers. In IEEE Transactions on Computational Social Systems (Vol. 10, Issue 6, p. 2971). Institute of Electrical and Electronics Engineers. DOI: 10.1109/TCSS.2023.3251729

Kim, C., Lee, J., Han, T., & Kim, Y. (2018). A hybrid framework combining background subtraction and deep neural networks for rapid person detection. *Journal of Big Data*, *5*(1), 22. DOI: 10.1186/s40537-018-0131-x

Kiran, B. R., Thomas, D. M., & Parakkal, R. (2018). An overview of deep learning based methods for unsupervised and semi-supervised anomaly detection in videos. *Journal of Imaging*, *4*(2), 36. DOI: 10.3390/jimaging4020036

Kitchin, R. (2016). *Getting smarter about smart cities: Improving data privacy and security. Data Protection Unit*. Department of the Taoiseach.

Klausen, J. (2014). Tweeting the Jihad: Social Media Networks of Western Foreign Fighters in Syria and Iraq. *Studies in Conflict and Terrorism*, *38*(1), 1–22. DOI: 10.1080/1057610X.2014.974948

KoÐºÐ¸Ð½, A. B., & Denisov, Yu. D. (2023). Artificial Intelligence in Criminalistics and Forensic Examination: Issues of Legal Personality and Algorithmic Bias. *Theory and Practice of Forensic Science*, *18*(2), 30â€"37. DOI: 10.30764/1819-2785-2023-2-30-37

Kolesnyk, V. (2021). Forensic analysis of crimes in the sphere of information technologies. *Information Security of the Person. Socialtjänst Statistik, 31–33*, 124–136.

Kommineni, M., & Baseer, K. K. (2024). An Architecture and Review of Intelligence Based Traffic Control System for Smart Cities. *EAI Endorsed Transactions on Energy Web, 11*. Advance online publication. DOI: 10.4108/ew.4964

Komninos, N. (2013). *Intelligent cities: Innovation, knowledge systems and digital spaces*. Routledge. DOI: 10.4324/9780203857748

Korkmaz, A. (2023). Public health emergencies and disaster risk management: A rural experience following the earthquake. *Turk Pediatri Arsivi, 58*(4), 353–354. DOI: 10.5152/TurkArchPediatr.2023.23061 PMID: 37144273

Koroniotis, N., Moustafa, N., & Sitnikova, E. (2020). A new network forensic framework based on deep learning for Internet of Things networks: A particle deep framework. In *Future Generation Computer Systems* (Vol. 110, p. 91). Elsevier BV., DOI: 10.1016/j.future.2020.03.042

Korotayev, A., Vaskin, I., Tsirel, T. (2021). Economic growth, education, and terrorism: A re-analysis. Terrorism and Political Violence, Taylor & Francis. Retrieved from: 2021_Economic_Growth_Education_and_Terrorism_A_Re_Analysis-libre.

Kotcher, J., Maibach, E., Miller, J., Campbell, E., Alqodmani, L., Maiero, M., & Wyns, A. (2021). Views of health professionals on climate change and health: A multinational survey study. *The Lancet. Planetary Health, 5*(5), e316–e323. DOI: 10.1016/S2542-5196(21)00053-X PMID: 33838130

Kouba, P., Kohout, P., Haddadi, F., Bushuiev, A., Samusevich, R., Sedlar, J., Damborsky, J., Pluskal, T., Sivic, J., & Mazurenko, S. (2023). Machine Learning-Guided Protein Engineering. *ACS Catalysis, 13*(21), 13863–13895. DOI: 10.1021/acscatal.3c02743 PMID: 37942269

Krähmer, K. (2020). Are green cities sustainable? A degrowth critique of sustainable urban development in Copenhagen. *European Planning Studies, 29*(7), 1272–1289. DOI: 10.1080/09654313.2020.1841119

Krishnan, S. R., Amudha, P., & Sivakumari, S. (2024). Comprehensive survey on video anomaly detection using deep learning techniques. *International Journal of Computational Vision and Robotics, 14*(4), 445–466. DOI: 10.1504/IJCVR.2024.139544

Kumar, A., & Navdeep, M. (2021). An approach-driven: Use of artificial intelligence and its applications in civil engineering. In Manoharan, K. G., Nehru, J. A., & Balasubramanian, S. (Eds.), *Artificial Intelligence and IoT: Smart Convergence for Ecofriendly Topography* (pp. 201–221). Springer Singapore., DOI: 10.1007/978-981-33-6400-4_10

Kumar, D., & Kumar, K. P. (2023, March 3–5). Artificial intelligence based cyber security threats identification in financial institutions using machine learning approach. In *Proceedings of the 2023 2nd International Conference for Innovation in Technology (INOCON)* (pp. 1–6). IEEE. DOI: 10.1109/INOCON57975.2023.10100967

Kumar, L., & Ailawalia, P. (2024). Advances in Answer Set Planning: A Comprehensive Survey and Integration with Mixed Integer Programming. *15th International Conference on Advances in Computing, Control, and Telecommunication Technologies (ACT 2024)*, vol. 2, pp. 4210-4214.

Kumar, L., & Ailawalia, P. (2024). Knowledge Extraction from Answer Set Programming based Encoding Selection. *15th International Conference on Advances in Computing, Control, and Telecommunication Technologies (ACT 2024)*, vol. 1, pp. 1494-1499, 2024.

Kumar, S., Pathak, S. K., & Singh, J. (2022). A comprehensive study of XSS attack and the digital forensic models to gather the evidence. *ECS Transactions*, *107*(1), 7153–7163. DOI: 10.1149/10701.7153ecst

Kumar, V. (2019). Dynamics of the "right to privacy": Its characterization under the Indian Constitution. *Journal of the Indian Law Institute*, *61*(1), 68–96. https://www.jstor.org/stable/27097351

Kummitha, R. K. R., & Nathalie, C. (2017). How do we understand smart cities? An evolutionary perspective. *Cities (London, England)*, *67*, 43–52. DOI: 10.1016/j.cities.2017.04.010

Kwok, A. O., & Treiblmaier, H. (2023). Blockchain technology as a driver of economic development in small economies: A dynamic capabilities framework. *Journal of Decision Systems*, •••, 1–26.

Laufs, J., & Borrion, H. (2022). Technological innovation in policing and crime prevention: Practitioner perspectives from London. *International Journal of Police Science & Management*, *24*(2), 190–209. DOI: 10.1177/14613557211064053

Lavin, A., Gilligan-Lee, C. M., Visnjic, A., Ganju, S., Newman, D., Ganguly, S., Lange, D., Baydin, A. G., Sharma, A., Gibson, A., Zheng, S., Xing, E. P., Mattmann, C., Parr, J., & Gal, Y. (2022). Technology readiness levels for machine learning systems. *Nature Communications*, *13*(1), 6039. DOI: 10.1038/s41467-022-33128-9 PMID: 36266298

Leal Filho, W., Mbah, M. F., Dinis, M. A. P., Trevisan, L. V., de Lange, D., Mishra, A., Rebelatto, B., Ben Hassen, T., & Aina, Y. A. (2024). The role of artificial intelligence in the implementation of the UN Sustainable Development Goal 11: Fostering sustainable cities and communities. *Cities (London, England)*, *150*, 105021. DOI: 10.1016/j.cities.2024.105021

Lee, J. Y., & Ji-In, C. (2019). The evolution of smart city policy of Korea. In Emergence, S. C. (Ed.), *Leonidas Anthopoulos* (pp. 173–193). Elsevier., DOI: 10.1016/B978-0-12-816169-2.00008-0

Leffa, D. T., Grevet, E. H., Bau, C. H. D., Schneider, M., Ferrazza, C. P., da Silva, R. F., Miranda, M. S., Picon, F., Teche, S. P., Sanches, P., Pereira, D., Rubia, K., Brunoni, A. R., Camprodon, J. A., Caumo, W., & Rohde, L. A. (2022). Transcranial direct current stimulation vs sham for the treatment of inattention in adults with attention-deficit/hyperactivity disorder: The TUNED randomized clinical trial. *JAMA Psychiatry*, *79*(9), 847–856. DOI: 10.1001/jamapsychiatry.2022.2055 PMID: 35921102

Lewis, B. (1970). On the revolutions in early Islam. *Studia Islamica*, *32*(32), 215–231. DOI: 10.2307/1595221

Liggett, R., Lee, J. R., Roddy, A. L., & Wallin, M. A. (2020). The Dark Web as a Platform for Crime: An Exploration of Illicit Drug, Firearm, CSAM, and Cybercrime Markets. In Holt, T., & Bossler, A. (Eds.), *The Palgrave Handbook of International Cybercrime and Cyberdeviance*. Palgrave Macmillan., DOI: 10.1007/978-3-319-78440-3_17

Li, S., Da Xu, L., & Wang, X. (2012). Compressed sensing signal and data acquisition in wireless sensor networks and Internet of Things. *IEEE Transactions on Industrial Informatics*, *9*(4), 2177–2186. DOI: 10.1109/TII.2012.2189222

Liu, W., Xia, X., Xiong, L., Lu, Y., Gao, L., & Yu, Z. (2021). Automated vehicle sideslip angle estimation considering signal measurement characteristic. *IEEE Sensors Journal*, *21*(18), 21675–21687. DOI: 10.1109/JSEN.2021.3059050

Lu, F. (2021, October 11–17). *HRegNet: A hierarchical network for large-scale outdoor LiDAR point cloud registration*. In *Proceedings of the IEEE International Conference on Computer Vision* (pp. 15994–16003). Montreal, BC, Canada. DOI: 10.1109/ICCV48922.2021.01571

Luo, L., & Qi, C. (2021). *An analysis of the crucial indicators impacting the risk of terrorist attacks: A predictive perspective*. Elsevier.

Luusua, A., Ylipulli, J., Foth, M., & Aurigi, A. (2023). Urban AI: Understanding the emerging role of artificial intelligence in smart cities. *AI & Society*, *38*(3), 1039–1044. DOI: 10.1007/s00146-022-01537-5 PMID: 36196366

Lv, H., Zhou, C., Cui, Z., Xu, C., Li, Y., & Yang, J. (2021). Localizing anomalies from weakly-labeled videos. *IEEE Transactions on Image Processing*, *30*, 4505–4515. DOI: 10.1109/TIP.2021.3072863 PMID: 33872149

Lynskey, O. (2023). Complete and effective data protection. *Current Legal Problems*, *76*(1), 297–344. DOI: 10.1093/clp/cuad009

Lyon, D. (2014). Surveillance, Snowden, and Big Data: Capacities, consequences, critique. *Big Data & Society*, *1*(2), 2053951714541861. Advance online publication. DOI: 10.1177/2053951714541861

Malhotra, C., & Malhotra, U. (2024). Putting interests of digital nagriks first: Digital Personal Data Protection (DPDP) Act 2023 of India. *The Indian Journal of Public Administration*, *70*(3), 516–531. DOI: 10.1177/00195561241271575

Malik, N. (2018). *Terror in the dark: how terrorists use encryption, the Darknet, and cryptocurrencies*. The Henry Jackson Society.

Malik, N. (2021). A study on different software used to perform cyber crime. *International Journal for Research in Applied Science and Engineering Technology*, *9*(6), 879–882. DOI: 10.22214/ijraset.2021.39395

Mandalapu, V., Elluri, L., Vyas, P., & Roy, N. (2023). Crime Prediction Using Machine Learning and Deep Learning: A Systematic Review and Future Directions. In Access, I. E. E. E. (Ed.), Vol. 11, p. 60153). Institute of Electrical and Electronics Engineers., DOI: 10.1109/ACCESS.2023.3286344

Manning, M., & Agnew, S. (2020). Policing in the Era of AI and Smart Societies: Austerity, Legitimacy, and Blurring the Line of Consent. In H. Jahankhani, B. Akhgar, P. Cochrane, & M. Dastbaz (Eds.), *Policing in the Era of AI and Smart Societies* (pp. 17–34). Advanced Sciences and Technologies for Security Applications. Springer, Cham. DOI: 10.1007/978-3-030-50613-1_2

Mannuru, N. R., Shahriar, S., Teel, Z. A., Wang, T., Lund, B. D., Tijani, S., Pohboon, C. O., Agbaji, D., Alhassan, J., Galley, J. K. L., Kousari, R., Ogbadu-Oladapo, L., Saurav, S. K., Srivastava, A., Tummuru, S. P., Uppala, S., & Vaidya, P. (2023). Artificial intelligence in developing countries: The impact of generative artificial intelligence (AI) technologies for development. *Information Development*, 02666669231200628. Advance online publication. DOI: 10.1177/02666669231200628

Mansoor, S. I., & Wani, S. A. (2025). Harnessing ethical AI: Measures of redressing hate speech in the social media context. In Chakraborty, S. (Ed.), *Ethical AI solutions for addressing social media influence and hate speech* (pp. 37–62). IGI Global Scientific Publishing., DOI: 10.4018/979-8-3693-9904-0.ch003

Mansur, T., Nizar, T. M., Ali, R., Baharudin, N., & Ananda-Rao, K. (2021). Performance analysis of smart lighting control system for sustainable campus operation. *International Journal of Advanced Technology and Engineering Exploration.*, *8*(74), 54–63. DOI: 10.19101/IJATEE.2020.S2762179

Marda, V. (2018). Artificial intelligence policy in India: A framework for engaging the limits of data-driven decision-making. *Philosophical Transactions. Series A, Mathematical, Physical, and Engineering Sciences*, *376*(2133), 20180087. DOI: 10.1098/rsta.2018.0087 PMID: 30323001

Marwaha, S., Dey, H. S., & Brar, T. S. (2024). The emerging role of Artificial Intelligence (AI) in urban and regional planning in India. *International Journal of Arts Architecture & Design*, *2*(2), 61–79. https://worlduniversityofdesign.ac.in/JAARD/wp-content/uploads/2024/07/4.-The-emerging-role-of-Artificial-Intelligence-AI-in-urban-and-regional-Planning-in-India.pdf. DOI: 10.62030/2024Julypaper4

Masih, E. A. (2022). Feasibility of using QR code for registration & evaluation of training and its ability to increase response rate–The learners' perception. *Nurse Education Today*, *111*, 105305. DOI: 10.1016/j.nedt.2022.105305 PMID: 35220149

Mazzucato, M. (2013). *The Entrepreneurial State: Debunking Public vs. Private Sector Myths*. Penguin Books.

McCluskey, Q. R., Chowdhury, M. M., Latif, S., & Kambhampaty, K. (2022, May 19–21). Computer forensics: Complementing cyber security. In *Proceedings of the 2022 IEEE International Conference on Electro Information Technology (eIT)*. IEEE. https://doi.org/DOI: 10.1109/eIT50749.2022.9813720

McKendrick, K. (2019). Artificial Intelligence Prediction and Counterterrorism. International Security Department. Chatham House. Retrieved from: https://www.chathamhouse.org/sites/default/files/2019-08-07-AICounterterrorism.pdf

Memarian, B., & Doleck, T. (2023). Fairness, Accountability, Transparency, and Ethics (FATE) in Artificial Intelligence (AI) and higher education: A systematic review. *Computers and Education: Artificial Intelligence*, *5*, 100152. DOI: 10.1016/j.caeai.2023.100152

Mennella, C., Maniscalco, U., De Pietro, G., & Esposito, M. (2024). Ethical and regulatory challenges of AI technologies in healthcare: A narrative review. *Heliyon*, *10*(4), e26297. DOI: 10.1016/j.heliyon.2024.e26297 PMID: 38384518

Mensah, G. B. (2023). Artificial intelligence and ethics: A comprehensive review of bias mitigation, transparency, and accountability in AI systems. *Journal of AI Ethics*.https://doi.org/DOI: 10.13140/RG.2.2.23381.19685/1

Meszaros, J., & Ho, C. (2021). AI research and data protection: Can the same rules apply for commercial and academic research under the GDPR? *Computer Law & Security Review*, *41*, 105532. DOI: 10.1016/j.clsr.2021.105532

Mishra, S., Yadav, S. S., Yadav, S., Verma, P., & Ojha, S. (2022). Artificial Intelligence: An Advanced Evolution In Forensic and Criminal Investigation. In Current forensic science (Vol. 1). Bentham Science Publishers. DOI: 10.2174/266648440 1666220819111603

Mliless, M. (2024). Artificial Intelligence (AI) in Law Enforcement and Criminal Activities A Dual-Use Dilemma. Geostrategic Pulse, No.296, May- June 2024.

Moalla, R., Lonc, B., Segarra, G., Laguna, M., Papadimitratos, P., Petit, J., & Labiod, H. (2014, April 14–17). *Experimentation with the PRESERVE VSS and the Score@F system*. In *Proceedings of the 5th Conference on Transport Research Arena (TRA)*. Paris, France. DOI: 10.1002/9781119307853.ch17

Moghimifar, F., & Stebila, D. (2016, February 2–5). *Predicting TLS performance from key exchange performance*. In *Proceedings of the Australasian Computer Science Week Multiconference* (pp. 44:1–44:4). Canberra, Australia. DOI: 10.1145/2843043.2843360

Mohamed, A., Dahl, G. E., & Hinton, G. E. (2011). Acoustic Modeling Using Deep Belief Networks. In IEEE Transactions on Audio Speech and Language Processing (Vol. 20, Issue 1, p. 14). Institute of Electrical and Electronics Engineers. DOI: 10.1109/TASL.2011.2109382

Montavon, G., Samek, W., & MÃ¼ller, K. (2017). Methods for interpreting and understanding deep neural networks. *Digital Signal Processing*, *73*, 1â€“15. DOI: 10.1016/j.dsp.2017.10.011

Mossberger, K., Tolbert, C. J., & McNeal, R. S. (2007). *Digital Citizenship: The Internet, Society, and Participation*. MIT Press. DOI: 10.7551/mitpress/7428.001.0001

Mukto, M. M., Hasan, M., Al Mahmud, M. M., Haque, I., Ahmed, M. A., Jabid, T., Ali, M. S., Rashid, M. R. A., Islam, M. M., & Islam, M. (2024). Design of a real-time crime monitoring system using deep learning techniques. *Intelligent Systems with Applications*, *21*, 200311. DOI: 10.1016/j.iswa.2023.200311

Najafi, M., Eshghi, S., & Eshghi, K. (2020). A framework for earthquake emergency response in Iran. *Scientia Iranica*, *27*(6), 2604–2620. DOI: 10.24200/sci.2019.52376.2168

Nale, R., Sawarbandhe, M., Chegogoju, N., & Satpute, V. (2021, September). Suspicious human activity detection using pose estimation and lstm. In *2021 International symposium of Asian control Association on Intelligent Robotics and Industrial Automation (IRIA)* (pp. 197-202). IEEE. DOI: 10.1109/IRIA53009.2021.9588719

Nasaruddin, N., Muchtar, K., Afdhal, A., & Dwiyantoro, A. P. J. (2020). Deep anomaly detection through visual attention in surveillance videos. *Journal of Big Data*, *7*(1), 87. DOI: 10.1186/s40537-020-00365-y

National Institute of Standards and Technology (NIST). (2022). Framework for Managing Bias in AI. NIST AI Framework. Retrieved from https://www.nist.gov/publications

Navalgund, U. V., & Priyadharshini, K. (2018, December). Crime intention detection system using deep learning. In *2018 International Conference on Circuits and Systems in Digital Enterprise Technology (ICCSDET)* (pp. 1-6). IEEE. DOI: 10.1109/ICCSDET.2018.8821168

Navarathna, P. J., MalagiInternational, V. P.,(2018). Artificial Intelligence in Smart City Analysis. In Conference on Smart Systems and Inventive Technology (ICSSIT). DOI: 10.1109/ICSSIT.2018.8748476

Nigatu, H. H., Tonja, A. L., Rosman, B., Solorio, T., & Choudhury, M. (2024). The Zenoâ€™s Paradox of â€˜Low-Resourceâ€™ Languages. In *Proceedings of the 2021 Conference on Empirical Methods in Natural Language Processing* (p. 17753). DOI: 10.18653/v1/2024.emnlp-main.983

Norris, P. (2001). *Digital divide: Civic engagement, information poverty, and the Internet worldwide*. Cambridge University Press. DOI: 10.1017/CBO9781139164887

Novelli, C., Taddeo, M., & Floridi, L. (2024). Accountability in artificial intelligence: What it is and how it works. *AI & Society*, *39*(4), 1871–1882. DOI: 10.1007/s00146-023-01635-y

Nowdehi, N., & Olovsson, T. (2014, June 8–11). *Experiences from implementing the ETSI ITS SecuredMessage service*. In *2014 IEEE Intelligent Vehicles Symposium Proceedings* (pp. 1055–1060). Dearborn, MI, USA. DOI: 10.1109/IVS.2014.6856587

O'Neil, C. (2016). *Weapons of Math Destruction: How Big Data Increases Inequality and Threatens Democracy*. Crown Publishing Group.

Ogunlade, G. I., & Clottey, E. (2024). Traffic congestion and air quality in Lagos, Nigeria—A public health perspective. *Liberty University*.https://digitalcommons.liberty.edu/cgi/viewcontent.cgi?article=2125&context=research_symp

Olivier, T. (2017, June 6). Artificial Intelligence Will Save Us from Cyberterrorism. DW documentary. Retrieved from: Bing Videos Oxford Dictionary, (2024) Terrorism definition, Available at: https://en.oxforddictionaries.com/definition/terrorism

Ortega-Bolaños, R., Bernal-Salcedo, J., Germán Ortiz, M., Galeano Sarmiento, J., Ruz, G. A., & Tabares-Soto, R. (2024). Applying the ethics of AI: A systematic review of tools for developing and assessing AI-based systems. *Artificial Intelligence Review*, *57*(5), 110. DOI: 10.1007/s10462-024-10740-3

Ouyang, X., Xu, S., Zhang, C., Zhou, P., Yang, Y., Liu, G., & Li, X. (2019). A 3D-CNN and LSTM based multi-task learning architecture for action recognition. *IEEE Access : Practical Innovations, Open Solutions*, *7*, 40757–40770. DOI: 10.1109/ACCESS.2019.2906654

Palmiotto, F., & Menéndez González, N. (2023). Facial recognition technology, democracy and human rights. *Computer Law & Security Review*, *50*, 105857. DOI: 10.1016/j.clsr.2023.105857

Pandiyan, P., Saravanan, S., Usha, K., Kannadasan, R., Alsharif, M. H., & Kim, M.-K. (2023). Technological advancements toward smart energy management in smart cities. *Energy Reports*, *10*, 648–677. DOI: 10.1016/j.egyr.2023.07.021

Pang, G., Shen, C., Cao, L., & Hengel, A. V. D. (2021). Deep learning for anomaly detection: A review. *ACM Computing Surveys*, *54*(2), 1–38. DOI: 10.1145/3439950

Papaioannidis, C., Mademlis, I., & Pitas, I. (2021, May 30–June 5). *Autonomous UAV safety by visual human crowd detection using multi-task deep neural networks*. In *Proceedings of the IEEE International Conference on Robotics and Automation (ICRA)* (pp. 11074–11080). Xi'an, China. DOI: 10.1109/ICRA48506.2021.9560830

Park, M.-S., & Lee, H. (2020). Smart City Crime Prevention Services: The Incheon Free Economic Zone Case. In Sustainability (Vol. 12, Issue 14, p. 5658). Multidisciplinary Digital Publishing Institute. DOI: 10.3390/su12145658

Patil et al. (2022). "Utilization of Artificial Intelligence in Healthcare System, Pharmaceutical Industry & Education". International Journal of Advanced Research in Science, Communication and Technology.

Patrikar, D. R., & Parate, M. R. (2022). Anomaly detection using edge computing in video surveillance system. *International Journal of Multimedia Information Retrieval, 11*(2), 85–110. DOI: 10.1007/s13735-022-00227-8 PMID: 35368446

Pauleen, D. J., Evaristo, R., Davison, R. M., Ang, S., Alanis, M., & Klein, S. (2006). Cultural Bias in Information Systems Research and Practice: Are You Coming From the Same Place I Am? In Communications of the Association for Information Systems (Vol. 17). Association for Information Systems. DOI: 10.17705/1CAIS.01717

Paulraj, D., Ezhumalai, P., & Prakash, M. (2024). A Deep Learning Modified Neural Network (DLMNN) based proficient sentiment analysis technique on Twitter data. *Journal of Experimental & Theoretical Artificial Intelligence, 36*(3), 415–434. DOI: 10.1080/0952813X.2022.2093405

Pawar, P. P., & Phadke, A. C. (2022, December). A survey on different techniques for anomaly detection. In International Conference on Computational Intelligence (pp. 365-380). Singapore: Springer Nature Singapore.

Pellatt, J., & Palfreman, J. (2023). Smart technology solution for a cleaner city: A Dar es Salaam, Tanzania case study. *GeoJournal, 88*, 5221–5245. DOI: 10.1007/s10708-023-10917-3

Perera, C., Ranjan, R., Wang, L., Khan, S. U., & Zomaya, A. Y. (2014). Privacy of Big Data in the Internet of Things Era. https://dblp.uni-trier.de/db/journals/corr/corr1412.html#PereraRWKZ14

Perilli, M., De Bonis, M., & Gallo, C. (2020). Computer forensics and cyber attacks. In Khosrow-Pour, M. (Ed.), *Handbook of research on cyber crime and information privacy* (pp. 132–150). IGI Global., DOI: 10.4018/978-1-7998-5728-0.ch008

Pesqueira, A. M., Sousa, M., & Pereira, R. (2023). Individual dynamic capabilities influential factors in blockchain technology innovation from hospital settings.

Pesqueira, A., & Sousa, M. J. (2022). Life Sciences Industry Blockchain Value Management, Investments, and Finance Impact Assessment: Global Questionnaire Survey of 1524 Industry Professionals and Executives. In Incorporating AI Technology in the Service Sector (pp. 67-107). Apple Academic Press.

Pesqueira, A., & Sousa, M. J. (2022). *12 Social Analytics Influencing KOLs Profiling in the Dissemination of Innovations and Scientific Knowledge in the Life Sciences Industry*. Innovations and Social Media Analytics in a Digital Society.

Piazza, JA. (2023). The Impact of Rural-Urban Economic Disparities on Terrorist Organizations' Survival and Attacks. On Terrorist Groups, taylorfrancis.com.

Pillai, A. S. (2024). Traffic management: Implementing AI to optimize traffic flow and reduce congestion. SSRN *Electronic Journal*.https://doi.org/DOI: 10.2139/ssrn.4916398

Pimenow, S., Pimenowa, O., & Prus, P. (2024). Challenges of artificial intelligence development in the context of energy consumption and impact on climate change. *Energies*, *17*(23), 5965. DOI: 10.3390/en17235965

Police1. (2024, November 8). Empowering investigations: AIâ€™s impact on law enforcement: Enhancing efficiency and solving complex crimes. Police1.

Pratama1, I., Suswanta, S., (2021). Artificial Intelligence in Realizing Smart City through City Operation Center, In Proceedings of the International Conference on Public Organization. 209.

Privacy and Civil Liberties Oversight Board (PCLOB). (2022). Guidelines on the Use of AI in Public Surveillance. PCLOB Report. Retrieved from https://www.pclob.gov/reports/

Privacy International. (2021). Human rights groups win European Court of Human Rights claim on UK mass surveillance regime. Retrieved in https://privacyinternational.org/press-release/4522/human-rights-groups-win-european-court-human-rights-claim-uk-mass-surveillance

Qadir, A. M., & Varol, A. (2020, June 1–2). The role of machine learning in digital forensics. In *Proceedings of the 2020 8th International Symposium on Digital Forensics and Security (ISDFS)* (pp. 1–5). IEEE. DOI: 10.1109/ISDFS49300.2020.9116298

Qu, F., Wu, Z., Wang, F., & Cho, W. (2015). A security and privacy review of VANETs. *IEEE Transactions on Intelligent Transportation Systems*, *16*(6), 2985–2996. DOI: 10.1109/TITS.2015.2439292

Raj, A. N. J., & Mahesh, V. G. (2017). Zernike-moments-based shape descriptors for pattern recognition and classification applications. In *Advanced Image Processing Techniques and Applications* (pp. 90–120). IGI Global. DOI: 10.4018/978-1-5225-2053-5.ch004

Rajendiran, K., Kannan, K., & Yu, Y. (2021). Applications of machine learning in cyber forensics. In Khosrow-Pour, M. (Ed.), (pp. 29–46). Advances in digital crime, forensics, and cyber terrorism. IGI Global., DOI: 10.4018/978-1-7998-4900-1.ch002

Ramesh, K., Sitaram, S., & Choudhury, M. (2023). Fairness in Language Models Beyond English: Gaps and Challenges. DOI: 10.18653/v1/2023.findings-eacl.157

Rashid, Y., Rashid, A., Warraich, M. A., Sabir, S. S., & Waseem, A. (2019). Case study method: A step-by-step guide for business researchers. *International Journal of Qualitative Methods, 18*, 1609406919862424. Advance online publication. DOI: 10.1177/1609406919862424

Revathi, A. R., & Kumar, D. (2017). An efficient system for anomaly detection using deep learning classifier. *Signal, Image and Video Processing*, *11*(2), 291–299. DOI: 10.1007/s11760-016-0935-0

Ribeiro, M., Lazzaretti, A. E., & Lopes, H. S. (2018). A study of deep convolutional auto-encoders for anomaly detection in videos. *Pattern Recognition Letters*, *105*, 13–22. DOI: 10.1016/j.patrec.2017.07.016

Richardson, R., Schultz, J. M., & Crawford, K. (2019). Dirty data, bad predictions: How civil rights violations impact police data, predictive policing systems, and justice. *New York University Law Review*, *94*, 192â€"248.

Ritchie, H., Samborska, V., & Roser, M. (2024). Urbanization: The world population is moving to cities. Why is urbanization happening and what are the consequences? *Our World in Data*. https://ourworldindata.org/urbanization

Robbins, M. (2016), 'Has a rampaging AI algorithm really killed thousands in Pakistan?', Guardian, 18 February 2018, https://www.theguardian.com/science/the-lay-scientist/2016/feb/18/has-a-rampaging-ai-algorithm-really-killed-thousands-in-pakistan

Roberts, H., Cowls, J., Morley, J., Taddeo, M., Wang, V., & Floridi, L. (2021). The Chinese approach to artificial intelligence: An analysis of policy, ethics, and regulation. *AI & Society*, *36*(1), 59–77. DOI: 10.1007/s00146-020-00992-2

Rodrigues, R. (2020). Legal and human rights issues of AI: Gaps, challenges and vulnerabilities. *Journal of Responsible Technology*, *4*, 100005. DOI: 10.1016/j.jrt.2020.100005

Romero-Ben, L., Alves, D., Blesa, J., Cembrano, G., Puig, V., & Duviella, E. (2023). Leak detection and localization in water distribution networks: Review and perspective. *Annual Reviews in Control*, *55*, 392–419. DOI: 10.1016/j.arcontrol.2023.03.012

Romney., ... (2024). Framework for Mitigating Extreme AI Risks. https://www.romney. senate.gov/wp-content/uploads/2024/04/AI-Framework_2pager.pdf

S Bhalshankar -, D. (2023). An Examination on the Consistency of Forensic Information in Criminal Courts in India. In International Journal For Multidisciplinary Research (Vol. 5, Issue 1). DOI: 10.36948/ijfmr.2023.v05i01.1756

Sabokrou, M., Fathy, M., & Hoseini, M. (2016). Video anomaly detection and localisation based on the sparsity and reconstruction error of auto-encoder. *Electronics Letters*, *52*(13), 1122–1124. DOI: 10.1049/el.2016.0440

Sabokrou, M., Fayyaz, M., Fathy, M., Moayed, Z., & Klette, R. (2018). Deep-anomaly: Fully convolutional neural network for fast anomaly detection in crowded scenes. *Computer Vision and Image Understanding*, *172*, 88–97. DOI: 10.1016/j.cviu.2018.02.006

Sabrina, M. (2016). New tools for emergency managers: An assessment of obstacles to use and implementation. *Disasters*, *40*(2), 207–225. DOI: 10.1111/disa.12141 PMID: 26281801

Sachoulidou, A. (2024). Harnessing AI for law enforcement: Solutions and boundaries from the forthcoming AI Act. *New Journal of European Criminal Law*, *15*(2), 117–125. DOI: 10.1177/20322844241260114

Saheb, T. (2023). Ethically contentious aspects of artificial intelligence surveillance: A social science perspective. *AI and Ethics*, *3*(2), 369–379. DOI: 10.1007/s43681-022-00196-y PMID: 35874304

Saini, D. K., Ahir, D., & Ganatra, A. (2016). Techniques and challenges in building intelligent systems: anomaly detection in camera surveillance. In *Proceedings of First International Conference on Information and Communication Technology for Intelligent Systems*: Volume 2 (pp. 11-21). Springer International Publishing. DOI: 10.1007/978-3-319-30927-9_2

Saini, J., Dutta, M., & Marques, G. (2020). Indoor Air Quality Monitoring Systems Based on Internet of Things: A Systematic Review. *International Journal of Environmental Research and Public Health*, *17*(14), 4942. DOI: 10.3390/ijerph17144942 PMID: 32659931

Salem, A. H., Azzam, S. M., Emam, O. E., & Abohany, A. A. (2024). Advancing cybersecurity: A comprehensive review of AI-driven detection techniques. *Journal of Big Data*, *11*(1), 105. DOI: 10.1186/s40537-024-00957-y

Samwine, T., Wu, P., Xu, L., Shen, Y., Appiah, E., & Yaoqi, W. (2017). Challenges and prospects of solid waste management in Ghana. *International Journal of Environmental Monitoring and Analysis*, *5*(4), 96. DOI: 10.11648/j.ijema.20170504.11

Sanchez, T. W., Brenman, M., & Ye, X. (2024). The ethical concerns of artificial intelligence in urban planning. *Journal of the American Planning Association*, •••, 1–14. DOI: 10.1080/01944363.2024.2355305

Sanso-Navarro, M. M., & Vera-Cabello, M. (2020). The socioeconomic determinants of terrorism: A Bayesian model averaging approach. Defence and Peace, Taylor & Francis. Retrieved from: https://zaguan.unizar.es/record/84207/files/texto_completo.pdf

Santhoshkumar, R., Jabez, I., Kannan, S. B., & Kumar, K. (2024, March). Intelligent Monitoring and Learning System for Electric Vehicle Charging Stations. In International Conference on Artificial Intelligence and Smart Energy (pp. 198-207). Cham: Springer Nature Switzerland. DOI: 10.1007/978-3-031-61475-0_16

Santos, G. L., Endo, P. T., Sadok, D., & Kelner, J. (2020). When 5G Meets Deep Learning: A Systematic Review. In Algorithms (Vol. 13, Issue 9, p. 208). Multidisciplinary Digital Publishing Institute. DOI: 10.3390/a13090208

Sarabdeen, J. (2022). Protection of the rights of the individual when using facial recognition technology. *Heliyon*, *8*(3), e09086. DOI: 10.1016/j.heliyon.2022.e09086 PMID: 35309394

Sarker, I. H., Furhad, M. H., & Nowrozy, R. (2021). AI-driven cybersecurity: An overview, security intelligence modeling and research directions. *SN Computer Science*, *2*(1), 173. DOI: 10.1007/s42979-021-00557-0

Sarzaeim, P., Mahmoud, Q. H., Azim, A., Bauer, G., & Bowles, I. (2023). A Systematic Review of Using Machine Learning and Natural Language Processing in Smart Policing. *Computers*, *12*(12), 255. DOI: 10.3390/computers12120255

Sayyed, H. (2024). Artificial intelligence and criminal liability in India: Exploring legal implications and challenges. *Cogent Social Sciences*, *10*(1), 2343195. Advance online publication. DOI: 10.1080/23311886.2024.2343195

Scanlon, M., Breitinger, F., Hargreaves, C., Hilgert, J.-N., & Sheppard, J. (2023). ChatGPT for Digital Forensic Investigation: The Good, The Bad, and The Unknown. https://doi.org/DOI: 10.20944/preprints202307.0766.v1

Schmidt, R., Lasowski, R., Leinmüller, T., Linnhoff-Popien, C., & Schäfer, G. (2010, December 13–15). *An approach for selective beacon forwarding to improve cooperative awareness.* In *Proceedings of the IEEE Vehicular Networking Conference* (pp. 182–188). Jersey City, NJ, USA. DOI: 10.1109/VNC.2010.5698243

Schuurman, B., & Carthy, S. L. (2023). The Makings of a Terrorist: Continuity and Change Across Left-, Right- and Jihadist Extremists and Terrorists in Europe and North-America, 1960s-Present. *Deviant Behavior, 44*(6), 953–974. DOI: 10.1080/01639625.2022.2118088

Seaberg, D., Devine, L., & Zhuang, J. (2017). A review of game theory applications in natural disaster management research. *Natural Hazards, 89*(3), 1461–1483. DOI: 10.1007/s11069-017-3033-x

Secinaro, , Calandra, D., Secinaro, A., Muthurangu, V., & Biancone, P. (2021). The role of artificial intelligence in healthcare: A structured literature review. *BMC Medical Informatics and Decision Making, 21*(1), 125. DOI: 10.1186/s12911-021-01488-9 PMID: 33836752

Shah, N., Bhagat, N., & Shah, M. (2021). Crime forecasting: a machine learning and computer vision approach to crime prediction and prevention. In Visual Computing for Industry Biomedicine and Art (Vol. 4, Issue 1). Springer Nature. DOI: 10.1186/s42492-021-00075-z

Shan, M., Narula, K., Wong, Y. F., Worrall, S., Khan, M., Alexander, P., & Nebot, E. (2020). Demonstrations of cooperative perception: Safety and robustness in connected and automated vehicle operations. *Sensors (Basel), 21*(1), 200. DOI: 10.3390/s21010200 PMID: 33396804

Shannon, C. E. (1948). A mathematical theory of communication. *The Bell System Technical Journal, 27*(3), 379–423. DOI: 10.1002/j.1538-7305.1948.tb01338.x

Sharma, A. (2017). India's Smart Cities Mission: Smart for Whom? *Cities (London, England), 91*, 70–78.

Shiwlani, A., Khan, M., Sherani, A. M. K., & Qayyum, M. U. (2023). Synergies of AI and Smart Technology: Revolutionizing Cancer Medicine, Vaccine Development, and Patient Care. International Journal of Social. *Humanities and Life Sciences, 1*(1), 10–18.

Shrivastava, A. (2024). AI in smart cities: Enhancing urban living. [JARET]. *Journal of Advanced Research Engineering and Technology, 3*(1), 213–222. https://iaeme.com/Home/issue/JARET?Volume=3&Issue=

Shughart, W. F.II. (2006). September 11, 2001. In Rowley, C. K., & Schneider, F. (Eds.), *The Encyclopedia of public choice* (Vol. II, pp. 520–524). Kluwer Academic Publishers.

Sikri, A. K. (2021). Proportionality—A balancing act for achieving constitutional rights: A comparative study. In M. John, V. H. Devaiah, P. Baruah, M. Tundawala, & N. Kumar (Eds.), *The Indian Yearbook of Comparative Law 2019* (pp. [specific pages if known]). Springer, Singapore. DOI: 10.1007/978-981-16-2175-8_6

Skillicorn, D. B., & Little, A. (2009). Patterns of Word Use for Deception in Testimony. In *Annals of information systems* (p. 25). Springer Nature., DOI: 10.1007/978-1-4419-1325-8_2

Smith, J., & Jones, A. (2022). The Role of Deep Learning in Fraud Detection. *Journal of Financial Security*, *13*(4), 132–145.

Smith, M., & Miller, S. (2022). The ethical application of biometric facial recognition technology. *AI & Society*, *37*(1), 167–175. DOI: 10.1007/s00146-021-01199-9 PMID: 33867693

Smuha, N. A. (2021). From a 'race to AI' to a 'race to AI regulation': Regulatory competition for artificial intelligence. *Law, Innovation and Technology*, *13*(1), 57–84. DOI: 10.1080/17579961.2021.1898300

Sokol, K., & Flach, P. (2020). One Explanation Does Not Fit All. In KI - KÃ¼nstliche Intelligenz (Vol. 34, Issue 2, p. 235). Springer Science+Business Media. DOI: 10.1007/s13218-020-00637-y

SolÃ -Sales, S., Alzetta, C., Moretâ€ Tatay, C., & Dellâ€™Orletta, F. (2023). Analysing Deception in Witness Memory through Linguistic Styles in Spontaneous Language. *Brain Sciences*, *13*(2), 317. DOI: 10.3390/brainsci13020317 PMID: 36831859

Spiel, K., Hornecker, E., Williams, R. M., & Good, J. (2022). ADHD and technology research–investigated by neurodivergent readers. In *Proceedings of the 2022 CHI Conference on Human Factors in Computing Systems* (pp. 1-21). DOI: 10.1145/3491102.3517592

Spiroiu, F. (2018). The Impact of Beliefs Concerning Deception on Perceptions of Nonverbal Behavior: Implications for Neuro-Linguistic Programming-Based Lie Detection. *Journal of Police and Criminal Psychology*, *33*(3), 244â€"256. DOI: 10.1007/s11896-018-9278-9

Srinivasan, R., & Chander, A. (2021). Biases in AI Systems. In Queue (Vol. 19, Issue 2, p. 45). Association for Computing Machinery. DOI: 10.1145/3466132.3466134

Strassel, S., & Tracey, J. (2016). LORELEI Language Packs: Data, Tools, and Resources for Technology Development in Low Resource Languages. In Proceedings of the Tenth International Conference on Language Resources and Evaluation (LRECâ€™16) (pp. 3273â€“3280). European Language Resources Association (ELRA). https://aclanthology.org/L16-1521/

Sultani, W., Chen, C., & Shah, M. (2018). Real-world anomaly detection in surveillance videos. In *Proceedings of the IEEE conference on computer vision and pattern recognition* (pp. 6479-6488).

Sun, C., Abbas, H. S. M., Xu, X., & Abbas, S. (2022). The impact of socio-economic and fractionalisation determinants on terrorism in ESNA. Socio-Economic Planning Sciences, Elsevier. Retrieved from: https://www.sciencedirect.com/science/article/abs/pii/S0038012121001300

Sundmaeker, H., Guillemin, P., Friess, P., & Woelfflé, S. (2010). Vision and challenges for realising the Internet of Things. European Commission, 3(3), 34-36. https://data.europa.eu/doi/10.2759/26127

Sun, L., Zhang, H., & Fang, C. (2021). Data security governance in the era of big data: Status, challenges, and prospects. *Data Science and Management*, *2*, 41–44. DOI: 10.1016/j.dsm.2021.06.001

Svoboda, J., & Lukas, L. (2019). Sources of threats and threats in the cyber security. In Katalinic, B. (Ed.), *DAAAM International Scientific Book 2019* (pp. 321–330). DAAAM International., DOI: 10.2507/daaam.scibook.2019.27

Szpilko, D., Jiménez Naharro, F., Lăzăroiu, G., & Nica, E. (2023). Artificial intelligence in the smart city — A literature review. *Engineering Management in Production and Services*, *15*(4), 53–75. DOI: 10.2478/emj-2023-0028

Tahiru, A.-W., Cobbina, S. J., Asare, W., & Takal, S. U. (2024). Unlocking energy from waste: A comprehensive analysis of municipal solid waste recovery potential in Ghana. *WORLD (Oakland, Calif.)*, *5*(2), 192–218. DOI: 10.3390/world5020011

Tallberg, J., Erman, E., Furendal, M., Geith, J., Klamberg, M., & Lundgren, M. (2023). The global governance of artificial intelligence: Next steps for empirical and normative research. *International Studies Review*, *25*(3), viad040. Advance online publication. DOI: 10.1093/isr/viad040

Tan Yigitcanlar, T., & Cugurullo, F. (2020). The Sustainability of Artificial Intelligence: An Urbanistic Viewpoint from the Lens of Smart and Sustainable Cities. In State of the Art and Future Perspectives in Smart and Sustainable Urban Development. 12(20), 8548; DOI: 10.3390/su12208548

Tariq, , Awan, M. J., Alshudukhi, J., Alam, T. M., Alhamazani, K. T., & Meraf, Z. (2022). Software Measurement by Using Artificial Intelligence. *Journal of Nanomaterials*, *2022*(1), 7283171. DOI: 10.1155/2022/7283171

Taskiran, M., Kahraman, N., & Erdem, C. E. (2020). Face recognition: Past, present and future (a review). *Digital Signal Processing*, *106*, 102809. DOI: 10.1016/j.dsp.2020.102809

Taylor, I. (2023). Justice by Algorithm: The Limits of AI in Criminal Sentencing. *Criminal Justice Ethics*, *42*(3), 193–213. DOI: 10.1080/0731129X.2023.2275967

Tennakoon, K., Serrao-Neumann, S., & Hanna, C. (2021). Examining the incorporation of small-scale recurring disasters in emergency management frameworks: Insights from Aotearoa—New Zealand. *International Journal of Disaster Risk Reduction*, *66*, 102595. DOI: 10.1016/j.ijdrr.2021.102595

Thakare, K. V., Sharma, N., Dogra, D. P., Choi, H., & Kim, I. J. (2022). A multistream deep neural network with late fuzzy fusion for real-world anomaly detection. *Expert Systems with Applications*, *201*, 117030. DOI: 10.1016/j.eswa.2022.117030

Thiebes, S., Lins, S., & Sunyaev, A. (2020). Trustworthy artificial intelligence. In Electronic Markets (Vol. 31, Issue 2, p. 447). Springer Science+Business Media. DOI: 10.1007/s12525-020-00441-4

Thorley, T. G., & Saltman, E. (2023). GIFCT tech trials: Combining behavioural signals to surface terrorist and violent extremist content online. *Studies in Conflict and Terrorism*, •••, 1–26.

Turner, S., Brown, D., Yiu, K., Housley, R., & Polk, T. (2009). *Elliptic Curve Cryptography Subject Public Key Information* (RFC 5480). Internet Engineering Task Force (IETF). DOI: 10.17487/rfc5480

Tutar, H., Güneş, A., Zontul, M., & Aslan, Z. (2024). A Hybrid Approach to Improve the Video Anomaly Detection Performance of Pixel-and Frame-Based Techniques Using Machine Learning Algorithms. *Computation (Basel, Switzerland)*, *12*(2), 19. DOI: 10.3390/computation12020019

U.S. Department of Justice (DOJ). (2024). Artificial Intelligence and Civil Rights. DOJ Report. Retrieved from https://www.justice.gov/crt/ai

Ukoba, K., Olatunji, K. O., Adeoye, E., Jen, T.-C., & Madyira, D. M. (2024). Optimizing renewable energy systems through artificial intelligence: Review and future prospects. *Energy & Environment*, *35*(7), 3833–3879. DOI: 10.1177/0958305X241256293

Ullah, A., Anwar, S. M., Li, J., Nadeem, L., Mahmood, T., Rehman, A., & Saba, T. (2024). Smart cities: The role of Internet of Things and machine learning in realizing a data-centric smart environment. *Complex & Intelligent Systems*, *10*(3), 1607–1637. DOI: 10.1007/s40747-023-01175-4

Ullah, H., Manickam, S., Obaidat, M., Laghari, S. U. A., & Uddin, M. (2023). Exploring the Potential of Metaverse Technology in Healthcare: Applications, Challenges, and Future Directions. *IEEE Access : Practical Innovations, Open Solutions*, *11*, 69686–69707. DOI: 10.1109/ACCESS.2023.3286696

Ullah, W., Ullah, A., Haq, I. U., Muhammad, K., Sajjad, M., & Baik, S. W. (2021). CNN features with bi-directional LSTM for real-time anomaly detection in surveillance networks. *Multimedia Tools and Applications*, *80*(11), 16979–16995. DOI: 10.1007/s11042-020-09406-3

United Nations Office of Counter-Terrorism and United Nations Interregional Crime and Justice Research Institute, (2021). Countering Terrorism Online with Artificial Intelligence: An Overview for Law Enforcement and Counter-Terrorism Agencies in South Asia and South-East Asia. A Joint Report. Retrieved from: countering-terrorism-online-with-ai-uncct-unicri-report-web.pdf

United Nations Office of the High Commissioner for Human Rights (OHCHR). (2022). *China's algorithms of repression: Reverse engineering a Xinjiang police mass surveillance app*. Retrieved from https://www.ohchr.org/en/press-releases/2022/08/un-human-rights-office-issues-assessment-human-rights-concerns-xinjiang

United States Department of State. (2022). Country Reports on Terrorism 2022: Morocco. retrieved from: https://www.state.gov/reports/country-reports-on-terrorism-2022/morocco

Urquhart, L., & Miranda, D. (2021). Policing faces: The present and future of intelligent facial surveillance. *Information & Communications Technology Law*, *31*(2), 194–219. DOI: 10.1080/13600834.2021.1994220

Vallentin, A., Thórisson, K. R., & Latapie, H. (2023). Addressing the Unsustainability of Deep Neural Networks with Next-Gen AI. In International Conference on Artificial General Intelligence (pp. 296-306). Cham: Springer Nature Switzerland. DOI: 10.1007/978-3-031-33469-6_30

Van Dijk, J. (2020). *The Digital Divide*. Polity Press.

Vedre, S., & Parulekar, W. (2022). (in press). Digital forensic and role of computers in digital forensic. *International Journal of Creative Research Thoughts (IJCRT), 10*(1). *Article ID, IJCRT2201030*. Advance online publication. DOI: 10.1729/IJCRT.2201030

Venkatesh, V. (2022). Adoption and use of AI tools: A research agenda grounded in UTAUT. *Annals of Operations Research, 308*(1), 641–652. DOI: 10.1007/s10479-020-03918-9

Villoria, C. (2023). The transformation of Medellín, from violence to innovation. *Where on Planet Earth, Journal Post #13*. https://www.whereonplanetearth.com/p/the-transformation-of-medellin

Vlasta, M. (2023). Methodological framework for European regulation of (artificial) intelligence and its limits.

Vlek, C. S., Prakken, H., Renooij, S., & Verheij, B. (2014). Building Bayesian networks for legal evidence with narratives: a case study evaluation. In Artificial Intelligence and Law (Vol. 22, Issue 4, p. 375). Springer Science+Business Media. DOI: 10.1007/s10506-014-9161-7

Vu, H. (2017, August). Deep Abnormality Detection in Video Data. In IJCAI (pp. 5217-5218). DOI: 10.24963/ijcai.2017/768

Vu, H., Nguyen, T. D., Travers, A., Venkatesh, S., & Phung, D. (2017, April). Energy-based localized anomaly detection in video surveillance. In *Pacific-Asia conference on knowledge discovery and data mining* (pp. 641–653). Springer International Publishing. DOI: 10.1007/978-3-319-57454-7_50

Wada, M., Noda, Y., Iwata, Y., Tsugawa, S., Yoshida, K., Tani, H., Hirano, Y., Koike, S., Sasabayashi, D., Katayama, H., Plitman, E., Ohi, K., Ueno, F., Caravaggio, F., Koizumi, T., Gerretsen, P., Suzuki, T., Uchida, H., Müller, D. J., & Nakajima, S. (2022). Dopaminergic dysfunction and excitatory/inhibitory imbalance in treatment-resistant schizophrenia and novel neuromodulatory treatment. *Molecular Psychiatry, 27*(7), 2950–2967. DOI: 10.1038/s41380-022-01572-0 PMID: 35444257

Wamba, S. F., Queiroz, M. M., Jabbour, C. J. C., & Shi, C. V. (2023). Are both generative AI and ChatGPT game changers for 21st-Century operations and supply chain excellence? *International Journal of Production Economics, 265*, 109015. DOI: 10.1016/j.ijpe.2023.109015

Wang, C., Shi, J., Zhang, Q., & Ying, S. (2017, July). Histopathological image classification with bilinear convolutional neural networks. In 2017 39th Annual International Conference of the IEEE Engineering in Medicine and Biology Society (EMBC) (pp. 4050-4053). IEEE. DOI: 10.1109/EMBC.2017.8037745

Wang, S., Zhu, E., Yin, J., & Porikli, F. (2018). Video anomaly detection and localization by local motion based joint video representation and OCELM. *Neurocomputing, 277*, 161–175. DOI: 10.1016/j.neucom.2016.08.156

Wang, X., Zhao, Y., & Pourpanah, F. (2020). Recent advances in deep learning. *International Journal of Machine Learning and Cybernetics, 11*(4), 747–750. DOI: 10.1007/s13042-020-01096-5

Wang, Y., & Gao, S. (2017). Application of DBNs for concerned internet information detecting. In *AIP conference proceedings* (Vol. 1808, p. 90005). American Institute of Physics., DOI: 10.1063/1.4977389

Wani, . (2022). Utilization of Artificial Intelligence in Disease Prevention: Diagnosis, Treatment, and Implications for the Healthcare Workforce. *Health Care*. PMID: 35455786

Wani, S. A., & Mansoor, S. I. (2025). Criminal justice system in the age of artificial intelligence: Exploring rights, risks, and responsibilities in the digital era. In Kaunert, C., Raghav, A., Ravesangar, K., Singh, B., & Riswandi, B. (Eds.), *Artificial intelligence in peace, justice, and strong institutions* (pp. 67–92). IGI Global Scientific Publishing., DOI: 10.4018/979-8-3693-9395-6.ch004

Ward, J., Kim, J., & Dey, A. K. (2015). Smart city sensors: A survey. *ACM Computing Surveys, 48*(1), 1–34.

Weismann, I. (2020). The Making of the Modern Arab Da'wa Discursive Field. In Malik, J., & Weismann, I. (Eds.), *Culture of Da'wa: Islamic preaching in the modern world* (pp. 15–30). The University of Utah Press.

Welle, D. (2021). Slahi and His Torturers - Life after Guantanamo. Documentary. Retrieved from https://www.dw.com/en/slahi-and-his-torturers-life-after-guantanamo/a-59629504

Whiting, D., Housley, R., & Ferguson, N. (2003). *Counter with CBC-MAC (CCM)* (RFC 3610). Internet Engineering Task Force (IETF). DOI: 10.17487/rfc3610

Williams, M., Burnap, P., & Sloan, L. (2016). Crime Sensing with Big Data: The Affordances and Limitations of using Open Source Communications to Estimate Crime Patterns. In *The British Journal of Criminology*. Oxford University Press., DOI: 10.1093/bjc/azw031

Wolniak, R., & Stecuła, K. (2024). Artificial intelligence in smart cities—Applications, barriers, and future directions: A review. *Smart Cities*, *7*(3), 1346–1389. DOI: 10.3390/smartcities7030057

Xi, J., Siegel, M., Labudde, D., & Spranger, M. (2024). Towards a joint semantic analysis in mobile forensics environments. In *Forensic Science International Digital Investigation* (Vol. 52, p. 301846). Elsevier BV., DOI: 10.1016/j.fsidi.2024.301846

Xue, R., Chen, J., & Fang, Y. (2020, October). Real-time anomaly detection and feature analysis based on time series for surveillance video. In 2020 5th International Conference on Universal Village (UV) (pp. 1-7). IEEE. DOI: 10.1109/UV50937.2020.9426191

Yadav, S. (2020). Cyber forensics. In Khosrow-Pour, M. (Ed.), (pp. 1–15). Advances in digital crime, forensics, and cyber terrorism. IGI Global., DOI: 10.4018/978-1-7998-6811-8.ch001

Yang, C., Su, G., & Chen, J. (2017, March 10–12). Using big data to enhance crisis response and disaster resilience for a smart city. In *Proceedings of the 2017 IEEE 2nd International Conference on Big Data Analysis (ICBDA)* (pp. 504–507). IEEE. DOI: 10.1109/ICBDA.2017.8078684

Yazdi, M., Zarei, E., Adumene, S., & Beheshti, A. (2024). Navigating the power of artificial intelligence in risk management: A comparative analysis. *Safety (Basel, Switzerland)*, *10*(2), 42. DOI: 10.3390/safety10020042

Yerriswamy, K., & Venumadhava, G. S. (2022). Cyber forensic tools and its application in the investigation of digital crimes: Preventive measures with case studies. [IJSR]. *International Journal of Scientific Research*, *11*(5), 71–73. DOI: 10.21275/SR22505102723

Yigitcanlar, T. (2014). Smart cities: An effective urban development and management model? *Australian Plants*, *52*(1), 27–34. DOI: 10.1080/07293682.2015.1019752

Yigitcanlar, T., Lee, S. H., & Kamruzzaman, M. (2019). Artificial intelligence and machine learning for smart cities: A bibliometric and systematic literature review. *Cities (London, England)*, *89*, 186–201.

Zahid, Y., Tahir, M. A., Durrani, N. M., & Bouridane, A. (2020). Ibaggedfcnet: An ensemble framework for anomaly detection in surveillance videos. *IEEE Access : Practical Innovations, Open Solutions*, *8*, 220620–220630. DOI: 10.1109/ACCESS.2020.3042222

Zaidan, E., & Ibrahim, I. A. (2024). AI governance in a complex and rapidly changing regulatory landscape: A global perspective. *Humanities & Social Sciences Communications, 11*(1), 1121. DOI: 10.1057/s41599-024-03560-x

Zanella, A., Bui, N., Castellani, A., Vangelista, L., & Zorzi, M. (2014). Internet of things for smart cities. *IEEE Internet of Things Journal, 1*(1), 22–32. DOI: 10.1109/JIOT.2014.2306328

Završnik, A. (2020). Criminal justice, artificial intelligence systems, and human rights. *ERA Forum, 20*(4), 567–583. DOI: 10.1007/s12027-020-00602-0

Zhang, H., Dai, X., & Qian, D. (2022). Strategic analysis of the modernization of emergency management enabled by new generation of information technology. *Bulletin of the Chinese Academy of Sciences, 37*(12), 1727–1737. DOI: 10.1360/TB-2022-0330

Zhang, X. (2022). Strengthen the construction of disaster prevention and disaster reduction and emergency management system in rural areas. *International Talent Exchange, 3*, 10.

Zhao, Y. (2016). Performance evaluation of Cubature Kalman filter in a GPS/IMU tightly-coupled navigation system. *Signal Processing, 119*, 67–79. DOI: 10.1016/j.sigpro.2015.07.014

Zhou, L. (2021). Social media and natural disaster governance in the era of big data. *Humanities Journal, 1*, 102–109.

Zhou, L., & Luo, Y. (2023). Digital intelligence and empowerment: Emergency management in the era of smart city. *Theoretical Discussion, 2*, 69–78.

Zhu, P., Hu, J., Zhang, Y., & Li, X. (2021). Enhancing traceability of infectious diseases: A blockchain-based approach. *Information Processing & Management, 58*(1), 102570. DOI: 10.1016/j.ipm.2021.102570 PMID: 35721004

Zuiderveen Borgesius, F. J. (2020). Strengthening legal protection against discrimination by algorithms and artificial intelligence. *International Journal of Human Rights, 24*(10), 1572–1593. DOI: 10.1080/13642987.2020.1743976

Zuiderwijk, A., Chen, Y.-C., & Salem, F. (2021). Implications of the use of artificial intelligence in public governance: A systematic literature review and a research agenda. *Government Information Quarterly, 38*(3), 101577. DOI: 10.1016/j.giq.2021.101577

About the Contributors

Mamdooh Abdelhameed Abdelmottlep is a Professor of Police Science and Law Enforcement and the Executive Chairman of the International Police Science Association (IPSA). He earned his Ph.D. in Police Sciences from the Egyptian Police University and holds additional graduate degrees in Criminal Justice, Law Enforcement, and Administration. Dr. Abdelmottlep has taught at numerous esteemed institutions including University of St. Thomas, Texas A&M International University, and Naif Arab University for Security Sciences. His academic contributions span topics such as police leadership, terrorism financing, and criminal justice, with publications addressing global security challenges and law enforcement practices. He is also a recognized foreign legal consultant with experience in international academic cooperation, legal advising, and arbitration. His work is widely recognized for advancing the field of policing science, contributing to the creation of indices like the World Internal Security & Police Index (WISPI).

***

Raed Awashreh is Professor of Management & Public Administration. He brings over 25 years of combined academic and industry experience, teaching undergraduate and postgraduate courses. Dr. Awashreh has authored 70 articles, several Book chapters, and 3 books spanning topics such as, human resources, governance, public policy, strategy, leadership, Entrepreneurship, Innovation, multidisciplinary linked AI, and management. In addition to his academic role, Dr. Awashreh serves as a consultant in business, management, governance, HR, and organizational development, working closely with government, private, and non-governmental sectors. He earned his degrees in Public Administration and Management from Flinders University, Australia, and Monterey, USA.

Komal Bhardwaj is currently working at the Maharishi Markandeshwar Institute of Management, Maharishi Markandeshwar University as Assistant Professor of Finance. She has a rich experience of more than eight years of teaching in the field of management. She has a research experience in the areas of assets pricing, derivatives, option pricing and study on stock volatility. Her research interest includes consumer behaviour, investments, corporate governance, and assets liability management. She also worked as a Thesis supervisor for a program called upgrad-LJMU MBA at upgrade education private limited.

Kyvalya Garikapati is currently working as Dean (Academics) at KIIT School of Law, KIIT Deemed to be University, Bhubaneswar.

Ritu Gupta is an Associate Professor at the Chandigarh University, Mohali, teaching Electronics and Communication. She has done Bachelor in Engineering in Electronics and Instrumentation, Kurukshetra University, India. Master in Engineering in Electronics and Communication, Thapar University, India. Ph.D. in Electronics Engineering, IKGPTU, Jalandhar, India. She is having 15 years of teaching experience. Published various research papers in Journals and international conferences. Her areas of interest are optical communication (wired and wireless) and IoT.

Lalit Bansal is an accomplished academic with 16 years of teaching experience, specializing in cybersecurity and artificial intelligence. Currently an Associate Professor in Computer Science and Engineering department at Maharishi Markandeshwar (Deemed to be University), Mullana-Ambala, Dr. Bansal's academic career has included impactful roles at Chandigarh University and Kurukshetra University-affiliated colleges. Dr. Bansal's contributions are underscored by multiple granted patents and a significant body of research published in Scopus-indexed journals and presented at prominent international conferences. A visionary educator, researcher, and mentor, Dr. Bansal is committed to nurturing the next generation of technology leaders and advancing the fields of cybersecurity and artificial intelligence.

Andréia de Bem Machado has a PhD in Engineering and Knowledge Management. Postdoctoral fellow at the Federal University of Santa Catarina. Evaluator of the National Institute of Educational Studies and Research Anísio Teixeira (Ministry of Education Brazil). She is an Ad Hoc evaluator of National and International Journals. Evaluator in the PNLD Infantile Education program. Consultant in the production of low vision UNESCO teaching material. She has been working in the educational field for over 25 years. She is part of the scientific committee of national and international journals. Currently the areas of study are:

innovation, innovation in the public sector, entrepreneurship, smart cities, education, special education and digital pedagogical model. She likes to innovate in the art of researching and disseminating knowledge.

Vijayalakshmi G V Mahesh received her BE in Electronics and Communication Engineering from Bangalore University, India in 1999, and M.Tech in Digital Communication and Networking from Visvesvaraya Technological University in 2005 and the Ph.D. degree from the Vellore Institute of Technology, Vellore, India. Currently she is working as an Associate Professor at BMS Institute of Technology and Management, Bangalore, India. She has been in academics for over 19 years and has published her research in various reputed journals and conferences. Her research interests include Machine Learning, Image Processing, Pattern Recognition and Deep learning, Affective computing. She has Memberships in Professional Bodies such as ISTE and IEI.

Sheikh Inam Ul Mansoor (BA.LLB Hon's, LLM, CCPT WIPO, Ph.D. International Trade Law) is a highly accomplished academician presently working as an Assistant Professor Law at the School of Law, Dayananda Sagar University in Bangalore, India. With a strong background in law and a passion for academia, Dr. Sheikh has made significant contributions to the field through his extensive research and publications. Pursued his BA. LLB (Hon's) from University of Kashmir, LLM from JNU Jaipur and Ph.D. International Trade Law from LPU Punjab. Prior to his academic career, Dr. Sheikh served as an Advocate and Solicitor at the Jammu and Kashmir High Court and other subordinate courts in Jammu and Kashmir. This experience as a legal practitioner has provided him with valuable insights into the practical application of law and enhanced his understanding of legal dynamics. As an Assistant Professor Law at Dayananda Sagar University, Dr. Sheikh Inam Ul Mansoor continues to make significant contributions to the legal field through his research, teaching, and involvement in various professional activities.

Abhinash Mohanta pursued a three-year LLB program at Ganjam Law College, Berhampur, under Berhampur University. He further advanced his academic journey by enrolling in the Master of Laws (LLM) program in Business Law at the P.G. Department of Law, Berhampur University, graduating in 2017. Currently, he is pursuing a Ph.D. in Law at KIIT Deemed to be University, with a research focus on critical areas such as refugee and human rights. In addition to his academic endeavors, Abhinash has authored several Scopus-indexed papers covering diverse topics, including AI, environment, migration, crime, intellectual property, and refugee studies.

Sanskruti Mohanty, a legal scholar who completed my B.A.LL.B (Hons.) from the prestigious University Law College, Utkal University, in 2024. Currently, I am pursuing my LL.M. at the P.G. Department of Law, Utkal University, with a keen interest in criminal justice, particularly focusing on rape laws and evidence. My academic journey reflects my commitment to understanding and contributing to these critical areas of the legal system.

Antonio Pesqueira is a healthcare and pharmaceutical commercial and supply chain management leader, with an emphasis on technological advancements and process improvement. Concurrently, he holds esteemed academic positions as a professor and research fellow at ISCTE/IUL. Within the Technology and Architecture Research Department, he contributes to the Ph.D. program, focusing his research on digital technologies, healthcare data management, blockchain, and the nexus of innovation and business management. He has notably chaired the Pharmaceutical Supply Chain & Security World Forum and is often invited as a keynote speaker at events such as the Pharma Track & Trace, and Serialization & Labeling Summit. Co-authored more than 20 scholarly articles and book chapters that have been featured in prestigious scientific journals. These include the Journal of Business Research, Future Generations Computer Systems, Journal of Medical Systems, Knowledge Management, WSEAS Transactions on Business and Economics, and Information Systems Frontiers, to name a few. Moreover, his outstanding contributions have been acknowledged at various peer-reviewed international conferences.

Shivani Samanta, a dynamic legal professional, going to complete my B.A.LL.B. (H) in 2024 from the esteemed University Law College, a constituent college of Utkal University and currently pursuing LL.M. at South Asian University, New Delhi. Throughout my academic journey, I've embraced various leadership roles, shaping my collaborative and team-oriented approach. Key Attributes: Leadership: I have a proven track record in diverse leadership roles, fostering teamwork and achieving collective goals. Communication: As an extrovert and creative contributor to any conversation, I am adept at articulating ideas and perspectives. Academic Excellence: Being a dedicated and driven student, I've built a strong academic foundation, complemented by an insatiable curiosity for legal intricacies. Career Aspirations: I am passionate about research related to the legal field and academia. I am committed to acquiring a comprehensive understanding of the legal field and honing skills for a positive impact. Eager to specialise in an area of law aligning with my passion, whether it's human rights, social justice, or constitutional law, I aspire to contribute to ethical practices. Future Goals: My aim is to utilise my legal expertise to effect meaningful change in society. I embrace challenges for personal and professional growth and am keen on connecting with like-minded professionals to explore opportunities and discussions in the legal domain. Let's build a network that fosters positive change!

Onam Singh is currently enrolled in the Economics Department at Dr B. R. Ambedkar University, Delhi, pursuing an undergraduate degree with Economics as a major and Sociology as a minor. As an early career scholar, he has actively engaged in academic writing, contributing articles and book chapters since his first year. His work has garnered positive feedback from various conferences and publications, highlighting its relevance and impact. His overarching goal is to foster inclusive and equitable economic development across all sectors. He firmly believes in addressing welfare, inclusion, and equal development across all industries. For far too long, these fundamental aspects have been overlooked. Now, with a fresh perspective and innovative ideas from the new generation, it is time to usher in a transformative era of inclusive growth and sustainable development. To this end, he is continuously refining programming codes and economic theories to enhance welfare and inclusivity.

Kamal Upreti is currently working as an Associate Professor in Department of Computer Science, CHRIST (Deemed to be University), Delhi NCR, Ghaziabad, India. He completed is B. Tech (Hons) Degree from UPTU, M. Tech (Gold Medalist), PGDM(Executive) from IMT Ghaziabad and PhD in Department of Computer Science & Engineering.He has completed Postdoc from National Taipei University of Business, TAIWAN funded by MHRD. He has published 50+ Patents, 32+Magazine issues and 110+ Research papers in in various reputed Journals and international Conferences. His areas of Interest such as Modern Physics, Data Analytics, Cyber Security, Machine Learning, Health Care, Embedded System and Cloud Computing. He has published more than 45+ authored and edited books under CRC Press, IGI Global, Oxford Press and Arihant Publication. He is having enriched years' experience in corporate and teaching experience in Engineering Colleges.

Renu Vij is a seasoned educator with a robust 16-year career in teaching at the master's level Strategic HR courses . She has made significant contributions to academic research, authoring over 15 research papers published in Scopus-indexed journals and contributing chapters to Scopus-indexed books. Her expertise extends beyond academia, as she is a certified trainer in HR analytics and an accomplished workplace psychologist. Additionally, she holds certification from AON, further solidifying her credentials in the field. Her work reflects a deep commitment to advancing knowledge in her areas of specialization, making her a respected figure in both academic and professional circles.

Index

www.ingramcontent.com/pod-product-compliance
Lightning Source LLC
LaVergne TN
LVHW080557300926
849162LV00005B/982